International Series on Public Policy

Series Editors
B. Guy Peters
Department of Political Science
University of Pittsburgh
Pittsburgh, PA, USA

Philippe Zittoun
Research Professor of Political Science
LET-ENTPE, University of Lyon
Lyon, France

The International Series on Public Policy—the official series of International Public Policy Association, which organizes the International Conference on Public Policy—identifies major contributions to the field of public policy, dealing with analytical and substantive policy and governance issues across a variety of academic disciplines. A comparative and interdisciplinary venture, it examines questions of policy process and analysis, policymaking and implementation, policy instruments, policy change & reforms, politics and policy, encompassing a range of approaches, theoretical, methodological, and/or empirical. Relevant across the various fields of political science, sociology, anthropology, geography, history, and economics, this cutting edge series welcomes contributions from academics from across disciplines and career stages, and constitutes a unique resource for public policy scholars and those teaching public policy worldwide. All books in the series are subject to Palgrave's rigorous peer review process: https://www.palgrave.com/gb/demystifying-peer-review/792492.

More information about this series at
http://www.palgrave.com/gp/series/15096

Sandra Eckert

Corporate Power and Regulation

Consumers and the Environment
in the European Union

Sandra Eckert
Goethe Universität Frankfurt
Frankfurt, Hesse, Germany

ISSN 2524-7301   ISSN 2524-731X (electronic)
International Series on Public Policy
ISBN 978-3-030-05462-5   ISBN 978-3-030-05463-2 (eBook)
https://doi.org/10.1007/978-3-030-05463-2

Library of Congress Control Number: 2019933870

This Palgrave Macmillan imprint is published by the registered company Springer Nature
Switzerland AG
The registered company address is: Gewerbestrasse 11, 6330 Cham, Switzerland

To Daniel

Preface

The history of the making of this book goes back to the time I spent at the European University Institute in Florence between 2004 and 2008. Back then I joined a research project entitled "New modes of governance in the shadow of hierarchy" led by Adrienne Héritier, which was funded by the European Union's Sixth Framework Programme in the context of an integrated project on "New Modes of Governance" (NEWGOV, Project ID 506392). As a research assistant I supported Adrienne's empirical work on such new modes of governance in environmental and energy regulation. In the course of the project, Burkard Eberlein joined us, and I had the pleasure to draw on his deep knowledge and understanding of the energy sector. I was also privileged to be able to participate in the events of the Florence School of Regulation (FSR) in the early days of its existence. I frequently attended FSR workshops and conferences on energy regulation and was able to interact with industry stakeholders and regulatory experts. I have fond memories of regular conversations with the directors of the FSR, Pippo Ranci and Jean-Michel Glachant, and I am furthermore deeply grateful to them for sharing their sector expertise with me. As a research assistant in the project I conducted numerous interviews with policy and industry experts at both the EU and national levels. I have learned a great deal about the specifics of industry activities and regulation in the energy, paper and plastics sectors in the course of these interviews, and about European policy-making more generally. I am grateful to all the experts who shared their views with me. Most importantly, I want to express my gratitude to Adrienne and Burkard to give permission that I use the NEWGOV material for the longitudinal analysis conducted in this book.

It is, however, not only the material gathered during the NEWGOV project which enabled me to write this book. It is also the intellectual history behind the very idea of the book, namely the study of "corporate power and regulation". Adrienne's theoretical framing of the NEWGOV project focused on the public side of the story, on the "shadow of hierarchy" and its effects on business actors. We found that the scope for non-hierarchical steering and the involvement of private actors proved pretty limited and would only work if public actors were able to cast a credible shadow of hierarchy. In our joint publications we have argued that industry self-regulation is ultimately triggered by a regulatory threat and can only work if there is some form of continued public or policy pressure. Unless there are important economic incentives, industry actors would find it difficult to overcome collective action problems through the use of various governance devices. This focus on governance, the shadow of hierarchy and regulatory threats is the starting point of my argument in the book. I owe the intellectual origins of this book to Adrienne, and I cannot thank her enough for everything that I have learned from her about European public policy and regulation.

My interest in governance and public policy did not come to an end with my time in Florence. I was lucky to learn from and work with colleagues studying similar topics since my time there. When finalising my Ph.D. at the Centre for European Integration of the Freie Universität Berlin in 2008–2009, I had the privilege to cooperate closely with my Ph.D. thesis supervisor and friend, Tanja A. Börzel. I discussed my work on policy-making and governance in the EU with Tanja and profited enormously from this exchange. Tanja is a great role model and has always given support and advice, for which I am deeply grateful. During my time in Berlin, I was also privileged to hold a Ph.D. completion grant within the Research College "The Transformative Power of Europe", financed by the German Research Foundation. This context has enabled me to engage in an exchange with the most excellent junior and senior colleagues in our discipline and beyond. Of particular relevance for my work, and the topic of this book, is the inspiring encounter with David Levi-Faur. I have learned a great deal about regulation, governance and politics from my discussions with David and would like to thank him for his continuous interest in my research.

Between 2009 and 2014, I worked as a postdoc academic assistant at the chair in European Integration held by Andrea Lenschow at the Universität Osnabrück. It was a pleasure to share my interests in European environmental policy with Andrea and profit from her deep and long-standing understanding of this policy field. I vividly remember our annual study trips to Brussels which usually focused on sustainable development policies and gave us new, fascinating insights into the dynamics of the European policy process and the distinct positions of the numerous actors involved on the ground. I owe Andrea special thanks for reading and commenting on parts of the book manuscript. During my time in Osnabrück, I also was lucky to meet Ingeborg Tömmel, who with her passion for European studies is a great source of inspiration to me. I am grateful for the continuing support, friendship and encouragement from Andrea and Ingeborg.

I joined the Institute for Political Science at the Goethe-Universität in Frankfurt in October 2014. I am grateful to work in such a stimulating intellectual environment at one of the largest political science departments in Germany. It is with great pleasure that I share my interest in political economy with various colleagues at the department. Here, I would like to express my particular gratitude to Andreas Nölke who is a great colleague and has provided me with useful comments on various occasions, also in preparation of this book. Further, I am glad to share my interest in, and my passion for European integration with my colleague and friend Sandra Seubert at the political science department. I enjoy promoting the European dimension in the life of the Goethe Universität together with Sandra and, beyond the disciplinary frontiers, with Pierre Monnet in his capacity as the director of the Franco-German Institute of History and Social Sciences (IFRA), and Matthias Lutz-Bachmann, director of the Research College in the Humanities (Forschungskolleg Humanwissenschaften).

Throughout the process of developing the ideas behind the book and writing it, I have presented my work on numerous occasions and have received insightful comments and suggestions for improvement. In particular, I would like to thank the participants of the following events: a conference organised at York University, Toronto, in 2012 on European governance; the workshops organised by the Political Science Standing Group on Regulatory Governance in Exeter in 2012 and during the Society for the Advancement of Socio-Economics annual conference held in 2013, in Milan; the third Florence conference on the regulation of infrastructure organised by the Florence School of Regulation at the European University Institute in 2014; a panel on energy and climate change policies during the ECPR 2014 General Conference at the University of Glasgow; a workshop on private governance at the Mannheim Centre for European Social Research (MZES) in 2014; a workshop on energy policy during the International Conference on Public Policy (ICPP) in Milan; a panel on the trajectories of EU regulatory governance during the 2016 Pan-European Conference on the European Union in Trento; and a panel on the judicialisation of politics during the ECPR General Conference 2018 in Hamburg. Helpful input was furthermore provided to me during presentations of the book project to the participants of the research college "The Transformative Power of Europe" at the Freie Universität in Berlin in 2017. Further, I would like to thank the colleagues Tim Büthe, Christoph Knill, Berthold Rittberger and Bernhard Zangl at the political science departments at the Technische Universität München and the Ludwig-Maximilians-Universität München for inviting me to attend and present my work at their research colloquia. Special thanks go to all the participants of these intellectually stimulating and challenging sessions. It was during these meetings, that I began to discuss regulatory policies with Dovile Rimkute, and I would like to thank her for providing thoughtful comments on my work on various occasions. Special thanks go further to the anonymous reviewer for giving very helpful and constructive comments that helped me improve the manuscript. Finally, I would like to thank the staff at Palgrave for their patience, editorial advice and guidance throughout the project.

Financial support to conduct this research is gratefully acknowledged. Funding has been received from the European Union in the framework of the FP 6 NEWGOV project coordinated at the European University Institute. I am also grateful for the financial support received from the Goethe Universität Frankfurt to cover travel expenses in my capacity as an Assistant Professor. Throughout the process of conducting the research, writing up and finalising the manuscript, thorough research assistance has been provided by Regina Ellenbracht, Janne Kriesch, David Mann and Victoria Siegismund. Further, I would also like to express my gratitude to my former student, David Royle, for providing excellent proofreading services. Many policy practitioners and experts have dedicated time and energy during several rounds of interviews conducted in Berlin, Bonn, Brussels, Florence, Frankfurt, Munich, Paris and

London between 2005 and 2018. Without their willingness to share their knowledge and insights, I would not have been in a position to write this book. Special thanks go to my dear friends Katharina Kastner, Livia Figà-Talamanca and Erika Schulze for hosting me during these various research trips.

On a more personal note, I would like to express my gratitude to my family and my partner. My parents, Doris and Siegfried, and my mother-in-law, Imke, have always been very supportive of my work. Together with my brother Ralf and his family, they have offered a wonderful sense of perspective beyond the world of academia. We keep fond memories of my father-in-law, Lüdmil, whose passing away in 2016 was a great loss to all of us. Lastly, I am delighted to dedicate this book to the love of my life and husband, to Daniel. He provided me with the encouragement and tireless support needed to complete this piece of work. But much more than that, I cherish every day we share our intellectual curiosity, our love and passion for good food, the cinema, dancing, literature, music, the opera, travel… and for each other. It is more than a lucky coincidence that our paths crossed in Brussels back in March 2001.

Munich, Germany   Sandra Eckert
March 2019

Contents

ABBREVIATIONS

ACE	The European Alliance for Beverage Cartons and the Environment
ACER	Agency for the Cooperation of European Energy Regulators
AESAG	Electricity Stakeholder Advisory Group
AFERA	European Adhesive Tape Association
AMDEA	Association of Manufacturers of Domestic Appliances
ANEC	European Association for the Coordination of Consumer Representation in Standardisation
APPLiA	Home Appliance Europe
ATSOI	Association of the Transmission System Operators of Ireland
BBP	Benzyl butyl phthalate
BEUC	The European Consumer Organisation (*Bureau Européen des Unions des Consommateurs*)
BPA	Bisphenol A
BPF	British Plastics Federation
BSI	British Standards Institute
CACM	Capacity Allocation and Congestion Management
CARACAL	Competent authorities for REACH and expert group
CBA	Chemical Business Association
CECED	European Committee of Domestic Equipment Manufacturers (*Conseil Européen de la Construction d'appareils Domestiques*), became APPLiA in 2018
CEER	Council of European Energy Regulators
CEFIC	European Chemical Industry Council
CEN	European Committee for Standardisation (*Comité Européen de Normalisation*)

CENELEC	European Committee for Electrotechnical Standardisation
CEPI	Confederation of European Paper Industries
CFI	Court of First Instance
CHEMSEC	International Chemical Secretariat
CHEM Trust	Chemicals, Health and Environment Monitoring, UK registered charity
CIA	Chemicals Industry Association, UK
CITPA	International Confederation of Paper and Board Converters in Europe
CLASP	Clean Energy Access Program
CLC	CENELEC, European Committee for Electrotechnical Standardisation
CLP	Classification, Labelling and Packaging
COM	European Commission
CPI	Confederation of Paper Industries
DBP	Dibutyl phthalate
DEFRA	Department for Environment, Food & Rural Affairs
DEHP	Bis(2-ethylhexyl) phthalate
DG	Directorate General (European Commission)
DG COMP	Directorate General for Competition Policy
DG ENVI	Directorate General Environment
DG GROWTH	Internal Market, Industry, Entrepreneurship and SMEs
DG SANTE	Directorate General for Health and Food Safety
DSO	Distribution System Operators
EAC	Environmental Audit Committee, House of Commons
EADP	European Association of Directory and Database Publishers
EC	European Communities
ECHA	European Chemicals Agency
ECJ	European Court of Justice
ECOS	European Environmental Citizens Organisation for Standardisation
ECPI	European Council for Plasticisers and Intermediates
ECVM	European Council of Vinyl Manufacturers
EDC	Endocrine Disruptors
EdF	*Electricité de France*
EEA	European Environmental Agency
EEB	European Environmental Bureau
EEE	Electrical and Electronic Equipment
EFSA	European Food Safety Agency
EFTA	European Free Trade Association
EGC	General Court of the European Union
EIAC	Electronic Industries' Association of Japan

EICTA	European Information and Communications Technology Association
EMF	Ellen MacArthur Foundation
EMFA	European Molded Fibre Association
EMMA	European Magazine Media Association
ENPA	European Newspaper Publishers Association
ENTSO	European Network of Transmission System Operators
EP	European Parliament
EPCoat	PVC Coated Fabric Sector Group
EPFLOOR	European PVC Flooring Manufacturers
EPPA	European PVC Window Profile and Related Building Products Association
EPRC	European Paper Recycling Council (European Recovered Paper Council, ERPC until April 2017)
ERGEG	European Regulators' Group for Electricity and Gas
ERPA	European Recovered Paper Association (ceased to exist as a legal entity in 2016 and became part of EuRIC)
ERPC	European Recovered Paper Council (European Paper Recycling Council, EPRC from April 2017)
ESPA	European Stabilisers Producers Association
ESWA	European Single Ply Waterproofing Association
ETS	European Tissue Symposium
ETSI	European Telecommunications Standards Institute
ETSO	European Transmission System Operators
EU	European Union
EUBA	European Bioeconomy Alliance
EuPC	European Plastics Converters
EuPIA	European Printing Ink Association
EURELECTRIC	Union of the electricity industry in Europe
EuRIC	European Recycling Industries
Euro-C	European Consumer Unit
FEAD	European Federation of Waste Management and Environmental Services
FEF	Florence Electricity Forum
FEFCO	European Federation of Corrugated Packaging
FEICA	Association of the European Adhesives and Sealant Industry
FEPE	European Federation of Envelope Manufacturers
FINAT	European Association for the self-adhesive label industry
FoE	Friends of the Earth
GDP	Gross Domestic Product
HEAL	Health and Environment Alliance
HL	House of Lords

HMRC	Her Majesty's Revenue and Customs
IAA	Independent Administrative Authority
ICT	Information and Communication Technology
IEC	International Electrotechnical Commission
IEM	Internal Energy Market
INTERGRAF	European Federation for Print and Digital Communication
IP	Press releases published by the European Commission
IPE	International Political Economy
IRA	Independent Regulatory Authority
ISO	International Organisation for Standardisation
	Independent System Operator
ITC	Inter-TSO Compensation
ITO	Independent Transmission Operator
IVK	Industrieverband Kunststoffbahnen e.V.
JTC 10	Joint Technical Committee 10 on Energy-related products—Material Efficiency Aspects for Ecodesign (CEN/ CLC/ JTC 10)
MEP	Member of European Parliament
MP	Member of Parliament
NAO	National Audit Office
NCA	National Competition Authority
NCC	National Competition Council
NGET	National Grid
NGO	Non-Governmental Organisation
NIE	National Ireland Electricity
NIRA	Network of Independent Regulatory Authorities
NRA	National Regulatory Authority
NRDC	Natural Resources Defense Council
OECD	Organisation for Economic Cooperation and Development
OFFER	Office of Electricity Supply
OFGEM	Office of Gas and Electricity Markets
ONP	Open Network Provision
OU	Ownership Unbundling
PCI	Projects of Common Interest
plc	public limited company
PRN	Packaging Recovery Note
RDI	Research, Development and Innovation
R&D	Research and Development
REACH	Registration, Evaluation, Authorisation of Chemicals
REFIT	Regulatory Fitness and Performance
RGI	Renewable Grid Initiative
RoHS	Restriction of Hazardous Substances

rreuse	Association of social enterprises active in reuse, repair and recycling
RTE	European Association for the Advancement of Radiation Curing by UV, EB and Laser Beams RadTech-Europe
SEC	Documents of the European Commission which cannot be classified in any of the other series
SVHC	Substances of Very High Concern
TEPPFA	European Plastic Pipes and Fittings Association
TEU	Treaty on European Union
TFEU	Treaty on the Functioning of the European Union
TSO	Transmission System Operator
TYNDP	Ten-Year Network Development Plan
UCPTE	Union for the Coordination of Production and Transmission of Electricity
UCTE	Union for the Coordination of Transmission of Electricity
UK	United Kingdom
UKTSOA	United Kingdom Transmission System Operators Association
VA	Voluntary Agreement
WEEE	Waste from Electrical and Electronic Equipment
WRAP	Waste and Resources Action Programme
WWF	World Wide Fund for Nature

List of Figures

List of Tables

CHAPTER 1

Introduction

This book is about how consumers and the environment are protected
through European regulation and, in particular, the role of corporate
actors in the policy process. But it is not a book only about European
consumer and environmental policy. Rather, it is about the extent to
which private actors, mainly firms and their associations, acquire a regulatory role. This book asks how corporations do so, and what resources
they draw upon, especially where they have to face media and NGO
pressure and are exposed to regulatory threats. Four examples show that
corporate power in regulation prevails in very diverse settings, addressing
quite distinct policy challenges.

Λ 2015 video of a sea turtle with a plastic straw up its nostril went
viral. The eight minute video taken by a team of biologists who were
on an expedition off the coast of Costa Rica has, at the time of writing, been seen more than thirty million times since it was uploaded on
YouTube. The heartbreaking video caused many people to re-think
their own consumption of plastic products, many of them for single use.
NGO-led public campaigns such as the global "Break free from Plastic
Movement", media coverage such as the BBC series "Blue Planet", or
the work of the renowned Ellen MacArthur Foundation (EMF) on the
"New Plastics Economy" further contributed to the upward momentum
for change. In 2018, a number of airlines, coffee house chains, hotels,
fast food restaurants and retailers, including large international companies such as McDonald's, Starbucks and Marriott Hotels, announced

© The Author(s) 2019
S. Eckert, *Corporate Power and Regulation*,
International Series on Public Policy,
https://doi.org/10.1007/978-3-030-05463-2_1

phase-outs or bans of plastic straws and other single-use plastic items in their business premises. Concurrently, policymakers seemed to engage in a race to the top, claiming leadership in the global fight against plastic pollution. In January 2018, China announced bans and restrictions on imported plastic waste. In the same month, the European Commission came forward with its plastics strategy, and the UK government announced its "world-leading micro-beads ban". In May 2018, the European Commission proposed to ban the top-ten single-use plastic products most commonly found in marine litter, including the famous plastic straw, and a provisional political agreement was reached by the European Parliament and the Council of the European Union (EU) in December 2018 on the proposed directive.

* * *

In summer 2015, the automotive manufacturing giant Volkswagen was discovered to have been falsifying emission testing results, leading to a large scandal and drawing massive media attention for many months. The Volkswagen emission scandal became a classic of corporate misbehaviour over false and misleading "clean Diesel" claims. Echoing such accusations presented in the "Dieselgate" scandal, British inventor Sir James Dyson sought to trigger a "Hoovergate" scandal (Crisp 2016), this time targeting German home appliance manufacturers. Dyson sued competitors for alleged misleading advertising of energy efficiency standards and challenged the European Commission for regulatory requirements concerning energy efficiency tests under unrealistic laboratory conditions (with empty receptacle), which he considered inappropriate. The European Commission in 2015 issued a standardisation mandate to review the testing requirements for vacuum cleaners, and NGOs voiced concerns whether testing methods were to undermine consumers' trust. While in a first ruling in 2015 the General Court rejected Dyson's request to annul a Commission regulation laying down the energy labelling requirements for vacuum cleaners, in its final November 2018 ruling the General Court upheld Dyson's argument.

* * *

From mid-January to March 2018, electric clocks slowed across 25 European countries, and power deviations were persisting throughout 2018. The change was caused by a decrease in the electric frequency in the continental transmission network. The imbalance in the continental European power system originated in Serbia and Kosovo: Serbia prevented Kosovo from importing energy from neighbouring Albania. Concurrently, Serbia's electrical power grid company blamed Kosovo to withdraw uncontracted electric energy from the synchronised European grid. A more dramatic energy crisis occurred in 2006, when several Western European countries were hit by a blackout. It started off in north-west Germany, when a ship ran into a set of overhead cables during a river crossing. Failure to communicate this routine interruption of cross-border electricity flows ahead of time to the neighbouring grid operator led to continued disruption, eventually causing a domino effect across Europe. Previously, in 2003, Italy was hit by a blackout due to a transmission line connecting Italy to Switzerland being damaged, leading to many trains being cancelled and numerous airports being closed across Europe. These incidents in 2003, 2006 and 2018 disrupted the technical, behind-the-scenes routines of network operators and brought their apparent failures to cooperate across national borders into the spotlight. Policymakers were alerted to prioritise security of supply issues and adopt measures in order to safeguard uninterrupted provision.

*   *   *

In June 2016, a majority of voters in the UK voted to leave the EU. The decision was made despite the many warnings that voting to leave would have a detrimental impact on the domestic economy. In the ensuing domestic debate, high profile Brexiteers brushed off corporate criticism about Brexit. It became apparent that politics had trumped economic reasoning. This outcome was particularly surprising given the business-friendly legacy of the Anglo-Saxon liberal market economy. The consequences that this political decision to disintegrate will have in the long run for the future business environment are at this stage uncertain, both with respect to regulatory decisions and trading patterns. Moreover, the continuous political struggles on acceptable conditions of an exit deal have created a level of uncertainty which in itself is detrimental in the short and medium run.

*   *   *

What all of these four examples have in common is that these are cases where corporate power is under pressure. In times of heightened media attention and targeted NGO campaigning industry has come into the spotlight in regard to the environmental and health damage caused by their products (plastics); alleged non-compliance with environmental regulatory standards (automobiles, vacuum cleaners); and a failure to secure reliable technical operation of essential infrastructure (electricity). Even worse, it seems that in times of the populist surge rational economic arguments are no longer heard and that political decisions are made on the basis of popular moods (Brexit). Corporations face enormous public pressure, which is amplified by modern means of communication in the age of digitalisation. This is illustrated by global campaigns such as the one on plastics and media coverage of corporate scandals such as "Dieselgate", which will cost the German automobile producer Volkswagen billions, not to mention the harm done to the reputation of the company, the automobile sector and the merchandise mark "made in Germany". The performance of companies as providers of goods and services is under continuous public scrutiny, and companies are easily targeted by NGOs. In short, these examples seem to run counter to the argument that "corporations rule the world" (Korten 2015).

At a closer look, however, the picture becomes more nuanced in all of these cases. In addressing the challenge posed by the global anti-plastics campaign, corporate actors in the retail and services sector have already seized on opportunities to "green" their image. Plastics manufacturers are following suit to their retail counterparts. European and national business associations publicise their voluntary activities against marine littering, their commitment to develop recycling methods and their efforts to boost the shares of recycled and recovered material. Similarly, brands such as Bosch and Siemens targeted by the "Hoovergate" scandal, fought hard to defend their reputation—both in court and publicly—and generated substantive evidence about their compliance with regulatory and testing requirements. Further, while electricity operators who draw their legitimacy from technical reliability and operational security suffer from blackouts, they can also benefit from such incidents: they can ask policymakers to invest more in the grid and expand cross-border capacity in order to avoid similar incidents in the future; and they can justify operational leeway on the grounds of security of supply arguments. Finally, Brexit, while bearing considerable risks of regulatory uncertainty for UK-based businesses, is also an opportunity for business to bring their interests in the de- and reconstruction of the regulatory state. The threat to leave the UK is particularly prevalent for big, transnational companies and gives them extra leverage in domestic politics.

In order to shed light on both sides of the equation, namely the ways in which corporate actors are put under pressure and targeted by media coverage, NGO activism and ultimately regulatory action, and also the ways in which business disposes of powerful tools to respond to, or even pre-empt such pressure, I submit the following research question to empirical scrutiny: *To what extent are corporations threatened by regulation, and to what extent do they themselves pose a challenge to regulation?*

In answering this research question, this book does not take sides by arguing that either type of actor is stronger than the other. Neither do I claim that corporations or their associations take over and control politics. Further, I do not argue that policymakers dispose of the power of last resort as they can always decide to regulate. This book does also not discuss the general lobbying power of corporations in policy formulation. There is already a huge literature on how organised business interests seek to influence the legislative output and what resources they draw upon (e.g. Dür et al. 2019). This book is about the role of corporate actors in the *regulatory process*, posing a second research question: *How do corporations use various power resources in order to prevent, shape, make or revoke regulation?*

The Argument

Thus, I am interested in the role of corporate actors in policy dynamics (Hogwood and Peters 1983), considering regulation as, broadly speaking, a specific type of policy (Lowi 1964: 39; Héritier 1987). In order to apprehend the role of corporate actors in the regulatory policy process, I suggest moving from the demand side to the supply side of private governance. Much has been written on the underlying motives of public actors when delegating authority to private actors, often times from an efficiency-driven transaction cost perspective (Williamson 1979). Starting out from resource dependency theory (Pfeffer and Salancik 2003: xiii), I seek to shed light on corporate actors' regulatory capacity. I opt for a power lens—based on seminal contributions such as those by Max Weber (1978), Peter Bachrach and Morton S. Baratz (1962), and Steven Lukes (2005)—in order to focus on what Doris Fuchs has conceptualised as "structural power", while also integrating aspects of "discursive power" (Clapp and Fuchs 2007; Fuchs 2007).

I suggest differentiating between three types of regulatory power that corporations dispose of as *experts, innovators and operators*. I argue that *distinct power resources*, both structural and discursive, are available to corporate actors in the regulatory process, and that they dispose of a discernible capacity to *cope with uncertainty* (Pfeffer 1981: 109–112), and that different risks of *acquired regulation* are involved each time. To be sure, this argument is made at the analytical level, while in the real world corporations will frequently dispose of more than one type of power resource. When corporations act as *experts*, they dispose of levels and types of knowledge on highly complex and specialised issues that cannot easily be reproduced in the public arena, nor can sufficient counter-expertise be mobilised outside the corporate world. This is not to say that the expert status of corporations remains unchallenged, nor that it is a resource that corporations automatically draw upon. Rather, they have to continuously make their case—using both structural and discursive power—that they can provide policy input that draws on knowledge that is *superior* to other information sources. Expertise, which is extremely well-researched in the literature (Ambrus et al. 2014; Fischer 1990; Fleck et al. 2016; Boswell 2009; Radaelli 1995; Schrefler 2013), can serve to prevent regulation altogether, it is required in both rule-shaping and rule-making, and also in challenging and revoking existing rules. Where expertise and the capacity to cope with epistemic uncertainty are unequally distributed between regulator and regulatee, there is an eminent risk of regulatory capture (Croley 2011: 3; Stigler 1971). Corporations are, in fact, ahead of their regulators when they act as *innovators*. The innovator is a specific type of expert, disposing of innovative know-how and a superior capacity to cope with technological, and related market uncertainty. Innovators will emphasise the societal benefits of innovation in order to legitimise their requests for a regulatory framework that supports innovative economic activity. Innovation, a well-established theme in various disciplines (Burgelman and Sayles 1986; Webster 2004; Witt and Jackson 2016; Corso and Pellegrini 2007; Ford 2017), can take more radical or more incremental paths, and thus involve different degrees of uncertainty for both the innovator and the regulator. The risk of acquired regulation is that it mainly protects market power. Finally, *operators* as the sole provider of a critical infrastructure dispose of a type of knowledge about technical and operational details that other actors cannot easily reproduce or verify. This also holds for the capacity to cope with uncertainty related to operation—the operator knows best, and under certain conditions has no interest to disclose full information. Operators will refer to their role as neutral facilitators who are technically reliable and strive for secure and uninterrupted supply. Their discursive power is considerable given that policymakers will shy away from any action that could involve the risk of a blackout. In a nutshell, regulation is likely to put security of supply front and centre, and therefore tends to amplify the autonomy of operators.

THE CONTRIBUTION

The book makes three key contributions: first, to the literature on governance and regulation, and second, to previous accounts of the international political economy (IPE) literature, with either a focus on private authority or business power. So far, both the literatures on governance and regulation as well as on private authority have overemphasised the demand side, i.e. the role of public actors. Third, the book makes a substantive contribution to various strands of policy analysis.

The governance literature has discussed the concept of hierarchy and the shadow of hierarchy extensively, which in essence questions the capacity of the public domain to engage in top-down intervention and revert to public regulation as a last resort (Héritier and Lehmkuhl 2008; Börzel 2010; Héritier and Rhodes 2010). The legislative and regulatory threat scenario takes on this line of reasoning, assuming that the mere possibility of public intervention alters incentive structures for private actors (Halfteck 2006, 2008; Glachant 2003). Crucially, these accounts approach private actors predominantly as the addressees of such hierarchical intervention or regulatory threats. The book thus contributes to this literature by addressing the flip side of the coin on the supply side of corporate regulatory power. Further, it incorporates the role of litigation as a business tool (Forcier 1994) in the regulatory process and questions the substantive effects of "regulation by litigation" (Morriss et al. 2009). Not enough attention has so far been dedicated to the rising importance of litigation in the regulatory process, not only as an instrument of revoking regulation but also when it comes to the substantive effects on regulatory outputs and outcomes.

Similarly, previous accounts of private authority have started out from asking why public actors would demand for, or legitimise private action. This appears quite paradoxical given the focus of the literature on *private* actors. The conceptualisation suggested by Jessica Green (2014), for example, differentiates between delegated and entrepreneurial private authority as two distinct types depending on the degree of *public* intervention. Drawing on existing work on corporate and business power (Clapp and Fuchs 2007; Fuchs 2007; May 2006; Mikler 2018), I provide a more nuanced conceptualisation of what Doris Fuchs has termed "structural" and "discursive" power, establishing an analytical distinction between the regulatory role of experts, innovators and operators.

In substantive terms, this book contributes to various strands of the vast literature on European public policy and governance, namely risk regulation, environmental policy, energy policy, and emerging scholarship on Brexit and disintegration. Broadly speaking, the book contributes to the field of European governance and integration (Börzel 2010; Peters and Borrás 2010) and complements the picture drawn by the thriving literature on a European administrative space (Trondal and Peters 2015; Heidbreder 2011) with its focus on private governance. The area of risk regulation has been discussed in numerous publications, yet again the focus is on public actors and regulators. The seminal contribution by David Vogel's longitudinal comparison of US-American and European regulatory regimes provides a rich and sharp analysis of international regulatory competition (Vogel 2012). As with other accounts (e.g. Tosun 2013), however, Vogel focuses on the public policy response to the risks caused by business activities and not on the role of corporations in the regulatory process. This is where my analysis of corporate power in regulation adds yet another angle to a rich literature.

The field of European environmental policy is mushrooming, and possibly one of the best researched policy fields in Europeanisation studies (Börzel and Risse 2006: 486). This also holds for aspects relating to the role of private governance and self-regulation (Rottmann and Lenschow 2008; Lenschow and Rottmann 2010; Héritier and Eckert 2008, 2009). Further, there is an intense discussion about the balance between corporate and diffuse interests, especially in the field of environmental policy, given the eminent role of environmental NGOs (Greenwood 2017; Newell and Grant 2000; Wurzel and Connelly 2011). Yet we still need to come to terms with the precise role of business actors in the process of specifying broad legislative frameworks, through self- or co-regulatory instruments, but also through committee and agency governance, standardisation and litigation. This is the field where the book contributes to existing research (Levi-Faur and Jordana 2004; Levi-Faur 2011; Büthe 2010; Büthe and Mattli 2010; Morriss et al. 2009; Wonka and Rittberger 2010; Trondal et al. 2012). Further, it addresses topical issues in European environmental policy. The case studies relate to new sustainability paradigms such as the circular economy (Geissdoerfer et al. 2017; Murray et al. 2017) and the bioeconomy (McCormick and Kautto 2013). With respect to the ambition and scope of regulatory activity, the discussion of recent developments in view of Europe's post-crisis growth agenda also raises issues around policy dismantling (Bauer 2005; Knill et al. 2009; Steinebach and Knill 2017). Finally, the book contributes to the emerging scholarship on the effects of disintegration and Brexit on environmental policy (Burns et al. 2016, 2019; Heyvaert and Čavoški 2018).

European energy policy has become a topical issue of political science research, and the number of publications is steadily increasing. Despite this growing interest, few publications have specifically focused on the role of TSOs. Existing research on European energy policy addresses various aspects of energy policy in the EU, such as emission trading, climate policy and renewables, internal gas markets, as well as the role of individual EU institutions and EU member states (e.g. Birchfield and Duffield 2011; Tosun et al. 2014; Dreger 2014; Schubert et al. 2016; Herweg 2017; Goldthau and Sitter 2014). In terms of actors and institutions, the focus thus far has been on policymakers, stakeholder fora and regulatory agencies (Labelle 2016; Mathieu 2016; Vasconcelos 2001; Jevnaker 2015). Burkard Eberlein, for example, has covered energy policy and governance in the Internal Energy Market (IEM) from various angles (Eberlein 2003, 2005, 2008, 2012). The role of infrastructure operators, by contrast, is clearly an under-researched area of European energy policy. In order to fill this gap, the book provides a crucial case study on private authority in the electricity market, and thereby challenges claims about the degree of centralised administrative capacity achieved in this policy field (Jevnaker 2015). Further, it discusses the possible impact of Brexit for the internal electricity market, linking to publications on the role of the UK for the European energy policy agenda (Solorio 2011; Buchan 2010) and contributing to an emerging research topic (Pollitt 2017; Fernandez 2018: 242–243).

Compared to renewables and climate change, energy efficiency also does not take centre stage in the literature on European energy policy. Existing research covers the rebound effect across countries and sectors (Herring and Sorrell 2009), or the role of white certificate instruments in steering end-use energy savings in Europe (Steuwer 2013). There are a number of contributions covering European Integrated Product Policy and Ecodesign, also with a focus on voluntary agreements (VAs) such as the one by Irina Tanasescu (2009). Research on the move from energy efficiency towards resource efficiency in European product policy is only emerging (Bundgaard et al. 2017). The same holds for issues related to the Information and Communication Technology (ITC) industry and sustainability (Belkhir and Elmeligi 2018; Haucke et al. 2019; Hilty and Aebischer 2014). The case study on innovation in energy and resource efficiency in European product policy thus contributes to both, an existing debate and an emerging field of research.

Finally, the book feeds into the ongoing debate about theorising and explaining the consequences of political disintegration (Vollaard 2014; Schimmelfennig 2018; Eckert 2018; Jones 2018). More specifically, it addresses the policy implications of Brexit and provides a timely contribution on the type of consequences we can anticipate in specific areas of regulation (chemicals, energy, product and waste regulation). The focus in the emerging literature on UK disintegration and political disengagement is so far on the politics dimension (Inglehart and Norris 2016; Glencross 2016; Clarke et al. 2017). By contrast, contributions addressing the substantive consequences for policies are only starting to complement the picture (Howarth and Quaglia 2017; Dennison and Geddes 2018; Dougan 2018: Part II; Burns et al. 2016, 2019). The Brexit chapter in the book gives us first hints about future regulatory alignment or divergence (Armstrong 2018).

Plan of the Book

Chapter 2 develops the book's conceptual framework. It revisits the discussion of the public–private divide in the literature on governance, regulation and IPE. I suggest moving from demand-side arguments about the shadow of hierarchy, regulatory threats and authority to considering what private actors have to offer on the supply side. Here I spell out expectations for the three types of corporate power in regulation: How the expert will use the power of knowledge; how the innovator disposes of decisive resources as a first mover; and how managing critical infrastructure gives the operator authority as the guarantor of secure supply. The last section presents the case study selection: paper and plastics industry (expert), home appliance and ICT industry (innovator) and electricity transmission industry (operator).

Chapter 3 provides readers with an introduction to policy dynamics in the European Union's (EU) consumer and environmental protection. It reviews the literature on the power balance between corporate interests and environmental and consumer interests. Next, expectations are formulated on how corporate regulatory strategies materialise at the

EU-level. To that end, I compare the role of VAs, secondary law and implementing measures, and litigation. I argue that EU-wide self-regulation is often too demanding for industry, and not necessarily rewarding. By contrast, it is expected that corporate power in non-legislative rule-making, i.e. agency governance, standardisation bodies and courts, is particularly pronounced. The chapter concludes by providing a brief overview of the areas of EU regulation to be covered in the industry case studies conducted in the subsequent chapters.

Exemplary cases for these three settings are analysed in Chapters 4–6. Chapter 4 is dedicated to the analysis of corporate expertise in managing the environmental and health impacts of materials. First, it introduces the European plastics and paper industries and discusses their varying exposure to public and NGO pressure. Next, it considers how measures proposed under the circular economy initiative might affect these industries in the future. A second part contrasts the diverging rationales of the two industry branches in the EU regulatory process: the paper industry as a producer and recycler of an organic material, which is asking for more stringent regulation of hazardous substances and waste management processes; and the plastics industry, which mainly seeks to relax regulatory requirements. The chapter finds that both industries have engaged in voluntary recycling schemes in order to pre-empt sector-specific regulation and raise their environmental credentials.

Chapter 5 presents the case study on innovation in the production of resource efficient electrical and electronic devices. Following the structure of the previous case study chapter, it first introduces the industry branches (home appliance and ICT products) and subsequently covers the role of consumer and environmental interests, the track record of industry influence and ongoing policy discussions. Further, it sheds light on industries' strategies in the regulatory process. A key finding is that home appliance producers seek binding energy efficiency standards in order to avoid freeriding and achieve market coverage, while the ICT industry mostly argues against regulatory requirements on the grounds of technological innovation and market incentives. Both industry branches take a cautious stance towards more encompassing, binding requirements on resource efficiency throughout the life cycle of their products.

Chapter 6 analyses the regulatory power of infrastructure operators. First, it introduces transmission system operators in the European electricity sector, addresses their relations with other market actors, NGOs and consumer interests, and explains how their cooperation within a dedicated European association has become a cornerstone of European energy governance. It also reflects on network aspects in the Clean Energy proposal, and how these could affect the governance architecture. Second, it analyses the regulatory role of grid operators in allocating the costs of the use of cross-border infrastructure, managing congestion, network development and the formulation of network codes. The findings suggest that the European TSOs effectively use their power resources in order to prevent, shape and even make regulation on highly technical infrastructure issues.

Chapter 7 looks at corporate power from a Brexit lens. It covers, firstly, the likely effects of leaving the EU for future chemical, waste and energy efficiency policies and, secondly, the consequences for the energy sector. It appears that in these areas of regulation UK-based business, rather than embracing the opportunity to do away with Brussels red tape, wants to safeguard the status quo. I argue that most of the industry branches can be expected to lose out in their power to shape regulation. The EU could, for instance, deny access to its databases and standardisation bodies in chemical and environmental regulation. It can be anticipated, however, that a different pattern emerges for energy where the relative influence of domestic TSOs, participating in technically driven cross-border cooperation, will increase.

Finally, the concluding Chapter 8 brings together the findings of the book and provides brief answers to the research questions. It posits that, in the areas of EU regulation studied, policymakers have limited capacity to effectively pose a regulatory threat. Rather, it is the experts, innovators and operators who pose a challenge to regulation. There is an eminent risk for regulators to reward gatekeeping (expert), protect market power (innovator), and amplify autonomy (operator). Further, the industry case studies and the analysis of Brexit back up the argument that corporations do not simply strive for deregulation but for power in regulation. The chapter concludes by summarising the contributions made to existing literature, and identifies perspectives for both future developments in relevant policy fields and future research.

References

Ambrus M, Arts K, Hey E, et al. (2014) *The Role of 'Experts' in International and European Decision-Making Processes: Advisors, Decision Makers or Irrelevant Actors?* Cambridge: Cambridge University Press.

Armstrong KA. (2018) Regulatory Alignment and Divergence After Brexit. *Journal of European Public Policy* 25(8): 1099–1117.

Bachrach P and Baratz MS. (1962) Two Faces of Power. *The American Political Science Review* 56(4): 947–952.

Bauer MW. (2005) Administrative Costs of Reforming Utilities. In: Héritier A and Coen D (eds) *Refining Regulatory Regimes: Utilities in Europe.* Cheltenham, Northampton: Edward Elgar, 53–88.

Belkhir L and Elmeligi A. (2018) Assessing ICT Global Emissions Footprint: Trends to 2040 and Recommendations. *Journal of Cleaner Production* 177: 448–463.

Birchfield VL and Duffield JS. (2011) *Toward a Common European Union Energy Policy: Problems, Progress, and Prospects.* Houndmills, Basingstoke: Palgrave Macmillan.

Börzel TA. (2010) European Governance: Negotiation and Competition in the Shadow of Hierarchy. *Journal of Common Market Studies* 48(2): 191–219.

Börzel TA and Risse T. (2006) Europeanization: The Domestic Impact of European Union Politics. In: Jørgensen KE, Pollack MA and Rosamond B (eds) *Handbook of European Union Politics.* London: Sage, 483–504.

Boswell C. (2009) *The Political Uses of Expert Knowledge: Immigration Policy and Social Research.* Cambridge: Cambridge University Press.

Buchan D. (2010) From Liberalisation to Intervention: Europe, the UK, and the Changing Agenda. In: Rutledge I and Wright P (eds) *UK Energy Policy and the End of Market Fundamentalism.* Oxford: Oxford University Press, Oxford Institute for Energy Studies, 401–420.

Bundgaard AM, Mosgaard MA and Remmen A. (2017) From Energy Efficiency Towards Resource Efficiency within the Ecodesign Directive. *Journal of Cleaner Production* 144: 358–374.

Burgelman RA and Sayles LR. (1986) *Inside Corporate Innovation: Strategy, Structure, and Managerial Skills.* New York: Free Press.

Burns C, Gravey V, Jordan A, et al. (2019) De-Europeanising or Disengaging? EU Environmental Policy and Brexit. Special Issue: The Future of European Union Environmental Politics and Policy. In: Zito A, Burns S and Lenschow A (eds) *Environmental Politics* 28(2): 271–292.

Burns C, Jordan A, Gravey V, et al. (2016) The EU Referendum and the UK Environment: An Expert Review. How has EU Membership Affected the UK and What Might Change in the Event of a Vote to Remain or Leave? *ESRC UK in a Changing Europe Initiative* 158.

Büthe T. (2010) Private Regulation in the Global Economy: A (P)Review. *Business and Politics* 12(3): 1–38.

Büthe T and Mattli W. (2010) International Standards and Standard-Standard-Setting Bodies. In: Coen D, Grant W and Wilson GK (eds) *The Oxford*

Handbook of Business and Government. Oxford: Oxford University Press, 440–471.

Clapp J and Fuchs D. (2007) *Corporate Power in Global Agrifood Governance. Challenges and Strategies*. Boston: MIT Press.

Clarke HD, Goodwin M and Whiteley P. (2017) *Brexit: Why Britain Voted to Leave the European Union*. Cambridge: Cambridge University Press.

Corso M and Pellegrini L. (2007) Continuous and Discontinuous Innovation: Overcoming the Innovator Dilemma. *Creativity and Innovation Management* 16(4): 333–347.

Crisp J. (2016) Commission Won't Regulate Toasters or Hairdryers after Hoovergate Scandal. *Euractiv*: 8.11.2016.

Croley SP. (2011) Beyond Capture: Towards a New Theory of Regulation. In: Levi-Faur D (ed) *Handbook on the Politics of Regulation*. Cheltenham, Northampton: Edward Elgar, 50–69.

Dennison J and Geddes A. (2018) Brexit and the Perils of 'Europeanised' Migration. *Journal of European Public Policy* 25(8): 1137–1153.

Dougan M. (2018) *The UK After Brexit: Legal and Policy Challenges*. Cambridge: Intersentia.

Dreger J. (2014) *The European Commission's Energy and Climate Policy: A Climate for Expertise*. Houndmills, Basingstoke: Palgrave Macmillan.

Dür A, Marshall D and Bernhagen P. (2019) *The Political Influence of Business in the European Union*. Ann Arbor: University of Michigan Press.

Eberlein B. (2003) Regulating Cross-Border Trade by Soft Law? The Florence Process in the Supranational Governance of Electricity Markets. *Journal of Network Industries* 4(2): 137–155.

Eberlein B. (2005) Regulation by Cooperation: The Third Way in Making Rules for the Internal Energy Market. In: Cameron P (ed) *Legal Aspects of EU Energy Regulation: Implementing the New Directives on Electricity and Gas Across Europe*. Oxford: Oxford University Press, 59–88.

Eberlein B. (2008) The Making of the European Energy Market: The Interplay of Governance and Government. *Journal of Public Policy* 28(1): 73–92.

Eberlein B. (2012) Inching Towards a Common Energy Policy: Entrepreneurship, Incrementalism, and Windows of Opportunity. In: Richardson J (ed) *Constructing a Policy-Making State? Policy Dynamics in the EU*. Oxford: Oxford University Press, 147–169.

Eckert S. (2018) The European Commission as a Negotiator: Evidence from the Disintegration Talks with the United Kingdom and Switzerland. In: Jörn E, Bauer MW and Becker S (eds) *The European Commission in Turbulent Times: Assessing Organizational Change and Policy Impact*. Baden-Baden: Nomos, 159–180.

Fernandez RM. (2018) Conflicting Energy Policy Priorities in EU Energy Governance. *Journal of Environmental Studies and Sciences* 8(3): 239–248.

Fischer F. (1990) *Technocracy and the Politics of Expertise*. Newbury Park: Sage.

Fleck J, Faulkner W and Williams R. (2016) *Exploring Expertise: Issues and Perspectives*. Houndmills, Basingstoke: Palgrave Macmillan.

Forcier JR. (1994) *Judicial Excess: The Political Economy of the American Legal System*. Lanham, New York, London: University Press of America.

Ford C. (2017) *Innovation and the State: Finance, Regulation, and Justice*. New York: Cambridge University Press.

Fuchs D. (2007) *Business Power in Global Governance*. London: Lynne Rienner.

Geissdoerfer M, Savaget P, Bocken NMP, et al. (2017) The Circular Economy: A New Sustainability Paradigm? *Journal of Cleaner Production* 143: 757–768.

Glachant M. (2003) Voluntary Agreements Under Endogenous Legislative Threats. *FEEM Working Paper* No. 36.2003.

Glencross A. (2016) *Why the UK Voted for Brexit: David Cameron's Great Miscalculation*. Houndmills, Basingstoke: Palgrave Macmillan.

Goldthau A and Sitter N. (2014) A Liberal Actor in a Realist World? The Commission and the External Dimension of the Single Market for Energy. *Journal of European Public Policy* 21(10): 1452–1472.

Green JF. (2014) *Rethinking Private Authority: Agents and Entrepreneurs in Global Environmental Governance*. Princeton: Princeton University Press.

Greenwood J. (2017) *Interest Representation in the European Union*. London: Palgrave Macmillan.

Halfteck G. (2006) *A Theory of Legislative Threats*. Tel Aviv: Tel Aviv University.

Halfteck G. (2008) Legislative Threats. *Stanford Law Review* 61: 629–710.

Haucke F, Lenschow A and Pollex J. (2019) Consumption for Sustainability? Exploring Societal and Political Dynamics in Digital Society. In: Boucher JL and Heinonen J (eds) *Sustainable Consumption: Promise or Myth? Case Studies from the Field*. Cambridge: Cambridge Scholars Publishing.

Heidbreder EG. (2011) Structuring the European Administrative Space: Policy Instruments of Multi-Level Administration. *Journal of European Public Policy* 18(5): 709–727.

Héritier A. (1987) *Policy Analyse: Eine Einführung*. Frankfurt/New York: Campus Verlag.

Héritier A and Eckert S. (2008) New Modes of Governance in the Shadow of Hierarchy: Self-Regulation by Industry in Europe. *Journal of Public Policy* 28(1): 113–138.

Héritier A and Eckert S. (2009) Self-Regulation by Associations: A Collective Action Problem in Environmental Regulation. *Business and Politics* 11(1): 1–22.

Héritier A and Lehmkuhl D. (2008) The Shadow of Hierarchy and New Modes of Governance. *Journal of Public Policy* 28(1): 1–17.

Héritier A and Rhodes M. (2010) *New Modes of Governance in Europe: Governing in the Shadow of Hierarchy.* Basingstoke, New York: Palgrave Macmillan.

Herring H and Sorrell S. (2009) *Energy Efficiency and Sustainable Consumption: The Rebound Effect.* Houndmills, Basingstoke: Palgrave Macmillan.

Herweg N. (2017) *European Union Policy-Making: The Regulatory Shift in Natural Gas Market Policy.* Cham: Palgrave Macmillan.

Heyvaert V and Čavoški A. (2018) UK Environmental Law Post-Brexit. In: Dougan M (ed) *The UK After Brexit: Legal and Policy Challenges.* Cambridge: Intersentia, 115–133.

Hilty LM and Aebischer B. (2014) *ICT for Sustainability: An Emerging Research Field.* London: Springer.

Hogwood BW and Peters BG. (1983) *Policy Dynamics.* Brighton, Sussex: Wheatsheaf Books.

Howarth D and Quaglia L. (2017) Brexit and the Single European Financial Market. *Journal of Common Market Studies* 55(S1): 149–164.

Inglehart RF and Norris P. (2016) Trump, Brexit, and the Rise of Populism: Economic Have-Nots and Cultural Backlash. *HKS Faculty Research Working Paper Series.* August 2016.

Jevnaker T. (2015) Pushing Administrative EU Integration: The Path Towards European Network Codes for Electricity. *Journal of European Public Policy* 22(7): 927–947.

Jones E. (2018) Towards a Theory of Disintegration. *Journal of European Public Policy* 25(3): 440–451.

Knill C, Tosun J and Bauer MW. (2009) Neglected Faces of Europeanization: The Differential Impact of the EU on the Dismantling and Expansion of Domestic Policies. *Public Administration* 87(3): 519–537.

Korten DC. (2015) *When Corporations Rule the World.* Oakland: Berrett-Koehler Publishers.

Labelle MC. (2016) Regulating for Consumers? The Agency for Cooperation of Energy Regulators. In: Andersen SS, Goldthau A and Sitter N (eds) *Energy Union: Europe's New Liberal Mercantilism?* London: Palgrave Macmillan, 147–164.

Lenschow A and Rottmann K. (2010) The Evolving Role of Industry in European Union Environmental Governance. In: O'Connor A (ed) *Managing Economies, Trade and International Business.* Houndmills, Basingstoke: Palgrave Macmillan, 67–85.

Levi-Faur D. (2011) Regulatory Networks and Regulatory Agencification: Towards a Single European Regulatory Space. *Journal of European Public Policy* 18(6): 810–829.

Levi-Faur D and Jordana J. (2004) *The Politics of Regulation: Institutions and Regulatory Reforms for the Age of Governance.* Cheltenham, Northampton: Edward Elgar.

Lowi T. (1964) American Business, Public Policy, Case-Studies, and Political Theory. *World Politics* 16(4): 677–715.

Lukes S. (2005) *Power: A Radical View.* Houndmills, Basingstoke: Palgrave Macmillan.

Mathieu E. (2016) *Regulatory Delegation in the European Union: Networks, Committees and Agencies.* London: Palgrave Macmillan.

May C. (2006) *Global Corporate Power.* Boulder: Lynne Rienner, 244.

McCormick K and Kautto N. (2013) The Bioeconomy in Europe: An Overview. *Sustainability* 5(6): 2589.

Mikler J. (2018) *The Political Power of Global Corporations.* Cambridge: Polity Press.

Morriss AP, Yandle B and Dorchak A. (2009) *Regulation by Litigation.* New Haven, London: Yale University Press.

Murray A, Skene K and Haynes K. (2017) The Circular Economy: An Interdisciplinary Exploration of the Concept and Application in a Global Context. *Journal of Business Ethics* 140(3): 369–380.

Newell PJ and Grant W. (2000) Environmental NGOs and EU Environmental Law. In: Somsen H (ed) *Yearbook of European Environmental Law. Volume 1.* Oxford: Oxford University Press, 225–252.

Peters GB and Borrás S. (2010) Governance and European Integration. In: Egan M (ed) *Research Agendas in EU Studies: Stalking the Elephant.* Houndmills, Basingstoke: Palgrave Macmillan, 117–133.

Pfeffer J. (1981) *Power in Organizations.* Marshfield, MA: Pitman Publishing.

Pfeffer J and Salancik GR. (2003) *The External Control of Organizations: A Resource Dependence Perspective.* Stanford: Stanford Business Books.

Pollitt MG. (2017) The Economic Consequences of Brexit: Energy. *Oxford Review of Economic Policy* 33(S1): S134–S143.

Radaelli C. (1995) The Role of Knowledge in the Policy Process. *Journal of European Public Policy* 2(2): 159–183.

Rottmann K and Lenschow A. (2008) 'Privatising' EU Governance: Emergence and Performance of Voluntary Agreements in European Environmental Policy. In: Conzelmann T and Smith R (eds) *Multi-Level Governance in the European Union: Taking Stock and Looking Ahead.* Baden-Baden: Nomos.

Schimmelfennig F. (2018) Brexit: Differentiated Disintegration in the European Union. *Journal of European Public Policy* 25(8): 1154–1173.

Schrefler L. (2013) *Economic Knowledge in Regulation: The Use of Expertise by Independent Agencies.* Colchester: ECPR Press.

Schubert SR, Pollak J and Kreutler M. (2016) *Energy Policy of the European Union.* Houndmills, Basingstoke: Palgrave Macmillan.

Solorio I. (2011) Bridging the Gap Between Environmental Policy Integration and the EU's Energy Policy: Mapping out the 'Green Europeanisation' of Energy Governance. *Journal of Contemporary European Research* 7(3): 396–415.

Steinebach Y and Knill C. (2017) Still an Entrepreneur? The Changing Role of the European Commission in EU Environmental Policy-Making. *Journal of European Public Policy* 24(3): 429–446.

Steuwer DS. (2013) *Energy Efficiency Governance: The Case of White Certificate Instruments for Energy Efficiency in Europe.* London: Springer.

Stigler GJ. (1971) The Theory of Economic Regulation. *The Bell Journal of Economics and Management Science* 2(1): 3–21.

Tanasescu I. (2009) *The European Commission and Interest Groups: Towards a Deliberative Interpretation of Stakeholder Involvement in EU Policy-Making.* Brussels: Brussels University Press.

Tosun J. (2013) *Risk Regulation in Europe: Assessing the Application of the Precautionary Principle.* New York: Springer Verlag.

Tosun J, Schmitt S and Schulze K. (2014) *Energy Policy Making in the EU: Building the Agenda.* London: Springer.

Trondal J, Busuioc M and Groenleer M. (2012) *The Agency Phenomenon in the European Union.* Manchester, New York: Manchester University Press.

Trondal J and Peters BG. (2015) A Conceptual Account of the European Administrative Space. In: Bauer MW and Trondal J (eds) *The Palgrave Handbook of the European Administrative System.* London: Palgrave Macmillan, 79–92.

Vasconcelos J. (2001) Cooperation Between Energy Regulators in the European Union. In: Henry C, Matheu M and Jeunemaître A (eds) *Regulation of Network Utilities: The European Experience.* Oxford: Oxford University Press, 284–289.

Vogel D. (2012) *The Politics of Precaution: Regulating Health, Safety and Environmental Risks in Europe and the United States.* Princeton: Princeton University Press.

Vollaard H. (2014) Explaining European Disintegration. *Journal of Common Market Studies* 52: 1142–1159.

Weber M. (1978) *Economy and Society.* Berkeley: University of California Press.

Webster E. (2004) Firms' Decisions to Innovate and Innovation Routines. *Economics of Innovation and New Technology* 13(8): 733–745.

Williamson OE. (1979) Transaction-Cost Economics: The Governance of Contractual Relations. *Journal of Law and Economics* 22(2): 233–261.

Witt MA and Jackson G. (2016) Varieties of Capitalism and Institutional Comparative Advantage: A Test and Reinterpretation. *Journal of International Business Studies* 47(4): 778–806.

Wonka A and Rittberger B. (2010) Credibility, Complexity and Uncertainty: Explaining the Institutional Independence of 29 EU Agencies. *West European Politics* 33(4): 730–752.

Wurzel RKW and Connelly J. (2011) Environmental NGOs: Taking a Lead? In: Wurzel RKW and Connelly J (eds) *The European Union as a Leader in International Climate Change Politics.* London: Routledge, 214–231.

CHAPTER 2

The Regulatory Power of Corporations

In order to grasp the regulatory role of corporations in regulation, I suggest adopting a power lens. Power is a multifaceted concept with a long tradition in the social sciences. The point of reference for this book is the discussion in international political economy (IPE) on business and corporate power (Clapp and Fuchs 2007; Fuchs 2007; May 2006; Mikler 2018). Further, I engage with the IPE literature on private authority, which has moved our focus towards instances of legitimate power held by private actors (Cutler et al. 1999; Green 2014). My starting point, however, is the governance approach, which has been dominating the literature on policy-making and regulation (Whitley and Kristensen 1997; Levi-Faur 2011; Pierre and Peters 2000). Crucially, governance scholars have mostly been silent about the notion of power (Mayntz 2005). Analysing the governance and regulation from a power lens thus adds to this literature in particular. What the IPE and governance literatures have in common, however, is their conceptual focus on public actors' demands in the policy process. In addressing the public–private divide various demand-side arguments have been put forward about the shadow of hierarchy, regulatory threats and delegated authority. Instead, there is a need to reconsider what private actors have to offer on the supply side. To that end, I spell out expectations for the three types of power in regulation corporations hold as experts, innovators and operators. Finally, I present the case study selection, explaining how the industry branches studied in the book represent the distinct types of corporate power.

© The Author(s) 2019   19
S. Eckert, *Corporate Power and Regulation*,
International Series on Public Policy,
https://doi.org/10.1007/978-3-030-05463-2_2

GOVERNANCE, REGULATION, POWER AND AUTHORITY

This section seeks to bridge the literatures on governance, regulation and IPE. Power (Clapp and Fuchs 2007; Fuchs 2007; May 2006; Mikler 2018) and the role of legitimate power as "authority" (Cutler et al. 1999; Green 2014) are central concepts in the IPE literature. The dominant angle in the scholarship on policy-making and regulation, by contrast, is on governance (Whitley and Kristensen 1997; Levi-Faur 2011; Pierre and Peters 2000). I will discuss, firstly, how my book links to and contributes to the literatures on governance and regulation, considering concepts such as the shadow of hierarchy and regulatory threats. Next, I will set out how my conceptual framework differs from previous accounts of business power developed in the IPE literature, and how it links to the concept of private authority.

The Governance Perspective

Originating in institutionalist economics, the governance literature has surely not focused on the notion of power front and centre. Rather, the governance literature has been dominated by what Cutler et al. have called "efficiency approaches" (Cutler et al. 1999: 337, 344–348). This perspective is rooted in rational choice theory, namely transaction cost theory and new institutional economics (Brousseau and Fares 2000; North 1990; Williamson 1975, 1996). These contributions posit that cooperation between firms and governance structures inside firms are required for effective market allocation, refuting the invisible-hand hypothesis of self-governing markets. From this angle, the raison d'être of any institution is to save transaction costs and to provide information. This applies to governance devices used inside and between firms, as well as for institutions governing the relations between firms and the state. Applied to self-regulation by industry (Héritier and Eckert 2008, 2009), the approach has been used to explain the emergence of voluntary cooperation between firms to address environmental concerns. It establishes a rationale for why firms prefer self-regulation over legislation and why public actors abstain from imposing regulation. From a transaction cost perspective, the state delegates tasks to private actors solely on the grounds of efficiency considerations, i.e. when private governance is supposed to be more efficient in achieving the desired outcomes.

The turn towards a governance perspective in political science has been driven by factors at the domestic and international level: it has sought to pay tribute to the long-standing legacy of the role of private actors in the policy process, and it has responded to the need to embrace policy-making beyond the nation state in international organisations and supranational institutions such as the EU (Mayntz 2005). Besides the level of policy-making and the type of actors involved, the governance literature has also sought to capture and differentiate between various steering modes. A typical distinction is a binary one between hierarchical and non-hierarchical coordination or, as it were, government as opposed to governance (Rhodes 1996; Héritier and Lehmkuhl 2008a). And there is, of course, the classical distinction developed by Walter W. Powell between hierarchies, networks and markets (1990). Adrienne Héritier has suggested to combine the type of actors involved (public versus private) and the steering mode (hierarchical versus non-hierarchical) in order to delineate government (public and hierarchical) from so-called new modes of governance—which either involves private actors, or is non-hierarchical, or both (Héritier and Lehmkuhl 2008b; Héritier and Rhodes 2010). A myriad of other concepts have also been developed in the literature, such as innovative (Tömmel and Verdun 2009) or experimentalist (Sabel and Zeitlin 2010) governance. The involvement of private actors in the policy process has been discussed under the broad category of "private governance" (Knill 2001; Lehmkuhl 2005; Graz and Nölke 2008), often times referring to very different governance settings.

Of particular relevance for this book is the "shadow of hierarchy", which as a conceptualisation is prevalent on its own merit (Scharpf 1997; Héritier and Eckert 2008; Smismans 2008; Héritier and Lehmkuhl 2008a; Börzel 2010; Héritier and Rhodes 2010). Its focus is on the relationship between hierarchical and non-hierarchical steering modes, and how the former casts a "shadow" on the latter. The shadow of hierarchy therefore alters the behaviour of those actors involved in non-hierarchical steering. This can work through both positive and negative incentives. The shadow of hierarchy is usually seen in its threatening form, i.e. negative sanctions such as the threatening of legislation, executive intervention or court rulings. However, it may also take the form of a positive incentive, for example where public actors grant financial support or publicly endorse private governance (Héritier and Lehmkuhl 2008a). When examining the interaction between public and private actors from that perspective, a "governance paradox" can be discerned, as suggested by Tanja A. Börzel (2008). In fact, the incentive structures of these two types of actors can be assumed as being diametrically opposed. In a setting where public actors dispose of a high level of governance capacity they are in a position to cast a strong shadow of hierarchy, while at the same time their incentives to cooperate with private actors are weak. By contrast, in a setting where public actors dispose of a low level of governance capacity they cannot cast a strong shadow of hierarchy, which is why their incentive to cooperate with private actors is high. This combines with the opposite pattern for private actors, who are incentivised to cooperate by a strong, rather than a weak shadow of hierarchy. Their incentive structures do only coincide where there is some middle ground, i.e. when there is a sufficiently credible shadow of hierarchy (Börzel 2008: 127).

The governance literature therefore already points to the limits and scope conditions on the demand side, that is, on the side of public actors, to cast a credible shadow of hierarchy. This leads me to consider the flipside of the coin, asking about the ways in which private actors pose a challenge to hierarchical, public intervention: *To what extent are corporations threatened by regulation, and to what extent do they themselves pose a challenge to regulation?* To that end, the following section lays out the distinct strategies of corporate actors in the regulatory process.

Corporate Strategies in the Regulatory Process

Governance perspectives have also been prominent in the political science literature on regulation (Levi-Faur and Jordana 2004; Scott 2004). Regulatory governance, broadly speaking, examines the steering modes in the area of regulatory policies, understood as rule-setting in contrast to distributive and re-distributive policies (Lowi 1964: 39; Héritier 1987). To be sure, some authors such as David Levi-Faur use the term regulation in a more concise way, distinguishing it from legislation or court action (Levi-Faur 2011). Following Lowi's seminal typology, regulation is conceived as a distinct policy type in this book: regulation is about prescriptive rules and encompasses several phases of the policy-cycle, such as formulation, implementation and enforcement. As mentioned in the Introduction, I am interested in studying the role of corporate actors in policy dynamics (Hogwood and Peters 1983), notably in *preventing, shaping, making and revoking rules*. The focus in this book is on the regulatory power of these actors and much less so on mere lobbying activities. It therefore links to strands in the interdisciplinary regulation literature which have emphasised the role of private actors, for instance by conceptualising categories of "private regulation" (Cafaggi 2006), or discarding a clear public–private divide in a setting of "decentred regulation" (Black 2002).

Rule prevention can be the result of successful lobbying activities already at the agenda-setting stage (Princen 2007; Considine 1998), yet in the area of regulatory policies is often complemented by means of voluntary, unilateral industry action in rule compliance. The benefit for the actors involved is first that they are autonomous in devising and managing their own rules without outside interference—this is commonly understood as (industry) self-regulation (Héritier and Eckert 2008; Haufler 2001). Other, alternative terms used are autonomous and voluntary regulation (Ronit and Schneider 2000: 23), unilateral commitment (OECD 1999: 16), voluntary agreements (VAs) (Hansen 1999), or voluntary private regulation (Cafaggi 2006). The second benefit for private actors is that they can prevent public regulation. Here, self-regulation functions as a pre-emptive strategy in the context of a (credible) regulatory threat. When industry actors face the risk to become subject to regulatory requirements, especially when these are costly and sector-specific, they prefer engaging in voluntary activities that potentially lift the policymakers' desire to introduce regulation. On the regulatory side, intervention involves controlling of externalities of economic activities. In contrast, on the side of regulated parties, regulation is mainly perceived as a cost. The regulatory threat reverses the cost-benefit analysis for economic actors where action to prevent (costly) regulation is preferable to non-action. A regulatory or legislative threat (Halfteck 2006, 2008; Glachant 2003) thus functions as an incentive and alters industry behaviour. It is a variant of public actors casting a "shadow of hierarchy" (Börzel 2010; Héritier and Rhodes 2010; Héritier and Lehmkuhl 2008b) in its threatening version. Public actors envisage or rather threaten to enact such legislation unless private actors comply with their demands. Halfteck has described such a deal as an "implicit political transaction, in which the legislator barters the non-use of legislative power […] in return for the firm's commitment to change its conduct" (Halfteck 2006: 6). To have an effect on corporate behaviour, it will be crucial whether private actors consider the threat as being credible and likely to be carried through (Halfteck 2006: 3–6; Erfle et al. 1990). This brings us back to the governance paradox of the "shadow of hierarchy" argument discussed earlier. Certain factors that strengthen credibility provide the basis of the formation of a supporting political coalition or alliance with actors that support legislation, such as NGOs (Halfteck 2006: 56–59). Contributions in both the governance and regulation literature have discussed the varying extent of the power of policymakers to pose such a threat or cast a shadow. Private actors, on the other hand, have mostly been dealt with as the recipients of such intervention. Yet, when successfully preventing public regulation through VAs, private actors become de facto *rule-makers*. Especially where voluntarily set objectives are reasonably ambitious and where the contracting parties comply with voluntary standards, this outcome might actually be quite stable. There are three possible outcomes for rule prevention: first, private actors succeed in temporarily removing regulatory pressure, i.e. they can at least delay regulation, but face regulatory intervention at a later point in time. Second, they achieve a tacit agreement with policymakers not to engage in regulation, which is to say that pre-emption works permanently. Third, policymakers endorse voluntary action and thus legitimise self-regulation ex post. The latter outcome reminds us that public actors hold the monopoly to offer legitimacy, while private actors never have full access to this type of authority (Genschel and Zangl 2014: 339). Such endorsement, however, might also shift the settings towards co-regulation where endorsement comes along with formalised requirements.

Rule-shaping is a broader category which can refer to rather different degrees of involvement in the policy process. Private influence in the policy formulation stage can be quite substantial and may alter policy output to a significant extent. Or, alternatively, private actors may have an active role in implementing and executing policies by generating epistemic input and giving advice or by holding a formalised mandate in implementation.

Where private interests de facto steer regulatory action without disposing of formalised rule-making capacity we encounter regulatory capture. The "capture" or "interest group" theory stipulates the likeliness of such "beneficial" or "acquired" regulation:

> Regulation may be actively sought by an industry, or it may be thrust upon it. A central thesis of this paper is that, as a rule, regulation is acquired by the industry and is designed and operated primarily for its benefit. There

are regulations whose net effects upon the regulated industry are undenia-
bly onerous [...] These onerous regulations, however, are exceptional and
can be explained by the same theory that explains beneficial (we may call it
"acquired") regulation. [...] (Stigler 1971: 3)

George J. Stigler, building on Mancur Olson's theory of collective action
(1965), argued that the regulatory process can be captured by relatively
small business industries. According to the logic of collective action, the
incentives for business to affect regulatory outcomes are a function of
the smallness of the group and its per capita stake. Stigler inferred that
members of an industry have a strong incentive to organise, contrary
to dispersed consumers with a low per capita stake. Therefore, the risk
that some firms or industries benefit disproportionally from regulation
has become a primary concern in the design of regulation (Wilson 1980;
Ayres and Braithwaite 1992). Specific challenges in this regard arise
when regulating experts, innovators and operators, as argued later in the
chapter.

Where private actors formulate and adopt rules they take on the role
of *rule-making*. This role is most pronounced in purely private, voluntary settings, as discussed above. But it can also take the form of co-regulation. Co-regulation constitutes the middle ground where rules or
policy objectives are defined by a public authority but are complemented
with regulatory detail and also implemented by private actors. Alternative
terms suggested in the literature are "regulated self-regulation", "delegated self-regulation" (Ronit and Schneider 2000: 23) or "negotiated
agreements" (OECD 1999: 18).

Finally, corporate actors may engage in activities aimed at *revoking
rules* in order to avoid the cost of current or future regulatory compliance. They can lobby policymakers, seeking to persuade them that existing rules are no longer appropriate or needed. Cutting red tape and
improving the investment climate can be powerful arguments in such an
endeavour, especially where companies can credibly threaten with dislo-
cation. Litigation is another means to achieve this goal. Adversarial legalism, which involves a systematic preference for litigation, has been on
the rise in the USA and EU context (Kelemen 2011; Kagan and Axelrad
2000). As a result, litigation has become a "business tool" and "an
inevitable part of any undertaking" (Forcier 1994: 140). As Robert A.
Kagan observes, the "powerful tools of adversarial legalism [...] are costly
to involve and clumsy and difficult to calibrate" (Kagan 2001: 226).

Business actors usually dispose not only of the financial means but also of sector-specific legal expertise they use to their benefit. This preference for litigation has a substantive effect on regulatory outcomes: in anticipation of or response to litigation regulation tends to be more prescriptive and detailed, plus it relies on legalistic enforcement (Kagan 2001: 187, 194). Further, litigation can impose "forward-looking substantive requirements [...] on the regulated entities" (Morriss et al. 2009: 48). Legal uncertainty can be costly for all parties involved, although in some instances it might be a preferable outcome to buy time, especially where interim non-compliance is beneficial for some parties. *Delay* can thus become in itself the goal of legal action (Forcier 1994: 164): when delay is costly for policymakers, the mere "threat of going to court" can become a "powerful negotiation tool in the hand of objectors" (Kagan 2001: 225). Threatening with litigation can thus be of strategic use in *preventing rules.*

Threats (regulatory or corporate) arise in an environment where public and private interests are opposed to each other. In the scenario where a regulatory threat occurs, the regulator pursues goals that differ from those held by the regulated business. Threatening with binding measures is thus utilised to alter the behaviour of the non-complying corporate actor. In order for regulation to be "threatening", it must impose costs that an actor would otherwise not engage in. The corporate threat scenario, in analogy to the regulatory threat scenario, would shift the focus towards the anticipatory reactions of policymakers to corporate action. This is particularly acute when business actors engage in litigation against regulators and have a good chance to win their case. Thus, rather than perceiving the constellation as one of self-regulation in the "shadow of public power" (Newman and Bach 2004), it is possible that public regulation will occur *in the shadow of corporate power.* Where interests of regulators and business actors coincide, the latter may engage in self- or co-regulation because it is economically beneficial or raises their reputation (Haufler 2001: 26–27), or they may ask for regulation to avoid freeriding and secure compliance by all market players. Industry strategies of rule-shaping and rule-making can thus also be in the public interest and make a valuable contribution to regulatory compliance.

Beyond Efficiency: Adopting a Power Approach

Compared to the regulatory governance perspective, a power approach refutes pure efficiency rationales. Here, we touch upon the main difference between resource dependence theory, as developed by Jeffrey Pfeffer and Gerald R. Salancik, and transaction cost theory, based on Oliver E. Williamson's seminal contribution (1975): "The emphasis on power as opposed to economic efficiency distinguishes resource dependence from transaction cost theory" (Pfeffer and Salancik 2003: xiii). Rather, the argument goes "that social institutions function to enhance the capacity of some actors to exercise power over others" (Cutler et al. 1999: 337). Power-centred explanations seek to shed light on both the emergence and durability of power in the policy process. Corporate power builds either on the established dominance of firms or their associations, or it is created to achieve dominance, especially in newly emerging markets and fields of industrial activity. The prior goal is thus to consolidate or create private dominance and *not* to save transaction costs. Hence, power and dominance do emerge and persist even though they do not produce efficient outcomes.

The argument developed in this book is about the extent to which corporations dispose of active rule-setting or "regulatory" power. The focus is on the material and political resources at the origin of corporate power (supply side) but also on the institutional context in which corporate actors operate. To be sure, the terms corporate and corporations are going to be used in a broad sense in this book. That is, they include companies that do not necessarily operate as corporations legally speaking, as is the case under US-American and Canadian law. I will thus not make a distinction between corporations and companies as used in American and British English, reflecting different legal schemes in corporate and company law. Further, I will set out how I define corporate power and how a power approach to the role of business actors in regulation contributes to existing research. In this context, it is appropriate to reconsider the classics in the literature on power, such as the ones by Max Weber (1978), Bachrach and Baratz (1962), and Steven Lukes (2005), and the contributions by Doris Fuchs and colleagues on corporate and business power (Clapp and Fuchs 2007; Fuchs 2007).

Max Weber defined power as "the probability that one actor within a social relationship will be in a position to carry out his own will despite resistance, regardless of the basis on which this probability rests" (Weber 1978: 5). Peter Bachrach and Morten Baratz, in their seminal article on the "Two Faces of Power" (Bachrach and Baratz 1962), highlighted that power is not only directly exerted in a sense that decisions made by actor A affect actor B but also where A succeeds in limiting the scope of possible actions for B: "Power is also exercised when A devotes his energies to creating or reinforcing social and political values and institutional practices that limit the scope of the political process to public considerations of only those issues which are comparatively innocuous to A" (Bachrach and Baratz 1962: 948). Power is thus exercised in a way to eliminate certain options from the political agenda; or to put it in Schattschneider's words, "organisation is the mobilisation of bias" (Schattschneider 1975: 69).

Steven Lukes (2005) proposed to differentiate three dimensions of power. The first view apprehends cases where power is observable in a sense that (measurable) resources are used to exert influence and achieve certain results. Actors' behaviour is assessed in relation to their expressed preferences and interests. Lukes' second perspective on power envisages the success of exerted influence on the decision-making process, i.e. it asks about actual impact. Resourceful actors can potentially change, delay or stop political decisions and thus effectively influence the policy output. The common denominator with the first dimension is that the kind of resources this type of explanation refers to are still material. By contrast, a third view of power includes ideational and normative aspects and shifts the focus of analysis to the agenda-setting phase in the policy process. It is at this early stage that power can be exerted by framing the debate, discarding certain venues of action and privileging others. Methodologically speaking, this type of research is more demanding, as it seeks to shed light on the real intention of actors and not only those that are articulated. Importantly, Lukes makes a case that all three dimensions of power need consideration, and limiting the analysis to either of them leaves the account incomplete (Lukes 2005: 21–25). In this book, I use the term power in an encompassing way that covers all three dimensions. More specifically, I will consider decision-making power and control over the political agenda broadly speaking, including areas of latent conflict (Lukes 2005: 25).

Doris Fuchs, in her work on "business power" (Fuchs 2007), draws much on Lukes' contribution and further suggests to combine rational choice and sociological institutionalist theories. Fuchs differentiates between three types of political influence corporations dispose of: instrumental, structural and discursive power (Fuchs 2007: 52–67). The instrumental logic comes close to Lukes' first dimension of power, that is, it refers to direct influence through lobbying, campaigning or party finance (Fuchs 2007: 7, Chapter 4). According to Fuchs, this concept is actor-centred and one-dimensional, as it looks into the power of business over other actors but does not acknowledge the relational nature of power (Fuchs 2007: 56). Structural power, by contrast, looks into the material fundamentals underlying behavioural options on the input side. It refers to both the agenda-setting and rule-setting power of business (Fuchs 2007: 7, 58: Chapter 5). Following Fuchs, the agenda-setting power of business relies on the threatening potential of capital mobility, resulting in quasi-regulation. Furthermore, structural power leads to concrete regulatory output produced by business, taking the form of public private partnerships or self-regulation (Fuchs 2007: 66). Finally, discursive power is used as a concept to capture ideational and normative conditions of business power. It examines the role of discourse, cultural norms and institutions, broadly understood. Here, the objective is to understand how private actors shape perceptions and identities, persuade and co-opt other actors. It does also put into focus the necessity for business actors to "face the issue of its moral legitimacy" (Fuchs 2007: 144). In concrete terms, the means to achieve such legitimacy are corporate social responsibility activities, coalition-building with NGOs, or corporate philanthropy (Fuchs 2007: 145–146). Fuchs emphasises that her three categories of power interlink one another, since instrumental power in the form of lobbying is often a pre-condition for structural power to emerge and operate, while discursive power is a pre-condition as well as a result of structural power (Fuchs 2007: 65). Christopher May, engaging with Fuchs' work, also places emphasis on the relevance of such discursive elements (May 2015). Further, John Mikler draws on the three faces of power identified by Fuchs in his recent account of the "political power of global corporations" (Mikler 2018: 35–49).

In this book, I suggest an alternative conceptualisation which puts the differentiation between types of resources on the supply side of what Fuchs calls structural and discursive power front and centre. Of particular interest are the dynamics that fuel the legitimacy of corporate activities. Fuchs does consider the legitimacy of business power, but in her account this mainly relates to the motives driving business discourse. Where power is considered as being legitimate, it is rather appropriate to operate with a distinct category.

Legitimate Power: Authority

An important distinction has to be made between authority and power, namely whether or not it is considered legitimate. Only those settings that are socially accepted and are in conformity with average expectations do hold legitimacy. Authority presupposes acceptance and legitimacy, while power may be imposed on subjects that do not give their consent (Pfeffer 1981: 4). According to Bachrach and Baratz, we deal with authority where "B complies because he recognizes that [A's] command is reasonable in terms of his own values – either because its content is legitimate and reasonable or because it has been arrived at through a legitimate and reasonable procedure" (Bachrach and Baratz 1970: 34, 37). In their seminal work on private authority, Cutler et al. posit that authority emerges "when an individual or organisation has *decision-making power* over a particular issue area and is *regarded to exercise that power legitimately*" (Cutler et al. 1999: 5, emphasis added). Similarly, in her contribution to the debate, Green emphasises the relational nature of authority requiring the consent of those who are subject to it. She defines private authority as "*situations in which nonstate actors make rules or set standards that other actors in world politics adopt*" (Green 2014: 6, emphasis in the original). Private authority is thus a special case of legitimate power held by private actors. To be sure, the literature on private authority considers a multitude of private actors, including civil society and environmental NGOs (as discussed by Büthe 2003). The literature is particularly interested in whether or not private authority constitutes a valuable substitute to state authority and public regulation in a globalised economy (Bartley 2018).

The interesting question, of course, is about how exactly power gains legitimacy, thus becoming authority. Pfeffer, inspired by Max Weber, reflected on the transformation of power into authority:

> The distribution of power within a social setting can also become legitimated over time, so that those within the setting expect and value a certain pattern of influence. When power is so legitimated, it is denoted as authority. Weber (1947) emphasized the critical role of legitimacy in the exercise of power. By transforming power into authority, the exercise of influence is transformed in a subtle but important way. In social situations, the exercise of power typically has cost. Enforcing one's way over others requires the expenditure of resources, the making of commitments, and the level of effort which can be undertaken only when the issues at hand are relatively important. On the other hand, the exercise of authority, power which has become legitimated, is expected and desired in the social context. Thus, the exercise of authority, far from diminishing through use, may actually serve to enhance the amount of authority subsequently processed. (Pfeffer 1981: 4)

When conducting my case studies, I will pay particular attention to strategies of private actors to acquire authority but also to contextual and structural factors that create or sustain authority.

Paradoxically, arguments about *private* authority strongly highlight the role of *public* and state actors. Cutler and others posit that "the cooperation among firms is either given legitimacy *by governments* or legitimacy is acquired through the special expertise or historical role of the private sector participants" (Cutler et al. 1999: 4, emphasis added). Green's conceptualisation of private authority is entirely derived from state preferences and institutional settings on the demand side of the equation (Green 2014). She differentiates between delegated and entrepreneurial private authority (Green 2014: 33–36). The difference relates to the origins of authority: "Claims of delegated authority are ultimately derived from the state" (Green 2014: 7). According to Green, this type of authority is de jure and involves a principal-agent relation between public and private actors. It is more likely to occur where powerful states are in agreement and a strong focal institution that can potentially monitor private action exists (Green 2014: 17, 41). By contrast, entrepreneurial authority "does not originate with the state" (Green 2014: 7). Rather, it results from "governance failure" (Green 2014: 17) and requires that "any private actor that projects authority must persuade others to adopt its rules or practices" (Green 2014: 7). Entrepreneurial authority only occurs where private actors succeed in this endeavour. As private actors will not forgo the use of coercion as a source for gaining legitimacy, they have to mobilise other sources such as expertise or moral arguments. Green goes on to argue that, in contrast to delegated authority, "entrepreneurial authority is de facto" (Green 2014: 7, emphasis in the original). These types of authority further also differ as to the timing when governments give their consent: "the governed grant their consent *ex ante* in the case of delegated authority, whereas it tends to be *ex post* in entrepreneurial authority" (Green 2014: 7, emphasis in the original). On the demand side, she identifies four types of benefits of private authority that states or other actors strive for, namely reduced transaction costs, enhanced credibility of commitments, first mover advantage, and improved reputation.

Accounts of private authority thus highlight the role of private actors as experts, but other than that heavily focus on demand-side arguments and institutional settings very alike relevant research on governance and regulation. I contribute to this literature by moving the focus towards conceptualising the supply side of private governance. In particular, I seek to address the following research question: *How do corporations use various power resources in order to prevent, shape, make or revoke regulation?*

Conceptualising Regulatory Power

Despite their different objectives, the literatures on regulatory governance and private authority share the same preoccupation with the role of public actors in the policy process. The regulatory and legislative threat scenarios are about the risk of negative sanctions issued by policymakers, and the shadow of hierarchy arguments more generally addresses the steering capacity of public actors over private ones. Similarly, accounts of private authority have analysed the role of public actors in granting authority, namely in the form of delegation (Green 2014) or orchestration (Abbott et al. 2014).

When moving to the supply side of the equation, an important point of reference is the resource dependence theory, as developed by Jeffrey Pfeffer and Gerald R. Salancik (2003). It highlights the relevance of the "external" social context and the environment of organisations, which are inherently dependent on financial and physical resources as well as on information. I acknowledge the relevance of these resources when discussing the economic importance of the industry sectors in the empirical Chapters (4–7), notably by looking at turnover, number of companies and employees, as well as trade shares. My conceptualisation, however, does not put economic and financial resources front and centre. I argue that other types of resources do hold more explanatory power for regulatory outcomes. More specifically, I argue that corporations dispose of distinct power resources in regulation as experts, innovators and operators. Corporations are expected to make instrumental use of these resources, to the effect that the capacity of public actors to exert effective control will be limited. In all three settings private actors dispose of a pronounced capacity to cope with uncertainty, yet for different reasons. Uncertainty coping capability figures prominently in resource dependence theory (Pfeffer 1981: 109–112). Katzenstein and Sybert, in their recent contribution to power in international relations, even go a step further and argue that the ability to adapt to uncertainty dynamics constitutes a different, understudied type of power that they dub "protean power" (Katzenstein and Seybert 2018). Finally, in all

Table 2.1   Regulatory power of corporations

Case	Expert	Innovator	Operator
Power resource	Specialised knowledge	Innovative know-how	Technical knowledge
Uncertainty coping	Epistemic uncertainty	Technological and market uncertainty	Operational uncertainty
Acquired regulation	Regulatory capture	Protect market position	Amplifies autonomy

Source Author's illustration

settings private actors will seek to create acceptance for the power they hold, i.e. they want to acquire authority. The conceptualisation set out in Table 2.1 presents the regulatory power of corporations. It differentiates between the power resources corporate actors hold each time and the way in which they are expected to cope with uncertainty. Further, I make an assumption about which type of *acquired regulation* is likely to emerge each time. In the subsequent section, I will elaborate in further detail on the three types of regulatory power. Next, I present and explain the selection of industry case studies.

Experts

Expertise as a source of power or authority has attracted most attention in the literature (Ambrus et al. 2014; Fischer 1990; Fleck et al. 2016; Boswell 2009). This holds for contributions on regulation (Thatcher and Stone Sweet 2002; Majone 1997; Radaelli 1999a, b; Schrefler 2013), on resource dependence theory (Pfeffer and Salancik 2003) or on private authority (Cutler et al. 1999: 5; Green 2014: 41; Sending 2015: 14–18; Price 2011: 587; Hall and Biersteker 2002). Expertise and competence have been considered as the main source of authority in the "epistemic communities" (Haas 1992) approach, echoed by the concept of "epistemic authority" (Quack 2016) in the global governance literature. Furthermore, this category empirically overlaps the most with the other two. In fact, it is reasonable to argue that innovators and operators hold specific types of expertise.

When corporations act as experts, they dispose of levels and types of specialised knowledge on highly complex issues which cannot easily be reproduced in the public arena. That said, expertise or epistemic authority shall not be regarded as a given but involves continuous competition for recognition (Sending 2015). Knowledge and technology play an increasingly important role in policy-making, and in many economic sectors expertise develops rapidly. Frank Fischer has even argued that a new type of politics has emerged which is "said to be more responsible *to the criteria of* knowledge. Politics, in short, becomes a *politics of expertise*" (Fischer 1990: 106, emphasis in the original). The literature has identified various types of knowledge usage, including instrumental, symbolic or strategic usage (Schrefler 2013: 16; Boswell 2009: 26). The instrumental usage of this resource aims at controlling specialised knowledge and monopolising the expert status. In that capacity, private actors claim to be capable of dealing with *epistemic uncertainty*, as the generation of new knowledge and evidence can challenge received wisdom. Symbolic usage is about gaining legitimacy (Schrefler 2013: 16; Radaelli 1995: 162) thanks to scientific soundness and the proof of competence. The strategic usage of expertise in regulation is expected to matter throughout the policy process, i.e. in preventing, shaping or even making rules, and in revoking regulatory measures. Approaching expertise from a power lens links to a Foucauldian rather than a Weberian perspective on the use of knowledge (Boswell 2009: 29). With the caveat that knowledge is never entirely neutral and cannot portray reality objectively without a bias (Schrefler 2013: 2), one could still assume that the prior objective of its usage is to improve the epistemic quality and problem-solving of policy outputs. This is the Weberian, technocratic vision, which perceives expert knowledge as being a-political, relying on technical rationality which redefines "political problems into administrative issues amenable to technical solutions" (Fischer 1990: 182). More specifically, "technocracy [...] refers to the adaptation of expertise to the tasks of governance" (Fischer 1990: 18). By contrast, the Foucauldian perspective suggests that the use of knowledge constitutes a "technique of social control" (Fischer 1990: 357). In fact, "technocratic politics changes the nature of power in that knowledge becomes the terrain of politics" (Radaelli 1999a: 6). Power struggles will thus translate into the production of "counter policy expertise" (Fischer 1990: 28). The "politics of expertise" involve dynamics of opposition which draw on competing sources of expertise aiming at supporting respective policy choices (Fischer 1990: 28; Boswell 2009: 5). Diverse actors will thus compete for the expert status and will contest the neutrality and validity of the expertise provided by their political opponents (Fleck et al. 2016;

Littoz-Monnet 2017: 2). Therefore, by considering these mechanisms of politicisation and power struggles, expertise can no longer be considered as being neutral. From the perspective of theorising empowerment, experts "have too often misappropriated their specialised knowledge to serve both their own interests and those of a power elite intent on maintaining its own dominance over the rest of society" (Fischer 1990: 357). As a result, experts only dispose of authority to the extent that the superiority and quality of the information they provide are socially accepted and trusted.

It is apparent that expertise can serve as a formidable power resource throughout the policy process. Corporate experts will seek to strategically use their knowledge to prevent regulation altogether, in both rule-shaping and rule-making, and also to challenge and revoke existing rules. They will succeed in achieving their goals to the extent that public actors, regulators and NGOs are not in a position to generate counter-expertise and compensate for information asymmetries. The important discursive strategy for corporations thus is to prove that they can provide policy input that draws on specialised knowledge that is superior to other information sources. This classical constellation of information asymmetries thus bears the risk of *regulatory capture* (Croley 2011: 3; Stigler 1971). The most pronounced form is where regulatees convince the regulator to abstain from taking any measures, i.e. where they succeed in rule prevention—for instance by engaging in voluntary industry action as a reaction to a regulatory threat (discussed above). Alternatively, private actors may also succeed in capturing the policy-making process. Indeed, "acquired regulation" (Stigler 1971: 3) is a likely outcome in areas where industry effectively monopolises the generation of expertise and evidence. As a remedy, regulators can specify information and transparency requirements and then in turn threaten with sanctions in case of non-compliance. Or they can seek to facilitate fire-bell-ringing (Aghion and Tirole 1997) by granting various stakeholders and civil society organisations access to the policy process and relevant information. In economic sectors involving a high level of branch-specific expertise, complexity and uncertainty, industry is likely to shape regulation to a significant extent. Industry actors may also be the formal or actual rule-makers, especially where their expert status is recognised and well respected. They will actively seek to steer an evidence-based regulatory process. In areas where evidence-based regulation draws on industry input, there are also good chances to challenge and revoke regulatory measures. The contestation of existing rules usually follows formalised, judicial procedures where a regulatee can appeal against regulatory decisions. In this perspective, litigation comes in at the end of the policy process (De Figuiredo and De Figuieredo 2002; Holburn and Vanden Bergh 2000).

While there is legitimate reason to doubt the objectivity and neutrality of expertise, there are also societal tendencies to object the validity of expertise altogether (Nichols 2017). The 2016 Brexit vote, discussed in Chapter 7, is an example that merits special attention. It is a showcase of why underexploiting expertise also bears risks. In times of fake news and heated debates, this reverse scenario has become more important (Collins and Evans 2017; Nichols 2017). While an output-oriented perspective emphasises the "pareto-optimal" nature of policy solutions provided by unelected experts and regulators (Majone 1999: 7, 9–11), others have emphasised that output-related legitimacy à la Easton can only generate a "shallow level of support for the political system" (Lacey 2017: 129; Easton 1957: 399). Especially in times of output crises, there is great potential to exploit an opposition between "we, the people" and "them bureaucrats/ technocrats" or "business lobbies" along the lines of a populist discourse (Bickerton and Accetti 2017; Brett 2013; March 2017).

In conclusion, the key challenge for regulators when dealing with corporate expertise is to generate or draw on adequate "counter policy expertise" (Fischer 1990: 28), as discussed before. Where there is complete reliance on business expertise, there is an eminent risk of the regulator being captured by corporate interests and rewarding gatekeeping.

Innovators

Corporations are, in fact, ahead of their regulators where they act as innovators. The innovator is a specific type of an *expert* disposing of *innovative know-how*, which gives him a competitive edge in a given market environment and further puts him into an advantageous position vis-à-vis his regulator. Innovation studies, building on the seminal work of Joseph Schumpeter, are a well-established field of research in various disciplines, and the points of reference in the literature are numerous (Burgelman and Sayles 1986; Webster 2004; Witt and Jackson 2016; Corso and Pellegrini 2007). Surprisingly enough, however, innovation has not taken center stage in the literature on regulation, though it surely should be thought of as a "regulatory challenge" (Ford 2017: 3). The "entrepreneur as innovator" (Hébert and Link 2006) disposes of the sole capacity to embark on new types of economic activity, and a high level of expertise, knowledge and investment is needed to both identify the direction of change and set the pace of change. Depending on the level and pace of innovation, the innovative process augments economic and technological complexity and uncertainty to a significant extent. The innovator is thus capable of dealing with a specific type of *uncertainty*, which relates both to the unknown in technological progress and newly emerging market segments.

The degree of uncertainty involved can of course vary, as we may deal with different kinds of innovation. The innovation literature typically distinguishes between radical as opposed to incremental innovation (Freeman and Soete 1997). Radical innovations involve big, transformative and paradigm-shifting changes. Incremental innovation results from a process of collective learning and small innovations, emerging bottom-up and motivated by economic self-interest. Christie Ford (2017) has suggested to rethink the dichotomy along the terms "seismic" versus "sedimental" innovation. Compared to radical innovation, in her view, seismic innovation highlights the "dislocating, ground-shaking and unpredictable character of innovation" (Ford 2017: 167), which for regulators raises particular challenges requiring "proactive and muscular regulatory responses" (Ford 2017: 170). Sedimental innovation, however, does not pose less of a regulatory challenge, not only because it occurs more frequently but also because its unsettling nature tends to be underestimated due to complex causation (Ford 2017, Chapter 8). At a much lower level of abstraction, various categories of innovation can be differentiated depending on who innovates. Technology-based firms, for example, can act as application innovators, market innovators, technology innovators and paradigm innovators (Autio and Lumme 1998). The challenge for regulators is therefore to adequately assess the type and scope of innovation in order to formulate regulatory responses.

More fundamentally, policy and regulatory responses will also depend on whether or not innovation is considered to be in the general interest. Intuitively, we highly value the potential economic and social benefits of innovation. Yet we might also think of innovative products that raise environmental, ethical or social concerns. Where this is the case, the regulator is likely to step in and engage in corrective regulatory action. As such regulation can hamper the innovative process, the innovator has an interest to pursue a discourse which publicises the beneficial nature of innovation. Ideally, the innovative firm secures benevolent regulation that supports and fuels innovation, and potentially also protects his market position. Industrial policy considerations can further drive regulation (or abstention thereof), mostly to the benefit of the innovator. Overall, we can expect that the innovator has substantial influence on rule-shaping and may become a rule-maker, for instance by engaging in voluntary action. Further, he may be rather successful in either preventing or revoking regulation, also by using litigation as a business tool. Where there is no alignment between the innovator's and regulator's preferences, the innovator will emphasise the mis-fit between existing regulatory approaches and innovative economic activity, formulating demands to either abolish existing rules, cease their application, or adapt them to new products and markets. In a less visible manner, innovation might also be oblivious to regulation, or actually seek to circumvent regulatory goals (Ford 2017: 3). Striking a balance between potentially counterveiling interests, regulation has to provide adequate levels of regulatory continuity and, where desirable, a regulatory environment supporting innovation. Posing credible regulatory threats appears rather counter-productive where the policy framework seeks to incentivise corporate innovation. Even where there is a desire to engage in corrective regulatory action the regulatory process risks to prove too lengthy and cumbersome to catch up with rapid evolutions on relevant markets. Overall, therefore, regulation (or the absence thereof) risks protecting the market position of the innovator position.

Operators

Operators manage a critical and costly infrastructure and in this capacity provide a public good. For that reason, they are not only heavily regulated entities but frequently still fully or partially state-owned. Operating assets or infrastructure creates information asymmetries in relation to the regulator and other market participants. Operators dispose of *technical knowledge* about operational details that other actors cannot easily reproduce or verify. We can therefore assume that operators have a strong incentive to seek and uphold such information asymmetries. In particular, they will seek to resist reforms that aim at enhancing regulatory oversight and transparency. Rather, they will favour arrangements that help to strengthen their position in the regulatory process. Ideally, they will welcome arrangements where they develop operational rules. Operators will typically be rule-shapers and, to some extent, rule-makers. They may also seek to prevent the introduction of new rules, for instance by engaging in voluntary action. In contrast, it is rather unlikely that these heavily regulated entities will go against their regulators by means of litigation, as the harm done to the regulatee-regulator relationship might be more significant than the actual gained benefit.

The operator disposes of a long-standing legacy of technical reliability. As a "high reliability organisation" (Bierly and Spender 1995; La Porte and Consolini 1991; La Porte 1996), the operator is in a position to cope with *operational uncertainty* and avoid security risks for society. Using the wording of Cutler et al. (1999: 4), the authority of operators thus resides in their "special expertise" and their "historical role" in securely operating technical systems. Operators can be expected to engage in a securitisation discourse (Buzan et al. 1998), given that security as a prior objective dominates the political agenda. Operators will thus highlight their public and neutral task to provide security.

Infrastructure operation is highly path dependent and involves important sunk costs. The operator will therefore legitimately claim return on costly investment, while the public sphere expects sufficient levels of investment as well as secure and reliable operation of the infrastructure. The operator has an interest in expanding his infrastructure and maximising his income. By contrast, it is not in the public interest to overinvest and underexploit existing infrastructure (Chick 2010: 686). The balance is difficult to strike. It is rational for the operator to exaggerate the need for investing in new infrastructure and to prioritise security over maximising capacity. This poses specific risks in terms of acquired regulation. Operators will refer to their role as neutral facilitators who are technically reliable and strive for secure and uninterrupted supply. Their discursive power is considerable given that policymakers will shy away from any action that could involve the risk of a blackout. When dealing with the operator, regulators need to get the incentives right in order to secure the reliability and security of the infrastructure. In short, in this area of regulation we can expect substantial asymmetries where regulatory oversight and operators' discretion are concerned, as well as a tendency of policymakers to grant generous funding for maintaining the existing, and building up new infrastructure in order to pre-empt the risk of shortage of supply. Regulation will put security of supply front and centre, and hence tend to *amplify the autonomy* of operators.

The operator is obviously an *expert* where the specificities of technical operation and related information are concerned. Furthermore, the operator may also be an *innovator* in areas where technological progress has the potential to change the operation of the infrastructure. That said, the high level of sunk costs involved in infrastructure investment is a serious barrier to innovation. We may therefore witness quite different types of operators depending on whether or not, and to what extent, they embrace innovative potential. The question here will for instance be whether regulators or other market participants can effectively exert pressure on operators in order to change their course of action.

Selection of Industry Sectors

Empirically, the book looks at industry sectors that represent the distinct constellations of corporate power, i.e. the case selection is guided by the analytical distinction (Peters 2013: Chapters 4 and 7). Table 2.2 summarises the selection of industry sectors to study the role of the expert, innovator and operator in the regulatory process. The areas of regulation covered relate to the protection of the environment and consumers. Relevant dossiers at European level will be presented in further detail in Chapter 3 (see Table 3.3).

The plastics and paper industries have an important role as *experts* in realising sustainable product life cycles (Chapter 4). A substantial level of scientific and technical complexity is involved in production and recycling processes, as well as for managing the risks of hazardous substances. To be sure, the paper industry derives its authority mainly from its specialised knowledge about the recycling process, whereas the plastics industry is the expert when it comes to the numerous chemical substances used in various materials. There is, moreover, significant variation as to the uncertainty coping capabilities (Pfeffer 1981: 109–112) required across sectors. The paper industry produces and recycles an organic material and has a fundamental interest in disposing of both maximum quantities and high quality of raw and collected material. For the paper sector, therefore, a crucial uncertainty relates to the amounts and properties of available raw and collected material. The plastics industry produces materials composed of sophisticated, often innovative chemical substances and mixtures. Assessing the health and environmental risks of these substances and materials involves costly and lengthy processes, and there is typically a time lag between the placing on the market

Table 2.2 Case selection industry sectors

Case	Expert		Innovator		Operator
Industry sectors	*Paper industry*	*Plastics industry*	*Home appliance industry*	*ICT industry*	*Transmission system operators*
Power resource	Specialised knowledge about recycling process	Specialised knowledge about chemical substances	Incremental technological know-how product innovation	Path-breaking technological know-how product and market innovation	Technical knowledge related to electricity infrastructure
Uncertainty coping	Quantities, price and quality of recovered materials	Health and environmental risks of materials	Product features	Market structure	Available (cross-border) capacity

Source Author's illustration

of new products and the generation of relevant knowledge. Recycling rates are still low in the sector, given that raw materials are relatively cheap compared to the cost of developing appropriate techniques and engaging in recycling. The comparison therefore contrasts a case characterised by well-established recycling techniques with a sector were such practice has yet to be developed.

The role of the *innovator* is the topic in Chapter 5, taking the producers of electrical and electronic devices as an example. More specifically, I look at the home appliance and the Information and Communication Technology (ICT) industries. These branches do both engage in innovation, but it is fair to say that (by now) the speed and paths of change vary: innovation is incremental in the sector of home appliances and radical in the ICT sector. Further, the more fragmented market structure in the home appliance sector involves a risk of freeriding in terms of non-compliance, which is less relevant in the ICT market dominated by fewer players. The type of uncertainty coping involved differs in line with innovation patterns: there is far more market uncertainty in the ICT industry, where new products may not generate profit in the long run or be outperformed by competitors. We can also expect varying interests inside the sector, where top runners may seek to consolidate their competitive edge through regulation, while producers that risk elimination from the market will want to delay or prevent such measures.

The third industry case study (Chapter 6) covers the role of the *operator*, analysing the electricity transmission system industry. In this sector, the policy goal is to provide, in the short term, secure supply and, in the medium to long term, adequate capacity. The transmission system operators (TSOs) who run the grid know best about the available and used capacity. In fact, there is a structural information asymmetry in this respect in comparison to other market actors, who are never entirely certain about the degree of available and used capacity. What is more, there is a fundamental tension where business interests are concerned: the operators have an interest in maximising security, while users of the grid have an interest in using maximum capacity. The need to cope with uncertainty increases with augmenting cross-border traffic, as there is a lack of knowledge about available capacity and a lack of capacity to generate such knowledge—given that, historically, regulatory oversight and reporting duties have been national in scope.

The qualitative case comparison draws on secondary literature, document analysis and insights gathered through half-structured interviewing.

Between 2005 and 2019, I have conducted a total of 93 interviews with policymakers and stakeholders, out of which 40 were with industry experts.

REFERENCES

Abbott KW, Genschel P, Snidal D, et al. (2014) Two Logics of Indirect Governance: Delegation and Orchestration. *Social Science Research Network* 46: 719–729.

Aghion P and Tirole J. (1997) Formal and Real Authority in Organizations. *Journal of Political Economy* 105(1): 1–29.

Ambrus M, Arts K, Hey E, et al. (2014) *The Role of 'Experts' in International and European Decision-Making Processes: Advisors, Decision Makers or Irrelevant Actors?* Cambridge: Cambridge University Press.

Autio E and Lumme A. (1998) Does the Innovator Role Affect the Perceived Potential for Growth? Analysis of Four Types of New, Technology-Based Firms. *Technology Analysis & Strategic Management* 10(1): 41–55.

Ayres I and Braithwaite J. (1992) *Responsive Regulation: Transcending the Deregulation Debate.* New York: Oxford University Press.

Bachrach P and Baratz MS. (1962) Two Faces of Power. *The American Political Science Review* 56(4): 947–952.

Bachrach P and Baratz MS. (1970) *Power and Poverty: Theory and Practice.* London, Toronto: Oxford University Press.

Bartley T. (2018) *Rules Without Rights: Land, Labor, and Private Authority in the Global Economy.* Oxford: Oxford University Press.

Bickerton C and Accetti CI. (2017) Populism and Technocracy: Opposites or Complements? *Critical Review of International Social and Political Philosophy* 20(2): 186–206.

Bierly PE and Spender J-C. (1995) Culture and High Reliability Organizations: The Case of the Nuclear Submarine. *Journal of Management* 21(4): 639–656.

Black J. (2002) Critical Reflections on Regulation. *Australian Journal of Legal Philosophy* 27: 1–35.

Börzel TA. (2008) Der „Schatten der Hierarchie". Ein Governance-Paradox? Special Issue: Governance in einer sich wandelnden Welt. *Politische Vierteljahresschrift* 41: 118–131.

Börzel TA. (2010) European Governance: Negotiation and Competition in the Shadow of Hierarchy. *Journal of Common Market Studies* 48(2): 191–219.

Boswell C. (2009) *The Political Uses of Expert Knowledge: Immigration Policy and Social Research.* Cambridge: Cambridge University Press.

Brett W. (2013) What's an Elite to Do? The Threat of Populism from Left, Right and Centre. *The Political Quarterly* 84(3): 410–413.

Brousseau E and Fares Mh. (2000) Incomplete Contracts and Governance Structures: Are Incomplete Contract Theory and New Institutional

Economics Substitutes or Complements? In: Ménard C (ed) *Institutions, Contracts and Organizations: Perspectives from New Institutional Economics.* Cheltenham, Northampton: Edward Elgar, 399–421.

Burgelman RA and Sayles LR. (1986) *Inside Corporate Innovation: Strategy, Structure, and Managerial Skills.* New York: Free Press.

Büthe T. (2003) Governance Through Private Authority? Non-state Actors in World Politics. *Journal of International Affairs* 57(1): 245–253.

Buzan B, Wæver O and de Wilde J. (1998) *Security: A New Framework for Analysis.* Boulder, CO: Lynne Rienner.

Cafaggi F. (2006) Rethinking Private Regulation in the European Regulatory Space. *SSRN Electronic Journal.*

Chick M. (2010) Network Utilities: Technological Development, Market Structure, and Forms of Ownership. In: Coen D, Grant W and Wilson GK (eds) *The Oxford Handbook of Business and Government.* Oxford: Oxford University Press, 685–702.

Clapp J and Fuchs D. (2007) *Corporate Power in Global Agrifood Governance: Challenges and Strategies.* Boston: MIT Press.

Collins H and Evans R. (2017) *Why Democracies Need Science:* Hoboken: Wiley.

Considine M. (1998) Making Up the Government's Mind: Agenda Setting in a Parliamentary System. *Governance* 11(3): 297–317.

Corso M and Pellegrini L. (2007) Continuous and Discontinuous Innovation: Overcoming the Innovator Dilemma. *Creativity and Innovation Management* 16(4): 333–347.

Croley SP. (2011) Beyond Capture: Towards a New Theory of Regulation. In: Levi-Faur D (ed) *Handbook on the Politics of Regulation.* Cheltenham, Northampton: Edward Elgar, 50–69.

Cutler CA, Haufler V and Porter TP. (1999) *Private Authority and International Affairs.* Albany, NY: Suny Press.

De Figuiredo J and De Figuieredo RJP. (2002) The Allocation of Resources by Interest Groups: Lobbying, Litigation and Administrative Regulation. *Business and Politics* 4(3): 343.

Easton D. (1957) An Approach to the Analysis of Political Systems. *World Politics* 9(3): 383–400.

Erfle S, McMillan H and Grofman B. (1990) Regulation via Threats: Politics, Media Coverage, and Oil Pricing Decisions. *Public Opinion Quarterly* 54(1): 48–63.

Fischer F. (1990) *Technocracy and the Politics of Expertise.* Newbury Park: Sage.

Fleck J, Faulkner W and Williams R. (2016) *Exploring Expertise: Issues and Perspectives.* Houndmills, Basingstoke: Palgrave Macmillan.

Forcier JR. (1994) *Judicial Excess: The Political Economy of the American Legal System.* Lanham, New York, London: University Press of America.

Ford C. (2017) *Innovation and the State: Finance, Regulation, and Justice.* New York: Cambridge University Press.

Freeman C and Soete L. (1997) *The Economics of Industrial Innovation.* Cambridge, MA: MIT Press.

Fuchs D. (2007) *Business Power in Global Governance*. London: Lynne Rienner.

Genschel P and Zangl B. (2014) State Transformations in OECD Countries. *Annual Review of Political Science* 17(1): 337–354.

Glachant M. (2003) Voluntary Agreements Under Endogenous Legislative Threats. *FEEM Working Paper* No. 36.2003

Graz J-C and Nölke A. (2008) *Transnational Private Governance and Its Limits*. London: Routledge.

Green JF. (2014) *Rethinking Private Authority: Agents and Entrepreneurs in Global Environmental Governance*. Princeton: Princeton University Press.

Haas PM. (1992) Introduction: Epistemic Communities and International Policy Coordination. *International Organization* 46(1): 1–35.

Halfteck G. (2006) *A Theory of Legislative Threats*. Tel Aviv: Tel Aviv University.

Halfteck G. (2008) Legislative Threats. *Stanford Law Review* 61: 629–710.

Hall PA and Soskice D. (2001) *Varieties of Capitalism*. Oxford: Oxford University Press.

Hall RB and Biersteker TJ. (2002) *The Emergence of Private Authority in Global Governance*. Cambridge: Cambridge University Press.

Hansen LG. (1999) Environmental Regulation Through Voluntary Agreements. In: Carraro C and Lévêque F (eds) *Voluntary Approaches in Environmental Policy*. Dordrecht: Springer, 27–54.

Haufler V. (2001) *A Public Role for the Private Sector: Industry Self-Regulation in a Global Economy*. Washington: Carnegie Endowment for International Peace.

Hébert RF and Link AN. (2006) The Entrepreneur as Innovator. *The Journal of Technology Transfer* 31(5): 589.

Héritier A. (1987) *Policy Analyse: Eine Einführung*. Frankfurt/New York: Campus Verlag.

Héritier A and Eckert S. (2008) New Modes of Governance in the Shadow of Hierarchy: Self-Regulation by Industry in Europe. *Journal of Public Policy* 28(1): 113–138.

Héritier A and Eckert S. (2009) Self-Regulation by Associations: A Collective Action Problem in Environmental Regulation. *Business and Politics* 11(1): 1–22.

Héritier A and Lehmkuhl D. (2008a) New Modes of Governance and the Shadow of Hierarchy: Sectoral Governance and Territorially Bound Democratic Government. Special Issue. *Journal of Public Policy* 28(1): 113–138.

Héritier A and Lehmkuhl D. (2008b) The Shadow of Hierarchy and New Modes of Governance. *Journal of Public Policy* 28(1): 1–17.

Héritier A and Rhodes M. (2010) *New Modes of Governance in Europe: Governing in the Shadow of Hierarchy*. Basingstoke, New York: Palgrave Macmillan.

Hogwood BW and Peters BG. (1983) *Policy Dynamics*. Brighton, Sussex: Wheatsheaf Books.

Holburn GLF and Vanden Bergh RG. (2000) Policy and Process: A Game-Theoretic Framework for the Design of Non-market Strategy. *Advances in Strategic Management* 19: 33–66.

Kagan RA. (2001) *Adversarial Legalism: The American Way of Law*. Cambridge, MA: Harvard University Press.

Kagan RA and Axelrad L. (2000) Regulatory Encounters: Multinational Corporations and American Adversarial Legalism. *California Series in Law, Politics and Society*. Berkeley: University of California Press.

Katzenstein PJ and Seybert LA. (2018) *Protean Power: Exploring the Uncertain and Unexpected in World Politics*. Cambridge: Cambridge University Press.

Kelemen RD. (2011) *Eurolegalism: The Transformation of Law and Regulation in the European Union*. Cambridge, MA: Harvard University Press.

Knill C. (2001) Private Governance Across Multiple Arenas: European Interest Associations as Interface Actors. *Journal of European Public Policy* 8(2): 227–246.

La Porte TR and Consolini P. (1991) Working in Practice but Not in Theory: Theoretical Challenges of High Reliability Organizations. *Journal of Public Administration Research and Theory* 1(1): 19–48.

La Porte TR. (1996) High Reliability Organizations: Unlikely, Demanding and at Risk. *Journal of Contingencies and Crisis Management* 4(2): 60–71.

Lacey J. (2017) *Centripetal Democracy: Democratic Legitimacy and Political Identity in Belgium, Switzerland, and the European Union*. Oxford: Oxford University Press.

Lehmkuhl D. (2005) How Private Governance Arrangements May Produce Binding Outcomes. *International Journal of Civil Society Law* 4(3): 34–55.

Levi-Faur D. (2011) Regulation and Regulatory Governance. In: Levi-Faur D (ed) *Handbook on the Politics of Regulation*. Cheltenham, Northampton: Edward Elgar, 3–21.

Levi-Faur D and Jordana J. (2004) *The Politics of Regulation: Institutions and Regulatory Reforms for the Age of Governance*. Cheltenham, Northampton: Edward Elgar.

Littoz-Monnet A. (2017) *The Politics of Expertise in International Organizations: How International Bureaucracies Produce and Mobilize Knowledge*. Abingdon: Taylor & Francis.

Lowi T. (1964) American Business, Public Policy, Case-Studies, and Political Theory. *World Politics* 16(4): 677–715.

Lukes S. (2005) *Power: A Radical View*. Houndmills, Basingstoke: Palgrave Macmillan.

Majone G. (1997) From the Positive to the Regulatory State: Causes and Consequences of Changes in the Mode of Governance. *Journal of Public Policy* 17(2): 139–167.

Majone G. (1999) The Regulatory State and Its Legitimacy Problems. *West European Politics* 22(1): 1–24.

March L. (2017) Left and Right Populism Compared: The British Case. *The British Journal of Politics and International Relations* 19(2): 282–303.

May C. (2006) *Global Corporate Power*. Boulder: Lynne Rienner.

May C. (2015) *Global Corporations in Global Governance*. Oxon, New York: Routledge.

Mayntz R. (2005) Governance Theory als Fortentwicklung der Steuerungstheorie? In: Schuppert GF (ed) *Governance-Forschung: Vergewisserung über Stand und Entwicklungslinien*. Baden-Baden: Nomos, 11–20.

Mikler J. (2018) *The Political Power of Global Corporations*. Cambridge: Polity Press.

Morriss AP, Yandle B and Dorchak A. (2009) *Regulation by Litigation*. New Haven, London: Yale University Press.

Newman AL and Bach D. (2004) Self-Regulatory Trajectories in the Shadow of Public Power: Resolving Digital Dilemmas in Europe and the United States. *Governance* 17(3): 387–413.

Nichols T. (2017) *The Death of Expertise. The Campaign Against Established Knowledge and Why it Matters*. Oxford: Oxford University Press.

North DC. (1990) *Institutions, Institutional Change and Economic Performance*. Cambridge: Cambridge University Press.

OECD. (1999) *Voluntary Approaches for Environmental Policy: An Assessment*. Paris: Organisation for Economic Co-operation and Development.

Olson M. (1965) *The Logic of Collective Action*. Cambridge, MA: Harvard University Press.

Peters BG. (2013) *Strategies for Comparative Research in Political Science*. Houndmills, Basingstoke: Palgrave Macmillan.

Pfeffer J. (1981) *Power in Organizations*. Marshfield, MA: Pitman Publishing.

Pfeffer J and Salancik GR. (2003) *The External Control of Organizations: A Resource Dependence Perspective*. Stanford: Stanford Business Books.

Pierre J and Peters BG. (2000) *Governance, Politics and the State*. Houndmills, Basingstoke: Palgrave Macmillan.

Powell WW. (1990) Neither Market Nor Hierarchy: Network Forms of Organization. *Research in Organizational Behavior* 12: 295–336.

Price R. (2011) Transnational Civil Society and Advocacy in World Politics. *World Politics* 55(4): 579–606.

Princen S. (2007) Agenda-Setting in the European Union: A Theoretical Exploration and Agenda for Research. *Journal of European Public Policy* 14(1): 21–38.

Quack S. (2016) Expertise and Authority in Transnational Governance. In: Cotterrell R and Del Mar M (eds) *Authority in Transnational Legal Theory. Theorising Across Disciplines*. Cheltenham, Northampton: Edward Elgar.

Radaelli C. (1995) The Role of Knowledge in the Policy Process. *Journal of European Public Policy* 2(2): 159–183.

Radaelli CM. (1999a) The Public Policy of the European Union: Whither Politics of Expertise? *Journal of European Public Policy* 6(5): 757–774.

Radaelli CM. (1999b) *Technocracy in the European Union*. London and New York: Longman.

Rhodes RAW. (1996) The New Governance: Governing Without Government. *Political Studies* 44(4): 652–667.

Ronit K and Schneider V. (2000) *Private Organizations in Global Politics*. London and New York: Routledge.

Sabel CF and Zeitlin J. (2010) *Experimentalist Governance in the European Union: Towards a New Architecture*. Oxford: Oxford University Press.

Scharpf FW. (1997) Introduction: The Problem-Solving Capacity of Multi-Level Governance. *Journal of European Public Policy* 4(4): 520–538.

Schattschneider E. (1975) *The Semi-Sovereign People: A Realist's View of Democracy in America*. Wadsworth: Cengage Learning.

Schrefler L. (2013) *Economic Knowledge in Regulation: The Use of Expertise by Independent Agencies*. Colchester: ECPR Press.

Scott C. (2004) Regulation in the Age of Governance: The Rise of the Post-regulatory State. In: Jordana J and Levi-Faur D (eds) *The Politics of Regulation. Institutions and Regulatory Reforms for the Age of Governance*. Cheltenham, Northampton: Edward Elgar, 145–174.

Sending OJ. (2015) *The Politics of Expertise: Competing for Authority in Global Governance*. Ann Arbor, MI: University of Michigan Press.

Smismans S. (2008) The European Social Dialogue in the Shadow of Hierarchy. *Journal of Public Policy* 28(1): 161–180.

Stigler GJ. (1971) The Theory of Economic Regulation. *The Bell Journal of Economics and Management Science* 2(1): 3–21.

Thatcher M and Stone Sweet A. (2002) Theory and Practice of Delegation to Non-majoritarian Institutions. *West European Politics* 25(1): 1–22.

Tömmel I and Verdun A. (2009) *Innovative Governance in the European Union: The Politics of Multilevel Policymaking*. Boulder: Lynne Rienner.

Weber M. (1978) *Economy and Society*. Berkeley: University of California Press.

Webster E. (2004) Firms' Decisions to Innovate and Innovation Routines. *Economics of Innovation and New Technology* 13(8): 733–745.

Whitley R and Kristensen PH. (1997) *Governance at Work: The Social Regulation of Economic Relations*. Oxford: Oxford University Press.

Williamson OE. (1975) *Markets and Hierarchies, Analysis and Antitrust Implications: A Study in the Economics of Internal Organization*. New York: Free Press.

Williamson OE. (1996) *The Mechanisms of Governance*. New York: Oxford University Press.

Wilson JQ (ed). (1980) *The Politics of Regulation*. New York: Basic Books, 357–394.

Witt MA and Jackson G. (2016) Varieties of Capitalism and Institutional Comparative Advantage: A Test and Reinterpretation. *Journal of International Business Studies* 47(7): 778–806.

CHAPTER 3

Protecting Consumers and the Environment in Europe

In times of disintegration and rising Euroscepticism, the added value of European policies in comparison with purely national solutions is often at stake. One of the major lines of criticism touches upon the topic which is at the very heart of this book, namely that the EU is mainly serving big business and not the man on the street. There is indeed evidence that Euroscepticism might at least partly be rooted in a critical attitude towards big corporations (Fuchs et al. 2017). Another line of criticism is about "Brussels red tape". It pictures European bureaucrats inventing unnecessary and burdensome rules which hinder, rather than help business activities. While both views are certainly oversimplifications, they touch upon crucial questions for European policymaking. And they are of concern for the areas of EU policymaking covered in this book, namely consumer and environmental protection. If taken seriously, these policies should indeed be beneficial for each of us and for nature and wildlife. And they should be designed in a way that those affected, notably companies, are willing to implement and comply with them. Sophisticated institutional structures and procedures are in place in order to strike this balance in the EU policymaking process. This chapter seeks to introduce the reader to our acquired knowledge about how these processes work. First, I will review the literature addressing the power balance between corporate interests on the one hand, and diffused interests (consumer and environmental interests), on the other hand. I will then briefly present the organisational structures of the industry sectors that

S. Eckert, *Corporate Power and Regulation*,
International Series on Public Policy,
https://doi.org/10.1007/978-3-030-05463-2_3

49

are going to be covered in the case studies (Chapters 4, 5 and 6). Next, I will formulate expectations about how the corporate regulatory strategies identified in Chapter 2 may materialise at EU-level. More specifically, I will reflect on the role of various policy instruments such as voluntary agreements (VAs), legislation, other types of rule specification and litigation. The chapter concludes by providing an overview of the EU regulatory policies addressed in the case studies.

CORPORATE VERSUS DIFFUSED INTERESTS

There is an ongoing discussion in EU studies about the relative influence of corporate versus "diffused" interests (Eising 2016: 189–190)—i.e. those interests which are overall less concentrated and expected to be more difficult to articulate. Environmental non-governmental organisations (ENGOs) and consumer organisations strive to overcome the collective action problem involved in representing these interests. The subsequent sections will revisit arguments about the influence of these interests in EU politics and briefly present the industry case studies in the context of EU-level interest politics.

Corporate Interests in EU Politics

The role of corporate interests in EU politics has attracted widespread attention in the literature. Already in Moravcsik's seminal liberal-intergovernmental integration theory, powerful domestic business interests are a key explanatory factor for integration dynamics (1998). Further, there is a vast literature on business lobbying in the EU, covering lobbying activities of sectoral and trans-sectoral, national and international business associations and individual TNCs since the 1990s (Fischer 1997; Ronit and Schneider 1997; Nollert 1997; Kohler-Koch et al. 2013; Coen 2009, 2010; Beyers et al. 2008). Empirical evidence points to high levels of activity, and successful business influence in various policy areas (Fuchs 2007; Klüver 2009, 2011; Mahoney 2007; Marshall 2010; Saurugger 2008).

EU policy-making is targeted by business activities, as it constitutes a unique laboratory of regulation beyond the nation state, and significantly affects corporate activity (Mikler 2018: 6). Further, the nature of EU policy-making makes it particularly receptive for the type of resources provided by corporate actors. The EU is predominantly a regulatory state due to its lack of financial resources (Majone 1994; McGowan and Wallace 1996; Lodge 2008; Eckert 2015). It has therefore been argued that "knowledge, rather than budget, is the critical resource in regulatory policy making" in the EU context (Radaelli 1999a: 759). Experts and epistemic communities (Richardson 1996) have been influential early into the integration process: indeed, their symbiotic relations with policymakers have been dubbed *copinage technocratique* (Radaelli 1999b). In all three constellations discussed in Chapter 2, we can expect that such interlinkage with industry actors is pronounced: in highly complex areas requiring specialised knowledge (expert); in areas where there is a high degree of technological and market uncertainty (innovator); and in technical areas where operational information on infrastructure capacity is required to make regulatory decisions (operator).

The power balance between corporate and diffused interests in EU policy-making has attracted much attention in the literature (Heinelt and Meinke-Brandmeier 2006; Bunea 2013; Eising 2016). The degree to which corporate interests dominate EU politics is controversial: some argue that the balance clearly tips to the disadvantage of diffuse interests (Krämer 2000: 167; Newell and Grant 2000; Dür et al. 2019). Doris Fuchs and her co-authors, for example, posit that the EU "may well be not only the world's largest but also the world's most asymmetric playground for business interest groups" (Fuchs et al. 2017). Indeed some of the peculiarities of EU politics, such as its fragmented institutional structure, and a low level of salience were found to be advantageous to business actors (Knill 2001; Cadot and Webber 2017). Others express a line of caution and identify scope conditions determining the relative influence of business, when compared to other interests (Eising 2016: 190; Dür 2008; Dür et al. 2015). In any case, the sheer number of business lobbies and their resources should not necessarily be conflated with actual influence (Adelle and Anderson 2013: 161). Although they are fewer in number and weaker in terms of financial and human resources when compared to business organisations, ENGOs and consumer organisations have proven to be an influential voice in European policy-making (Dür and Mateo 2014, 2016: 47–49). Intuitively, we could assume that business influence predominates in such an area which involves high levels of economic and technological expertise, and there is evidence that supports this claim (Knill 2001; Klüver 2012). However, public attention and politicisation are relevant factors, too. For example, research has identified a pattern where consumer organisations and environmental groups have been more effective in shaping EU GMO regulation than industry branches specialised in biotechnology (Falkner 2007: 513).

The increasing politicisation of EU issues (Hooghe and Marks 2009) therefore has the potential to affect the power balance between corporate and diffuse interests. In particular, European policymakers face a challenge where the perception of corporate power fuels opposition towards the EU. Drawing on Eurobarometer data from 2005 to 2020, Doris Fuchs and colleagues analysed the relationship between public attitudes towards transnational corporations and the EU. The research found a positive correlation between public (dis)trust in big business and the EU (Fuchs et al. 2017: 318). Indeed, these perceptions may link to support for party-based Euroscepticism (Taggart 1998) where parties on the far left and far right invoke the spectre of a "Europe of corporations" (Fuchs et al. 2017: 327). It is against this background that we could expect that EU elites will seek to strive for actions that visibly go against the interests of big business.

On the other hand, however, increased politicisation coincided with the economic and financial crisis and the subsequent economic downturn across Europe and internationally. In EU policy-making, the crisis context gave some extra weight to a growth-oriented paradigm and deregulatory ambition. Take the example of the Europe 2020 strategy (European Commission 2010): The strategy is complemented by the Commission's "better regulation" and the regulatory fitness checks (REFIT) programmes with the declared objectives to reduce the regulatory burden for business, to boost growth, and to create jobs (European Commission 2005a, b).

The Rising Power of Diffused Interests

Both environmental and consumer organisations are an influential voice in today's EU policy-making process (Burns and Carter 2012; Long 1995; Lehmann 2009; Rauh 2019). ENGOs were a driving force alongside DG Environment, the European Parliament and some pioneering member states in developing a European environmental policy (Judge 1992; Knill and Liefferink 2007; Burns and Carter 2012; Weale et al. 2000; Liefferink and Andersen 1998; Lenschow 2015). ENGOs, from their national and international base, have progressively built up EU-specific policy expertise and opened up Brussels-based offices. The player with the longest history is the European Environmental Bureau

(EEB). It opened its premises in 1974 with the goal to monitor environmental policy developments at the EU-level and coordinate responses from its member organisations at the national level (Hontelez 2012: 398–399). The EEB was the main environmental grouping until 1985. Thereafter, other environmental NGOs such as Friends of the Earth (FoE), Greenpeace, and the World Wide Fund for Nature (WWF) entered the Brussels scene throughout the 1980s. These ENGOs subsequently formed the "Green Eight" (Hontelez 2012: 400–401), and the "Green Ten" (Adelle and Anderson 2013: 154; Wurzel and Connelly 2011). ClientEarth, an ENGO made up of activist lawyers, is one of the latest additions to this range of actors, opening an office in Brussels in 2008.

Similarly, consumer organisations have been established and have diversified their portfolio over time (Greenwood 2017: 155–161) as a response to increased Europeanisation of the policy field and consumer rights (Micklitz and Weatherill 1993; Howells et al. 2017). These organisations include the European Consumer Organisation (Bureau Européen des Unions de Consommateurs [BEUC]) and the European Association for the Coordination of Consumer Representation in Standardisation (ANEC), which is the standardised offshoot of BEUC (Greenwood 2017: 50). European consumer policy has been developed against the background of very different national traditions in consumer protection (Trumbull 2010: 627–628). One of them follows an interest group approach aiming at overcoming collective action problems through the organisation of the diffused consumer interest, by assisting consumers in their effort to represent their own interest and by granting access to decision-making. It is in this logic that European policymakers lent support to the creation of consumer organisation bodies and granted these bodies access to decision-making and judicial processes.

Several factors give diffused interests, represented by ENGOs and consumer organisations, a relative advantage over business interests at European level: first, they attract support from supranational institutions because they are considered to represent the civil society and the public interest; second, they are part of larger, often global organisations with significant grass-root membership; third, these groups might find it easier to align to a common cause and engage in concerted action; finally, these groups have normative power in that they can claim to be the "good guys" going against the self-interested goals of business elites. The creation and rise of ENGOs and consumer organisations has been supported by European policymakers and thus has very much been an elite-driven process (Warleigh 2000: 230). The EEB, for instance, has been created at the request and with the help of the European Commission (Hontelez 2012: 412). Its umbrella and confederal structure has been designed on purpose in order to establish a link to nationally and regionally based organisations (Lehmann 2009). In today's EU, numerous civil society organisations receive funding from EU budget lines (Greenwood 2017: 134–139). Empirical evidence shows that the Brussels elites address public interests when issues are salient and attract intensive mobilisation by civil society groups (De Bruycker 2017), and that especially the European Commission seeks giving a voice to, and being responsive to diffused interests in times of rising politicisation (Rauh 2019). Second, the fact that many ENGOs are not solely based in Brussels but are rather part of wider, global organisations gives them additional leverage. International players have considerable resources in terms of staff, finance and reputation at their disposal (Gullberg 2008b). An organisation such as Greenpeace, which does not finance its activities through EU-funding but raises its resources independently through membership and donations, can effectively claim to represent the environmental interest and exert considerable pressure on business actors. ENGOs vocally refer to their grass-root membership in order to boost their legitimacy (Adelle and Anderson 2013: 164). These groupings, though representing "diffused interests", might further find it easier to align their interests and join forces. There is indeed evidence that these groups which, unlike business actors do not have to face each other on competitive markets, turn their relative organisational weakness into a strength. ENGOs and consumer organisations frequently cooperate and agree on work-sharing task attributions and joint campaigns (Wurzel and Connelly 2011; Mazey and Richardson 1992). Finally, their voice may be better heard where it is considered to represent the public interest rather than private interests (Adelle and Anderson 2013: 161). In comparison with business organisations, ENGOs and consumer organisations draw on a different type of authority: and, normatively speaking, they are on the "good side", representing the interests of consumers, animals and the earth. Overall, the rise of environmental and consumer issues at the supranational level has provided diffused interests with a new and promising opportunity structure.

The activities that these groups engage in range from providing policy input, and offering expertise and information to the Commission and other various institutions as "access goods" (Bouwen 2002: 370), to more classical tools of campaigning and awareness raising. These different strategies can also been categorised as insider versus outsider lobbying (Junk 2016). Accordingly, more radical environmentalist organisations such as Greenpeace would rather opt for outsider lobbying, while WWF or the EEB would lean towards insider lobbying, that is exerting influence as participants in the policy process (Grant et al. 2000). At a closer look, all Brussels-based ENGOs to some extent engage in insider lobbying and thus provide access goods to policymakers. In this endeavour, several organisations frequently join forces with one another and build alliances in order to advocate specific topics, or engage in work-sharing strategies in order to cover a multitude of dossiers (Wurzel and Connelly 2011; Warleigh 2000).

ENGOs and consumer protection organisations can put considerable pressure on business and regulators alike. For instance, they can raise the reputational cost of corporate or regulator's non-action through targeted campaigns (Hendry 2003). This is why it is important to note that corporate and diffused interests are not necessarily opposed. Where corporations fit the environmentalist frame, we also see so-called green alliances between ENGOs and industry (Stafford et al. 2000).

Responsiveness of Policymakers

The policymakers involved in the EU legislative process have a reputation that differs in terms of responsiveness to political interests. The European Commission with its policy of initiative rights and the European Parliament as a co-legislator are usually considered to be the most promising access points, while influencing the Council mostly works through indirect, national channels (Greenwood 2017: Chapter 2; Bouwen 2002; Coen and Richardson 2009b). Attempts to influence the legislative process are promising at the early stage of agenda-setting, which makes the Commission as the policy initiator the obvious venue for these activities (Bouwen 2009: 20–21, Mazey and Richardson 1996: 208; 2003).

Having limited staff and financial resources, the Commission is especially in need of and depends on a high level of technical and scientific information and knowledge both in its policy entrepreneurship and regulatory activities (Coen and Richardson 2009a: 7; Majone 1994; Cram 1993). This facilitates access to decision-making through insider lobbying, both, by corporate interests and diffuse interests. Further, ENGOs and consumer organisations represent and constitute a link to the European "civil society" (European Commission 2001: 11, 13). Especially in view of rising politicisation of EU issues, the European Commission is responsive to diffused interests (Rauh 2016). As mentioned, however, the Commission also drives the EU's growth and better regulation agenda, which favours business interests. Besides the legacy of sectoral DGs, responsiveness to distinct types of interests as well as policy goals do also depend on personal ambition and the ownership of policy leaders (Tömmel and Verdun 2017). In her capacity as Commissioner for Environment, Margot Wallström (1999–2004) had the reputation of being quite outspoken and strived for ambitious policy change in comparison with her successors, who preferred to keep a relatively low profile (Schön-Quinlivan 2013: 98). Inside the Commission, there is a process of *"institutionalisation of consultation"* (Mazey and Richardson 1996: 210, emphasis in original) through advisory committees, expert groups and the like, which typically include business actors (Bouwen 2009: 29; Mazey and Richardson 2003: 222–223). Early examples are the Scientific Committee for Toxicity, Ecotoxicity and Environment, set up in 1978; the Consultative Forum on the Environment and Sustainable Development, set up in 1993 (Krämer 2000: 158); or the Energy Consultative Committee, which represents all energy interests and was created in 1996 (Mazey and Richardson 1996: 210). It has been argued that these groups are an element of an "elite pluralist arrangement where industry is perceived as an integral policy player" (Coen 2010: 293). There is, however, variation across the Commission's Directorates General (DGs) as to their corresponding private interest constituencies (Mazey and Richardson 2003: 220, 222–223). The DG dealing with industrial policy and internal market issues (in the Juncker Commission DG Growth for Internal Market, Industry, Entrepreneurship and SMEs) traditionally attracts a high degree of business lobbying. By contrast, DG Environment typically maintains dialogues with civil society organisations and NGOs (Bouwen 2009: 24; Greenwood 2017: 40). Since several DGs are involved in preparing secondary and delegated legislation (Scully and van Schendelen 2004: 6), there is however a need to engage in inter-service consultation (Schön-Quinlivan 2013: 106–107). Thus organised interests cannot limit the focus of lobbying activities on one single DG (Hontelez 2012; Mazey and Richardson 1992), but instead need to target both "friends" and their "foes" (Gullberg 2008a).

Because of its ever increasing co-legislative powers, the European Parliament (EP) has become an important target of interest politics (Greenwood 2017: 41–44; Mazey and Richardson 1996: 209). Overall the EP, in comparison with the European Commission, pursues a different rationale in its consultation practice: it strives for "political rather than policy legitimacy" (Coen 2010: 292). The European Parliament will formulate public interest positions on salient issues and cultivate its role as being the voice of the European people (Dür and Mateo 2014: 200–201, 204–205; Justin and Christilla 2015). As a consequence, non-technical approaches as well as the emphasis of regional and local political priorities have been identified as preconditions for lobbying success in the EP (Lehmann 2009: 40). Members of European Parliament (MEPs) are in general more responsive to diffused interests (Pollack 1997), and empirical research has shown that civil society interests can be more successful than business interests in issue areas where the European Parliament has a strong role as a legislator (Dür et al. 2015). That said, the rising legislative power has shifted the focus of parliamentary work towards the committee stage, a level at which policy-specific expertise can be a game changer (Smith 2008; Rasmussen 2012, 2015; Marshall 2010; Lehmann 2009: 51–53). In any case, lobbying EP committees involved in legislation is the best way to make a difference at an early stage in the process. Interest politics thus increasingly target committees, which vary substantially as to their responsiveness to different interests (Rasmussen 2012; Ripoll Servent 2015). In environmental policy, the environmental committee has traditionally been an influential player for the EP position which "normally called for stronger environmental measures than proposed by the Commission or the Council" (Krämer 2000: 160). There is, however, also evidence that the increase in competencies has come along with a less radical environmentalist stance over time (Burns 2013: 144–145; Schön-Quinlivan 2013: 104–105; Burns and Carter 2010), notwithstanding changing political majorities.

The Council and the European Council are the "least accessible but not inaccessible" (Hayes-Renshaw 2009), holding a reputation to be much less approachable than both the European Commission and the European Parliament (Dinan 2010: Chapter 8; Sherrington 2000; Eising 2007). Especially the Council has cultivated this image, arguing that secrecy is a necessary condition for effective negotiations between member states, and has rejected demands for more transparency and openness (Hayes-Renshaw 2009: 73–74). What further complicates access for lobbyists is that, compared to other institutions, the Council has fewer staff and less permanent personnel at its disposal, making it difficult for interest groups to build up long term relationships and trust. Its rotating presidency, for instance, holds important agenda-setting powers, and yet relevant input must be addressed to different national delegations each time. Furthermore, the Council is, if at all, responsive to a different type of interest, a "domestic encompassing interest" (Bouwen 2004) rather than a European one. The Council is thus a venue for those opting for the "national route" (Greenwood 2017: 29–32) in European interest politics. National interest groups are more likely to engage in effective lobbying vis-à-vis the Council (and its individual members), whereas European federations will consider this approach where there is a need to orchestrate the individual lobbying efforts of national trade associations in order to target several Council members (Bouwen 2002; Hayes-Renshaw 2009). Further, lobbyists will select the institutional venue depending on the goals they pursue. Cornelia Woll, in her research on interest politics in European trade policy, has shown that the proponents of pan-European solutions target the European Commission, while the proponents of protectionism take the national route (Woll 2009).

Member state interests generally diverge considerably: they derive from acquired levels of domestic environmental regulation (Börzel 2002) and, one might add, domestic economic interests. There is a traditional divide between the more affluent Northern member states on the one hand and the Southern and Eastern member states on the other (Liefferink and Andersen 1998; Wurzel 2008; Veenman and Liefferink 2012). Where governments identify environmental issues that matter for domestic business interests, they may go a long way to push through their priorities. The German government, for instance, used its leadership role as Council presidency in the course of adopting the End-of-life Vehicle Directive in 1999 (Wurzel 2013: 83; Greenwood 2017: 31). Overall, the role of the Council in pushing for ambitious environmental policies has been less impactful than the role of the European Commission and the Parliament—with the notable exception of certain energy and climate change policies (Jordan et al. 2010; Oberthür and Dupont 2011).

The Industry Sectors at EU-Level

Table 3.1 shows how the industry sectors covered in the case studies are organised at the EU-level. European associations vary as to whether they

Table 3.1 Industry organisations at European level

Case studies	Expert		Innovator		Operator
Industry sectors	Paper industry	Plastics industry	Home appliance industry	ICT industry	Transmission system operators
EU-association Members	CEPI	PlasticsEurope	APPLiA (CECED)	Digital Europe	ENTSO-E
	18 associations	>100 firms	21 firms 25 associations	64 firms 39 associations	43 TSOs (36 countries)

Source Information retrieved from websites: 2018 APPLiA, CEPI, PlasticsEurope, Digital Europe, ENTSO-E

allow for direct membership, or whether they are EU-level peak organisations of national or branch-specific trade associations. Historically, most business associations started out as peak organisations, but many of them evolved to become "hybrid" associations allowing for direct firm membership from the 1990s onwards (Coen 2010: 300). The focus is on the most important EU-level associations each time.

The European pulp and paper industry is organised through the Confederation of the European Paper Industries (CEPI), created in 1992. CEPI only allows for direct membership of national associations, while its partnership programme is open to individual firms. At the time of writing, it brings together national associations from 18 countries representing 495 companies, and 5 partners, such as machine or chemical suppliers with a direct link to paper manufacturing. European plastics manufacturers are represented by PlasticsEurope, a trade association representing more than 100 member-companies. PlasticsEurope is one out of four industry sector organisations of the European Chemical Industry Council (CEFIC) that exist alongside the CEFIC horizontal programme. CEFIC includes both associations and firms as members. Producers of home appliance electronics are organised in the EU-association APPLiA, formerly known as CECED. In 2018, APPLiA comprised of 21 member firms and 25 national associations (APPLiA 2018). Digital Europe brings together the world's leading ICT firms such as Microsoft or Google, but also smaller, specialised players through its national trade association members. It comprises of 64 firms as direct members, and an additional

39 national associations (DigitalEurope 2018). Finally, the European Network of European Transmission System Operators in Electricity (ENTSO-E) with national Transmission System Operators (TSOs) as direct members has a structure that differs from the other sectors. This is due to the specificities of the electricity business as a network industry, in which the infrastructure constitutes a natural monopoly. Accordingly, there are few players in network operation. In 2017, ENTSO-E was composed of 43 TSOs from 36 countries (ENTSO-E 2018).

CORPORATE REGULATORY STRATEGIES

Chapter 2 identified corporate strategies in preventing, shaping, making and revoking regulation, taking the varying power resources of experts, innovators and operators into account. In what follows, these expectations are to be specified for the context of EU-level regulatory policies focusing on VAs , secondary law and its implementation, as well as litigation. Finally, I will briefly discuss the areas of EU regulation relevant for the case studies.

Voluntary Agreements

In theory, VAs can be in the interest of business and political actors alike. On the supply side, business actors dispose of the required time, staff, sector-specific knowledge and capacity to engage in self-regulation, which ultimately eliminates the need for public regulation. On the demand side, policymakers save transaction costs when delegating the adoption and implementation of rules to private actors. How does this materialise at EU-level? Research on private governance and self-regulation has shown that the preconditions at the European level are quite demanding for voluntary instruments to be effective and legitimate (Héritier 2003; Rottmann and Lenschow 2008; Lenschow and Rottmann 2010; Héritier and Eckert 2008).

Corporations acting as experts, innovators and operators certainly dispose of the sector-specific knowledge required to formulate rules that can address certain policy issues. They also frequently have the required financial and human resources to engage in voluntary action, yet of course there are certain opportunity costs involved. The capacity to effectively organise at the EU-level with full industry support across the EU-28 already presents a challenge. Branches with numerous players and high levels of market fragmentation may actually prefer binding European regulation rather than self-regulation. Another issue is the question of whether costly voluntary action is indeed rewarding in that it substantially lowers the risk of being regulated. If there is no real risk of policymakers taking action that negatively affects the industry, there is no given incentive to come up with voluntary measures in the first place (Halfteck 2006, 2008; Héritier and Eckert 2008). On the other hand, where regulatory capacity is high, policymakers do not easily abstain from taking action, which can make voluntary action for industry even less rewarding. This has been discussed as the "governance paradox" (Börzel 2008: 127) in Chapter 2. In such a setting, industry does not eliminate the risk of regulation for good when committing to VAs. Rather, it exposes itself to heightened public scrutiny and this more so than when being subject to binding requirements. Therefore, the regulatory threat must be credible, and the type of regulation threatened likewise costly—for example, the ban of a material or a product manufactured by a particular industry branch. Public and ENGO pressure may moreover function as an incentive where industry seeks to avoid and lower reputational cost (Doner and Schneider 2000; Bell 2008; Héritier and Eckert 2009; Haufler 2001: 26–27).

On the side of EU policymakers (demand side), self-regulation is seen as appealing because it fits the goal of reducing the supranational regulatory burden. At the beginning of the New Millennium, the EU's so-called better regulation agenda was defined by a high-level advisory group established in December 2000 and chaired by the French civil servant Dieudonné Mandelkern. The better regulation action plan was adopted by the Prodi Commission in 2002 (European Commission 2002a). Since then, better regulation has been declared a priority of subsequent Commission Presidents, such as José Manuel Barroso in 2009 (EurActiv 2009), and Jean Claude Juncker in 2014 (Heath 2017). There would therefore be a reputational gain for the European Commission to cut Brussels red tape. Further, policymakers could save both decision-making and implementation costs. The European process of formulating and agreeing on rules is riddled with veto points, leading to lengthy and cumbersome negotiations so that European policymakers may well be caught in the famous joint-decision trap (Scharpf 2006). In the implementation phase, supranational bodies hold very limited enforcement power. There is a vast literature on implementation and compliance which compares change in the member states (Falkner et al. 2004; Angelova et al. 2012; Börzel 2001; Falkner et al. 2007; Toshkov 2008; Mastenbroek 2005; Bondarouk and Mastenbroek 2018; Groenleer et al. 2010). In the specific EU context, self-regulation by industry may therefore save transaction costs already in the phase of formulating policies and has the potential to ensure compliance of actors that voluntarily abide to certain rules (Héritier and Eckert 2008). Another advantage of voluntary measures is that their territorial scope is driven by functional needs rather than territorial boundaries (Héritier and Lehmkuhl 2008). This is attractive in a situation where uniform rules for the EU-28 countries do not meet the needs of certain regions in which the regulation is actually needed, either because they are too encompassing in certain areas, or not encompassing enough in others. Furthermore, the legislative process lacks the flexibility and adaptation required for ever-changing circumstances and conditions. This holds especially true in European policy-making, where it takes on average two years (usually more) to complete the adoption or revision of legislation. In areas where swift regulatory action is needed, such as in sectors with rapid technological innovation, legislation is hence often times not the adequate instrument.

In the light of these considerations, one would expect that VAs are promoted by policymakers. These have, however, not become a standard instrument in the EU policy toolbox, neither legally, nor de facto. In fact European environmental policy continued to be dominated by hierarchical rule-making despite the new governance agenda (Holzinger et al. 2009). The use of VAs was first considered in the field of environmental policy. In 1996, the European Commission adopted the Fifth Environmental Action Programme as well as a communication on voluntary environmental agreements, which mainly discussed examples at national level (European Commission 1996). In the context of the better regulation agenda, a second communication followed in 2002, which envisaged the potential for VAs at the community level (European Commission 2002b). This communication defined the assessment criteria for environmental agreements and some procedural requirements and differentiated between settings of self-regulation and co-regulation. Yet not much followed from there, for a number of reasons (Interview COM 2005; Schnabl 2005): There are no treaty provisions that would give legal status to VAs, hence it is not possible to formulate a legal framework for their use, and it is also difficult to formally endorse them. Further, there is disagreement about the policy effectiveness and legitimacy of the instrument both between Commission DGs, and between the Commission, the EP and the Council. For all these reasons, the instrument has scarcely been used at the supranational level, and the European Commission was reluctant to lend support to the instrument. There was also no follow-up to the 2002 Communication. That said, several legislative measures have incorporated the use of voluntary instruments as a means of implementation. One example, to be discussed in the case study on product innovation, is the Ecodesign framework directive.

Beyond Legislation

Legislation at the EU-level frequently sets only a broad regulatory framework that leaves room for interpretation at the national level, and often it involves the prescription of more detailed rules at later stages (also discussed by Scully and van Schendelen 2004: 5–7). It is therefore important to consider non-legislative types of rule-setting at EU-level such as Comitology (Wessels 1998; Blom-Hansen and Brandsma 2009), agency governance (Rittberger and Wonka 2011; Trondal et al. 2012) and standardisation (Büthe and Mattli 2010; Wettig 2002) in order to fully capture corporate power. The bulk of legislation originating at the EU-level has steadily increased over time. Environmental policy is one of the areas with the highest levels of Europeanisation (Töller 2010). Likewise, consumer policy has become more Europeanised through negative and positive integration (Weatherill 2013). Business therefore has an interest in seeking to shape European legislation. As discussed previously, the responsiveness to business and diffused interests inside the EU's institutional triangle varies. Especially the European Commission and EP committees will be responsive to the more sector-specific and technical input of experts, innovators and operators. Both institutions have developed consultation procedures to that end.

The adoption of rules through committees involves a great deal of procedural detail and has evolved considerably over time. Policymakers and "in-sourced experts" (van Schendelen 2004) gather in the various committees and interact on a regular basis, they adopt implementation measures which not only refine but constitute a substantial part of the European regulatory framework (Everson and Joerges 2006; Héritier et al. 2013). The institutional and procedural structure of committee governance has evolved significantly over time, especially as the European Parliament has sought to gain access to this type of policy-making (Bradley 1997, 2008; Christiansen and Dobbels 2012). Under the Lisbon treaty, the Commission can adopt delegated and implementing acts. There are substantive as well as procedural differences between the two: implementing acts are deemed to execute the law in a uniform way and shall not modify the legislation; delegated acts amend and complement existing legislation and provide for regulatory detail. Further, in procedural terms, implementing acts are developed by the Commission, without EP involvement ("Comitology"), whereas delegated acts can only enter into force when the Parliament and Council do not object. In most areas where the Commission adopts implementing acts (regulation EU no. 182/2011), the EU bureaucracy is assisted by committees that give member state representatives either a vote in the process (examination procedure), or an advisory role (advisory procedure). In the period from 2009 to 2014, the number of Comitology committees ranged from 259 to 302 (European Commission 2016: 3). Similarly, delegated acts rely on input from expert groups. Although since the Lisbon treaty delegated acts no longer fall into the realm of Comitology strictly speaking, the term is still being used in both cases (Delreux and Happaerts 2016: 108–113; Brandsma 2013).

The European Commission secures policy input through numerous expert groups and fora, (Bouwen 2009: 29; Mazey and Richardson 2003: 222–223). Decisions taken by these bodies are not binding, yet they provide a significant level of expert knowledge and legitimacy to the Commission (Bouwen 2002: 369–371, 373; 2009: 29–31). The Commission has a high degree of discretion in designing such expert groups and fora: it can select the policy area, the participants, and determine the procedures (Mahoney 2004: 447–449). Such fora and expert bodies include a number of policy experts, representing industry stakeholders but also regulatory or standard-setting bodies.

Given the non-delegation principle—known as the Meroni doctrine (for a discussion of recent case law, see Simoncini 2018: 6)—EU-level regulatory agencies usually dispose only of limited stand-alone regulatory powers and often merely advise the committees. However, there is evidence from various sectors that their recommendations frequently get rubber-stamped by the committees (Groenleer 2011; Gehring and Krapohl 2007). Business interests also play a role in agency governance, as the regulators do rely on input from their regulated stakeholders and engage in intense practices of consulting with, and reporting to their constituencies (Ossege 2015; Kelemen 2012; Nesti 2018; Williams 2005; Borrás et al. 2007). In view of such interaction between regulators and regulatees the risk of regulatory capture is real especially for relatively weak EU agencies (Shapiro 1997). EU agencies frequently depend on and demand stakeholder input (Pérez Durán 2018; Arras and Braun 2017). Quantitative research shows that interest organisations have frequent contacts with both national and EU regulatory agencies (Dür and Mateo 2016: 62–63).

Standardisation bodies are another type of expert organisation which develop rules that can become binding regulation where policymakers decide to endorse them (Büthe and Mattli 2010). Examples at the EU-level include the European Committee for Standardisation (CEN) and the European Committee for Electrotechnical Standardisation (CENELEC), or the European Telecommunications Standards Institute (ETSI). Though from the outset, these bodies were open to the participation of ENGOs or consumer organisations, they were basically composed of industry representatives, as civil society lacked the required financial resources to cover the cost of participation (Krämer 2000: 167). Under the directive 94/62/EC on packaging and packaging waste, for instance, the general requirements for the safety and environmental aspects of packaging formulated in the directive were elaborated under the authority of CEN. In the view of Ludwig Krämer, former DG ENVI official and today ClientEarth lawyer, the process was captured by industry, leading to outcomes with no visible environmental added value (Krämer 2000: 165). To go against such industry dominance, the European Commission has started to provide funding to help organisations such as BEUC participate in the standards bodies (Greenwood 2017: 50). For that purpose, BEUC has created a dedicated branch organisation in 1995, the ANEC. Similarly, ENGOs have created a structure in 2001, the European Environmental Citizens Organisation for Standardisation (ECOS, Interview ENGO 2019). ECOS is supported by EU public funding and recognised as part of the European Standardisation System (regulation EU 1025/2012). Further, it is a partner organisation of CEN and CENELEC, and a member of ETSI.

Due to the many veto players and their diverse interests, the hurdles for effective policy-shaping in the legislative arena may actually be quite high for corporate actors, especially in visible and politicised areas. It is therefore crucial to consider non-legislative venues for corporate regulatory power.

The Use of Litigation

Another avenue of business influence is via the judiciary. Generally speaking this route is less pronounced than in the US context for both institutional and cultural reasons (Coen and Richardson 2009a: 11; McCown 2009: 90–91). Yet there are contextual factors that favour judicial politics at EU-level, one of them being that drafting legislation in a multi-level and multilingual context is "prey to drafting defects [... as a consequence of which] it falls to the European Court of Justice to give a definitive meaning to a text which secured adoption by virtue of its opaqueness or ambiguity" (Wyatt 1998). For corporate actors, litigation strategies constitute not only an alternative to, but can complement and support traditional lobbying activities (Alter and Vargas 2000; Conant 2002; Fligstein and Stone Sweet 2002). As Pieter Bouwen and Margaret McCown emphasise, litigation is far more than a second-best solution where lobbying has failed at earlier stages in the policy process. Rather, it can actually initiate policy change:

> The ECJ's rulings can be quite prescriptive and when it makes rulings that strike down national rules, and widen the applicability of EU ones, it is often rather explicit about what the amended national or European rules should look like in order to be in conformity with the treaties. In this way, interest groups that successfully litigate in order to shape EU policy not only effect the removal of national rules, on the basis of EU law, but also shape the form of future legislation. (Bouwen and McCown 2007: 426)

Litigation demands not only a comparatively high level of material resources and know-how, but also a clear-cut position with respect to the desired outcome of court proceedings. Individual firms and business groups are the most likely candidates to engage in resource-intense, long term litigation (Conant 2002; Harlow and Rawlings 2013), and even more so in "repeat player" strategies (Galanter 1974). This is due to both their financial and human resources, as well as their organisational characteristics with a well-defined mandate (Bouwen and McCown 2007: 429–430). Business associations are far less likely to go for litigation. Especially where they assemble a wide and diverse range of members it will be difficult to reach the necessary consensus for a longer period of time and cope with situations in which court rulings may go against the interests of some of their members (Alter and Vargas 2000: 473; Bouwen and McCown 2007: 427). Success in court is very appealing to businesses, as a decision is not easily overturned and comparatively insulated from other policy challenges (McCown 2009). Business actors, where affected by European regulation, may have an interest in bringing non-compliance to the attention of the Commission and thus trigger infringement proceedings. The Commission has an interest to receive such information on potential non-compliance, given that its instruments to enforce European law are limited. In a highly Europeanised area of regulation such as environmental policy the Commission will thus welcome the information from private complainants on potential non-compliance (Krämer 2000: 177).

Access to justice for diffuse groups such as consumers became a salient issue with the increasing role of litigation in the EU context (Kelemen 2013: 255). Responding to pressure to make it easier for EU citizens and companies to enforce their rights in a European area of justice, access to the judiciary has opened up in member states (Kelemen 2011: 56–79, 2013: 253–256). Privatised approaches to litigation funding (Faure et al. 2013) and altered rules concerning collective action (Tait and Sherwood 2005; Hodges 2009) have changed traditional patterns of litigation. On the side of ENGOs, new organisations such as ClientEarth or Deutsche Umwelthilfe have emerged. Until ClientEarth set up its Brussels office in 2008, ENGOs only disposed of limited legal expertise (Thornton and Goodman 2017; Interview ENGO 2017; Smedley 2016). Bringing his legal experience from the US-based organisation Natural Resources Defense Council (NRDC), ClientEarth founder James Thornton sought to tip the balance:

> Nobody in Europe was doing this type of work. Greenpeace had one external lawyer they would call upon when people were arrested…[but] there simply wasn't an NRDC-type organisation […]. There are about 15,000 corporate lobbyists in Brussels, many with very highly paid lawyers. Our idea was to balance that. (Smedley 2016)

Further, access to justice has been strengthened in the area of consumer protection. The legal doctrine which characterises "consumer capitalism"

(Trumbull 2006) is giving consumers a strong voice in legal proceedings. According to Trumbull, the emergence of the principle of consumer citizenship in Europe has caused a major shift, away from the traditional legal doctrine positing caveat emptor (let the buyer beware), towards producer responsibility. It is this "revolution in legal doctrine of product liability" (Trumbull 2006: 2) which has transformed consumers into a legal class recognised by the courts.

From an enforcement perspective, however, NGO access to justice was also discussed as an instance of policy retrenchment. Hofmann, in his longitudinal analysis of enforcement patterns of EU environmental law, finds evidence that the Commission is increasingly withdrawing from its role as the central actor in enforcing European law. While NGOs would partially take over this task, they would lack the capacity to be as effective as the Commission, and private enforcement would further heavily depend on national opportunity structures (Hofman 2019). From the perspective of this book, this also raises the question whether Commission inactivity ultimately goes to the advantage of corporate power.

Areas of EU Regulation

Table 3.2 presents the areas of regulation covered in the book. These are grouped into four broad categories, namely the regulation of chemicals, waste, products and electricity. The period covered in the book allows me to capture the dynamics in the regulatory process by considering the secondary law currently in force, the ensuing process of rule-specification and the processes of reviewing and recasting existing regulation. The time of adoption of existing legislation broadly falls into the first decade of the New Millennium, while at the time of writing revisions are currently under discussion for all three dossiers. The two most relevant policy proposals for the case studies are the measures under the Clean Energy and the Circular Economy Packages proposed between 2014 and 2018.

The case study on the role of the expert (paper and plastics sectors) concerns the areas of EU chemical and waste regulation. Legislation in both areas is limited to formulating broad rules, whereas much of the actual rule-setting takes place at a later stage in implementing the law. The supranational framework governing the regulation, evaluation and authorisation of chemicals (REACH) has been adopted in 2006 to streamline a huge number of pre-existing material-specific legislative

Table 3.2 Areas of EU regulation

	Chemicals	Waste	Products	Electricity
Legislation	REACH (2006)	Waste Framework directive (2008), WEEE directive (2012), RoHS directive (2011), Packaging Waste directive (2015)	Ecodesign framework directive (2009), Energy Labelling directive (2010), Ecolabel directive (2010), Green Public Procurement (2014)	Third Energy Package (2009)
Rule-specification	Implementing acts, agency advice and decisions	Implementing decisions, delegated acts	Implementing regulations, VAs	Delegated acts, agency advice and decisions, network codes
Reviews, recast	REACH review (2017), Circular Economy Strategy (2015)	Circular Economy Strategy (2015), Waste Framework directive, Packaging Waste directive, Plastics Strategy (2018)	Circular Economy Strategy (2015), Clean Energy Package (2016), Energy Labelling regulation (2017)	Energy Union Strategy (2015), Clean Energy Package (2016)

Source Author's illustration

measures (Delreux and Happaerts 2016: 166–167). It is therefore not surprising that policy formulation was the target of considerable lobbying efforts (Lenschow 2015: 333; Long and Lörinczi 2009: 176–177). Implementation relies on delegated legislation through committees, but also on assessment by the European Chemicals Agency (ECHA) (Martens 2012). From the vantage point of this book, REACH is the prime example of a regulatory framework which requires a high level of scientific information and expertise with its principle "no data, no market" (Heyvaert 2007). Similarly, waste regulation incorporates a contingent tension between targeted, specific measures concerning certain products and waste streams, as opposed to an overall architecture to deal with cross-cutting issues not only in the waste phase but increasingly with the ambition to tackle the entire life cycle of products and substances (idea of a "circular economy"). Waste legislation was developed from the mid-1970s onwards, and the overarching waste framework directive adopted in 1975 was subject to review in 2005, 2008 (Delreux and Happaerts 2016: 164–165) and in 2018. It was subsequently complemented by legislation targeting specific waste streams and the end-of-life of products, e.g. on the Waste of Electrical and Electronic Equipment (WEEE), on the Restriction of Hazardous Substances (RoHS) in such equipment, or on packaging waste (Weale et al. 2000: 410–434). Overall, there was a shift in EU and national policies towards recycling and recovery of waste (Fischer 2011). Different from the areas of chemical and energy regulation, implementation does not rely on a supranational regulatory agency, while "delegated legislation" through committees (van Schendelen 2004: 28) is equally important in both fields. At the time of writing, both areas of regulation go through substantial review: the REACH review (2017) and the Circular Economy Strategy (2015–2018), comprising of initiatives such as the Plastics Strategy (2018). Thirty-seven interviews on issues related to EU waste and chemical regulation were conducted for this book with policymakers and policy experts at the European Commission (7), the European Parliament (6), ministries (2), national parliament (1), industry (16), ENGOs and consumer organisations (5).

The case study on product innovation with an environmental impact touches upon an area of regulation with a high level of specificity. In fact, the boundaries between product, chemicals and waste regulation are fluid (Delreux and Happaerts 2016: 164–168). Product policy combines measures under the Ecodesign framework directive (last recast 2009), the Energy Labelling regulation (last recast 2017), the Ecolabel directive, introduced in 1992 and subject to recasts in 2000 and 2010, and Green Public Procurement (2014). Implementing Ecodesign relies on a process of adopting product-specific implementing regulations as set out in multi-annual working plans. While operating in a legislative context, third parties are heavily involved in defining and implementing specified rules (Tanasescu 2009: 151–184). In this process, industry can agree to adopt VAs, to become formally recognised implementing measures. Twenty-four expert interviews have covered issues related to product policy, with a double focus on energy efficiency in the use phase as well as on resource efficiency throughout the life cycle of products. Interviews were conducted with Commission officials (7), ministerial officials (4), ENGOs (4) and industry (9).

Finally, the case study on the operators of transmission electricity grids relates to Internal Energy Market (IEM) regulation. A European energy policy, while being an early example of supranational cooperation, has emerged as a policy in its own right over the last few decades, and was formalised as an EU competence with the treaty of Lisbon (Eckert 2016; Buchan 2009, 2015). Secondary law has been adopted and revised through three legislative packages. Their implementation involves a substantial amount of non-legislative rule-setting, for instance through the so-called network codes adopted between 2009 and 2017. Rules prepared by committees as well as by the Agency for the Cooperation of Energy Regulators (ACER) deserve particular attention. Finally, I will discuss the current proposals affecting the internal electricity market as part of the Clean Energy Package. Thirty-two interviews have been conducted for the energy case at the European Commission (6), ministries (3), regulators (6) TSOs (9), energy industry representatives (6), and with academic and ENGO experts (2).

References

Adelle C and Anderson J. (2013) Lobby Groups. In: Jordan A and Adelle C (eds) *Environmental Policy in the EU: Actors, Institutions and Processes.* 3rd ed. London, New York: Routledge, 152–169.

Alter KJ and Vargas J. (2000) Explaining Variation in the Use of European Litigation Strategies: European Community Law and British Gender Equality Policy. *Comparative Political Studies* 33(4): 452–482.

Angelova M, Dannwolf T and König T. (2012) How Robust Are Compliance Findings? A Research Synthesis. *Journal of European Public Policy* 19(8): 1269–1291.

APPLiA. (2018) *APPLiA. About Us.* Available at: https://www.applia-europe.eu/about-us (accessed 24.10.2018).

Arras S and Braun C. (2017) Stakeholders Wanted! Why and How European Union Agencies Involve Non-state Stakeholders. *Journal of European Public Policy* 25(9): 1257–1275.

Bell S. (2008) Rethinking the Role of the State: Explaining Business Collective Action at the Business Council of Australia. *Polity* 40(4): 464–487.

Beyers J, Eising R and Maloney W. (2008) Researching Interest Group Politics in Europe and Elsewhere: Much We Study, Little We Know? *West European Politics* 31(6): 1103–1128.

Blom-Hansen J and Brandsma GJ. (2009) The EU Comitology System: Intergovernmental Bargaining and Deliberative Supranationalism? *Journal of Common Market Studies* 47(4): 719–740.

Bondarouk E and Mastenbroek E. (2018) Reconsidering EU Compliance: Implementation Performance in the Field of Environmental Policy. *Environmental Policy and Governance* 28(1): 15–27.

Borrás S, Koutalakis C and Wendler F. (2007) European Agencies and Input Legitimacy: EFSA, EMeA and EPO in the Post-delegation Phase. *Journal of European Integration* 29(5): 583–600.

Börzel TA. (2001) Non-compliance in the European Union: Pathology or Statistical Artefact? *Journal of European Public Policy* 8(5): 803–824.

Börzel TA. (2002) Pace-Setting, Foot-Dragging, and Fence-Sitting: Member-State Responses to Europeanization. *Journal of Common Market Studies* 40(2): 193–214.

Börzel TA. (2008) Der „Schatten der Hierarchie". Ein Governance-Paradox? Special Issue: Governance in einer sich wandelnden Welt. *Politische Vierteljahresschrift* 41: 118–131.

Bouwen P. (2002) Corporate Lobbying in the European Union: The Logic of Access. *Journal of European Public Policy* 9(3): 365–390.

Bouwen P. (2004) Exchanging Access Goods for Access: A Comparative Study of Business Lobbying in the European Union Institutions. *European Journal of Political Research* 43(3): 337–369.

Bouwen P. (2009) The European Commission. In: Coen D and Richardson J (eds) *Lobbying the European Union: Institutions, Actors, and Issues.* Oxford: Oxford University Press, 19–38.

Bouwen P and McCown M. (2007) Lobbying Versus Litigation: Political and Legal Strategies of Interest Representation in the European Union. *Journal of European Public Policy* 14(3): 422–443.

Bradley KSC. (1997) The European Parliament and Comitology: On the Road to Nowhere? *European Law Journal* 3(3): 230–254.

Bradley KSC. (2008) Halfway House: The 2006 Comitology Reforms and the European Parliament. *West European Politics* 31(4): 837–854.

Brandsma GJ. (2013) *Controlling Comitology: Accountability in a Multi-Level System.* London, New York: Palgrave Macmillan.

Buchan D. (2009) *Energy and Climate Change: Europe at the Crossroads.* Oxford, New York: Oxford University Press.

Buchan D. (2015) Energy Policy: Sharp Challenges and Rising Ambitions. In: Wallace H, Pollack MA and Young AR (eds) *Policy-Making in the European Union.* 7th ed. Oxford: Oxford University Press, 344–366.

Bunea A. (2013) Issues, Preferences and Ties: Determinants of Interest Groups' Preference Attainment in the EU Environmental Policy. *Journal of European Public Policy* 20(4): 552–570.

Burns C. (2013) The European Parliament. In: Jordan A and Adelle C (eds) *Environmental Policy in the EU: Actors, Institutions and Processes.* 3rd ed. London, New York: Routledge, 132–151.

Burns C and Carter N. (2010) Is Co-decision Good for the Environment? An Analysis of the European Parliament's Green Credentials. *Political Studies* 58(1): 123–142.

Burns C and Carter N. (2012) Environmental Policy. In: Jones E, Menon A and Weatherill S (eds) *The Oxford Handbook of the European Union.* Oxford: Oxford University Press, 511–525.

Büthe T and Mattli W. (2010) International Standards and Standard-Standard-Setting Bodies. In: Coen D, Grant W and Wilson GK (eds) *The Oxford Handbook of Business and Government.* Oxford: Oxford University Press, 440–471.

Cadot O and Webber D. (2017) Banana Splits: Policy Process, Particularistic Interests, Political Capture, and Money in Transatlantic Trade Politics. *Business and Politics* 4(1): 5–39.

Christiansen T and Dobbels M. (2012) Comitology and Delegated Acts After Lisbon: How the European Parliament Lost the Implementation Game. *European Integration Online Papers (EIoP)* 16.

Coen D. (2009) Business Lobbying in the European Union. In: Coen D and Richardson J (eds) *Lobbying the European Union: Institutions, Actors, and Issues.* Oxford: Oxford University Press, 145–168.

Coen D. (2010) European Business-Government Relations. In: Coen D, Grant W and Wilson GK (eds) *The Oxford Handbook of Business and Government.* Oxford: Oxford University Press, 285–306.

Coen D and Richardson J. (2009a) Learning to Lobby the European Union: 20 Years of Change. In: Coen D and Richardson J (eds) *Lobbying the European Union: Institutions, Actors, and Issues.* Oxford: Oxford University Press, 3–15.

Coen D and Richardson J. (2009b) Lobbying the European Union: Institutions, Actors, and Issues. *Lobbying the European Union: Institutions, Actors, and Issues.* Oxford: Oxford University Press.

Conant LJ. (2002) *Justice Contained: Law and Politics in the European Union.* Ithaca, NY: Cornell University Press.

Cram L. (1993) Calling the Tune Without Paying the Piper? Social Policy Regulation: The Role of the Commission in European Community Social Policy. *Policy & Politics* 21(2): 135–146.

De Bruycker I. (2017) Politicization and the Public Interest: When Do the Elites in Brussels Address Public Interests in EU Policy Debates? *European Union Politics* 18(4): 603–619.

Delreux T and Happaerts S. (2016) *Environmental Policy and Politics in the European Union.* London, New York: Palgrave Macmillan.

DigitalEurope. (2018) *DigitalEurope: About Us.* Available at: http://www.digitaleurope.org/About-Us (accessed 27.7.2018).

Dinan D. (2010) *Ever Closer Union: An Introduction to European Integration.* London: Palgrave Macmillan.

Doner RF and Schneider BR. (2000) Business Associations and Economic Development: Why Some Associations Contribute More Than Others. *Business and Politics* 2(3): 261–288.

Dür A. (2008) Interest Groups in the European Union: How Powerful Are They? *West European Politics* 31(6): 1212–1230.

Dür A, Bernhagen P and Marshall D. (2015) Interest Group Success in the European Union: When (and Why) Does Business Lose? *Comparative Political Studies* 48(8): 951–983.

Dür A, Marshall D and Bernhagen P. (2019) *The Political Influence of Business in the European Union.* Ann Arbor: University of Michigan Press.

Dür A and Mateo G. (2014) Public Opinion and Interest Group Influence: How Citizen Groups Derailed the Anti-counterfeiting Trade Agreement. *Journal of European Public Policy* 21(8): 1199–1217.

Dür A and Mateo G. (2016) *Insiders Versus Outsiders: Interest Group Politics in Multilevel Europe.* Oxford: Oxford University Press.

Eckert S. (2015) *The Social Face of the Regulatory State: Reforming Public Services in Europe.* Manchester: Manchester University Press.

Eckert S. (2016) The Governance of Markets, Sustainability and Supply. Toward a European Energy Policy. *Journal of Contemporary European Research* 12(1): 502–517.

Eising R. (2007) The Access of Business Interests to EU Institutions: Towards Élite Pluralism? *Journal of European Public Policy* 14(3): 384–403.

Eising R. (2016) Interest Groups and the European Union. In: Cini M and Pérez-Solórzano Borragán N (eds) *European Union Politics.* Oxford: Oxford University Press.

ENTSO-E. (2018) *ENTSO-E: About. Our Members.* Available at: https://www. entsoe.eu/about (accessed 6.7.2018).

EurActiv. (2009) Barroso Seizes Control of 'Better Regulation' Agenda. *Euractiv*, 21.9.2009.

European Commission. (1996) Communication from the Commission. *On Environmental Agreements.* COM (96) 561 final. Luxembourg: Office for Official Publications of the European Communities.

European Commission. (2001) *European Governance: A White Paper.* COM (2001) 428. Luxembourg: Office for Official Publications of the European Communities.

European Commission. (2002a) Communication from the Commission. *Action plan 'Simplifying and Improving the Regulatory Environment'.* COM (2002) 278 final. Luxembourg: Office for Official Publications of the European Communities.

European Commission. (2002b) Communication from the Commission. *Environmental Agreements at Community Level.* Within the Framework of the Action Plan on the Simplification and Improvement of the Regulatory Environment. COM (2002) 412 final. Luxembourg: Office for Official Publications of the European Communities.

European Commission. (2005a) Communication from the European Commission. *Better Regulation for Growth and Jobs in the European Union.* COM (2005) 97 final. Luxembourg: Office for Official Publications of the European Communities.

European Commission. (2005b) *Communication from the European Commission to the European Parliament, the Council, the European Economic and Social Committee and the Committee of the Regions. EU Regulatory Fitness.* COM (2012) 746 final. Luxembourg: Office for Official Publications of the European Communities.

European Commission. (2010) Europe 2020. *A European Strategy for Smart, Sustainable and Inclusive Growth.* COM (2010) 2020. Luxembourg: Office for Official Publications of the European Communities.

European Commission. (2016) Report from the Commission on the Implementation of Regulation (EU) 187/2011. COM (2016) 92. Luxembourg: Office for Official Publications of the European Communities.

Everson M and Joerges C. (2006) Re-conceptualising Europeanisation as a Public Law of Collisions: Comitology, Agencies and an Interactive Public Adjudication. In: Hofmann HCH and Türk AH (eds) *EU Administrative Governance.* Cheltenham, Northampton: Edward Elgar, 512–540.

Falkner G, Hartlapp M, Leiber S, et al. (2004) Non-compliance with EU Directives in the Member States: Opposition Through the Backdoor? *West European Politics* 27(3): 452–473.

Falkner G, Hartlapp M and Treib O. (2007) Worlds of Compliance: Why Leading Approaches to European Union Implementation Are Only 'Sometimes-True Theories'. *European Journal of Political Research* 46(3): 395–416.

Falkner R. (2007) The Political Economy of 'Normative Power' Europe: EU Environmental Leadership in International Biotechnology Regulation. *Journal of European Public Policy* 14(4): 507–526.

Faure M, Fernhoiut F and Philipsen N. (2013) No Cure, No Pay and Contingency Fees. In: Tuil M and Visscher L (eds) *New Trends in Financing Civil Litigation in Europe: A Legal, Empirical, and Economic Analysis.* Cheltenham, Northampton: Edward Elgar, 33–56.

Fischer C. (2011) The Development and Achievements of EU Waste Policy. *Journal of Material Cycles and Waste Management* 13(1): 2–9.

Fischer KH. (1997) *Lobbying und Kommunikation in der Europäischen Union.* Berlin: Berliner Wissenschaftsverlag.

Fligstein N and Stone Sweet A. (2002) Constructing Polities and Markets: An Institutionalist Account of European Integration. *American Journal of Sociology* 107(5): 1206–1243.

Fuchs D. (2007) *Business Power in Global Governance.* London: Lynne Rienner.

Fuchs D, Gumbert T and Schlipphak B. (2017) Eurosecpticism and Big Business. In: Leruth B, Startin N and Usherwood S (eds) *The Routledge Handbook of Euroscepticism.* New York: Routledge, 317–330.

Galanter M. (1974) Why the 'Haves' Come Out Ahead: Speculations on the Limits of Legal Change. *Law & Society Review* 9(1): 95–160.

Gehring T and Krapohl S. (2007) Supranational Regulatory Agencies Between Independence and Control: The EMEA and the Authorization of Pharmaceuticals in the European Single Market. *Journal of European Public Policy* 14(2): 208–226.

Grant W, Matthews D and Newell PJ. (2000) *The Effectiveness of European Union Environmental Policy.* Houndmills, Basingstoke: Palgrave Macmillan.

Greenwood J. (2017) *Interest Representation in the European Union.* London: Palgrave Macmillan.

Groenleer M. (2011) Regulatory Governance in the European Union: The Role of Committees, Agencies and Networks. In: Levi-Faur D (ed) *Handbook on the Politics of Regulation.* Cheltenham: Edward Elgar, 548–560.

Groenleer M, Kaeding M and Versluis E. (2010) Regulatory Governance Through Agencies of the European Union? The Role of the European Agencies for Maritime and Aviation Safety in the Implementation of European Transport Legislation. *Journal of European Public Policy* 17(8): 1212–1230.

Gullberg AT. (2008a) Lobbying Friends and Foes in Climate Policy: The Case of Business and Environmental Interest Groups in the European Union. *Energy Policy* 36(8): 2964–2972.

Gullberg AT. (2008b) Rational Lobbying and EU Climate Policy. *International Environmental Agreements: Politics, Law and Economics* 8(2): 161–178.

Halfteck G. (2006) *A Theory of Legislative Threats.* Tel Aviv: Tel Aviv University.

Halfteck G. (2008) Legislative Threats. *Stanford Law Review* 61: 629–710.

Harlow C and Rawlings R. (2013) *Pressure Through Law.* London, New York: Taylor & Francis.

Haufler V. (2001) *A Public Role for the Private Sector: Industry Self-Regulation in a Global Economy.* Washington: Carnegie Endowment for International Peace.

Hayes-Renshaw F. (2009) Least Accessible But Not Inaccessible: Lobbying the Council and the European Council. In: Coen D and Richardson J (eds) *Lobbying the European Union: Institutions, Actors, and Issues.* Oxford: Oxford University Press, 70–88.

Heath R. (2017) Commission's Better Regulation Agenda Slammed in New Study. *Politico,* 29.1.2017.

Heinelt H and Meinke-Brandmeier B. (2006) Comparing Civil Society Participation in European Environmental Policy and Consumer Protection. In: Smismans S (ed) *Civil Society and Legitimate European Governance.* Cheltenham: Edward Elgar, 196–218.

Hendry JR. (2003) Environmental NGOs and Business: A Grounded Theory of Assessment, Targeting, and Influencing. *Business & Society* 42(2): 267–276.

Héritier A. (2003) New Modes of Governance in Europe: Increasing Political Capacity and Policy Effectiveness? In: Börzel TA and Cichowski RA (eds) *The State of the European Union: Law, Politics and Society.* Oxford: Oxford University Press, 105–126.

Héritier A and Eckert S. (2008) New Modes of Governance in the Shadow of Hierarchy: Self-Regulation by Industry in Europe. *Journal of Public Policy* 28(1): 113–138.

Héritier A and Eckert S. (2009) Self-Regulation by Associations: A Collective Action Problem in Environmental Regulation. *Business and Politics* 11(1): 1–22.

Héritier A and Lehmkuhl D. (2008) New Modes of Governance and the Shadow of Hierarchy: Sectoral Governance and Territorially Bound Democratic Government. Special Issue. *Journal of Public Policy* 28(1): 113–138.

Héritier A, Moury C, Bischoff CS, et al. (2013) *Changing Rules of Delegation: A Contest for Power in Comitology.* Oxford: Oxford University Press.

Heyvaert V. (2007) No Data, No Market: The Future of EU Chemicals Control Under the Reach Regulation. *Environmental Law Review* 9(3): 201–206.

Hodges C. (2009) From Class Actions to Collective Redress. *Civil Justice Quarterly* 28(1): 41–66.

Hofman A. (2019) Left to Interest groups? On the Prospects for Enforcing Environmental Law in the European Union. Special Issue: The Future of the

European Union in Environmental Politics and Policy. Eds. A. Zito, S. Burns and A. Lenschow. *Environmental Politics* 28(2): 342–364.

Holzinger K, Knill C and Lenschow A. (2009) Innovative Governance in the European Union. In: Tömmel I and Verdun A (eds) *Innovative Governance in the European Union: The Politics of Multilevel Policymaking*. Boulder, CO: Rienner, 45–61.

Hontelez J. (2012) The Influence of Non-governmental Environmental Organisations on EU Policies. In: Wijen F, Zoeteman K and Pieters J (eds) *A Handbook of Globalisation and Environmental Policy, Second Edition: National Government Interventions in a Global Arena*. Cheltenham, Northampton: Edward Elgar, 663–683.

Hooghe L and Marks G. (2009) A Postfunctionalist Theory of European Integration: From Permissive Consensus to Constraining Dissensus. *British Journal of Political Science* 39(1): 1–23.

Howells G, Twigg-Flesner C and Wilhelmsson T. (2017) *Rethinking EU Consumer Law*. Abingdon: Taylor & Francis.

Interview COM. (2005) Legislative Officer and Acting Head of Unit, DG ENVI, Brussels, 23.11.2005.

Interview ENGO. (2017) Programmes Director Client Earth, London, 20.10.2017.

Interview ENGO. (2019) Senior Programme Manager, ECOS, Brussels, 10.1.2019.

Jordan A, Huitema D, van Asselt H, et al. (2010) *Climate Change Policy in the European Union: Confronting the Dilemmas of Mitigation and Adaptation?* Cambridge: Cambridge University Press.

Judge D. (1992) 'Predestined to Save the Earth': The Environment Committee of the European parliament. *Environmental Politics* 1(4): 186–212.

Junk WM. (2016) Two Logics of NGO Advocacy: Understanding Inside and Outside Lobbying on EU Environmental Policies. *Journal of European Public Policy* 23(2): 236–254.

Justin G and Christilla RR. (2015) The 'Europeanization' of the Basel Process: Financial Harmonization Between Globalization and Parliamentarization. *Regulation & Governance* 9(4): 325–338.

Kelemen RD. (2011) *Eurolegalism: The Transformation of Law and Regulation in the European Union*. Cambridge, MA: Harvard University Press.

Kelemen RD. (2012) European Union Agencies. In: Jones E, Menon A and Weatherill S (eds) *The Oxford Handbook of the European Union*. Oxford: Oxford University Press, 392–403.

Kelemen RD. (2013) Eurolegalism and the European Legal Field. In: Vauchez A and de Witte B (eds) *Lawyering Europe: European Law as a Transnational Social Field*. Oxford and Portland, OR: Hart Publishing, 243–257.

Klüver H. (2009) Measuring Interest Group Influence Using Quantitative Text Analysis. *European Union Politics* 10(4): 535–549.

Klüver H. (2011) The Contextual Nature of Lobbying: Explaining Lobbying Success in the European Union. *European Union Politics* 12(4): 483–506.

Klüver H. (2012) Biasing Politics? Interest Group Participation in EU Policy-Making. *West European Politics* 35(5): 1114–1133.

Knill C. (2001) Private Governance Across Multiple Arenas: European Interest Associations as Interface Actors. *Journal of European Public Policy* 8(2): 227–246.

Knill C and Liefferink D. (2007) *Environmental Politics in the European Union: Policy-Making, Implementation and Patterns of Multi-Level Governance.* Manchester: Manchester University Press.

Kohler-Koch B, Quittkat C, Buth V, et al. (2013) *De-Mystification of Participatory Democracy: EU-Governance and Civil Society.* Oxford: Oxford University Press.

Krämer L. (2000) Thirty Years of EC Environmental Law: Perspectives and Prospectives. In: Somsen H (ed) *Yearbook of European Environmental Law: Volume 1.* Oxford: Oxford University Press, 155–182.

Lehmann W. (2009) The European Parliament. In: Coen D and Richardson J (eds) *Lobbying the European Union: Institutions, Actors, and Issues.* Oxford: Oxford University Press, 39–69.

Lenschow A. (2015) Environmental Policy: Contending Dynamics of Policy Change. In: Wallace H, Pollack MA and Young AR (eds) *Policy-Making in the European Union.* 6th ed. Oxford: Oxford University Press, 319–343.

Lenschow A and Rottmann K. (2010) The Evolving Role of Industry in European Union Environmental Governance. In: O'Connor A (ed) *Managing Economies, Trade and International Business.* Houndmills, Basingstoke: Palgrave Macmillan, 67–85.

Liefferink D and Andersen MS. (1998) Strategies of the 'Green' Member States in EU Environmental Policy-Making. *Journal of European Public Policy* 5(2): 254–270.

Lodge M. (2008) Regulation, the Regulatory State and European Politics. *West European Politics* 31(1): 280–301.

Long T. (1995) Shaping Public Policy in the European Union: A Case Study of the Structural Funds. *Journal of European Public Policy* 2(4): 672–679.

Long T and Lörinczi L. (2009) Business Lobbying in the European Union. In: Coen D and Richardson J (eds) *Lobbying the European Union: Institutions, Actors, and Issues.* Oxford: Oxford University Press, 169–185.

Mahoney C. (2004) The Power of Institutions: State and Interest Group Activity in the European Union. *European Union Politics* 5(4): 441–466.

Mahoney C. (2007) Lobbying Success in the United States and the European Union. *Journal of Public Policy* 27(1): 35–56.

Majone G. (1994) The Rise of the Regulatory State in Europe. *West European Politics* 17(2): 77–101.

Marshall D. (2010) Who to Lobby and When: Institutional Determinants of Interest Group Strategies in European Parliament Committees. *European Union Politics* 11(4): 553–575.

Martens M. (2012) Executive Power in the Making: The Establishment of the European Chemicals Agency. In: Trondal J, Busuioc M and Groenleer M (eds) *The Agency Phenomenon in the European Union.* Manchester, New York: Manchester University Press, 42–62.

Mastenbroek E. (2005) EU Compliance: Still a 'Black Hole'? *Journal of European Public Policy* 12(6): 1103–1120.

Mazey S and Richardson J. (1992) Environmental Groups and the EC: Challenges and Opportunities. *Environmental Politics* 1(4): 109–128.

Mazey S and Richardson J. (1996) The Logic of Organisation: Interest groups. In: Richardson J (ed) *European Union: Power and Policy-Making.* London, New York: Routledge, 200–215.

Mazey S and Richardson J. (2003) Interest Groups and the Brussels Bureaucracy. In: Hayward J and Menon A (eds) *Governing Europe.* Oxford: Oxford University Press, 208–227.

McCown M. (2009) Interest Groups and the European Court of Justice. In: Coen D and Richardson J (eds) *Lobbying the European Union: Institutions, Actors, and Issues.* Oxford: Oxford University Press, 89–104.

McGowan L and Wallace H. (1996) Towards a European Regulatory state. *Journal of European Public Policy* 3(4): 560–576.

Micklitz H-W and Weatherill S. (1993) Consumer Policy in the European Community: Before and After Maastricht. *Journal of Consumer Policy* 16(3): 285–321.

Mikler J. (2018) *The Political Power of Global Corporations.* Cambridge: Polity Press.

Moravcsik A. (1998) *The Choice for Europe: Social Purpose and State Power from Messina to Maastricht.* Ithaca: Cornell University Press.

Nesti G. (2018) Strengthening the Accountability of Independent Regulatory Agencies: From Performance Back to Democracy. *Comparative European Politics* 16(3): 464–481.

Newell PJ and Grant W. (2000) Environmental NGOs and EU Environmental Law. In: Somsen H (ed) *Yearbook of European Environmental Law. Volume 1.* Oxford: Oxford University Press, 225–252.

Nollert M. (1997) Verbändelobbying in der Europäischen Union. In: Alemann U and Weßels B (eds) *Verbände in vergleichender Perspektive.* Berlin: Sigma, 107–136.

Oberthür S and Dupont C. (2011) The Council, the European Council and International Climate Policy. In: Wurzel RKW and Connelly J (eds) *The*

European Union as a Leader in International Climate Change Politics. London: Routledge, 74–91.

Ossege C. (2015) Driven by Expertise and Insulation? The Autonomy of European Regulatory Agencies. *Politics and Governance* 3(1): 13.

Pérez Durán I. (2018) Interest Group Representation in the Formal Design of European Union Agencies. *Regulation & Governance* 12(2): 238–262.

Pollack MA. (1997) Representing Diffuse Interests in EC Policy-Making. *Journal of European Public Policy* 4(4): 572–590.

Radaelli CM. (1999a) The Public Policy of the European Union: Whither Politics of Expertise? *Journal of European Public Policy* 6(5): 757–774.

Radaelli CM. (1999b) *Technocracy in the European Union.* London and New York: Longman.

Rasmussen MK. (2012) Is the European Parliament Still a Policy Champion for Environmental Interests? *Interest Groups & Advocacy* 1(2): 239–259.

Rasmussen MK. (2015) The Battle for Influence: The Politics of Business Lobbying in the European Parliament. *Journal of Common Market Studies* 53(2): 365–382.

Rauh C. (2016) *A Responsive Technocracy? EU Politicisation and the Consumer Policies of the European Commission.* Colchester: ECPR Press.

Rauh C. (2019) EU Politicization and Policy Initiatives of the European Commission: The Case of Consumer Policy. *Journal of European Public Policy* 6(3): 344–365.

Richardson J. (1996) Actor-Based Models of National and EU Policy-Making. In: Kassim H and Menon A (eds) *The European Union and National Industrial Policy.* London: Routledge, 26–51.

Ripoll Servent A. (2015) *Institutional and Policy Change in the European Parliament: Deciding on Freedom, Security and Justice.* London: Palgrave Macmillan.

Rittberger B and Wonka A. (2011) Introduction: Agency Governance in the European Union. *Journal of European Public Policy* 18(6): 780–789.

Ronit K and Schneider V. (1997) Organisierte Interessen in nationalen und supranationalen Politökologien: Ein Vergleich der G7-Länder mit der Europäischen Union. In: Alemann U and Weßels B (eds) *Verbände in vergleichender Perspektive.* Berlin: Sigma, 29–62.

Rottmann K and Lenschow A. (2008) 'Privatising' EU Governance: Emergence and Performance of Voluntary Agreements in European Environmental Policy. In: Conzelmann T and Smith R (eds) *Multi-Level Governance in the European Union: Taking Stock and Looking Ahead.* Baden-Baden: Nomos, 232–254.

Saurugger S. (2008) Interest Groups and Democracy in the European Union. *West European Politics* 31(6): 1274–1291.

Scharpf FW. (2006) The Joint-Decision Trap Revisited. *Journal of Common Market Studies* 44(4): 845–864.

Schnabl G. (2005) The Evolution of Environmental Agreements at the Level of the European Union. In: Croci E (ed) *The Handbook of Environmental Voluntary Agreements: Design, Implementation and Evaluation Issues.* Berlin, Heidelberg and New York: Springer, 93–106.

Schön-Quinlivan E. (2013) The European Commission. In: Jordan A and Adelle C (eds) *Environmental Policy in the EU: Actors, Institutions and Processes.* 3rd ed. London, New York: Routledge, 95–112.

Scully R and van Schendelen R. (2004) *The Unseen Hand.* London: Routledge.

Shapiro M. (1997) The Problems of Independent Agencies in the United States and the European Union. *Journal of European Public Policy* 4(2): 276–277.

Sherrington P. (2000) *Council of Ministers: Political Authority in the European Union.* London: Bloomsbury Academic.

Simoncini M. (2018) *Administrative Regulation Beyond the Non-delegation Doctrine: A Study on EU Agencies.* Oxford: Bloomsbury Publishing.

Smedley T. (2016) At Work with the FT Interview: James Thornton, ClientEarth. *Financial Times,* 11.5.2016.

Smith MP. (2008) All Access Points are Not Created Equal: Explaining the Fate of Diffuse Interests in the EU. *The British Journal of Politics & International Relations* 10(1): 64–83.

Stafford ER, Polonsky MJ and Hartman CL. (2000) Environmental NGO–Business Collaboration and Strategic Bridging: A Case Analysis of the Greenpeace–Foron Alliance. *Business Strategy and the Environment* 9(2): 122–135.

Taggart P. (1998) A Touchstone of Dissent: Euroscepticism in Contemporary Western European Party Systems. *European Journal of Political Research* 33(3): 363–388.

Tait N and Sherwood B. (2005) Class Actions Across the Atlantic. *Financial Times,* 16.5.2005.

Tanasescu I. (2009) *The European Commission and Interest Groups: Towards a Deliberative Interpretation of Stakeholder Involvement in EU Policy-Making.* Brussels: Brussels University Press.

Thornton J and Goodman M. (2017) *ClientEarth.* Melbourne: Scribe Publications.

Töller AE. (2010) Measuring and Comparing the Europeanization of National Legislation: A Research Note. *Journal of Common Market Studies* 48(2): 417–444.

Tömmel I and Verdun A. (2017) Political Leadership in the European Union: An Introduction. *Journal of European Integration* 39(2): 103–112.

Toshkov D. (2008) Embracing European Law: Compliance with EU Directives in Central and Eastern Europe. *European Union Politics* 9(3): 379–402.

Trondal J, Busuioc M and Groenleer M. (2012) *The Agency Phenomenon in the European Union*. Manchester, New York: Manchester University Press.

Trumbull G. (2006) *Consumer Capitalism. Politics, Product Markets, and Firm Strategy in France and Germany*. Ithaca, New York: Cornell University Press.

Trumbull G. (2010) Consumer Policy. In: Coen D, Grant W and Wilson GK (eds) *The Oxford Handbook of Business and Government*. Oxford: Oxford University Press, 622–642.

van Schendelen R. (2004) The In-Sourced Experts. In: Scully R and van Schendelen R (eds) *The Unseen Hand*. London: Routledge, 25–35.

Veenman S and Liefferink D. (2012) Different Countries, Different Strategies: 'Green' Member States Influencing EU Climate Policy. In: Wijen F, Zoeteman K and Pieters J (eds) *A Handbook of Globalisation and Environmental Policy, Second Edition: National Government Interventions in a Global Arena*. Cheltenham, Northampton: Edward Elgar, 387–414.

Warleigh A. (2000) The Hustle: Citizenship Practice, NGOs and 'Policy Coalitions' in the European Union—The Cases of Auto Oil, Drinking Water and Unit Pricing. *Journal of European Public Policy* 7(2): 229–243.

Weale A, Pridham G, Cini M, et al. (2000) *Environmental Governance in Europe: An Ever Closer Ecological Union?* Oxford: Oxford University Press.

Weatherill S. (2013) *EU Consumer Law and Policy*. Cheltenham, Northampton: Edward Elgar.

Wessels W. (1998) Comitology: Fusion in Action—Politico-Administrative Trends in the EU System. *Journal of European Public Policy* 5(2): 209–234.

Wettig J. (2002) New Developments in Standardisation in the Past 15 Years: Product Versus Process Related Standards. *Safety Science* 40(1): 51–56.

Williams G. (2005) Monomaniacs or Schizophrenics? Responsible Governance and the EU's Independent Agencies. *Political Studies* 53(1): 82–99.

Woll C. (2009) Trade Policy Lobbying in the European Union: Who Captures Whom? In: Coen D and Richardson J (eds) *Lobbying the European Union: Institutions, Actors, and Issues*. Oxford: Oxford University Press, 277–297.

Wurzel RKW. (2008) Environmental Policy: EU Actors, Leader and Laggard States. In: Hayward J (ed) *Leaderless Europe*. Oxford: Oxford University Press, 66–88.

Wurzel RKW. (2013) Member States and the Council. In: Jordan A and Adelle C (eds) *Environmental Policy in the EU: Actors, Institutions and Processes*. 3rd ed. London, New York: Routledge, 75–94.

Wurzel RKW and Connelly J. (2011) Environmental NGOs: Taking a Lead? In: Wurzel RKW and Connelly J (eds) *The European Union as a Leader in International Climate Change Politics*. London: Routledge, 214–231.

Wyatt DWC. (1998) Litigating Community Environmental Law: Thoughts on the Direct Effect Doctrine. *Journal of Environmental Law* 10(1): 9–19.

CHAPTER 4

The Expert:
Striving for a Circular Economy

The concept of the "circular economy" has been in use since the 1960s, though it has been diffused widely as a new framing of waste and resource management policies only since the mid-1980s (Blomsma and Brennan 2017; Murray et al. 2017; Geissdoerfer et al. 2017). It has been taken up by policymakers around the globe, and by today, it is arguably the sustainable development concept with most traction (EMF 2014). The advocacy work of various actors, in particular of the Ellen MacArthur Foundation (EMF), has spurred the concept's diffusion. The EMF published a first report on the circular economy in 2012 and various follow-ups since then (EMF 2013, 2014). The work of the EMF on circular economy is widely considered by expert observers to have had a decisive impact on the rise of the concept as a new sustainability paradigm (Geissdoerfer et al. 2017; Interview COM 2017, 2019; Lieder and Rashid 2016; Carus and Dammer 2018: 2). The idea behind the circular economy is to cover the entire process of industrial production in a resource-efficient manner, from resource extraction to the waste phase. There is, however, no commonly agreed understanding of what the circular economy entails, and the blurriness of the concept has been critically discussed (Blomsma and Brennan 2017; Geissdoerfer et al. 2017). In fact, more than 100 definitions currently in use have been identified through stock-taking of existing literature (Kirchherr et al. 2017). In substance, many definitions embrace either the 3Rs (reduce, reuse, recycle) or the 6Rs (reuse, recycle, redesign, remanufacture,

© The Author(s) 2019
S. Eckert, *Corporate Power and Regulation*,
International Series on Public Policy,
https://doi.org/10.1007/978-3-030-05463-2_4

reduce, recover). Another sustainability paradigm is the "bioeconomy" which tackles the issue of resource scarcity from a different angle. It promotes the replacement of fossil resources with biogenic ones in industrial production and products (McCormick and Kautto 2013). A discussion document by the Canadian environment think tank Pollution Probe published in 2002 and an Organisation for Economic Cooperation and Development (OECD) report issued in 2004 contributed to the diffusion of the concept (Patermann and Aguilar 2018, OECD 2004). The bioeconomy concept links to resource efficiency aspects promoted under the circular economy heading (Bugge et al. 2016). The synergies of combining both approaches are advocated as a "circular bioeconomy" (Carus and Dammer 2018; D'Amato et al. 2017: 724–725) or as a "bio-based circular economy" (Borrello et al. 2016). At the European level, the European Commission has come up with a Bioeconomy Strategy in 2012 (European Commission 2017c) and Circular Economy policy proposals in 2014 and 2015 (European Commission 2014b, 2015). The 2015 Action Plan promotes the idea of circularity for European product, waste and chemical legislation.

In the transition towards a circular (bio-)economy producers are *experts* thanks to the knowledge and information about the complex materials and substances they produce. Their expertise input plays a central role in the area of assessing risks, which is important at several stages in the life cycle, namely when licensing new substances, when phasing out or banning substances in use, and when disposing of (hazardous) waste. They further act as *innovators* in developing new possibilities to recover and recycle used materials and products, or in developing bio-based materials and products. All in all, the area of regulation covered in this chapter exhibits features that could lead to a situation where the regulatory process is captured by industry experts, while there is correspondingly a lack of "counter policy expertise" (Fischer 1990: 28), as discussed in Chapter 2. I will study two industry branches, the paper and the plastics industries, which face different sustainability challenges and varying degrees of public pressure. The following four sections present these two sectors and their associative structure, address activities of consumer protection and environmental groups, and the evolution of relevant EU regulation. A second part examines the role of industry in the regulatory process in more detail. Here I discuss voluntary industry initiatives and the ways in which industry organisations have been able to prevent, shape, make or revoke regulation.

European Paper and Plastics Industries

The paper and plastics industries are economically important and resource-intense sectors, and at their end-of-life these products constitute significant shares in waste. In 2014, 406.5 million tonnes of paper and cardboard were produced globally (RISI 2015). The global production of plastics has grown significantly over the last few decades, from 15 million tonnes produced in 1964 to 311 million tonnes produced in 2014 (EMF 2016: 25). For both industries, the growing production and consumption poses a challenge in terms of scarce resources and raw materials. While the paper industry draws on renewable biomass and recyclable feedstocks, there is nevertheless an issue of using up biogenic resources and deforestation. The plastics industry uses up finite sources of fossil feedstocks, today at a level of four to eight per cent of global oil production. With the exponential growth of production, however, this share is forecast to account for 20 per cent by 2050 (EMF 2016: 27). In accordance with a relatively short lifespan of many paper, cardboard as well as plastics products, these materials also generate massive volumes of waste. In 2012, each European produced, on average, 72.75 kg of paper and cardboard waste and 23.8 kg of plastic waste (Bourguignon 2015: 2). A big share of plastic and paper waste originates from packaging waste. In 2015, 166.3 kg of packaging waste was generated per inhabitant in the EU. Paper and cardboard accounted for 41% of packaging waste, plastics for 19% (Eurostat 2018b: 1–2). Thus, in 2015, Europeans produced 31.6 kg plastic waste per capita from packaging alone—a share which is higher than the total share reported for 2012, illustrating the rapid growth rate of plastic waste in general and plastic wage from packaging in particular (EMF 2016).

In 2016, around 8.4 million tonnes of plastic waste were collected to be recycled (PlasticsEurope 2017), compared to 59.5 million tonnes of paper (ERPC 2016b). In paper recycling, Europe achieves a rate of more than 70%, which is substantially above the global paper recycling rate of around 58%, and significantly higher than the very low rates of recycling for plastics materials (EMF 2016: 17). These rates do, however, usually include the material exported for recycling, mostly to China. In 2016, for example, 1.6 million tonnes of plastic waste was sent to China, and around eight million tonnes of paper waste (Tamma 2018).

Paper Industry

The production of paper is centuries old (Hunter 1978) and part of our civilisational history (Basbanes 2013). Similarly, practices of recovery and reuse rely on a strong legacy. In Europe, recycling techniques were developed as early as in the sixteenth century, and national schemes for paper collection flourished, especially during wartime periods (Cooper 2008).

European paper manufacturers are organised at the Confederation of European Paper Industries (CEPI). CEPI was created as a European umbrella organisation of national trade associations in 1992. In 2018, it brought together national associations from 18 countries representing 495 companies. Through its national associations, CEPI comprises of very big companies (located in Germany and Scandinavia), medium-sized companies and small companies that are specialised in niche products (Interview paper industry 2006b). As producers of an organic material, CEPI members further adhere to the concept of the bioeconomy, voicing their interest in the European Bioeconomy Alliance (EUBA). EUBA brings together organisations representing sectors active in the bioeconomy in Europe in order to provide input to the EU's dedicated strategy (European Bioeconomy Alliance 2018).

The paper industry operates at the two ends of the life cycle and thus has a vital interest in getting information about the stages in between, that is, the converting and printing phase and the usage phase. Put simply, any chemical added to the organic material is problematic at the end-of-life and recycling stage. In this respect, additives and inks used downstream in the value chain pose a problem for the paper industry as a recycling business (Interview paper industry 2017). From the viewpoint of the paper industry, recovered material should be as clean as possible, while the processing industries pledge for more flexibility. The extent to which the usage of inks and the need to improve deinking techniques matter to the paper industry is illustrated by the fact that the industry maintains specialised organisational structures bringing together their deinking departments in the International Association of the Deinking Industry, INGEDE, founded in 1989 by European paper manufacturers (28 paper mills and research departments).

The paper industry value chain can be classified into four groups: first, the producers of inks, additives and adhesives; second, converters; third, the printing and publishing industry; fourth, the waste management and recovery industry. The first group is organised in various associations, namely the Association of the European Adhesives and Sealant Industry, the European Association for the Self-adhesive Label Industry (FINAT), the European Adhesive Tape Association (Afera) and the European Association for the Advancement of Radiation Curing by UV, EB and Laser Beams RadTech-Europe (RTE); second, the industry converting paper and cardboard into various products gathers inside the International Confederation of Paper and Board Converters in Europe (CITPA), the European Federation of Corrugated Packaging (FEFCO), the European Tissue Symposium (ETS), the European Federation of Envelope Manufacturers (FEPE) and the European Alliance for Beverage Cartons and the Environment (ACE). Thirdly, the printing and publishing industry comprises the European Federation for Print and Digital Communication (INTERGRAF), the European Printing Ink Association (EuPIA), the newsprint associations such as European Newspaper Publishers Association (ENPA) and the European Magazine Media Association (EMMA, until 2011 FAEP). Lastly, the recycling and recovery business is organised inside the association which brings together the European recycling industries through European and national recycling associations (EuRIC), and, since 2016, also incorporates the European Recovered Paper Branch (ERPA). Further, the European Federation of Waste Management and Environmental Services (FEAD) represents national associations of waste management and environmental services, whose members are primarily private waste management companies.

These actors within the paper, cardboard and recycling businesses build alliances where they share a common interest. The availability of virgin fibre as well as recovered material, which hits certain limits due to alternative usage, export or constraints in collection, is of key concern to the whole paper value chain. That said, interests diverge between the suppliers of recovered materials and the mill buyers of recovered paper and board organised inside CEPI and FEFCO, who ask for high-quality material at a reasonable price. The price of virgin fibre, amounts of recovered material exported to third countries and constraints in collection affect market prices for recovered paper. Additionally, the use of water and heat makes the industry vulnerable to rising energy prices. An important and growing market segment for paper and board products is packaging, and there is fierce competition between paper and plastics (Hansen 2018). The cardboard industries, for instance, are profiting from increased demand for packaging material with the rise of

E-Commerce (Business Wire 2017). In order to live up to the ambitions of the circular and bioeconomy, industries compete with regard to their respective environmental performance, especially in segments where they produce substitute materials such as in packaging.

Besides their specialised knowledge as experts in sustainable production and resource efficiency, industry actors do also hold structural power which resides in their economic importance, as discussed in the relevant literature (Fuchs 2007: 66). The economic importance of the European paper industry, both at the aggregate level and in some member states, is summarised in Fig. 4.1. In 2017, the European paper industry employed 177,000 people across Europe, with a 82 billion Euros annual turnover in around 675 companies. European producers have a share of 26.1% in global paper and board production—compared to 20% for North America and 46.4% for Asia, respectively. The most

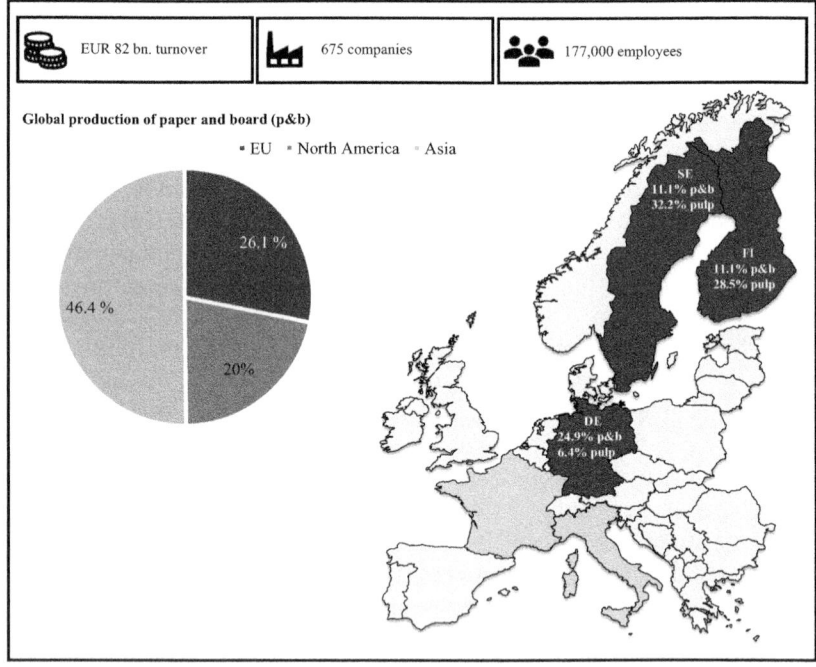

Fig. 4.1 Economic importance of European paper industry (*Source* 2017 data [CEPI 2018a], own figure)

important producers in Europe are: Sweden with 32.2% of pulp, 11.1% of paper and board production; Finland with 28.5% of pulp, 11.1% of paper and board production; and Germany with 6.4% of pulp, 24.9% of paper and board production (CEPI 2018a: 3, 4, 8, 10, 13, 16).

The European paper industry was significantly affected by the economic crisis and the ensuing downturn, but recently went back to pre-crisis growth and investment rates (CEPI 2017). For 2009, CEPI had reported a decline in production and consumption of paper and board compared to 2008 levels at around 10%, and a decline in exports at 12% (CEPI 2010). For 2017, by contrast, CEPI reported that in comparison with 2016 consumption was up by 0.5%, "benefiting from a more favourable economic environment and from conditions promoting sustainable solutions", exports were on the rise with an increase of 5.2%, and investments were on a growth path with 7.5% (CEPI 2018b).

Plastics Industry

Plastic is *the* material of the twentieth century (Fenichell 1996). The use of plastics has significantly altered the economic and industrial activities of mankind and also the daily life of every individual. The plastics industry is an important branch of the European chemical industry, which is organised inside the European Chemical Industry Council (CEFIC). The plastics industry includes a number of different actors across the value chain, ranging from big multinational corporations that manufacture plastics and resins (such as BASF and Bayer) to small SMEs in the area of plastics converters. Plastics manufacturers are organised inside PlasticsEurope, which is a CEFIC partner association and represents 56 company members (PlasticsEurope 2018c). Inside the plastics industry, producers of specific applications are organised within the European Plastics Converters (EuPC), an association which, in 2018, brought together 28 national plastics associations as well as 18 sector associations (EuPC 2018). Plastics converters are an important branch in the sector, as they represent 90.40% of employees (1,600,000), 94.34% of the companies (50,000) and 71.82% of turnover. Companies and organisations active in the recycling business form the European Plastics Recyclers (EuPR) association. Further, the industry branch diversifies along the lines of a declared transition towards a circular bioeconomy. Producers of plastics that are bio-based, biodegradable or both, gather in the association European Bioplastics (EUBP 2018a), which forms part of the EUBA.

Resin-specific value chains do rely on their distinct organisational structures. A case in point is the polyvinyl chloride (PVC) industry (PVC 2018). PVC is a synthetic plastic polymer that, as a rigid material, is widely used in the construction and building sector, while flexible applications, which require the use of plasticisers, are used in a variety of products. In terms of plastics converter demand (figures for 2015, 2016) by resin type, PVC comes fourth (PlasticsEurope 2018e: 23), and as a polymer type used by plastics converters its share is 10% (PlasticsEurope 2018e: 24). The European Council of Vinyl Manufacturers (ECVM) is a division of PlasticsEurope and represents six major European PVC resin-producing companies that account for 70% of EU production. Further, there are numerous product-specific branch organisations, e.g. on PVC film, flooring or window profiles. Separate organisations bring together the PVC additives producers: the European Council for Plasticisers and Intermediates (ECPI), which gathers eight chemical companies that together produce more than 80% of the plasticisers manufactured in Europe, and the European Stabiliser Producers Association (ESPA), which as a pan-European trade association represents four European sub-associations (ESPA 2018). In addition to such value chain structures, PlasticsEurope also addresses specific product segments, for instance through its packaging working group (PlasticsEurope 2018a: 23).

The economic importance of the European plastics industry is summarised in Fig. 4.2. While the EU-wide turnover and employment is significantly higher than in the paper and cardboard industry, the share in global production is however smaller. The European plastics industry in 2017 employed around 1.5 million people in 60,000 companies and generated a turnover of close to 350 billion Euros (PlasticsEurope 2018a). In 2016, the European plastics industry ranked second in world production with a share of around 19%. This share compares to 50% for Asian producers—out of which China held 29%—and a share of 18% for NAFTA countries (PlasticsEurope 2018e: 17). The most important plastics producers in Europe (measured in plastics converter demand per country) are: Germany at 24.5%, Italy at 14.2%, France at 9.6%, Spain at 7.7%, the UK at 7.5% and Poland at 6.3%. The plastics industry experienced a significant downturn of production between 2008 and 2010 of between 20 and 40% in the various industry branches, which since then went back to pre-crisis levels and are steadily growing (PlasticsEurope 2018e: 40).

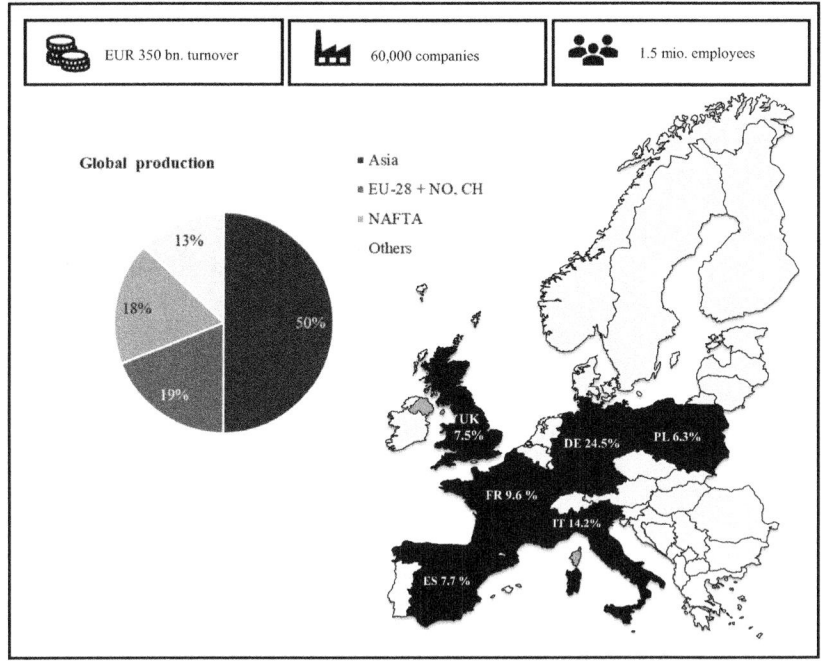

Fig. 4.2 Economic importance of European plastics industry (*Source* 2017 data [PlasticsEurope 2018b], own figure)

Consumer Protection and Environmental Groups

Both the paper and plastics industries have been subject to targeted NGO campaigning, though to a different extent so. The paper and pulp industry mainly deals with a natural raw material which itself poses specific sustainability challenges (Matthews 2016). Global plastics production is using up finite fossil feedstocks. Moreover, plastics products are perceived as a problem for human health when there is exposure to hazardous substances in the use phase, and for the environment due to their durability in the waste phase.

Concerning the paper and board industry, NGOs have been active in campaigning and raising awareness on three issues: first, on resource use; second, on sustainable consumption; and third, on health and safety issues. On the issue of a responsible use of wood as a valuable resource, the industry's reputation has suffered in the context of the international fight against deforestation as one of the major causes of global warming. Around the globe, ENGOs have joined forces under the umbrella of the "Environmental Paper Network" (EPN 2018). Environmentalists in their campaigns specifically targeted the paper industry's activities in the developing world. Unsustainable forestry practices in Asia have come to the ENGOs' attention, particularly so the dubious business activities of the Asia Pulp and Paper (APP) company (Eyes on the Forest 2011). Criticism from NGOs is less prevalent in the regions of North America and Western Europe which globally hold the largest share of certified sustainable forest areas. Major Asian producers, by contrast, do not have such certification programmes in place (Matthews 2016). That said, NGO campaigning is also now and then targeting Western producers. Over the last two decades the ENGO Dogwood Alliance has combatted the deforestation in the southern states of the USA (Dogwood Alliance 2017). In Europe, the paper industry occasionally also had to deal with the deforestation debate. For instance, the EPN network issued a public letter to the Swedish Ministry of Environment in 2015 to protest against what they saw as unsustainable forestry practice (EPN 2015). More spectacularly, Poland was taken to the European Court of Justice (ECJ) by ClientEarth and other organisations for allowing increased logging by the State Forests administration in Bialowieza Forest, a UNESCO natural world heritage site. Once they had won the case in April 2018, ENGOs continued to exert pressure on Poland which proved reluctant to comply with the ruling (ClientEarth 2018). European NGOs also campaigned on the theme of sustainable consumption, urging consumers to "reduce" or even "refuse" the use of paper or cardboard products (EPN 2017). Examples are World Wide Fund for Natures (WWF's) "Save Paper" initiative and slogans such as "think before you print" or "skip the slip". The latter slogan not only urges consumers to reduce their demand for paper receipts in order to reduce the waste of resources. Further, it seeks to avoid human exposure to thermal paper used for receipts which is usually covered with layers containing additives known to have detrimental health effects (Matthews 2016). Similarly, the traces of unwanted substances in recycled paper and board products pose another challenge to industry, especially in food contact material. Studies and tests conducted in Denmark found traces of endocrine disruptors (EDCs) such as BPA in paper and board packaging and pizza boxes (CHEM Trust 2016: 6). Further, scientific evidence provided by a report that the German health ministry commissioned showed that unwanted substances used for printing such as mineral oils, had migrated from recycled paper packaging into certain food products (Chemisches und Veterinäruntersuchungsamt Stuttgart et al. 2012). Besides NGOs exerting pressure on industry on these three themes, both sides might also align their interests. This constellation can emergy where NGO backing helps industry not only in publicising and communicating its sustainability track record but also to defend its interests. Such a win-win situation emerged when the Commission envisaged to end the Ecolabel scheme of recycled paper and tissue products. Industry and NGOs issued a joint letter addressed to the European Commission, which was signed by CEPI, ETS, EuroCommerce, BEUC and the EEB. In this letter business and NGOs pledged for the continuation of the Ecolabel (CEPI et al. 2016).

The European plastics industry has continuously faced NGO pressure and criticism. Chemical and waste policies, the two domains of regulation under scrutiny in this case study, do attract the attention of NGOs, though to a far lower degree than climate and wildlife issues. Relative to these other topics and the intensity of corporate lobbying, "chemical policy is poorly supported" from the NGO side (Interview ENGO 2017). Only a handful of ENGO experts work on the EU's chemicals policy, the most important players being BEUC, CHEM Trust, ClientEarth, Greenpeace, the European Environmental Bureau (EEB), and ChemSec. On waste issues, ENGOs and consumer organisations seek to raise awareness with respect to sustainable consumption and health issues. At EU-level, the European Environmental Bureau (EEB) is following waste issues, Greenpeace addresses mainly issues related to toxic waste, while CHEM Trust is focusing on EDCs throughout the life cycle of products. Environmental concerns relate mainly to the production and the waste phase of plastics, while concerns to the consumers' health and safety risks have been addressed for the use phase. Although these issues came up to varying degrees over time, it is fair to say that individual health aspects have proven to be a more salient issue for consumers in comparison to a collective concern about planet Earth, at least in Western societies (Interview ENGO 2006). In this respect, especially the endocrine-disrupting characteristics of additives in plastic products such as Bisphenol-A (BPA) or DEHP have been the subject of NGO campaigning. In the 1980s and 1990s, ENGOs targeted PVC as the most harmful und environmentally damaging plastic. Greenpeace campaigned for a total ban on PVC products in Scandinavia, Germany and Austria, and from the 1990s onwards also at European level (Interview ENGO 2006; Interview EP 2005c). The organisation generated evidence that identified hazardous chemicals in numerous PVC products, which put into question the recyclability of the material, and listed PVC-free alternatives (Greenpeace 2000, 2002, 2003; Preuss 1997). The debate on PVC subsequently moved on from environmental aspects, with a focus on plastic waste, to consumer and health aspects. These concerned the flexible applications of the material that involve the use of plasticisers, mainly phthalates. The health issues posed by phthalates (e.g. EDCs) became subject to targeted ENGO activism, putting considerable pressure on producers (Interview plastics industry 2006a). Throughout the mid-1990s, various Greenpeace campaigns on phthalates in toys and the related health risks proved highly successful across Europe (Interview ENGO 2006, Vogel 2012: 203–204). Several member states enacted restrictions and brought their concerns to the attention of EU authorities. In 1999, the European Commission issued an emergency ban on phthalates in toys (European Commission 1999), which was renewed several times and transformed into a permanent ban with the adoption of a directive in 2005. Due to a lack of responsiveness of EU policymakers and their shifting focus on the new European chemicals regulation proposed in 2001, the debate subsequently moved away from PVC. As a result, ENGOs stopped to target the industry by engaging in sustained campaigning as they had done in the past (Interview EP 2005c). Greenpeace still publicly criticised the industry occasionally (Greenpeace 2012), but the high tide of activism had passed. Other ENGOs, such as the EEB, which used to be an important campaigning partner of Greenpeace, entirely removed the PVC dossier from their working programme.

It was only in the time towards 2010 that ENGO campaigning on plastics made headlines once again. The issue of marine litter has attracted global attention through television documentaries (e.g. BBC series "Blue Planet"), movies (e.g. "Plastic Planet") and publications (e.g. Coe and Rogers 2012). The success of the campaign certainly relates to the powerful images of sea life and death (e.g. a sea turtle with a plastic straw up its nostril, rf. Lee 2018), as well as the smart issue linkage of environmental and (individual) health issues. The marine litter story joins both ends: there are obvious negative effects of plastic waste for wildlife but also for human health once microplastics contaminate soil, water and food. Special focus goes to the environmental and health impact of microplastics, used in personal care products, industrial scrubbers, and paints and other applications. The big international ENGOs maintain targeted campaigns, including Greenpeace (The Ocean Plastic Crisis), WWF (Marine litter) or ClientEarth (Oceans). Arguably, the immediate causes of marine littering are mostly located in Asia, which in 2015 contributed by over 80% to ocean leakage. However, European industry also has an eminent role to play as a major producer (EMF 2016: 38). At EU-level, ENGOs have joined forces in the alliance "Rethink Plastic" (Rethink Plastic 2018). Internationally, European ENGOs form part of the global "Break free from Plastic Movement" (#breakfreefromplastic 2018) which aims to develop scenarios for a plastic-free future.

Due to the scarcity of financial and human resources, NGOs usually focus on the policy formulation stage and lack the capacity to work on non-legislative measures such as agency governance or Comitology, or to fully engage in the implementation process. Registration, Evaluation, Authorisation of Chemicals (REACH) is an excellent example to illustrate the varying levels of NGO activity. In the run-up to new chemical legislation being adopted, ENGOs joined efforts and generated resources to provide policy input to the debate. They built an advocacy coalition with environmental ministers from progressive member states such as Sweden who were driving the EU's move towards new chemical legislation (Vogel 2012: 158, 177; Pesendorfer 2006: 104). The Gotheborg-based NGO International Chemical Secretariat (chemsec 2018), for instance, is a key provider of counter-expertise in the EU policy process. The EEB, in close cooperation with BEUC, trade unions and animal protection groups, voiced opposition against the European Commission's proposals tabled in 2001 (Hontelez 2012: 406). The EEB succeeded in visibly attacking animal-testing in the chemical industry, targeting and building coalitions with retailers such as Marks & Spencer, Kingfisher and B&Q. WWF attracted massive attention with its EU-wide DetoX campaign which was conducted between 2003 and 2006. The campaign combined both insider and outsider lobbying, including visible actions such as publicly testing human blood or food for chemical contamination (WWF 2007). The relative success of ENGOS in influencing REACH has been disputed in the literature (Persson 2007). Long and Lörinczi argued that without the "persistent and very strong lobbying from the environmental NGOs" the proposal would not have been tabled in the way it was (Long and Lörinczi 2009). Indeed, REACH does explicitly incorporate the precautionary principle

(Article 1.3), and compared to the weak US regulatory scheme, it has proven to be a powerful regulatory framework diffusing globally (Vogel 2012; Interview ENGO 2017). By contrast, Pesendorfer assesses REACH as being "neoliberal" and constituting a "dangerous shift in environmental policy making" (Pesendorfer 2006b). It is certainly fair to argue that due to massive industry lobbying, exacerbated by a looming economic downturn (Vogel 2012: 166), REACH proved to be "weaker than it was supposed to be" (Interview ENGO 2017). In particular, ENGOs would have welcomed a scheme that committed to a phase-out of dangerous and hazardous chemicals and that wasn't excluding so many substances from authorisation requirements (Vogel 2012: 167).

ENGO attention and resources spent on chemical policy decreased considerably once the new framework was adopted, and went to the post-legislative phase of rule-specification and implementation (Interview EP 2017; Interview Consumer Organisation 2017; Interview ENGO 2017). Only a few NGOs continued working on the dossier. These scrutinised industry compliance with registration deadlines (2004, 2018) and provided input to the 2013 and 2018 reviews. In particular, they signalled that they were unsatisfied with the authorisation practice of European Chemicals Agency (ECHA), which they considered far too lenient (Interview Consumer Organisation 2017; Interview EP 2017; ClientEarth 2017; ClientEarth and chemsec 2018). At the time of the first REACH registration deadline in 2004, for instance, ENGOs voiced their concern about compliance, given that a rather small number of chemicals had been listed with ECHA (Vogel 2012: 168). These shortcomings could have been rectified by the 2013 and 2017–2018 REACH reviews which, however, basically maintained the status quo. On the occasion of the ten-year review, NGOs toned down their criticism in reaction to the political climate in certain member states and the Commission's ambition to ease the regulatory burden. As interviewees argued, it was preferred to adopt a moderate tone in order to be heard at all and not risk opening up REACH once again (Interview Consumer Organisation 2017; Interview ENGO 2017). NGOs do not have at their disposal the type of resources required to fully participating in the implementation process. Contributing to expert groups is extremely time-consuming, and NGOs are not able to participate in all relevant expert groups all the time (Interview Consumer Organisation 2017). Even in groups where the number of participants from NGOs and industry seems well balanced—for the Competent Authorities for REACH and CLP (CARACAL) expert group we count nine NGOs (including ChemSec, HEAL, EEB, BEUC, ClientEarth) and ten business and trade associations (e.g. CEFIC)—we cannot assume that NGOs will be following the process throughout. As one interviewee put it, the NGO side simply could not sit at "week-long" meetings such as those held by ECHA in Helsinki (Interview ENGO 2017). However, there is evidence that ENGOs do at least engage in "firebell-ringing" activities (McCubbins and Schwartz 1984). ENGOs and consumer organisations frequently write public letters to express their concern about the work in Comitology or about ECHA decisions: in June 2017, six ENGOs criticised that ECHA was unduly responsive to industry concerns in the process of generating and assessing evidence on microplastics (ClientEarth et al. 2018). In July 2018, a joint letter by the EEB and CHEM Trust addressed to the Commission objected plans to grant exemptions for phthalates in food contact materials and for the use of the phthalate DEHP in PVC consumer products (EEB 2018b).

Apart from REACH, targeted campaigns have addressed the health effects of specific substances, such as the "EDC Free Europe" coalition (EDC Free Europe 2018) on EDCs which brings together more than 70 ENGOs and consumer organisations including ClientEarth, the EEB, Greenpeace and HEAL. Overall, however, the 2000s kicked off with a focus on climate change as the prime issue, absorbing public and ENGO attention, and somehow side-lining the technical and scientifically complex challenges raised by chemicals and plastics (Interview ENGO 2017).

To conclude, we see significant differences between sectors when it comes to outsider lobbying and campaigning. Plastics producers, in particular the producers of PVC, have faced continuous ENGO and public pressure across member states of the EU for the environmental and health impact of their products. Further, the recent marine litter campaign has been highly successful worldwide and places significant pressure on industry. Paper products, in contrast, enjoy a higher degree of public acceptance, while occasionally their reputation as a sustainable industry was put into question. Deforestation campaigns and awareness-raising activities about the wastefulness of single-use paper and board products pose a challenge to the paper industry. The discussion of NGO activities on chemicals regulation has further illustrated that the main focus of NGOs is on policy formulation in the legislative arena, while there is far less work done on non-legislative regulatory measures.

Regulating Paper and Plastics

Over the last few decades, the paper and plastics industries have been substantially affected by EU regulation in various areas, as highlighted in the Commission's assessment of the regulatory burden for these sectors (Maroulis et al. 2016; Rivera León et al. 2016). Before moving on to discussing the role of industry expertise in the regulatory process, in this section I will briefly outline how EU chemical and waste regulation has evolved over time.

A European dimension to waste legislation emerged as early as in the mid-1970s, yet wide discrepancies and tensions between national, regional and local policy practice remain (Weale et al. 2000: Chapter 12; Delreux and Happaerts 2016: 164–165; Krämer 2000: 176). Essentially, there are four types of legislation as far as its scope is concerned: horizontal provisions, specific provisions on hazardous waste, a regime on shipment of waste, and targeted measures for specific waste streams. The waste framework directive, first adopted in 1975 with recasts adopted in 2005 and 2008, sets a broad framework and provides an EU-wide definition of waste, while regulatory detail is added through daughter directives. These target specific waste streams such as packaging waste (Weale et al. 2000: 410–434). The first version, adopted in 1994 (amended in 2004, 2005, 2009, 2013, 2015), followed the so-called new approach in environmental policy which aimed at setting general safety and environmental requirements, while allowing for flexibility and tailor-made solutions in the implementation process. That said, the directive initially set maximum targets which undermined the pre-existing regulatory strictness in some member states, leading to several legal disputes (Vogel et al. 2012: 337–341).

With the shift in national and EU policies towards sustainable waste streams, regulation increasingly sought to boost recovery and recycling (Fischer 2011; Vogel et al. 2012: 249–250). In doing so, European policy combined push- and pull-factors, and further focused on two "Rs" which later on would figure prominently in the debate on the Circular Economy. Legislation on waste treatment, recovery and recycling seeks to push producers to sustainable production and recycling. The packaging waste framework directive, for example, which was adopted in 1994 and amended several times, imposes material-specific recycling targets. In addition, the labelling of recycled products should pull consumers to sustainable consumption. Paper products are covered by the European Ecolabel scheme and Green Public Procurement recommendations (European Commission 2018f, g). In fact the stipulation of recycling as a European policy goal has been helped by ECJ case law already in the 1980s, when in a ruling on a Danish recycling scheme (case 302/86) the ECJ stipulated that nationally set recycling targets are acceptable even where they pose a barrier on trade (Sands 1990: 696–697). Whether industry supports recycling targets or not depends on both the industry's track record in recycling and the targets' nature and ambition. Usually, industry opposes binding rules on minimum recycled content as a rather inflexible and strict instrument. The paper industry faced a real risk of being subject to such requirements at the end of the 1990s, when the European Commission envisaged minimum recycled fibre content in the course of the discussions in the so-called Recycling Forum. There was, however, intra-institutional conflict between the DGs Enterprise, having the lead in the Forum, and Environment. DG Enterprise prioritised economic and industrial policy aspects, while DG Environment, with the support of ENGOs, sought to regulate minimum recycled content (Directorate General Enterprise 2000; Directorate General Environment 2000). At about the same time, PVC waste streams were targeted by a Commission proposal, also in response to the debates in the member states and NGO pressure. From the mid-1990s onwards, the Commission sought to generate evidence on the environmental impact of the material, commissioning several studies (AEA Technology 2000; ARGUS 2000; PROGNOS 2000). These raised concern as to the use of some additives and increasing amounts of post-consumer waste. By the late 1990s, pressure on the Commission gained momentum in the context of the negotiations of the directive on end-of-life vehicles proposed in 1997. Responding to Member of European Parliament (MEP) pressure, the directive, adopted in 2000, announced that the Commission would address the environmental impacts of PVC in a policy proposal (consideration 12 of directive 53/2000). A Commission Green Paper on the environmental issues of PVC, published in July 2000 (European Commission 2000), found that a significant increase in PVC waste quantities was to be expected and that alternatives to landfilling should be developed. By that time, industry had already committed to a voluntary agreement on recycling, which was welcomed by DG Enterprise. DG Environment, in contrast, called for binding command-and-control measures on PVC. Similarly, the EP committees reporting on PVC (ENVI and ITRE) were split on the issue. The rapporteur on the Green Paper (PSE, Italy), who later became the relevant rapporteur on REACH, stressed the negative externalities of PVC throughout its life cycle and urged for targeted measures (Interview EP 2005b). As mentioned previously, the PVC dossier was overshadowed by REACH, and a new incoming Commission set new priorities and moved away from a sector-specific approach (Interview EP 2005b, c). While issues regarding certain substances and additives in PVC were thus going to be covered through REACH, the Green Paper's focus on waste and recycling was somehow lost out of the sight.

European chemicals regulation (Vogel 2012: 153–158) kicked off in the late 1960s with regulation that required dangerous substances to be listed, classified, packaged and labelled following certain rules, however without restricting their usage. From the 1970s, some member states had started to introduce testing requirements before products could be placed on the market, considered as market distortions by the Commission. An amendment adopted in 1979 significantly changed the initial framework, differentiating between existing substances and new substances to be placed on the market—with the caveat that the former were not subject to testing requirements. REACH, proposed in 2001 and adopted in 2006, was a complete overhaul of this approach, as it did away with this distinction in order to cover all chemical substances. Differently from previous regulation, REACH may result in the restriction of the manufacture, import and availability on the market of a substance, posing either certain conditions or completely banning its use. Chemicals placed on the market are subject to registration, following a gradual approach moving on from high-volume to low-volume chemicals. Registration deadlines had to be met in 2010, 2013 and 2018. ECHA expected that compared to the previous registration deadlines in 2010 and 2013, the number of registrations and the type of registrants would triple with up to 60,000 registrations for up to 25,000 substances (ECHA 2016). Yet after the May 2018 deadline had passed, the agency reported only 33,636 registrations for 11,114 substances (ECHA 2018). As ClientEarth noted in a critical report, the low number of notifications raises questions about industry compliance (2017: 13).

REACH targets the paper and plastics industries where it requires that substances of high concern, either contained in virgin or recycled material, go through an authorisation and evaluation procedure: in the paper industry this applies to inks or coating. An example is the use of BPA in the coating of thermal papers used for standard receipts. Such receipts will be banned EU-wide by 2020. For the plastics industry, and especially the PVC industry, it is mostly additives that are subject to REACH procedures. Many stabilisers and plasticisers used in PVC need to go through registration. Some of them have been classified as substances of very high concern (SVHCs) and are thus included in the candidate list for authorisation. This holds for lead-based stabilisers and phthalates-based plasticisers (DBP, BBP, DEHP). Polymers, the main ingredients in PVC, in contrast, have been excluded from the scope of the regulation, as these occur in indefinite combinations (Interview EP 2005a). The exemption granted to polymers was subject to scrutiny (bio by Deloitte 2014) after the 2013 REACH review. In its second REACH review published in March 2018, the Commission took a cautious stance on additional registration requirements, arguing that these would nega-tively affect the SMEs in the sector. The Commission merely announced that there is a need for further assessment (European Commission 2018c: 10–11).

The recycling activities of the industries have been affected by REACH where regulation requires that recyclers declare the presence of SVHCs once these are contained above a specific threshold. Under REACH (Article 2.7d), recovered substances are exempted from regis-tration under certain conditions. The Commission granted an exemption to the PVC industry, allowing recyclers to use DEHP irrespective of a non-binding resolution adopted in the European Parliament and ENGO opposition (European Parliament 2015a; McGrath 2016; EEB 2018b). In the 2018 REACH review, the European Commission highlighted that further action was needed to find workable solutions for information requirements asked from recycling industries (European Commission 2018c: 6).

Revised legislation to be adopted under the Circular Economy package and China's decision to put a ban on imports of certain waste streams such as plastics will transform recycling and waste man-agement. As an immediate consequence of China's import ban on certain types of plastic waste, introduced in January 2018, market prices for waste as secondary raw material have fallen drastically, lead-ing to more incineration and landfill and less recycling across the EU (Tamma 2018). The Circular Economy concept, in line with the eco-logical modernisation paradigm, sees environmental policies as a means to achieve economic growth. Especially in the medium to long term, resource efficiency will become a crucial asset for industry branches competing for scarce resources. In the short term, however, introducing new recycling goals means imposing additional cost on the industry. The immediate economic cost of new environmental regulation have certainly been a driving factor of what can be described as policy dismantling (Bauer and Knill 2012: 44) in the process of adopting a Circular Economy agenda for Europe. A first communication adopted by the late Barroso Commission in July 2014 (European Commission 2014b) was withdrawn by the incoming Juncker Commission in February 2015. In replacement, the Commission put forward a new action plan in December 2015 (European Commission 2015). The new proposal proved less ambitious than the previous one (Interview EP 2017; Interview Consumer Organisation 2017), and rumours said that the European Commission responded to pressure exerted by the trade association Business Europe (*Confino* 2015). The initial proposal strived for a "zero waste programme for Europe", aiming at a minimum 70% reuse and recycling target for municipal waste by 2030, an 80% recycling target for packaging by 2030, and a ban on sending recyclable materials (plastics, metals, glass, paper and cardboard) to landfill by 2025, with the ambition to "virtually eliminate landfill by 2030" (European Commission 2014b: 9). By contrast, the new action plan lowered the 2030 goal for municipal waste to 65% and for packaging waste to 75% and envisions a ban on landfilling separately collected waste. To put these figures into perspective: currently eight countries have landfill restrictions on recyclable and recoverable waste (PlasticsEurope 2018e: 33); the current packaging waste directive sets a new target of 22.5% for plastic packaging, and in 2016, the EU industry achieved a share of 40.8% (PlasticsEurope 2018e: 37). By May 2018, the Council approved legislation that further lowered these targets by 5% each, setting the 2030 recycling targets at 60% for municipal waste and at 70% for packaging (with a 55% target for plastic and a 85% target for paper waste). Further, policymakers agreed on a landfill reduction target of no more than 10% of the total amount of municipal waste by 2035. Finally, new requirements for extended producer responsibility are introduced, imposing the introduction of mandatory schemes on all packaging producers by 2024 (European Commission 2018b).

These newly set targets, but also several other proposed measures under the circular economy heading would greatly change the regulatory environment for the two industries. Moreover, the plastics producers are targeted by a dedicated EU Strategy for Plastics in the Circular Economy, proposed by the Commission in January 2018 (European Commission 2018e). It envisioned all plastic packaging on the EU market as being recyclable by 2030, that the consumption of single-use plastics is reduced, and finally that the use of microplastics is more heavily restricted. Following up on the phase-out of lightweight plastic carrier bags which was adopted in 2015 (directive 2015/720), in May 2018 the Commission further suggested to ban the ten single-use plastic products most frequently found in marine litter, urging the Parliament and the Council to adopt the proposed directive (2018/172) before the elections in May 2019 (European Commission 2018h). A provisional political agreement concluding trilogue negotiations on the single-use plastics directive between the Council and the European Parliament was reached in December 2018 (European Council 2018a). Policymakers decided on a ban on eight product categories—namely cutlery, plates, straws; food containers, beverage containers and cups made of expanded polystyrene; products from oxo-degradable plastic and cotton bud sticks—as well as on measures to reduce the consumption of certain product groups. Further, the directive will introduce a binding target of at least 25% and 30% of recycled plastic for PET beverage bottles from 2025 and 2030 onwards, respectively. In its plenary sitting in March 2019 MEPs voted in favour of the directive, which will come into force by 2021 (European Parliament 2019). The move to ban certain single-use products was welcomed by some ENGOs as an important step to reduce plastic waste (EEB 2018a). There were also critical voices, however, assessing the bans as symbolic activism running short of a more substantive overhaul of EU packaging regulation deemed necessary (German Environment Aid 2018). As part of the Circular Economy package, the Commission also put forward measures concerning the interface between chemicals, products and waste legislation (European Commission 2018d), as well as a recast of waste legislation.

Figure 4.3 summarises how European regulation has affected the two industry branches over time and how industry initiatives have responded to EU policies. These initiatives and the role of industry in the regulatory process will be the topic of the following sections.

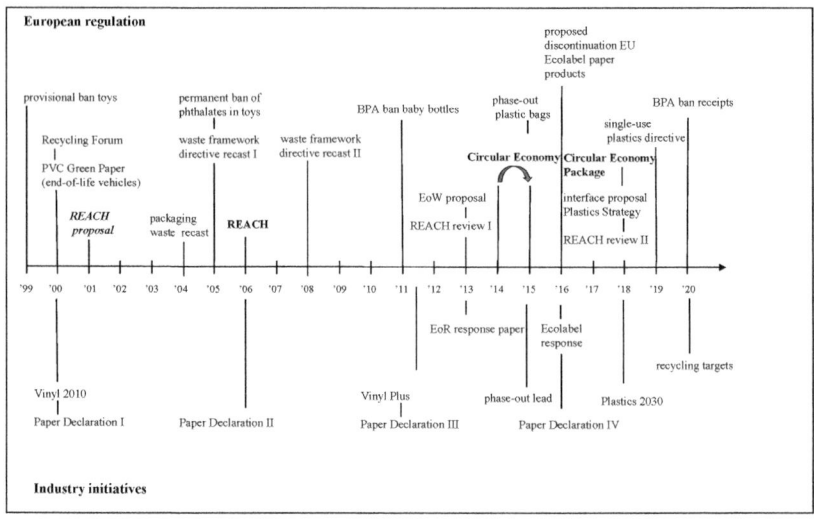

Fig. 4.3   Timeline of European chemicals and waste regulation and industry initiatives (*Source* Author's illustration)

EXPERT OR GATEKEEPER?

As outlined in Chapters 2 and 3, specialised knowledge is a powerful resource in regulating highly complex fields that require specific and detailed information at the implementation and rule specification stage. There is therefore an eminent risk for the regulator to be captured by industry interests and reward gatekeeping. On the other hand, while industry actors are experts in dealing with epistemic uncertainty, they may find it harder to manage the uncertainties of the political process and public debate. In short, their discursive power may prove more shaky. There is solid evidence that media news coverage of health and environmental issues follows specific dynamics which are often disproportional to "actual" policy problems (Anderson 2010, 2014). How does industry address this double challenge of being an insider in the regulatory process while also responding to the need to and communicate effectively to a wider public? To shed light on this question, the following sections examine self-regulation activities as well as regulatory strategies pursued by the two industry sectors.

The Paper Industry: We Are the Recycling Experts!

Despite its legacy as a recycling champion and its distinctiveness as a user of organic material, we have seen that the paper industry has come under pressure to prove its sustainability record. In the context of international debates about deforestation and clear-cutting, industry had to develop effective communication strategies:

> But the recyclability and sustainability of our products, we lost it a little bit out of sight - because it didn't need so much attention, because it was so obvious (to us); this has been misused by other industries who tried to make stories about things which are not really true [...] we are cutting trees, we are cutting forests. We should also say: we should cut the forest at a certain point, otherwise the forest will kill itself. The people have a different understanding. If you cut a tree now, you are almost categorised, this is bad behavior [...]. (Interview paper industry 2006d)

To address such concerns, the European paper and pulp industry visibly commits to sustainable forest management. It posits that most European forests are managed "in compliance with the principles of Sustainable Forest Management" (CEPI 2005). The industry engages in numerous public relations and educational activities which aim at improving the sector's reputation. Examples include the various campaigning and publicity initiatives run by the industry forum "Two Sides" (Two Sides 2018). One such initiative is entitled "Myths and Facts". It seeks to "separate verifiable facts from opinion and misleading information" regarding the sustainability of print and paper, addressing issues such as deforestation in Europe, global warming and packaging waste (Two Sides 2017). Further, Two Sides runs an "Anti-Greenwashing Campaign" which checks for and seeks to rectify greenwashing claims used by other industries, such as "go green – go paperless". Finally, the industry commits to recycling, engaging in voluntary schemes at national and EU-level.

The most visible voluntary commitment of the industry is its EU-wide paper recycling initiative launched in 2000. Between 2000 and 2005, the European Declaration on Paper Recovery set a recycling rate of 56% and formulated objectives related to improving the quality of recycled paper. Between 2006 and 2010, a new agreement was decided on, the European Paper Declaration on Recycling, which set a quantitative recycling target of 66%. A third commitment was signed for the period 2011–2015, this time committing to 70%. Finally, a fourth generation declaration was agreed upon in 2016, with the goal to achieve 74% paper recycling by 2020. As illustrated in Fig. 4.4, industry reached or even exceeded the voluntary targets set for the first three agreements, which makes it likely to achieve the target set for 2020. The latest recycling rate, reported for 2016, amounts to 72.5% (EPRC 2018: 3). It includes material exported to third countries to be recycled outside the EU—in 2016, 9.8 million tonnes, amounting to a share of 16.5%, was exported (EPRC 2018: 3). By way of comparison, the new binding recycling target for paper packaging, adopted under the Circular Economy package, amounts to 85% by 2030 (European Commission 2018b).

CEPI, bringing together the mill buyers interested in stabilising the market for recovered material, owned the process from the outset and gave the decisive impulse by drafting the agreement and providing the statistics (Interview paper industry 2006e). As discussed above, the paper

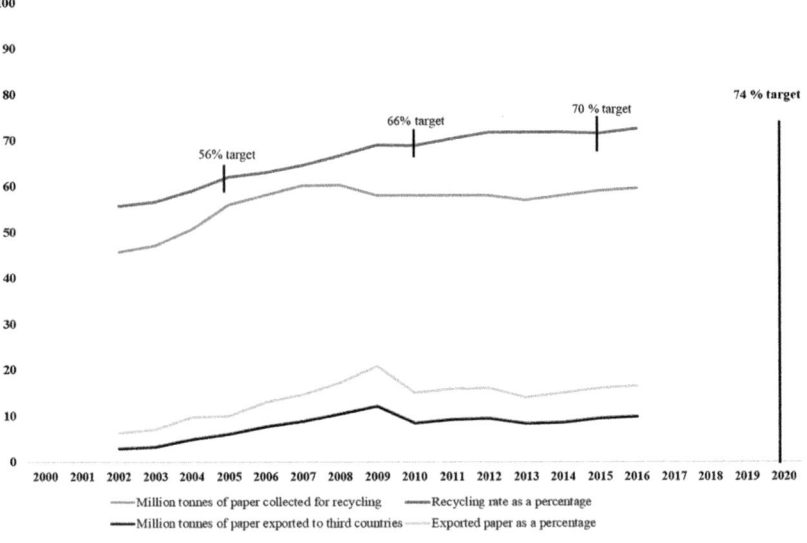

Fig. 4.4 Recycling European paper industry (*Source* Own figure based on ERPC/EPRC Monitoring Reports 2002–2018 [no annual report available before 2002, and for 2005; 2005 values for million tonnes collected and exported have been estimated])

industry has an interest to improve the flow of information throughout the value chain and also to be able to recover maximum amounts of paper and improve its quality. Paper mills are a costly venture, and owners therefore seek to reduce market uncertainties as to the amounts and price of available material. Towards the end of the 1980s, the European industry faced significant volatility, as sometimes there was a surplus of recycled fibre, resulting in a negative price, and at other times, there was a deficit of recycled fibre available, making the price positive and rather expensive. There was therefore an intrinsic incentive to commit to some targets in order to create more stability for the sector and send the right signals to the market (Interview paper industry 2006b). Besides the market stabilising effect, the agreement also is of strategic planning value to the actors involved (Interview COM 2006). At the time when the commitment was initiated, it was easy to predict that there would be a move to use more recycled fibres, because the price for virgin fibre had increased. CEPI developed statistical methods to predict the amounts of recovered material available on the market in order to calculate aggregate recycling targets. In this respect, the declaration works as an "uncertainty coping" (Pfeffer 1981: 109–112) tool for industry.

The paper industry managed to bring on board additional organisations throughout the four generations of the agreement. The founding associations of the European Paper Declaration in 2000 were CEPI and ERPA, joined by FEFCO in 2001. Three associations (EUGROPA, FEAD, INTERGRAF) were supporting members. The 2006–2010 declaration was backed by seven member associations (CEPI, CITPA, ERPA, ETS, INGEDE, INTERGRAF, FEPE) and supporters (EADP, ENPA, EuPIA, FAEP/EMMA, FEICA, FINAT, RTE). The 2011–2015 declaration brought together nine member associations (CEPI, CITPA, EMFA, ERPA, ETS, FEPE, INGEDE, INTERGRAF, BEVERAGE CARTON) and four supporters (Afera, EuPIA, FINAT, RADTECH). Finally, the declaration 2016–2020 maintains almost the same membership and support structure, with the exception of ERPA (ERPC 2016b). Through voluntary cooperation member associations sought to overcome diverse interest constellations along the chain (as discussed by Héritier and Eckert 2009), for instance between collectors organised inside EuRIC (formerly in ERPA) and mill buyers organised within CEPI. The collectors want to make a decent income for the material they offer, whereas the paper mills as buyers will seek to reduce cost. Similarly, the paper industry urges collectors to provide not only maximum quantity, but also high-quality material (Interview paper industry 2006a). Collectors and waste management companies, in contrast, favour more flexibility. For instance, FEAD has been critical about the strictness of the standard EN 643 in terms of moisture content (Interview paper industry 2006c). This standard has been agreed to by CEPI and ERPA, and was subsequently endorsed by the European Committee for Standardisation (CEN). The association supported the first declaration but was no longer willing to take part in the following agreements.

Besides internal divergence the paper value chain does, however, pursue a common interest, and gains from voluntary activity in several aspects. The first, most immediate gain is to prevent regulation that prescribes a minimum recycled content for certain product groups. According to an interviewee at DG Environment (Interview COM 2005), industry was motivated to become proactive as a result of the discussions in the EU Recycling Forum with the possibility of regulating recycled products. From an industry perspective, binding targets across the EU would not lead to more sustainability but only lead to "more trucks on European roads" (Interview paper industry 2017). The production of virgin fibre and the amounts of material collected are very uneven across the EU member states, and larger companies can more easily organise ambitious recycling schemes compared to smaller players (Interview paper industry 2006b). In Scandinavia, for instance, the amount of collected paper is not sufficient for their level of production. So if one would impose recycling content at the European level, countries with more recycled material available, e.g. Germany, would need to export this to the Scandinavian countries so that they could meet the targets in their production. The voluntary aggregate target set by the Paper Declaration, by contrast, leaves flexibility to the companies as to how and through what methods this target is to be achieved. In fact, industry self-regulation involves a number of governance devices that facilitate burden-sharing amongst companies inside market segments, across the value chain and between national associations (Héritier and Eckert 2009).

While the VA of the paper chain may therefore be interpreted as a proactive move by industry to avoid legislation, it is at the same time a powerful tool to effectively voice shared interests in the dynamic regulatory process. The thematic focus of the subsequent declarations has shifted in reaction to EU-level policy debates addressing issues such as

Ecodesign or the Circular Economy. Moreover, with the very idea of circularity, a single-material approach would no longer deliver the desired results, and from an industry perspective, cooperation across the value chain and beyond is seen as a precondition in order to design new products and engage in innovation (Interview paper industry 2017).

> Crucially, the Paper Declaration should be seen as a sustained effort to make positive publicity about the sustainability record of the industry chain and its expertise in recycling [...] It was also about effectively communicating our achievements in the recycling of paper to the public [...] to show how well paper recycling actually works and to demonstrate which huge amounts of used paper are going into the process. (Interview paper industry 2006e: own translation)

With the Paper Declaration, the industry aims to prove its sustainability record as it approaches the theoretical limit of 79% recycling of paper with the fourth agreement running up until 2020 (Interview paper industry 2017). In its regular reporting on the declaration, industry claims "sustainable leadership" and promotes itself as a "global leader in paper recycling" (ERPC 2007: 2). It provides data that underpin why "Europe is the paper recycling champion" globally, and when comparing packaging waste streams, paper is "the most recycled packaging material in Europe" (ERPC 2016a: 3, 5).

The Regulatory Power of the Paper Industry

The paper fibre loop can serve as the perfect model for circularity. (ERPC Chairman Henri Vermeulen 2016c)

The above quote by European Recovered Paper Council (ERPC) Chairman Henri Vermeulen illustrates how the paper industry chain seeks to position itself as a role model in the transition towards a circular economy. Through its VA the European industry has sought to anchor and publicise its reputation as a recycling expert. Compared to all other materials, paper has the longest history of recycling and in the highest rates. In the case of the paper industry, private authority relies both on "special expertise" and on a "historical role" (Cutler et al. 1999: 4). The paper industry has invested in setting up recycling capacity and developing recycling techniques over a long period of time, and as of today has a significant advantage when compared to other sectors such as the plastics industry. Further, industry has developed structures to bring together actors along the industry chain and to improve the data and knowledge base of recycling activities. In doing so, it has been particularly successful in avoiding binding regulation on minimum recycled content for specific products and safeguarding market flexibility instead. However, the two major issues for the paper industry that remain to be solved, potentially through regulatory requirements, are the collection of recovered materials and information about impurities and unwanted substances.

Regulation concerning the collection of recovered materials is mostly national, given that waste management schemes vary widely between member states. That said, European regulation can set certain incentives, for instance by pursuing a producer-pays and producer responsibility approach. The packaging waste directive adopted in the 1990s (directive 94/62/EC) did already impose costs on the packaging industry, and the scheme of extended producer responsibility envisaged as part of the Circular Economy package clearly indicates further movement towards that direction (European Commission 2018b). While the European landfill directive aims at diverting waste from landfill, it leaves significant flexibility to the member states to adopt measures such as incineration, separate collection or landfill bans (EEA 2009). The ban on landfill, which was proposed in the Commission's 2014 Circular Economy Communication, was no longer envisaged in the 2015 Action Plan. The paper industry would certainly have welcomed such a ban, as it asks for regulatory incentives for separate collection and recycling throughout the value chain (Interview paper industry 2017). Another issue which affects the industry's recycling activities is the definition of "end-of-waste". The paper industry strives for definitions that stipulate the non-waste status as a valuable secondary raw material of used cardboard and paper products. This does have substantial consequences for the value chain, notwithstanding the normative connotation of the term "waste": paper mills have been requested to be registered as waste treatment installations, subject to waste permit requirements and other obligations; collectors and recovered paper merchants have been required to be licensed as waste operators; in transportation, different value added tax levels for waste and non-waste apply. The paper industry favours a definition which sets the end-of-waste point at the stage where recovered material reaches the paper mills. The waste framework directive (2008/98/EC, Article 6.1) defines the criteria according to which waste ceases to be waste after it has undergone recovery, delegating material-specific decisions to Comitology. The Commission proposed end-of-waste (EoW) criteria for waste paper in 2013 (COM (2013) 502) which were, however, not adopted. In the view of the paper industry the proposal, by moving the end-of-waste point forward in the collection cycle, would have failed to increase the quality and availability of paper for recycling. Instead, it would have threatened recycling practice altogether, thus constituting the end-of-recycling (EoR) rather than the end-of-waste (CEPI 2013). Another example where CEPI voiced criticism of, in this case, deregulatory proposals was in 2016 when the Commission considered discontinuing the EU Ecolabel for paper products. In a joint letter with NGOs, industry voiced its support for safeguarding the Ecolabel for tissues and newsprint, arguing that the EU label was far more visible and reliable than national or private initiatives (CEPI et al. 2016).

The second challenge for the paper industry is that as recyclers they would want to have maximum information about impurities and unwanted substances in the recovered material. This is why they ask for stricter rather than more flexible rules under REACH when it comes to chemicals and waste:

> On waste and chemicals there is simply no support for us from European and national legislation [...] The Commission is pushing us, the industry, to be circular – and as a matter of fact we are already circular; but at the same time, much of EU regulation is not circular, take the REACH as an example which is linear apart from one exemption granted for recovery. We, as an industry, we don't need any loopholes, we need legislation that supports us in doing what we do. (Interview paper industry 2017)

"Circular regulation" from an industry point of view would thus introduce strict regulation on unwanted materials, and thereby help to clean up the material's life cycle and introduce strict regulation on unwanted materials. This is naturally not a view shared throughout the value chain where converters and inkers will ask for more flexibility. In order to avoid unwanted substances at the recovery and recycling stage, many widely used substances such as inks formulated from mineral oils would need to be substituted, e.g. by vegetable-based inks. Strict rules on legacy materials and recycling can indeed hamper recycling rates, as it is virtually impossible to identify all the substances that are present in recovered material. To improve the traceability of unwanted substances in the material stream, the industry funds research into innovative methods bringing together big data and chemistry (Interview paper industry 2017). The paper industry's concern about this lack of available information figures as an example in the European Commission's communication on the interface between chemicals and waste regulation, referencing the problems posed by ink residues and mineral oils that can be found in food packaging (European Commission 2018d: 2–3). ENGOs, for their part, have also deplored EU regulation as failing to address chemicals in food contact materials and not giving enough attention to the problems posed by inks in paper and cardboard packaging (Interview ENGO 2017). For recycled material it is apparent that "in the case of food contact materials made from paper and card, there is essentially minimal regulatory oversight [and] there is no scientific justification for regulating recycled plastics in food contact applications but not regulating recycled paper and card in the same applications" (CHEM Trust 2016: 6, 11). This leaves us with the question of how competing materials can be regulated in order to protect consumers and the environment adequately but also without giving an unfair economic advantage to one industry branch over the other. In a public letter signed by eleven associations the paper industry value chain expressed "deep concern[s]" about the Commission's forthcoming Plastics Strategy. The letter pointed to the effects of competing materials and technologies, the "evident market failures of plastic prices" and financial benefits to the plastics industry through oil and gas subsidies in the EU, and highlights that the circular economy targets would remain lower than for other materials:

> We find it unfair to have a strategy that rewards the laggards whilst other materials who have done the work and paid for it themselves in the past decades risk being penalised. It would be a strange outcome if the final strategy were to favour a material that remains problematic over less problematic ones. (CITPA et al. 2017)

The Plastics Industry: We Go Green!

Targeted NGO campaigning and public attention placed considerable pressure on the European plastics industry at the various life-cycle stages of plastics. At the production stage there is the issue of using up finite sources of fossil feedstock. In view of the exponential growth of plastics production forecasted for the years to come, there is thus a need to either re-use these resources and keep them in the circle (circular economy logic), or replace them by renewable feedstock (bioeconomy logic). At the usage stage health and safety risks have been raised for various, widely used substances. Finally, at the waste stage the environmental impact proves largely problematic. As we have seen in the previous sections, over time the public debate moved on from a targeted PVC campaign towards the health issues posed by toxic chemicals and, finally, to a broader campaign addressing the environmental and health impact of plastics more generally. The plastics industry, in response, has voluntarily committed to environmental measures, and sought to publicise its transition towards circularity.

The first phase of the PVC debate, initiated by Greenpeace and leading to the publication of the Commission's Green Paper on PVC, has brought about the industry voluntary commitment "Vinyl 2010". The VA was backed by four sector associations bringing together resin manufacturers, converters and additive producers (ECVM, EuPC, ECPI, ESPA). It was concluded in March 2000 even before the Green Paper on PVC was published (July 2000). The PVC industry value chain committed to a ten-year programme which included activities on recycling in the non-packaging segments (packaging being covered by mandatory recycling targets already), the phase-out of hazardous substances along with research and public relation activities. The most visible quantitative targets set were to phase out lead as a stabiliser until 2015 (50% until 2010) and to recycle an additional 200,000 tonnes of available post-consumer PVC waste per year in 2010 (Vinyl 2010 2001). Since 2010, VinylPlus runs as the renewed ten-year voluntary commitment of the PVC industry in order to pursue sustainability goals in the sector. It addresses five challenges, namely "controlled loop, organochlorine emissions, sustainable additives and sustainability awareness" (VinylPlus 2011: 3). The first challenge upgrades the industry's recycling target to 800,000 tonnes per year, including 100,000 tonnes per year of "difficult-to-recycle" PVC material. VinylPlus is backed by eleven members comprising the initial four and seven incoming associations representing the manufacturers of various PVC products, namely flooring, window profile and related building products, rigid PVC film, plastic pipes and fittings, coated fabrics, and thermoplastic roofing (EPFLOOR, EPPA, ERPA, IVK, TEPPFA, EPCoat, ESWA). As depicted in Fig. 4.5, the PVC industry

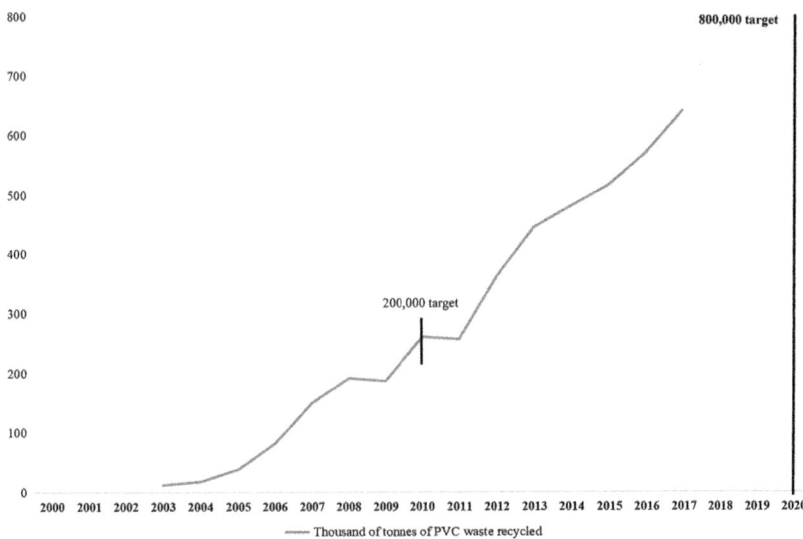

Fig. 4.5   Recycling European PVC industry (*Source* Own figure using data provided by Monitoring Reports Vinyl 2010 and VinylPlus 2004–2018)

achieved the goal set for 2010 and has been steadily increasing the volumes for the second agreement.

Not all branches of the PVC value chain were equally enthusiastic to commit to voluntary action (Héritier and Eckert 2009). From the outset, the driving association was the ECVM which brings together the big resin producers. Not only do the companies organised under the roof of the ECVM have the financial resources and manpower to drive such a process, they also were visibly targeted by the anti-PVC campaign. The small and medium-sized companies in the plastics converting sector, in contrast, do not have the same amount of resources, and it is far more difficult to achieve sector coverage in their associations. To combat the problem of free-riding in this segment, the so-called Vinyl Foundation had been initiated halfway through the implementation of the VA, with the task to collect the contributions in the converting sector (Interview plastics industry 2006b). The expanding membership of VinylPlus illustrates that the organisational structure of converters has evolved and that the coverage of the commitment has been increased. Finally, the producers of additives have been targeted by ENGO campaigning in a different way than the resin producers and the converters. Their major concern was not so much the sustainability and waste issue but the health risks attributed to phthalates. In the framework of Vinyl 2010, with its heavy focus on recycling, securing the commitment of the additives producers association (ECPI) proved difficult, especially at the high time of the ENGO phthalates and toys campaign. To accommodate the companies' concerns, ECPI's financial contribution was reduced halfway through the implementation process (Interview plastics industry 2006b). The renewed VinylPlus agreement adds strong emphasis on "sustainable additives" and thus takes on board the key concerns of this industry branch as well (VinylPlus 2011: 13).

Back in 2000, the overarching common interest for the whole chain was to set off regulatory pressure, which was very concrete in the run-up to the publication of the Commission's Green Paper. The industry chain joined forces to avoid the worst-case scenario: the introduction of stringent material-specific regulation, let alone a complete ban on PVC. The regulatory threat scenario, as discussed in the literature on self-regulation (Halfteck 2006, 2008; Glachant 2003), was thus the main trigger for the emergence of Vinyl 2010 (Héritier and Eckert 2008). Once introduced, the commitment had been continued after the first ten years, and this did not come as a surprise given the increased emphasis of EU regulation on sustainability and life cycle thinking. The challenges and goals defined by the renewed commitment very much mirror the evolution of the EU's chemicals (legacy additives, sustainable additives), environmental (controlled loop, emissions, sustainability awareness, e.g. through labelling) and energy policy (sustainable energy use). VinylPlus thus continues to prove the industry's proactive stance in many regulatory domains, and seeks to send a positive message about the environmental sustainability of the PVC industry. PVC industry representatives portray themselves as pioneers in the transition towards circularity of the plastics industry as a whole (Interview plastics industry 2019). Compared to the other branches the PVC supply chain was under pressure to act much earlier than the other branches, and now seeks to draw on this legacy in its legitimising discourse.

Compared to the long-standing track record of the paper industry in the recycling business, the PVC industry had to develop recycling techniques from scratch. It is safe to argue that without the paramount pressure from ENGOs and policymakers, the industry would probably not have committed to a recycling target in the first place (Héritier and

Eckert 2008). In fact, there was both a lack of expertise and know-how about how to recycle the material, and given the comparatively low cost of producing virgin PVC there was also a lack of economic incentives to do so (Interview EP 2005c). In order to generate expertise on possible recycling techniques, the PVC industry had to innovate, and embarked on an arduous process of trial and error in doing so. Here industry had to take on the role as an *innovator* in the process of developing appropriate recycling methods and procedures. Over the course of 2000–2015, the PVC industry invested 100 million Euros to further develop their recycling capabilities (Simon 2016). Without going into too much technical detail, two recycling options should be differentiated, namely chemical and mechanical recycling (PE Europe et al. 2004: 83–86; EMF 2016: 47–48). Vinyl 2010 launched several costly projects on chemical recycling—sponsored by the resin producers as part of the chemical industry—which failed spectacularly. Mechanical recycling, relying on the expertise of the plastics converters, proved more promising (Interview plastics industry 2006b). The dynamics of recycling over time are therefore quite different from the paper industry where, given the high share achieved, the marginal cost increases disproportionally as industry comes close to the theoretical maximum. In contrast, the initial levels of recycling achieved in the PVC sector were disappointing and far below the target set. The PVC industry, in its 2007 report, did, however, stress that the tonnages increased considerably: from 18,077 in 2004 to 82,812 in 2006 (Vinyl 2010 2007: 7). Underperformance during the first years was attributed to the failure of chemical recycling but also to miscalculations on the availability of post-consumer waste. Lower amounts of waste went into recycling, industry argued, both because products were used longer and exported to other parts of Europe or the world. Industry generated evidence, conducting studies for the current and incoming member states (Vinyl 2010 2007: 11; 2008: 16). As Fig. 4.5 shows, the tonnage of waste recycled also grew considerably during the second half of the agreement, and the PVC industry reported that 640,648 tonnes of post-consumer PVC waste was recycled in 2017—compared to a total of 8.4 million tonnes of recycled plastic waste reported for 2016 by PlasticsEurope (2018d: 13). If this trend continues, the 2020 recycling goal is on track to be fulfilled. In proportion to total waste volumes, however, the fraction going into recycling will remain small. At the time when the agreement was initiated, a study for the Commission reported 3.6 million tonnes of post-consumer PVC waste for 2000 and estimated an increase up to 6.4 million tonnes for 2020 for the EU-21. Recycling was at a rate of 3%, with 82% going to landfill and 15% to incineration (AEA Technology 2000). Accordingly, the two million tonnes recycled in 2020 would amount to 12.5% of this estimate for the EU-21, keeping in mind that the total volume of plastic waste in the EU-27 will be expectedly higher. Besides comparatively low recycling rates, the sustainability of the recycling process, involving emissions and hazardous waste, and the presence of legacy materials in recycled products pose problems. Naturally, incinerating and landfilling PVC waste are not viable solutions either, and according to the European waste hierarchy should be avoided.

As highlighted already, ENGO campaigning (Greenpeace 2001) in the mid-1990s targeted the use of plasticisers in toys, and ultimately triggered stringent regulation for this product group. Dealing with this campaign used up the financial and human resources of plasticisers producers in particular. The reputational damage was however caused to the whole chain. Especially the pledges of several big retailers to go PVC-free were highly visible for the general public. Moreover, this type of voluntary action can have a concrete pull effect on the demand side (EMF 2016: 60). The NGOs' claims met with a significant level of counter-expertise generated through various studies and assessments (e.g. TNO Nutrition and Food Research 2001). These suggested that the risks involved from exposure to PVC toys were not at significant levels. From an industry perspective, therefore, the health impact had been heavily exaggerated and was in contradiction with scientific findings (ECPI 2003, 2005). Given the reputational damage caused by a highly emotional campaign industry had to respond despite the negligeable economic relevance of the product segment, as one interviewee explained:

> [...] the amount of phthalates sold into the toys is and was always negligible, it was tiny. In fact, if you took away the amount of phthalates that was sold into it and you looked at the sales of phthalates, it wouldn't have even made a little bit in the annual sales. But the reason that it was defended, and it has cost a lot of money to defend, was really because of the whole domino effect. [...] the danger was that if toys had been given in from the very beginning – and there is no scientific reason to do so - then what would have been next? [...] that wouldn't have satisfied the people who were attacking it. Because they would have turned around immediately and said, the industry has admitted that phthalates shouldn't be used in toys,

these must be really bad for you, and so on and so forth. (Interview plastics industry 2006a)

All in all, the phthalates in toys discussion is a case study in how the intensity of public pressure is an important explanatory factor for adopting more risk-averse regulation (Vogel 2012: 202–206).

In the New Millennium the wider debate on plastics (over-)consumption and waste has moved far beyond PVC as a particularly problematic material. In response, industry branches have joined forces. At the global level, in 2011, plastics organisations initiated the "Global Action Plan for Solutions to Marine Litter", with 74 signatories in 2018 (Marine Litter Solutions 2001, 2018). At the European level, PlasticsEurope announced its voluntary commitment "Plastics 2030" the very same day that the Commission came forward with its Plastics Strategy. The European plastics industry strived to increase circularity and resource efficiency (PlasticsEurope 2018d), setting three key priorities, namely to increase reuse and recycling, prevent plastics leakages into the environment and improve resource efficiency—which very much mirror the ongoing EU policy debate. More specifically, industry abides to a target to reuse and recycle 60% of plastic packaging by 2030, indeed setting a more ambitious target than the 55% in the new waste legislation, and further, to increase that share to 70% by 2040 (in 2016 industry recycled 40.8%, rf. PlasticsEurope 2018e: 37); it also commits to recycle 50% of total plastic waste. On leakages, the industry announced measures to prevent pellet loss and launched educational and awareness-raising initiatives.

The Regulatory Power of the Plastics Industry

We will never recover this investment. But we believe it does have a value, and we are very proud of what we have done because it demonstrates that PVC can be 100 percent recycled. It is such a durable material that it can be recycled several times without destroying the molecules – the properties remain the same. (Brigitte Dero, General Manager of VinylPlus 2016)

This statement by the PVC boss illustrates how the industry frames its voluntary commitment as a successful endeavour towards sustainability and circularity. In any event, Vinyl 2010 was a success in taking off public and ENGO pressure from the industry. The continued voluntary efforts of the plastics industry under VinylPlus and Plastics 2030 further prove the added value of self-regulation in making a case that industry knows best how to generate expertise, and how to innovate production and recycling processes in order to achieve environmental and resource efficiency targets. Further, the industry branch has sought to claim authority based on a successful track record of voluntary action which in their view serves as a role model for other branches.

A major difference compared to the paper industry—though faced with some pressure concerning unwanted substances in recycled paper products—is that the plastics industry deals with an ongoing debate about the need to phase out and substitute hazardous substances and even types of plastics such as PVC. Industry has to cover enormous costs once a substance falls into the remit of REACH. First of all, there is an immediate reputational damage for having a substance listed. Already the listing as a SVHC has a massive signalling effect: the use of DEHP, for example, decreased massively as soon as it was classified (Simon 2016). Second, there are significant reporting and information obligations that come together with the listing. Lastly, there is the real risk that the substance will be subject to a phase-out or, worse still, an immediate ban. In the process of assessing the risk of chemicals, NGOs, regulators and industry engage in turf wars to generate compelling evidence (e.g. HEAL 2018; ClientEarth and chemsec 2018). Consumer organisations and ENGOs point to irresponsible and lenient industry practices in their dealings with hazardous and toxic materials and also routinely criticise ECHA's regulatory practice for a lack of transparency and strictness (ClientEarth 2017). Industry, by contrast, frequently deplores that political decisions are not based on a sound, scientific assessment of risks. The ban on plasticisers in toys was a showcase in that respect, as it involved a heated and indeed highly emotional debate on the health and well-being of children (Vogel 2012: 202–206). Industry lost the battle in this case. The exemptions achieved for the use of DEHP in PVC recycling, by contrast, are a case where industry managed to achieve the desired outcome. The generation of expertise and counter-expertise (Fischer 1990) is thus an essential part in these regulatory battles.

In those cases where industry looses the regulatory battle it typically engages in litigation. Industry actors dispose of the required specialised knowledge and the resources to challenge regulatory decisions before the courts with a view to revoke decisions taken, or at least delay the required adjustment. According to policy insider information, ECHA decisions are frequently contested by industry (Interview EP 2017; Interview Consumer Organisation 2017). An illustrative example is the regulatory struggle on BPA. PlasticsEurope filed several complaints: first, the association fought the French ban on BPA in food packaging. The French Constitutional Council partially lifted the ban in 2015, overturning it for food containers destined for the export market, while maintaining the ban for the French market (decision no. 2015-480, 15 September 2015). Second, industry challenged decisions of the European chemicals agency (ECHA) (Teffer 2018a, b; Oziel 2017): industry disputed ECHA's decision to include BPA in the candidate list on the grounds that most of its applications were as an intermediate and that as such the substance was excluded from REACH. Another case was brought to the ECJ against ECHA's decision to upgrade the classification of BPA, thus classifying the substance twice based on different regulatory provisions under REACH. While these cases are still pending, all the obligations of being on the candidate list still apply. Litigation is therefore an important "business tool" (Forcier 1994: 140) for industry. In this case, it did not bring immediate relief, yet it still served the purpose to put into doubt the soundness of regulatory assessment in the hope of re-establishing trust.

Finally, the plastics industry has also sought to set the regulatory agenda and to shape policy discussions. The voluntary commitments are not only used as instruments to pre-empt and prevent regulation but also to set the themes for future policy developments. Take the example of Plastics 2030 where industry explicitly asks for regulatory support to ban landfill of recyclable post-consumer waste to secure separate collection of packaging waste and to remove regulatory obstacles for recycling (PlasticsEurope 2018d: 16). The latter, industry specifies, requires alignment of the EU's chemical, waste and product regulation. The Commission's 2018 non-legislative communication on the interface between chemical, product and waste legislation does indeed refer to examples from PVC recycling on multiple occasions, namely when it comes to regulating legacy substances, the end-of-waste definition and the classification of hazardous substances (European Commission 2018d: 4, 5, 6). From an industry perspective, regulation under the Circular Economy package should "give certainty to the industry and investors to boost recycling" (General Manager of VinylPlus 2016). From an ENGO side, it has been argued that the European Commission's Plastics Strategy was industry-driven and actually serves their interests. In any case, from an environmentalist perspective circularity would require to "take PVC out" and not to facilitate its recycling (Interview ENGO 2017; Interview EP 2017). The ban on single-use plastic products, as envisaged with the introduction of the single-use plastics directive, is the first visible step taken in a direction that hurts the European plastics industry's reputation irrespective of its actual share in sales of the type of product banned. Accordingly, PlasticsEurope has been critical about the proposed bans:

> We [...] urge the European Commission to avoid shortcuts – plastic product bans are not the solution and will not achieve the structural change needed to build the foundation for a sustainable and resource efficient economy; as alternative products may not be more sustainable. (PlasticsEurope 2018b)

While the "traditional" industry branches—i.e. the majority of firms relying on fossil fuels in their production—thus oppose the "R" for refuse in the Commission's approach to circularity, the producers of bioplastics have yet other concerns with regard to the ban. In their view, the decision "fails to acknowledge the potential of biodegradable plastics", which is why they urged policymakers to "clearly define the difference between oxo-degradable and biodegradable plastics" (EUBP 2018b). The example illustrates how industry sectors and, within sectors, industry branches compete for regulatory support from policymakers. They engage in this battle by using their specialised knowledge as experts in production and recycling processes, in some instances also acting as innovators when developing new recycling procedures or new types of materials. Further, they proactively engage with the dominant policy discourses such as circular and bioeconomy in order to make legitimate claims about their sustainability record and, ultimately, to acquire authority in the regulatory process.

References

#breakfreefromplastic. (2018) *Break Free from Plastic Global Movement.* Available at: https://www.breakfreefromplastic.org/about/ (accessed 4.8.2018).
AEA Technology. (2000) *Economic Evaluation of PVC Waste Management.* A Report Produced for European Commission Environmental Directorate. Oxfordshire: AEA Technology.

Anderson A. (2010) Communicating Chemical Risks: Beyond the Risk Society. In: Eriksson J, Gilek M and Rudén C (eds) *Regulating Chemical Risks: European and Global Challenges*. Dordrecht: Springer, 29–44.

Anderson AG. (2014) *Media, Environment and the Network Society*. Houndmills, Basingstoke: Palgrave Macmillan.

ARGUS. (2000) *The Behaviour of PVC in Landfill*. Final Report February 2000. Brussels: European Commission DGXI.E.3.

Basbanes NA. (2013) *On Paper: The Everything of Its Two-Thousand-Year History*. New York: Knopf Doubleday Publishing Group.

Bauer MW and Knill C. (2012) Understanding Policy Dismantling: An Analytical Framework. In: Bauer MW, Jordan A, Green-Pederson C, et al. (eds) *Dismantling Public Policy: Preferences, Strategies, and Effects*. Oxford: Oxford University Press, 30–51.

bio by Deloitte. (2014) *Technical Assistance Related to the Review of REACH with Regard to the Registration Requirements on Polymer*. Final Report Prepared for the European Commission (DG ENV), in collaboration with PIEP. Brussels: European Commission.

Blomsma F and Brennan G. (2017) The Emergence of Circular Economy: A New Framing Around Prolonging Resource Productivity. *Journal of Industrial Ecology* 21(3): 603–614.

Borrello et al. (2016) The Seven Challenges for Transitioning into a Bio-based Circular Economy in the Agri-food Sector. *Recent Patents on Food, Nutrition & Agriculture* 8(1): 39–47.

Bourguignon D. (2015) *Understanding Waste Streams. Treatment of Specific Waste*. Briefing July 2015. PE 564.398. Brussels: EPRS European Parliamentary Research Service. Available at: http://www.europarl.europa.eu/EPRS/EPRS-Briefing-564398-Understanding-waste-streams-FINAL.pdf (accessed 18.3.2019).

Business Wire. (2017) Corrugated Box Market in Europe to Grow at a CAGR of 6.2% by 2021: Key Players are DS Smith, Georgia-Pacific, International Paper, Mondi, Smurfit Kappa & WestRock—Research and Markets. *Business Wire*: 22.8.2017.

Carus M and Dammer L. (2018) *The "Circular Bioeconomy"—Concepts, Opportunities and Limitations*. Hürth: nova-Institute Institute for Ecology and Innovation.

CEPI. (2005) *Sustainable Forest Management*. Position Paper: 1.3.2015. Available at: http://www.cepi.org/position-paper/sustainable-forest-management (accessed 18.3.2019).

CEPI. (2010) *Annual Statistics 2009*. European Pulp and Paper Industry. Brussels: Confederation of European Paper Industry. Available at: http://www.cepi.org/system/files/public/documents/publications/statistics/Annual%20Statistics%202009.pdf (accessed 18.3.2019).

CEPI. (2013) *End-of-Waste = End of Recycling?* Brussels: Confederation of European Paper Industry. Available at: http://www.cepi.org/press-release/end-waste-end-recycling (accessed 18.3.2019).

CEPI. (2017) *Key Statistics 2016. European Pulp and Paper Industry.* Brussels: Confederation of European Paper Industry. Available at: http://www.cepi.org/publication/key-statistics-2016 (accessed 18.3.2019).

CEPI. (2018a) *Key Statistics 2017. European Pulp and Paper Industry.* Brussels: Confederation of European Paper Industry. http://www.cepi.org/keystatistics2017 (accessed 18.3.2019).

CEPI. (2018b) *Latest Market Data Demonstrates Strong Performance for the European Pulp and Paper Industry in 2017.* Press Release: 16.07.2018. Brussels: Confederation of European Paper Industry. Available at: Latest Market Data Demonstrates Strong Performance for the European Pulp and Paper Industry in 2017 (accessed 18.3.2019).

CEPI, ETS, EuroCommerce, et al. (2016) Letter to the European Commission President Juncker and First Vice-President Timmermans: 19.12.2016. *Concerns on the Potential Discontinuation of EU Ecolabel Product Groups.* Brussels: Council of the European Paper Industry, European Tissue Symposium, The European Consumer Organisation, European Environmental Bureau. Available at: http://www.cepi.org/press-release/letter-european-commission-president-juncker-and-first-vice-president-timmermans (accessed 18.3.2019).

CHEM Trust. (2016) *Chemicals in Food Contact Materials: A Gap in the Internal Market, a Failure in Public Protection.* Policy Briefing. Brussels. Available at: https://chemtrust.org/food-contact (accessed 18.3.2019).

Chemisches und Veterinäruntersuchungsamt Stuttgart, Landesuntersuchungsanstalt für das Gesundheits- und Veterinärwesen Sachsen, Technische Universität Dresden, et al. (2012) *Abschlussbericht zur wissenschaftlichen Studie. Ausmaß der Migration unerwünschter Stoffe aus Verpackungsmaterialien aus Altpapier in Lebensmitteln.* Bonn: Bundesministerium für Ernährung, Landwirtschaft und Verbraucherschutz.

chemsec. (2018) *The International Chemical Secretariat.* Available at: http://chemsec.org/about-us/ (accessed 4.8.2018).

CITPA, CEPI, ACE, et al. (2017) *Letter to European Commission Vice President Timmermans on Plastics Strategy.* 16.11.2017. Brussels: CITPA et al. Available at: http://www.cepi.org/news/letter-european-commission-vice-president-timmermans-plastics-strategy (accessed 18.3.2019).

ClientEarth. (2017) *10 Years In: Time for ECHA to Disseminate Strategic Information to Empower Third Parties.* Brussels: ClientEarth. Available at: https://www.documents.clientearth.org/wp-content/uploads/library/2017-12-18-10-years-in-time-for-echa-to-disseminate-strategic-information-to-empower-third-parties-ce-en.pdf (accessed 18.3.2019).

ClientEarth. (2018) *Poland's Forests.* Available at: https://www.clientearth.org/polands-forests/ (accessed 4.8.2018).

ClientEarth and chemsec. (2018) *How to Find and Analyse Alternatives in the Authorisation Process*. London, Stockholm: ClientEarth, International Chemical Secretariat. Available at: https://chemsec.org/publication/authorisation-process,reach/how-to-find-and-analyse-alternatives-in-the-authorisation-process (accessed 8.3.2019).

ClientEarth, EEB, chemsec, et al. (2018) *Call for Evidence on Microplastics: Concerns and Recommendations*. London: ClientEarth.

Coe JM and Rogers D. (2012) *Marine Debris: Sources, Impacts, and Solutions*. New York: Springer.

Confino J. (2015) Future of Europe's Circular Economy Mired in Controversy. *The Guardian*: 3.2.2015.

Cooper T. (2008) Challenging the 'Refuse Revolution': War, Waste and the Rediscovery of Recycling, 1900–50. *Historical Research* 81(214): 710–731.

Cutler CA, Haufler V and Porter TP. (1999) *Private Authority and International Affairs*. Albany, NY: Suny Press.

D'Amato et al. (2017) Green, Circular, Bio Economy: A Comparative Analysis of Sustainability Avenues. *Journal of Cleaner Production* 168: 716–734.

Delreux T and Happaerts S. (2016) *Environmental Policy and Politics in the European Union*. London, New York: Palgrave Macmillan.

Directorate General Enterprise. (2000) *Recycling Forum*. Final Report. Brussels: European Commission.

Directorate General Environment. (2000) *Study on Minimum Quantity of Recycled Material in Certain Paper and Cardboard Applications*. Darmstadt: Technische Universität Darmstadt, Institut für Papierfabrikation.

Dogwood Alliance. (2017) *The Great American Stand: US Forsts and the Climate Emergency—Why the United States Needs an Aggressive Forest Protection Agenda Focused in Its Own Backyard*. Asheville: Dogwood Alliance.

ECHA. (2016) REACH 2018: *Registration Deadline for Low-Volume Chemicals*. Press Release REACH 2018: 1.4.2018. Helsinki: European Chemicals Agency. Available at: https://echa.europa.eu/de/press/press-material/pr-for-reach-2018 (accessed 18.3.2019).

ECHA. (2018) *Summary: The REACH 2018 Deadline*. ECHA REACH 2018 Registration Results. Helsinki: European Chemicals Agency.

ECPI. (2003) *US Product Safety Authority Agrees with Use of DINP in Toys*. ECPI Press Release. Brussels: European Council for Plasticisers and Intermediates.

ECPI. (2005) *EU Decision to Restrict Use of Phthalates in Toys Ignores EU Risk Assessment*. Brussels: European Council for Plasticisers and Intermediates.

EDC Free Europe. (2018) *The EDC-Free Europe Coalition of Public Interest Groups*. Available at: http://www.edc-free-europe.org/about-us/ (accessed 4.8.2018).

EEA. (2009) *Diverting Waste from Landfill. Effectiveness of Waste-Management Policies in the European Union*. Copenhagen: European Environment Agency.

EEB. (2018a) *The European Commission Steps Forward to Cut Down on Single-Use Plastics: But It's Just the Beginning.* EEB Press Release: 28.5.2018. Brussels: European Environmental Bureau. Available at: https://eeb.org/european-commission-steps-forward-to-cut-on-single-use-plastics-but-its-just-the-beginning (accessed 18.3.2019).

EEB. (2018b) *Towards an EU Product Policy Framework Contributing to the Circular Economy.* EEB proposals: 20.2.2019. Brussels: European Environmental Bureau.

EMF. (2012, 2013) *Towards a Circular Economy. Vol. 1. Economic and Business Rationale for an Accelerated Transition.* First published 25.1.2012. Cowes: Ellen MacArthur Foundation. Available at: https://www.ellenmacarthurfoundation.org/assets/downloads/publications/Ellen-MacArthur-Foundation-Towards-the-Circular-Economy-vol.1.pdf (accessed 20.3.2019).

EMF. (2014) *Towards the Circular Economy, Vol. 3: Accelerating the Scale-up across Global Supply Chains.* Cowes: Ellen MacArthur Foundation. Available at: https://www.ellenmacarthurfoundation.org/publications/towards-the-circular-economy-vol-3-accelerating-the-scale-up-across-global-supply-chains (accessed 20.3.2019).

EMF. (2016) *The New Plastics Economy: Rethinking the Future of Plastics.* Cowes: Ellen MacArthur Foundation.

EPN. (2015) *Letter to the Minister for Climate and the Environment, Government of Sweden.* Lochinver: Environmental Paper Network Europe.

EPN. (2017) *Annual Report 2016. Europe and Beyond.* Lochinver: European Environmental Paper Network.

EPN. (2018) *Environmental Paper Network.* Available at: http://environmental-paper.org/ (accessed 4.8.2018).

EPRC. (2018) *Monitoring Report 2016. European Declaration on Paper Recycling 2016–2020.* Brussels: European Paper Recycling Council.

ERPC. (2007) *European Declaration on Paper Recycling 2006–2010. Monitoring Report 2007.* Brussels: European Recovered Paper Council.

ERPC. (2016a) *European Declaration on Paper Recycling 2011–2015. Monitoring Report 2015.* Brussels: European Recovered Paper Council.

ERPC. (2016b) *European Paper Declaration 2016–2020.* Brussels: European Recovered Paper Council.

ERPC. (2016c) *Paper Recycling Chain Exceeds its Voluntary Commitment.* Press Release: 20.10.2016. Brussels: European Recovered Paper Council. Available at: http://www.cepi.org/press-release/paper-recycling-chain-exceeds-its-voluntary-commitment (accessed 18.3.2019).

ESPA. (2018) *European Plasticisers.* Available at: https://www.europeanplasticisers.eu/about-us (accessed 4.8.2018).

EUBP. (2018a) *Members & Membership.* Brussels: European Bioplastics. Available at: https://www.european-bioplastics.org/about-us/members-membership (accessed 7.1.2019).

EUBP. (2018b) *Single-Use Plastics Directive Fails to Acknowledge Potential of Biodegradable Plastics.* Position Paper: 23.1.2019. Brussels: European Bioplastics. Available at: https://www.european-bioplastics.org/single-use-plastics-directive-fails-to-acknowledge-potential-of-biodegradable-plastics (accessed 18.3.2019).

EuPC. (2018) *European Plastics Converters.* Available at: https://www.plastics-converters.eu (accessed 4.8.2018).

European Bioeconomy Alliance. (2018) *About Us.* Available at: https://bioeconomyalliance.eu/about-euba-bioeconomyalliance (accessed 7.1.2019).

European Commission. (1999) *Ban of Phthalates in Childcare Articles and Toys.* Press Release IP-99-829: 10.11.1999. Brussels: European Commission.

European Commission. (2000) *Green Paper. Environmental Issues of PVC.* COM (2000) 469 final. Brussels: Commission of the European Communities.

European Commission. (2012a) *Innovating for Sustainable Growth: A Bioeconomy for Europe.* Brussels: European Commission. Directorate General for Research and Innovation.

European Commission. (2014b) *Communication: Towards a Circular Economy: A Zero Waste Programme for Europe.* COM (2014) 398 final. Brussels: European Commission.

European Commission. (2015) *Closing the Loop: An EU Action Plan for the Circular Economy.* COM (2015) 614 final. Brussels: European Commission.

European Commission. (2017c) *Expert Group Report: Review of the EU Bioeconomy Strategy and Its Action Plan.* Brussels: European Commission. Directorate General for Research and Innovation.

European Commission. (2018a) *Circular Economy: Implementation of the Circular Economy Action Plan.* Available at: http://ec.europa.eu/environment/circular-economy/index_en.htm (accessed 7.8.2018).

European Commission. (2018b) *Circular Economy: New Rules Will Make EU the Global Front-Runner in Waste Management and Recycling.* Press Release IP-18-3846: 22.5.2018. Brussels: European Commission.

European Commission. (2018c) *Commission General Report on the Operation of REACH and Review of Certain Elements: Conclusions and Actions.* COM (2018) 116 final. Brussels: European Commission.

European Commission. (2018d) *Communication on the Implementation of the Circular Economy Package: Options to Address the Interface Between Chemical, Product and Waste Legislation.* COM (2018) 32 final. Brussels: European Commission.

European Commission. (2018e) *Communication: A European Strategy for Plastics in a Circular Economy.* COM (2018) 28 final. Brussels: European Commission.

European Commission. (2018f) *EU Ecolabel Paper Products.* Available at: http://ec.europa.eu/ecat/category/en/35/printed-paper (accessed 18.3.2019).

European Commission. (2018g) *Green Public Procurement.* Available at: http://ec.europa.eu/environment/gpp/eu_gpp_criteria_en.htm (accessed 25.6.2018).

European Commission. (2018h) *Single-Use Plastics: New EU Rules to Reduce Marine Litter.* Press Release IP-18-3927: 28.5.2018. Brussels: European Commission.

European Commission. (2018i) *A Sustainable Bioeconomy for Europe: Strengthening the Connection Between Economy, Society and the Environment.* Updated Bioeconomy Strategy. Brussels: European Commission. Directorate General for Research and Innovation.

European Council. (2018a) *Single-Use Plastics: Presidency Reaches Provisional Agreement with Parliament.* Press Release 818/18: 19.12.2018. Brussels: Council of the EU. Available at: https://www.consilium.europa.eu/de/press/press-releases/2018/12/19/single-use-plastics-presidency-reaches-provisional-agreement-with-parliament (accessed 18.3.2019).

European Council. (2018b) *Waste Management and Recycling: Council Adopts New Rules.* Press Release 259/18: 22.5.2018. Brussels: Council of the EU. Available at: https://www.consilium.europa.eu/en/press/press-releases/2018/05/22/waste-management-and-recycling-council-adopts-new-rules (accessed 18.3.2019).

European Parliament. (2015a) *Don't Allow Recycling of Plastics that Contain Toxic Phthalate DEHP, Warn MEPs.* Press Release: 25.11.2015. Brussels: European Parliament. Available at: http://www.europarl.europa.eu/news/en/press-room/20151120IPR03616/don-t-allow-recycling-of-plastics-that-contain-toxic-phthalate-dehp-warn-meps (accessed 18.3.2019).

European Parliament. (2019) *Parliament Seals Ban on Throwaway Plastics by 2021.* Press Release: 27.3.2019. Strasbourg: European Parliament.

Eurostat. (2018b) *Packaging Waste Statistics. Statistics Explained.* Brussels: Eurostat. Available at: https://ec.europa.eu/eurostat/statistics-explained/index.php/Packaging_waste_statistics (accessed 1.10.2018).

Eyes on the Forest. (2011) *The Truth Behind APP's Greenwash. Investigative Report Eyes on the Forest.* Eyes on the Forest: Riau, Sumatra.

Fenichell S. (1996) *Plastic: The Making of a Synthetic Century.* Grand Rapids, MI: Harper Business.

Fischer C. (2011) The Development and Achievements of EU Waste Policy. *Journal of Material Cycles and Waste Management* 13(1): 2–9.

Fischer F. (1990) *Technocracy and the Politics of Expertise.* Newbury Park: Sage.

Forcier JR. (1994) *Judicial Excess: The Political Economy of the American Legal System.* Lanham, New York, London: University Press of America.

Fuchs D. (2007) *Business Power in Global Governance.* London: Lynne Rienner.

Geissdoerfer M, Savaget P, Bocken NMP, et al. (2017) The Circular Economy: A New Sustainability Paradigm? *Journal of Cleaner Production* 143: 757–768.

German Environment Aid. (2018) *Deutsche Umwelthilfe befürwortet EU-Verbot von Plastikgeschirr und fordert verbindliche Einführung von Mehrwegalternativen.* Berlin: Deutsche Umwelthilfe.

Glachant M. (2003) Voluntary Agreements Under Endogenous Legislative Threats. *FEEM Working Paper No. 36.2003.*

Greenpeace. (2000) *Hazardous Chemicals in PVC Flooring.* A Report Compiled for He Healthy Flooring Network, Greenpeace Research Laboratories Technical Note No. 14/00. Exeter: Greenpeace Research Laboratories, Department of Biological Sciences, University of Exeter.

Greenpeace. (2001) *Toxic Chemicals in a Child's World: An Investigation into PVC Plastic Products.* Exeter: Greenpeace Research Laboratories, Department of Biological Sciences, University of Exeter.

Greenpeace. (2002) *Exposing the Dirty Path of PVC.* Amsterdam: Greenpeace International.

Greenpeace. (2003) *PVC-Free Future: A Review of Restrictions and PVC free Policies Worldwide: A List Compiled by Greenpeace International.* 9th ed. June 2003. Amsterdam: Greenpeace International.

Greenpeace. (2012) PVC ist übel. Die harte Wahrheit über weiches PVC. *Greenpeace Magazin* 2012(6), Hamburg: Greenpeace Deutschland.

Halfteck G. (2006) *A Theory of Legislative Threats.* Tel Aviv: Tel Aviv University.

Halfteck G. (2008) Legislative Threats. *Stanford Law Review* 61: 629–710.

Hansen S. (2018) *A Storm Is Raging Over the EU Plastics Packaging Sector.* January 2018. Utrecht: RaboResearch Food & Agribusiness.

HEAL. (2018) *HEAL's Response to the EU Commission's Proposed Roadmap 'Towards a More Comprehensive Framework on Endocrine Disruptors'.* Brussels: Health and Environment Alliance (HEAL).

Héritier A and Eckert S. (2008) New Modes of Governance in the Shadow of Hierarchy: Self-Regulation by Industry in Europe. *Journal of Public Policy* 28(1): 113–138.

Héritier A and Eckert S. (2009) Self-Regulation by Associations: A Collective Action Problem in Environmental Regulation. *Business and Politics* 11(1): 1–22.

Hontelez J. (2012) The Influence of Non-governmental Environmental Organisations on EU Policies. In: Wijen F, Zoeteman K and Pieters J (eds) *A Handbook of Globalisation and Environmental Policy, Second Edition: National Government Interventions in a Global Arena.* Cheltenham, Northampton: Edward Elgar, 663–683.

Hunter D. (1978) *Papermaking: The History and Technique of an Ancient Craft.* New York: Dover Publications.

Interview COM. (2005) Policy Officer Sustainable Production and Consumption, DG ENVI, Brussels, 23.11.2005.

Interview COM. (2006) Policy Officer Sustainable Production and Consumption, DG ENVI, Brussels, 23.3.2006.

Interview COM. (2017, 2019) Head of Unit, DG ENVI, Brussels, 10.4.2017 and 9.1.2019.

Interview Consumer Organisation. (2017) Project Officer, BEUC, Brussels, 12.4.2017.

Interview ENGO. (2006) Head of Office, Greenpeace European Unit, 22.2.2006, Brussels.

Interview ENGO. (2017) Executive Director, CHEM Trust, London, 17.7.2017.

Interview EP. (2005a) MEP, EPP-DE, IMCO, Brussels, 22.2.2006.

Interview EP. (2005b) MEP, PSE-IT, ENVI, Florence, 2.6.2006.

Interview EP. (2005c) Polic Officer Greens/EFA, Brussels, 23.11.2005.

Interview EP. (2017) Polic Officer Greens/EFA, Brussels, 12.4.2017.

Interview paper industry. (2006a) Managing Director, Recycling and EU Affairs Manager, GesPaRec, VDP, Bonn, 8.5.2006.

Interview paper industry. (2006b) Recycling Director, CEPI, Brussels, 5.5.2006.

Interview paper industry. (2006c) Deputy Secretary General, FEAD, Phone, 24.1.2006.

Interview paper industry. (2006d) EU Affairs Manager, Technical Director, FEFCO, Brussels, 5.5.2006.

Interview paper industry. (2006e) Managing Director, BVSE, ERPA, Bonn, 8.5.2006.

Interview paper industry. (2017) Deputy Director General, CEPI, Brussels, 11.4.2017.

Interview plastics industry. (2006a) Deputy Director, ECPI, Brussels, 23.2.2006.

Interview plastics industry. (2006b) Director Infraserv Höchst, Frankfurt/Main, 24.4.2006.

Interview plastics industry. (2019) Technical and Environmental Affairs Manager, Public Affairs Senior Manager, ECVM, Brussels, 11.1.2019.

Kirchherr J, Reike D and Hekkert M. (2017) Conceptualizing the Circular Economy: An Analysis of 114 Definitions. *Resources, Conservation and Recycling* 127: 221–232.

Krämer L. (2000) Thirty Years of EC Environmental Law: Perspectives and Prospectives. In: Somsen H (ed) *Yearbook of European Environmental Law: Volume 1.* Oxford: Oxford University Press, 155–182.

Lee JJ. (2018) How Did Sea Turtle Get a Straw Up Its Nose? *National Geographic:* 2.6.2018.

Lieder M and Rashid A. (2016) Towards Circular Economy Implementation: a Comprehensive Review in Context of Manufacturing Industry. *Journal of Cleaner Production* 115: 36–51.

Long T and Lörinczi L. (2009) Business Lobbying in the European Union. In: Coen D and Richardson J (eds) *Lobbying the European Union: Institutions, Actors, and Issues.* Oxford: Oxford University Press, 169–185.

Marine Litter Solutions. (2001) *Delcaration of the Global Plastics Associations for Solutions on Marine Litter.* Marine Litter Solutions. Available at: https://www.marinelittersolutions.com/about-us/joint-declaration (accessed 22.3.2019).

Marine Litter Solutions. (2018) *The Delcaration of the Global Plastics Associations for Solutions on Marine Litter. 4th Progress Report.* March 2018. Marine Litter Solutions.

Markus B, Hansen T and Klitkou A. (2016) What Is the Bioeconomy? A Review of the Literature. *Sustainability* 8(7): 691.

Maroulis N, Kettenis Pd, Bougas K, et al. (2016) *Cumulative Cost Assessment for the EU Chemical Industry.* Final Report. Brussels: Technopolis group, European Commission.

Matthews D. (2016) Sustainability Challenges in the Paper Industry. *ChEnected—Where Chemical Engineers Mix Up—Online Community:* 12.10.2016. Available at: https://www.aiche.org/chenected/2016/10/sustainability-challenges-paper-industry (accessed 22.3.2019).

McCormick K and Kautto N. (2013) The Bioeconomy in Europe: An Overview. *Sustainability* 5(6): 2589.

McCubbins MD and Schwartz T. (1984) Congressional Oversight Overlooked: Police Patrols and Fire Alarm. *American Journal of Political Science* 28(1): 165–179.

McGrath M. (2016) *EU Approves Use of Recycled Plastics Containing DEHP.* Reuters: 21.4.2016.

Murray A, Skene K and Haynes K. (2017) The Circular Economy: An Interdisciplinary Exploration of the Concept and Application in a Global Context. *Journal of Business Ethics* 140(3): 369–380.

OECD. (2004) *Biotechnology for Sustainable Growth and Development.* Paris: Organisation for Economic Cooperation and Development (accessed 6.3.2019).

Oziel C. (2017) *PlasticsEurope Files Second Case Against Echa Over BPA. Latest Action Focuses on Substance's Candidate List Entry as EDC.* ChemicalWatch: 16.11.2017. Available at: https://chemicalwatch.com/61101/plasticseurope-files-second-case-against-echa-over-bpa (accessed 23.6.2018).

Patermann C and Aguilar A. (2018) The Origins of the Bioeconomy in the European Union. *New Biotechnology* 40: 20–24.

PE Europe, IKP Universität Stuttgart, IPU, et al. (2004) *Life Cycle Assessment of PVC and of Principal Competing Materials.* Brussels: European Commission.

Persson T. (2007) Democratizing European Chemicals Policy: Do Consultations Favour Civil Society Participation? *Journal of Civil Society* 3(3): 223–238.

Pesendorfer D. (2006) EU Environmental Policy Under Pressure: Chemicals Policy Change Between Antagonistic Goals? *Environmental Politics* 15(1): 95–114.

Pfeffer J. (1981) *Power in Organizations*. Marshfield, MA: Pitman Publishing.

PlasticsEurope. (2017) *Plastics: The Facts 2016. An Analysis of European Plastics Production, Demand and Waste Data*. Brussels, Wemmel: Association for Plastics Manufacturers, European Association of Plastics Recycling.

PlasticsEurope. (2018a) *Annual Review 2017–2018*. Brussels: PlasticsEurope.

PlasticsEurope. (2018b) *Industry Urges Commission to Avoid Shortcuts and to Focus on Improving Waste Management. PlasticsEurope Reacts on Directive on Single Use Plastics*. Brussels: PlasticsEurope, 29.5.2018.

PlasticsEurope. (2018c) *Membership*. Available at: https://www.plasticseurope.org/en/about-us/membership (accessed 4.08.2018).

PlasticsEurope. (2018d) *Plastics 2030. PlasticsEurope's Voluntary Committment to Increasing Circularity and Resource Efficiency*. Brussels: PlasticsEurope. Available at: https://www.plasticseurope.org/en/newsroom/press-releases/archive-press-releases-2018/plastics-2030-voluntary-commitment (accessed 22.3.2019).

PlasticsEurope. (2018e) *Plastics: The Facts 2017. An Analysis of European Plastics Production, Demand and Waste Data*. Brussels, Wemmel: Association for Plastics Manufacturers, European Association of Plastics Recycling.

Preuss O. (1997) PVC: Die Recycling-Lüge. *Greenpeace Magazin*: 1997(2). Hamburg: Greenpeace Deutschland.

PROGNOS. (2000) *Mechanical Recycling of PVC Wastes*. Brussels: European Commission DG XI.

PVC. (2018) *The PVC Industry*. Available at: http://www.pvc.org/en/p/pvc-industry (accessed 4.8.2018).

Rethink Plastic. (2018) *Rethink Plastic Alliance of Leading European NGOs*. Available at: http://www.rethinkplasticalliance.eu/ (accessed 4.8.2018).

RISI. (2015) *Global Paper and Board Production Hit Record Levels in 2014*. Boston: RISI, 17.12.2015.

Rivera León L, Bougas K, Zoboli E, et al. (2016) *An Assessment of the Cumulative Cost Impact of Specified EU Legislation and Policies on the EU Forest-Based Industries*. Final Report. Brussels: Technopolis Group, European Commission.

Sands P. (1990) European Community Environmental Law: Legislation, the European Court of Justice and Common-Interest Groups. *The Modern Law Review* 53(3): 685–698.

Simon F. (2016) PVC Boss: We Will Not Change Our Reputation in One Day. *Euractiv*: 16.9.2016.

Tamma P. (2018) China's Trash Ban Forces Europe to Confront Its Waste Problem. *Politico*: 21.8.2018.

Teffer P. (2018a) How France Escaped EU Legal Action Over Chemical Ban. *EU Observer.* 18.5.2018.

Teffer P. (2018b) Plastics Lobby in Court to Keep Toxic Item Off EU List. *EU Observer.* 12.3.2018.

TNO Nutrition and Food Research. (2001) *Migration of Phthalate Plasticisers from Soft PVC Toys and Childcare Articles.* Final Report. Brussels: DG Enterprise, European Commission.

Two Sides. (2017) *Print and Paper Myths and Facts.* Daventry, UK.

Two Sides. (2018) *Two Sides Forum from the Graphic Communications Supply Chain.* Available at: https://www.twosides.info/about/ (accessed 4.8.2018).

Vinyl 2010. (2001) *The Voluntary Commitment of the European PVC Industry.* Brussels: Vinyl 2010.

Vinyl 2010. (2007) *Vinyl 2010. Progress Report 2007.* Report on the Activities of the Previous Year. Brussels: Vinyl 2010.

Vinyl 2010. (2008) *Vinyl 2010. Progress Report 2008.* Report on the Activities of the Year 2007. Brussels: Vinyl 2010.

VinylPlus. (2011) *The Voluntary Commitment of the European PVC Industry.* Brussels: VinylPlus.

Vogel D. (2012) *The Politics of Precaution: Regulating Health, Safety and Environmental Risks in Europe and the United States.* Princeton: Princeton University Press.

Vogel D, Toffel M and Post D. (2012) Environmental Federalism in the European Union and the United States In: Wijen F, Zoeteman K and Pieters J (eds) *A Handbook of Globalisation and Environmental Policy, Second Edition: National Government Interventions in a Global Arena.* Cheltenham, Northampton: Edward Elgar, 321–361.

Weale A, Pridham G, Cini M, et al. (2000) *Environmental Governance in Europe: An Ever Closer Ecological Union?* Oxford: Oxford University Press.

WWF. (2007) *DETOX. Campaigning for Safer Chemicals.* Brussels: World Wildlife Fund for Nature.

CHAPTER 5

The Innovator:
Boosting Resource Efficiency

In this chapter, I discuss sectors in which innovation is crucial to provide for common goods. Producers of resource-efficient products have a key role as *innovators* in the transition to a green, resource efficient economy. I will conduct two industry case studies that look at the producers of home appliances as well as Information and Communication Technology (ITC) manufacturers. We have seen a massive technological upgrading with home appliances of households for over two centuries (Woersdorfer 2017), and in the last century with consumer electronics and computers (Chandler 2005). The substantive uptake on such energy-using devices has caused a dramatic increase in per capita energy consumption. Therefore, the energy saving potential has been targeted by regulatory measures. In addition, since these products typically contain hazardous substances, at their end-of-life these substances need to be taken care of. With rising awareness about the scarcity of valuable materials used in electrical and electronic products, broader aspects of resource efficiency increasingly become subject to product regulation. This widening policy focus poses inherent challenges in an innovative sector and raises the question about the adequate balance between binding, public regulation, voluntary industry initiatives and market drivers.

To address all these issues, the chapter is structured as follows. First, I will present the two industry branches, namely producers of home appliances and ICT products. Then, I will elaborate on EU-level activities of consumer protection and environmental groups, before envisaging regulatory measures on energy efficiency and the whole life cycle of these

S. Eckert, *Corporate Power and Regulation*,
International Series on Public Policy,
https://doi.org/10.1007/978-3-030-05463-2_5

product groups. In the second step, the regulatory power of innovators will be examined by looking at the role of industry sectors in the regulatory process and their (voluntary) activities.

EUROPEAN HOME APPLIANCE AND ICT INDUSTRIES

The resource efficiency of electrical and electronic equipment (EEE) constitutes a key component in a circular economy, as these product markets are vibrant with rapid replacement rates. The amount of energy used in EU households for lighting and appliances in 2016 accounted for 13.8% of total energy use (Eurostat 2018). Although 64.7% of the total amount used by EEE goes to heating, product-related energy consumption is still significant. While many devices have become more energy efficient, we use more devices more often. There is a direct rebound effect where increased usage is directly caused by lower usage cost, but there are also indirect rebound effects leading to an overall increase in energy consumption (Herring and Sorrell 2009; Sorrell 2009).

Another sustainability challenge associated with EEE is that the amounts of waste generated are already quite considerable, and the waste keeps growing. A key problem is that a massive share of waste escapes waste treatment. The European home appliance industry reports that, in 2017, 2.2 million tonnes were mixed with metal scraps, 0.75 tonnes were estimated to end in the waste bin, 3.3 million tonnes were reported by member states as collected and recycled, which leaves a gap of 3.2 million tonnes (APPLiA 2018a). For the ICT segment, ENGOs have calculated reuse and repair rates of below 5% out of the products placed on the market and e-waste collected, respectively: in 2014, 1.27 million tonnes of IT and telecommunications equipment were placed on the market, 621,210 tonnes of waste were collected, but only 28,000 tonnes of that waste were shipped for repair and reuse (DigitalEurope 2017a; ECOS et al. 2017).

The Home Appliance Industry

Producers of home appliances in Europe are organised in the association APPLiA, formerly known as CECED. APPLiA brings together national trade associations (25 in 2018) and also allows for direct firm membership (21 in 2018). The European home appliance association CECED was created back in 1958, opened its Brussels office in 1997, and in 2018 on the occasion of its 60th anniversary rebranded as APPLiA (2018b).

Direct members include large players, such as BSH (Bosch Hausgeräte, with brands such as Bosch, Siemens and Gaggenau), Dyson, Electrolux, Panasonic or Whirlpool, some of which are headquartered outside of the EU. The market has seen some consolidation over the last decades, with a few multinational players dominating market segments. The US-headquartered Whirlpool Corporation, for instance, has European headquarters in Italy and is the third largest appliance producer in Europe. Whirlpool acquired Bauknecht in 1991 (Industry Europe 2011). The inclusion of big multinational companies in both national and European associations has drastically changed the working culture inside the organisations (Interview home appliance industry 2018a, 2019a, b).

Other companies in the supply chain fall into at least three categories: firms that supply home appliance manufacturers with components; those that provide goods and services to final consumers; and business that recovers and recycles waste from EEEs. The second category includes construction firms installing home appliances, retailers selling domestic appliances to consumers directly, wholesale distributors selling them to retailers, as well as cleaning contractors, public sector bodies and other organisations that use domestic appliances in the delivery of commercial services (Europe Economics 2015: 4–5). The supply industry is affected by chemical regulation and Restriction of Hazardous Substances (RoHS), the retailers and wholesalers by labelling schemes as well as take-back obligations at the end-of-life of EEEs. In accordance with such regulatory requirements, there is a need for the home appliance industry to cooperate along the supply chain. In regard to suppliers, manufacturers have an interest in a full disclosure of information about the substances used in order to comply with requirements under Registration, Evaluation, Authorisation of Chemicals (REACH) and RoHS. In their dealings with retailers, there are issues concerning producer responsibility under waste from electrical and electronic equipment (WEEE). The share of WEEE that "disappears" from official waste streams poses enforcement problems, and manufacturers continue to emphasise that due to dispersed retail and wholesale patterns the producer responsibility principle does not go far enough. Finally, in regard to recyclers, it is the manufacturers who have an obligation to pass on information about the presence of materials and components in WEEE that require separate treatment.

The economic importance of the European home appliance industry is summarised in Fig. 5.1. In 2016, the home appliance industry had an annual turnover of 47.6 billion Euros in the EU and contributed 53 billion Euros both directly and indirectly to EU Gross Domestic Product (GPD). Direct employment amounted to 202,089 jobs, while

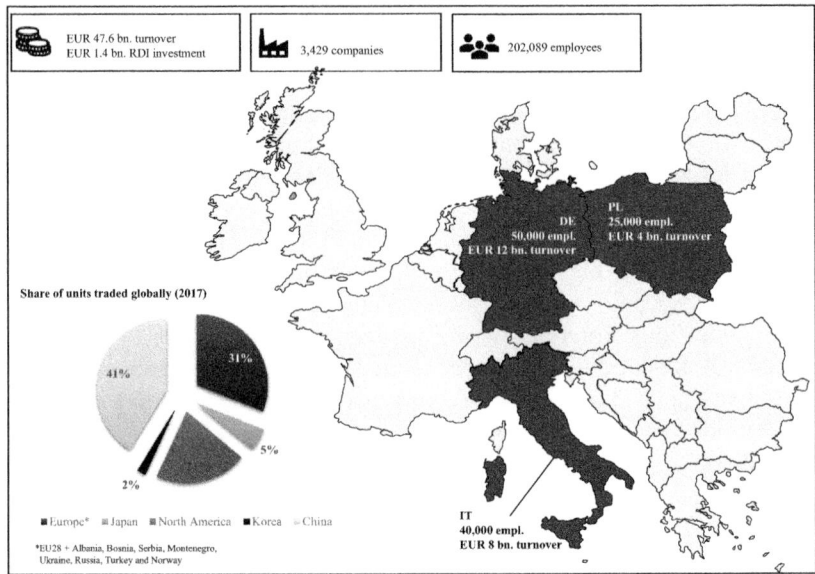

Fig. 5.1 Economic importance of European home appliance industry (*Source* 2016 and 2013 data (APPLiA 2018a; Europe Economics 2015: 1, 9, 11, 12), own figure)

total employment resulting from the presence of the sector is estimated to amount to approximately 889,192 jobs. The sector is comprised of 3429 companies in the EU and has invested 1.4 billion Euros in research and development activities (APPLiA 2018a). Inside the EU, the home appliance industry is most important in Germany, Italy and Poland. In 2013, the German home appliance industry comprised 50,000 employees and generated a turnover of above 12 billion Euros. In Italy, in the same year close to 40,000 employees worked in the sector, and a turnover of above 8 billion Euros was generated. Finally, in Poland, the industry was at a level of approximately 25,000 employees with a turnover of above 4 billion Euros (Europe Economics 2015: 1, 9, 11, 12). APPLiA membership also includes producers in Turkey, Switzerland and Norway. Amongst these non-EU members, Turkey is an increasingly important location for manufacturing, with around 40,000 employees and a turnover of 6 billion Euros in 2013 (Europe Economics 2015: 9, 12). In terms of global trade, in 2017, China held the largest share of units traded globally (41%), followed by Europe at 31%, North America at 21%, Japan at 5% and Korea at 2% (for Europe, these shares include non-EU countries and also Turkey).

The European home appliance industry has been under significant economic pressure over the last decade. In the aftermath of the economic and financial crisis turnover declined from around 52 billion Euros in 2008 to 44 billion Euros in 2012, with a recovery to 48 billion Euros in 2013 and 47.6 billion Euros in 2017; similarly, employment has been in decline, from 231,000 jobs in 2009 to 211,000 in 2012 and 202,000 in 2017 (Europe Economics 2015: 1; APPLiA 2018a).

The ICT Industry

Producers of consumer electronics in Europe are organised inside DigitalEurope. DigitalEurope represents a wide range of companies using and producing digital technologies. In 2018, DigitalEurope is comprised of 64 corporate direct members and 39 national trade associations from across Europe (DigitalEurope 2018). The predecessor organisation of DigitalEurope was the European Information and Communications Technology Association (EICTA). EICTA was created in 1999, merging several pre-existing sector associations in the information and telecommunications industry. One of these sector organisations was the European Association of Consumer Electronics Manufacturers (EACEM) which joined EICTA in 2001 (henceforward the associations' full name included consumer electronics technology in its title). Ten years after its creation, EICTA, in 2009, rebranded as DigitalEurope in order to reflect rapid technological innovation in its segment. The history of EICTA, EACEM (discussed by Knill 2001: 229–230) and DigitalEurope illustrates two aspects: first, the need to broaden the scope of associational structure as the boundaries between industry branches became increasingly blurred due to technological progress; and second, the need to allow for direct company membership in order to secure policy influence at the European level, thanks to a sufficient coverage of the entire industry. In the consumer electronics segment, there was initially an organisational split between a home-grown association of national, European trade associations and a "Japanese" body (Electronic Industries' Association of Japan, EIAJ). To overcome this divide, EACEM therefore allowed for direct corporate membership, including Japan-based firms, as of 1996.

DigitalEurope, with its diverse membership that includes large, transnational market leaders, has a daunting task to act on behalf of its membership. The regulatory power of individual companies, especially where they dominate a market segment, is immense. Company members as well as national trade associations generate specific technical expertise in many regulatory areas and deal with complex and fast-evolving issues such as data protection. That said, DigitalEurope is quite active on environmental issues which are of interest in this chapter, monitor the association's regulatory developments and formulate industry positions on Ecodesign and Energy Labelling. The association also frequently aligns with the home appliance association APPLiA (formerly CECED) where industries share similar interests, given that both are essentially targeted by the same type of EU regulation (Interview ICT industry 2017, Interview home appliance industry 2019a). The regulatory issues for ICT manufacturers in their value chain are similar to those of the home appliance industry—requirements under REACH and RoHS are relevant to the manufacturing and recycling phase, labelling and Ecodesign for the use phase. What differs, however, is the pace of technological change as well as the nature of the goods provided and regulated. ICT products typically hold hardware and software components, and these are not necessarily provided by the same company.

The ICT industry is of great economic importance across the EU, as illustrated by Fig. 5.2. The sector generated a 581 billion Euros of value added in 2015, with 5.8 million employees, and invested 30 billion Euros in research and development (R&D) activities. The ICT sector represented 3.9% of GDP in 2015, out of which 3.6% was generated by the ICT services sector, compared to only 0.3% by the manufacturing sector. The ICT manufacturing industry amounted to 635,000 employees and generated a value added of 0.5 billion Euros (JRC 2018). The biggest ICT nations in Europe are the UK and Germany, followed by France, Italy, Spain, Poland, the Netherlands and Romania (see Fig. 5.3). In relative size (value added as a share of GDP), the ICT sector is most important in Ireland, Malta, Luxembourg, Sweden and Romania with rates of above 5% (JRC 2018: 9).

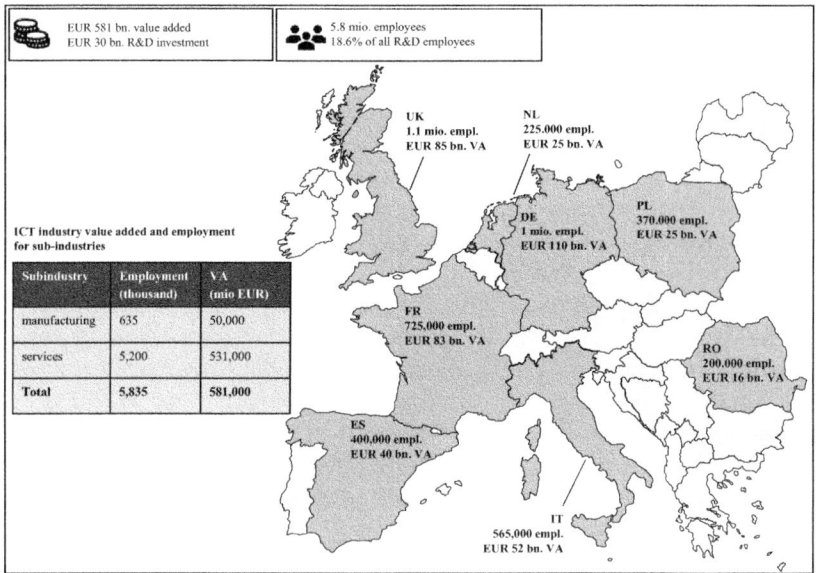

Fig. 5.2 Economic importance of European ICT industry (*Source* 2015 data (JRC 2018), own figure; VA: value added)

The European ICT sector was struck to differing extents by the economic crisis. The ICT manufacturing subsector experienced a sharp decline in terms of both value added and business expenditure on R&D. Between 1995 and 2017 employment halved in the manufacturing sector which continues to be affected by a slowdown since 2013. By contrast, employment and R&D have experienced rapid growth in the ICT services subsector (JRC 2018: 7–8). Overall, we can expect that the ICT branch and its association wield significant economic power and thus political influence in the post-crisis European policy agenda, which puts growth and jobs first (European Commission 2010, 2015c) and pursues an ambitious Digital Single Market strategy (European Commission 2015b).

Consumer Protection and Environmental Groups

If you talk to the industry, every time you ask them what made them shift or made them innovate, they will talk about: it is requirements or a shift in requirements - health, safety, or environmental requirements. (Interview ENGO 2006)

NGO activism targeting the home appliance and ICT industries is not as pronounced as in the area of the chemical and plastics industries discussed in Chapter 4, yet some of the environmental and consumer concerns raised for the latter are also relevant to brown and white goods, especially where their end-of-life is concerned. There are issues surrounding sustainable production and consumption in terms of resource efficiency more broadly speaking, including energy use. In particular, these goods typically contain not only valuable raw materials but also hazardous chemicals that pose a danger to human health and the environment where they leak (e.g. in the waste phase). And the manufacturing industry is a heavy user of plastics. The product replacement rates of electrical and electronic products are highly problematic from a resource efficiency viewpoint. Finally, appropriate management of WEEE is of growing concern around the globe, since considerable shares of electronic waste "disappear" from official waste streams in Europe to reappear elsewhere in the world, especially in Asia and Africa. Once China introduced restrictions and bans in January 2018, Thailand has become the largest dumpsite for electronic waste (Senet 2018).

All of these issues are covered by ENGOs and consumer organisations through insider lobbying and outsider lobbying. As the above quote indicates, ENGOs frame binding requirements and innovation as a win-win setting and not as a trade-off. In their view, industry needs to be exposed to regulatory pressure in order to engage in innovation. With respect to the wider circular economy ambition, this line of argumentation would go that if resources become ever more scarce and expensive it pays off to change to resource-efficient practices sooner rather than later. The European Consumer Organisation (BEUC) and the European Association for the Coordination of Consumer Representation in Standardisation (ANEC) are particularly active on the Ecodesign, Energy Labelling and the Ecolabel dossiers. BEUC provides and collects comments from consumer organisations on related measures (BEUC 2018). Both organisations have repeatedly voiced their concern about priority being given to voluntary agreements (VAs) under the Ecodesign scheme and have called for this option to be deleted altogether (ANEC and BEUC 2013). Further, they have urged policymakers to rescale the Energy Labelling Scheme in order to secure the effectiveness of the instrument as an incentive to produce top-class products for industry and as a visible pull-factor for consumers towards the most energy-efficient products (ANEC and BEUC 2015).

On the side of ENGOs, the European Environmental Bureau (EEB) generates significant expertise on resource efficiency issues, namely on circular economy, waste prevention, product policy and EU Ecolabel (EEB 2018c). For example, the EEB has provided detailed policy input on the way forward for product policy (EEB 2018d) and on the contribution of Ecodesign and Energy Labelling for a circular economy (EEB 2018a). The ENGOs' standardisation branch, the European Environmental Citizens Organisation (ECOS) created in 2001, mirrors ANEC as the body on the consumers' side. ECOS is a partner organisation of CEN and CENELEC, and a member of ETSI. The organisation generates standardisation counter-expertise on Ecodesign and Energy Labelling, with a special focus on compliance testing, product regulation and market surveillance (ECOS 2018, Interview ENGO 2019). More on the side of outsider lobbying and awareness raising, Greenpeace seeks to create reputational pressure for industry to go green by publishing an annual "Green Electronics Guide" which gives consumers advice about the sustainability features of distinct product categories such as smartphones or notebooks, and engages in visible naming and shaming (Greenpeace 2018).

NGOs frequently team up to effectively campaign for change, EU-wide and internationally. Typically, ENGOs and their respective standardisation branches—the EEB and ECOS, BEUC and ANEC—publish common positions. In October 2016, for instance, the four NGOs urged European Commission President Juncker to abstain from deregulatory activities on Ecodesign and the Ecolabel (EEB et al. 2016). In terms of issues addressed by NGO coalitions, we can see how the focus has moved from energy efficiency to broader issues of resource efficiency. For example, the EEB-lead campaign "Coolproducts. Green NGOs campaigning for energy efficient products" (coolproducts 2018a), launched in 2011, clearly had an energy efficiency focus. The "Make Resources Count" campaign, launched in 2016 by the EEB, has a broader focus along the life cycle of products (make resources count 2018). Another campaign with an end-of-life focus is the "zero waste network", which since 2011 has brought together ENGOs, consumer organisations and business that subscribe to the goal to eliminating waste in our society and relies on a decentralised structure with member-state-based zero-waste organisations (zerowasteeurope 2018). ENGOs also cooperate with business branches that advocate the circular economy transformation, such as the US-based Internet company IFIXIT (IFIXIT 2018) which provides a platform for diffusing information about the repair and reuse of electronic devices, or the association "rreuse" which brings together social enterprises active in reuse, repair and recycling (rreuse 2018). These alliances seek to generate counter-expertise to powerful industry branches such as the ICT industry. In December 2017, for instance, an NGO and stakeholder alliance responded to Digital Europe's circular economy proposals (ECOS et al. 2017).

Regulating Home Appliances and Consumer Electronics

I am convinced that voluntary agreements are an important instrument under the framework of IPP [Integrated Product Policy]. As a matter of fact, dealing with products has proved to be more difficult than dealing with industry pollution, where filters can be used, or other point-sources of environmental impact. The products that we have today didn't exist 5 or 10 years ago. You have products with a very short (market) life cycle and with more diffuse environmental impacts. They are really changing every now and then, and when you complete the (environmental) life cycle analysis for the product, the product doesn't look like it did in the past. (Interview COM 2006a)

The interview quote highlights the challenges involved in product regulation, especially for market segments with high degrees of technological innovation. The interviewee back in 2006 was of the opinion that VAs will constitute an important policy tool for regulating this sector. This assessment will be subject to empirical scrutiny in this chapter.

European product policy on white and brown goods has so far predominantly focused on the energy savings in the use phase but is slowly moving towards a circular approach targeting other stages along the life cycle. Product-specific regulatory measures are adopted under the Ecodesign and the Energy Labelling Framework Directives and combine push- and pull-factors: Ecodesign pushes producers to design and manufacture more energy (and resource)—efficient products. Energy Labelling pulls the consumer towards better products. Ecodesign and Energy Labelling are powerful harmonisation tools, as they are binding and restrict access to the Internal Market (Henningsen 2011: 133). Importantly, the Ecodesign gives priority to

VAs over mandatory regulation as an implementing measure. Further, producers can apply for the Ecolabel, which often sets more ambitious and comprehensive requirements. It thus pushes producers to voluntarily strive for more sustainability and signals the most environmentally friendly products to consumers (Haucke et al. 2019). Another policy instrument is Green Public Procurement (GPP) which seeks to pull public authorities to purchase environmentally friendly products. All of these instruments, binding and voluntary, are seen as complementary elements in the Integrated Product Policy (IPP) for energy using devices, as highlighted in the above interview quote (Interviews COM 2006a, 2017b). Finally, environmental and health issues at the end-of-life stage of EEEs are addressed by the WEEE directive and the RoHS in the EEE directive. In the subsequent sections, I will present how these measures regulate home appliances and consumer electronics throughout their life cycle. Figure 5.3 gives a timeline of European product regulation and industry initiatives over the last two decades.

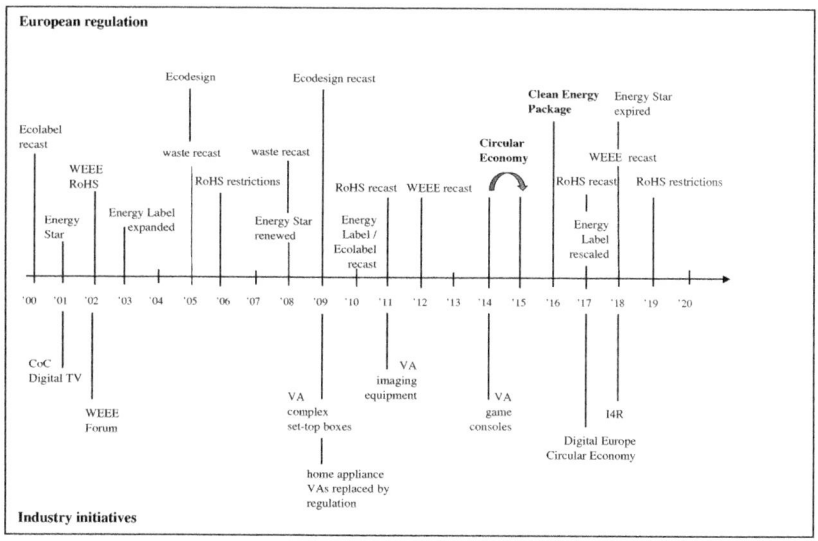

Fig. 5.3 Timeline of European product regulation and industry initiatives (*Source* Author's illustration)

European product policy had a strong focus on energy efficiency from the outset and started out by targeting home appliance products. The first measure was the 1992 Council Directive (92/75/EEC) on energy consumption labelling for this product segment. In 2003, the Energy Label was expanded to allow for a differentiation within the A-energy class for refrigerators—i.e. this was the first product group to be marketed with A+ labels (ANEC and BEUC 2015). In 2005, the Ecodesign directive (2005/32/EC) was adopted. In substantive terms, its focus was on energy-using products (EuPs), mostly home appliances, which is why the measure was frequently called the EuP directive (Interview COM 2006b). In procedural terms, it was a "new approach directive" seeking to reduce the regulatory burden and giving priority to new policy instruments, in this case VAs (Interview COM 2006a). From the outset, the Commission proposal for the 2005 directive gave priority to self-regulatory over binding regulatory measures (Tanasescu 2009: 152). For a VA to be accepted, the EuP directive stipulated it needed to be discussed at the EuP Consultation Forum and during implementation would be subject to scrutiny and monitoring through Comitology. Further, the Commission could always envisage regulation where a VA was not working (Interview COM 2006c). According to ENGO observers (Interview ENGO 2006), the initial ambition of Ecodesign was more comprehensive, however, namely to adopt a life cycle approach and include the waste phase and recycling. Yet throughout the policy formulation process, which took into account stakeholder input across the spectrum (discussed by Tanasescu 2009: 156–162), the focus of the directive had shifted towards energy-related aspects. In any case, the Ecodesign framework started out to harvest the "low-hanging fruit" (Interview ministry 2017) with its focus on product groups where the energy saving potential was particularly high. The Ecodesign recast adopted in 2009 (directive 2009/125/EC) came along with a recast of the Energy Labelling Directive (directive 2010/30/EU). In the post-crisis and pro-growth policy environment, strong emphasis was placed on reducing the regulatory burden for industry. This might explain that VAs were maintained as an implementing instrument alongside binding regulations, although evidence about their effectiveness was mixed (Interview COM 2017a; mure and Fraunhofer 2014b, e). An important difference between the VA procedure and the Ecodesign implementing acts procedure is that for VAs the Parliament and the Council do not hold a right of scrutiny, while for the adoption of implementing acts they do. In fact, the EuP directive was one of the first legislative acts which followed the new regulatory procedure with EP scrutiny (Tanasescu 2009: 166). The Commission did, however, not include a recast of the Ecodesign directive in its Circular Economy proposals put forward since 2014. From a policy dismantling standpoint, this could be considered as a case of "dismantling by default"—that is, there are no dismantling decision and low visibility, yet a lack of adjusting existing policies to changing conditions (Bauer and Knill 2012: 43). Instead, the Commission committed itself to shift the focus of regulatory measures from the realisation of energy efficiency towards resource efficiency goals, which it deems is possible under the existing scheme (European Commission 2016c; Interview COM 2017b). It also issued, in 2016, guidelines for self-regulation measures under Ecodesign (European Commission 2016b). The Energy Labelling Directive has been replaced by a new Energy Labelling Regulation (regulation (EU) 2017/1369) in 2017, launching a process of rescaling the energy efficiency classes.

As a framework directive, Ecodesign only sets broad targets and lays down the procedures to be followed to adopt product-specific measures. Product-related regulatory requirements are, therefore, defined outside the legislative arena. According to the directive, product groups shall be identified in accordance with a set of criteria including the environmental benefits, market shares, and potential for improvement while not entailing excessive costs. These product groups are identified by means of multi-annual Ecodesign working plans. Energy Labelling complements the Ecodesign framework, seeking to signal energy-efficient products to consumers. The first Energy Labelling Directive, adopted in 1992, was entirely focusing on home appliances. The scheme introduced mandatory labelling, assessing energy performance in categories from A to G in line with decreasing energy performance. The framework, however, soon proved ineffective, with most products falling into the highest energy efficiency class and the category being overcrowded. Therefore, a differentiation inside the highest category (A+, A++, etc.) was introduced, first for refrigerators and freezers in 2003, and then for further product groups with a recast in 2010 (directive 2010/30/EU). Rescaling adopted in 2017 (regulation 2017/1369/EU), in contrast, goes back to the initial A-G classification. To avoid that a rescaling will be needed in the coming years, the best-performing classes ought to remain empty in an initial phase and shall only be filled with subsequent energy efficiency improvements. The rescaling will take place according to a phased process: regulations for washing machines, refrigerators and freezers as well as dishwashers are the first to be targeted, with the goal to introduce the new A-G labelling by 2020. Drying tumblers, stoves and vacuum cleaners will only be rescaled to the new system by 2024 or later. Finally, the new directive introduces an online database providing Ecodesign information to consumers, so that they have easy access to information for a whole product segment on the market.

The voluntary Ecolabel complements the binding measures under Ecodesign and the Energy Label. The EU-wide label is a voluntary scheme introduced in 1992 and revised in 2000 and 2010. The green brand gives visibility to the top 10–20% of the best-performing products. Ecolabel is a third-party certified international standard (Type I ISO 14024). The product groups covered include electronic equipment, namely imaging equipment, personal notebooks, tablet computers and televisions. In the context of its Regulatory Fitness and Performance (REFIT) programme, in 2016 the European Commission considered discontinuing the label for certain products groups, and there were rumours that the label could be abolished altogether. In June 2017, responding to pressure from member states, industry and NGOs (BEUC 2017), the Commission decided to maintain the Ecolabel and announced it would seek to strengthen its application (European Commission 2018b).

Further, requirements and recommendations for GPP at the European level are meant to enhance the effectiveness of the Ecodesign, Energy Labelling and Ecolabel instruments. The Energy Labelling directive (Article 9 of directive 2010/30/EU) stipulated that public authorities shall "endeavour to procure only such products which comply with the criteria of having the highest performance levels and belonging to the highest energy efficiency class", a provision which is no longer included in the 2017 recast. Further, the Public Procurement directive (directive 2014/24/EU, consideration 75) points out that contracting parties should be able to refer to labels such as the EU Ecolabel. The European Commission is regularly publishing a handbook that gives guidance on GPP (European Commission 2016a) and sets voluntary EU GPP criteria for certain product groups. With respect to the industry branches studied in this chapter, these include computer and monitors (published in 2016) and imaging equipment (published in 2014, European Commission 2018h). One of the Commission experts considered GPP to be an effective pull-factor for public purchasers, especially in areas where it is difficult to incentivise and "push" the manufacturers to abide to mandatory or voluntary rules (Interview COM 2017a).

In their implementation, Ecodesign and labelling measures are linked to standardisation procedures. The Commission can direct standardisation requests to the European standardisation organisations in support of regulation. In the run-up to the adoption of the 2005 Ecodesign framework directive, the European Commission issued a standardisation mandate to CEN, CENELEC and ETSI on the programming of standardisation work in the field of Ecodesign and EuPs already in 2004 (M 341—EN, 7 January 2004). In 2015, it requested the European Committee for Electrotechnical Standardisation (CENELEC) to revise harmonised standards for vacuum cleaners (M/540, consultation date 20 July 2015). Typically, such standardisation bodies do not put particular emphasis on stakeholder consultation when drafting their reports and input (Tanasescu 2009: 178). Standardisation lends additional, even international regulatory influence (Bach and Newman 2007). In fact, European standardisation bodies such as CENELEC frequently coordinate their work with respective international bodies, in this case the International Electrotechnical Commission (IEC). It is a common practice that the two organisations mutually endorse their decisions (Büthe and Mattli 2011: 157–158). Another means of international cooperation were the coordination of energy labelling programmes with the USA. An agreement with the US government was concluded in 2001 and renewed twice, which formed the basis for the EU Energy Star scheme. Energy Star is a voluntary scheme that aims to endorse the best-performing products, typically around 20% of the market. The collaboration agreement between the USA and the EU covered ICT product groups, namely computers, displays, imaging equipment, enterprise servers and power supplies. On the European side, it was laid down in regulation 106/2008/EC on the energy efficiency labelling of office equipment. As Energy Star faces an uncertain future under the Trump administration in the USA (Cama 2018), the agreement with the EU expired in February 2018 (European Commission 2018c).

So far, energy savings achieved through product policy are the success story of the EU's energy efficiency policy, which lags behind its potential in many other areas such as housing or transport. Negotiations to agree on a recast of the horizontal energy efficiency directive (2012/27/EU) were completed in December 2018 with the adoption of a new directive (directive 2018/2002). The beneficial effect of the existing scheme is estimated at a level of 490 Euros of energy savings for each household in Europe by 2020, and product-related energy savings contribute about 50% to achieving the EU's energy efficiency goals (EEB 2018b). Figure 5.4 displays the evolution of energy consumption for distinct product groups between 1990 and 2014. The downwards trend is tangible for washing machines and refrigerators, whereas energy consumption has increased for televisions between 2006 and 2012. Energy savings through product standards will continue to contribute to the EU's "efficiency first" policy under the Clean Energy package and its target of achieving 30% energy savings by 2030 (Commission 2016: 4).

The end-of-life of EEE is covered by specific legislative measures, namely the WEEE (directive 2002/96/EC) and the RoHS, both introduced in 2002. The waste from EEE directive takes a producer responsibility approach and imposed the introduction of collection schemes of WEEE free of charge for consumers. In view of a fast-increasing waste stream, the WEEE directive was revised in 2012 (directive 2012/19/EU). This 2012 recast set a collection target of products sold at 45 and 65%, to be achieved by 2016 and 2019, respectively. Further, it was envisaged to extend WEEE to all categories of electronic waste as of 2018. The recast

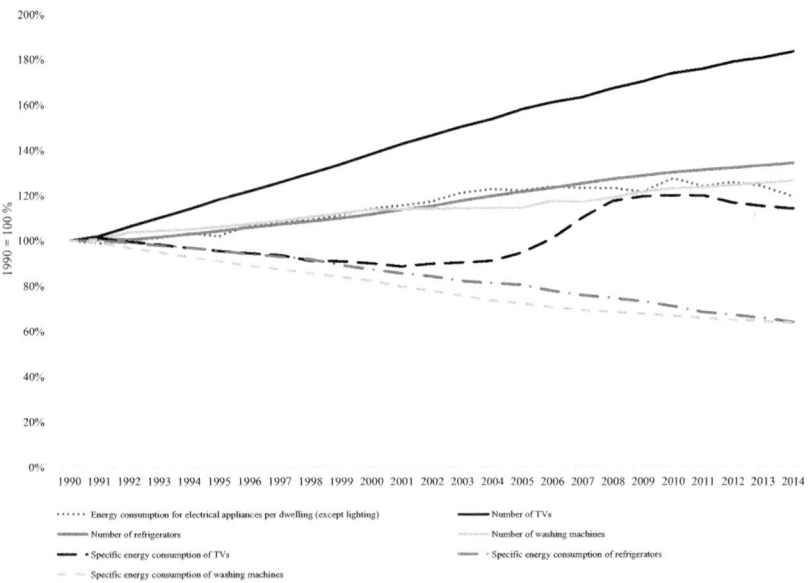

Fig. 5.4 Product-related energy consumption 1990–2014 (*Source* Own figure based on data from European Environmental Agency [EEA 2016])

that was adopted in 2018 (directive 2018/849/EU) foresees another revision by the end of 2020. The RoHS directive was first introduced in 2002 and revised in 2006, 2011 and 2017 (directive 2017/2102/EU). In short, RoHS is a "mini-REACH" which regulates the presence of hazardous substances in EEEs. The directive that was adopted in 2002 covered home appliances, IT and consumer equipment, and required the substitution of lead, mercury, cadmium, hexavalent chromium and flame retardants by safer alternatives. Alongside REACH, RoHS has also contributed to a trans-Atlantic shift in regulatory stringency (Vogel 2012), as it banned these materials at a time when these were still permitted in the USA. The 2011 recast broadened the scope of the directive to all electronic equipment, cables and spare parts. Further, the 2011 recast aimed at reducing the administrative burden and brought RoHS in line with chemicals legislation under REACH. The list of banned substances was subject to ongoing revision, and in 2015 was amended to add four phthalates (DEHP, BBP, DBP and DIBP, Commission delegated directive 2015/863/EU), the use of which in EEE is going to be restricted from 2019 at a concentration of maximum 0.1% each. A 2017 recast clarifies the scope of the RoHS directive and specifies the criteria for exemption.

Table 5.1 displays how the two industry branches have been targeted under subsequent Ecodesign working plans. The rows enumerate the

Table 5.1 Ecodesign working plans (2005–2019)

Working Plan	Home appliance	ICT
2005–2008		
Product groups	Heating and water-heating equipment (boilers and water heaters only), domestic appliance	Office equipment in both the domestic and tertiary sectors, consumer electronics
2009–2011		
Product groups	Food preparing equipment, water-using equipment, refrigerating and freezing	Sound and imaging equipment, network, data processing and data storing equipment
2012–2014		
Product groups	Wine storage appliances	Enterprise servers, data storage and ancillary equipment
2016–2019		
Product groups	Electric kettles, hand dryers, high-pressure cleaners	*Separate track approach, possible inclusion:* Gateways (home network equipment), mobile/smartphones, base stations

Source Author's illustration

product groups that have been identified for each period. The time lag between the adoption of the working plans 2012–2014 and 2016–2019 was caused by negative media coverage about Brussels "red tape" in the run-up to the Brexit vote (ANEC and BEUC 2016; Barbière 2016). The product groups identified for the first three phases until 2014 included various devices in both product branches, whereas the last working plan for the period 2016–2019 announced a separate track for ICT products.

Table 5.2 displays how the two industry branches have been regulated under the Ecodesign directive, including Energy Labelling, Ecolabel

Table 5.2 Ecodesign and Energy Labelling measures (2005–2019)

Measures	Home appliance	ICT
Regulations		
Ecodesign	7 (refrigerators and freezers 2009, dishwashers 2010, washing machines 2010, tumble driers 2012, vacuum cleaners 2013, domestic ovens 2014, domestic cooking appliances 2014)	4 (single set-top boxes 2009, televisions 2009 and 2013, external power supplies 2009, computers and computer servers 2013)
Energy Label	6 (refrigerators and freezers 2010, dishwashers 2010, washing machines 2010, tumble driers 2012, vacuum cleaners 2013, domestic ovens 2014)	1 (televisions 2010)
VAs		
In force	None	3 (complex set-top boxes 2012, imaging equipment 2013, game consoles 2015)
Expired	3 (dishwasher 2004, washing machines 2008, refrigerators and freezers 2009)	1 (televisions, DVDs 2010)
Ecolabel		
Uptake	n.a.	1 (televisions 2009)
No uptake/*expired*	n.a.	2 (*imaging equipment 2013,* personal, notebook and tablet computers 2011)
GPP	n.a.	Imaging equipment (2014) Computers, monitors (2016)

Source Author's illustration

and Green Public Procurement (GPP) measures. The rows enumerate the regulations and the VAs adopted under Ecodesign, the uptake of the Ecolabel and the use of GPP. We can see that four VAs have been replaced by binding regulation, while all three VAs that are still in force apply to ICT products. Further, the Ecolabel scheme is in use for one single product group (televisions), and public procurement applies to two categories of ICT products.

Innovator or Top Dog?

The innovator, as discussed in Chapter 2, has strong arguments against regulation especially in areas of radical technological change: formulating, agreeing on and implementing rules appears too time-consuming, results in output that does no longer fulfil its initially envisaged goals, and at worst works against market-driven progress and innovation. Industry, however, also has arguments for regulation and standards: namely, rules that protect innovative features or make them mandatory, thus securing an innovator's market share or regulating access to markets. There is therefore a challenge for regulators to find the right balance of providing regulatory certainty and clarity in fast-moving markets, yet without inhibiting innovation or protecting market power. In the following sections, I will first take stock of the measures taken under the Ecodesign framework (as summarised in Tables 5.1 and 5.2) and then consider the ways in which corporate actors intervene in the regulatory process in the two sectors.

The Home Appliance Industry: Binding Regulation!

We started with voluntary agreements because, after introduction of the label, manufacturers believed that voluntary agreements would have been the best way to provide further energy saving avoiding mandatory requirements […] But at some point, this didn't work anymore, because several market actors, not being part of the voluntary agreement, would still sell less efficient and cheaper products. The presence of less efficient and cheaper products was not considered acceptable by manufacturer's part of the agreements, committed to specific minimum requirements. Manufacturer's part of the agreement would risk losing part of the market because of other market actors supplying the products that were no longer supplied by manufacturers that obeyed the agreement. So a bit more than ten years ago, we decided that we would stop. We made a press conference where we said that our industry supported mandatory minimum standards that would be respected by all market actors. The possibility to create a level playing field was among the main reasons for abandoning voluntary measures. (Interview home appliance industry 2019a)

The main pattern that emerges from the types of measures adopted under the Ecodesign directive is, as we have seen (Table 5.2), that the home appliance industry is covered by binding regulation, both under Ecodesign and Energy Labelling. The fact that the three VAs that ran prior to the introduction of the new framework directive were subsequently replaced by binding measures mirrors the industry's overall preference for binding standards expressed in the above interview quote. In fact, in the home appliance sector, the 2009 Ecodesign framework directive was implemented entirely through regulations, accompanied by an Energy Label in each case (except for cooking appliances). As a consequence, we see no voluntary measures—no VA adopted after 2010, no Ecolabel and no measures under GPP.

There are at least two reasons why the home appliance industry preferred binding over voluntary regulation. The first reason is, as highlighted by the industry expert quoted above, market coverage. The home appliance manufacturing sector lacks the degree of market concentration which is generally thought to be an important precondition for VAs to work (Interviews home appliance industry 2017, 2018a, b, 2019a, b; Interview ministry 2017). In a concentrated market, it is not only easier to agree on voluntary standards but also to enforce them.

These preconditions were still fulfilled when the home appliance industry, through its association CECED, committed to VA from the mid-1990s onwards. These voluntary measures complemented existing regulation on energy labelling of home appliances, often by using the energy efficiency categories to set quantitative targets. Manufacturers of washing machines concluded a voluntary commitment in 1996, the Commission was notified in 1997, and then it was published in the Official Journal in 1998 and given final approval in January 2000. Market coverage of participating manufacturers reached almost 97%. They voluntarily committed to reducing the energy consumption of washing machines by 20% between 1994 and 2000. Further, manufacturers used the energy label system, as laid down in the directive 92/12/EC on energy labelling of household washing machines, to set phase-out targets: to stop producing or importing machines with energy efficiency classes E, F and G after 1997; to stop producing and importing machines with energy classes D and E after 1999. Industry reached all of these hard targets, yet the energy saving impact of the VA was assessed to be at a low level (mure and Fraunhofer 2014d). A follow-up agreement ran from 2002 to 2008, notified to the European Commission in November 2002 and given approval in June 2003. Participating manufacturers represented more than 90% of the market in 2002 (CECED 2002). They committed to further reduce energy consumption, amounting to at least 33% compared to 1994, and phase-out targets (energy efficiency class D until the end of 2003). The quantitative energy saving target was reached in 2003, and D-class devices were phased out to a significant extent, amounting to 1.2% in 2003, compared to around 20% in 1996 (mure and Fraunhofer 2014a). The energy saving impact of this VA was assessed as being at a medium level (mure and Fraunhofer 2014a). Other VAs were adopted for various product groups (for an overview rf. Tanasescu 2009: 142–144; Schnabl 2005). In 1999, CECED members signed up to a VA covering the energy efficiency of dishwashers, engaging in self-regulation until 2004. This VA complemented the Energy Labelling Directive 97/17/EC for dishwashers and again aimed at reducing energy consumption (by 20% for the year 2002) and phasing out the least efficient dishwashers from the market. While the number of suppliers and brands was relatively high at the time the agreement was concluded, CECED secured coverage of more than 90% of the market which was dominated by eight major manufacturers (mure and Fraunhofer 2014c). Further, CECED issued a VA on reducing energy consumption of household refrigerators, freezers and their combinations in 2002. It complemented mandatory minimum requirements under the directive 96/57/EC on these product groups. Manufacturers represented more than 95% of the market when concluding the agreement (mure and Fraunhofer 2014b). Industry committed to withdrawing the majority of devices with an energy label class C and above, as well as chest freezers and electric compressor-based chest freezers having an energy label class D and above, by 31 December 2004. The agreement was successful in achieving its targets and was renewed in 2004 (Bertoldi and Rezessy 2007). As illustrated in

Fig. 5.4, these product groups have seen a significant decline in specific energy consumption during the duration of these VA.

In a first phase, the adoption of VAs was preferable over regulation for the home appliance industry as being more flexible, avoiding market distortions and securing faster implementation (Meli 1999; Interview home appliance industry 2019a). Over time, however, these VAs proved ineffective due to diversification and internationalisation on the manufacturing side but also due to increasingly diverse channels of retail and wholesale distribution. In 2009, for example, industry chose to replace the VA on household refrigerators by means of binding regulation to tackle the problem of free-riding (VHK and ARMINES 2015: 39). As highlighted by the interview quoted at the beginning of this section, industry voluntarily gave up on VAs to move to binding regulation. Products that do not comply with regulations set under the Ecodesign directive cannot be placed on the market, including imports. By contrast, under a VA there is a risk of free-riding where manufacturers outside the agreement do not comply with the standards and can effectively undercut European manufacturers (Interview ministry 2017). Binding regulation, however, does not discard the issue of non-compliance altogether. Especially, the increase in online sales poses a problem from an enforcement perspective, as responsibility, which also applies to importers of goods, is increasingly dispersed. Online marketplaces such as Amazon cannot be held liable for compliance with Ecodesign standards, as it is the numerous marketplace sellers that place products on the market. According to the Commission's estimate, around 10–25% of the goods marketed in the EU do not comply with Ecodesign requirements (European Commission 2016d: 9). This is an issue for domestic enforcement authorities which may find it difficult to target dispersed retailers and manufacturers that are less trustworthy, while it is relatively easy to secure the compliance of the big producers based in Europe (Interview home appliance industry 2018b). In the light of these developments, it is apparent that harmonised standards and their enforcement should therefore be in the interest of both industry and regulators.

A second reason why the home appliance industry has been comparatively proactive on energy efficiency is that the energy label does in fact work as a pull-factor. There is evidence that the energy efficiency ranking does matter for consumers' purchasing decisions (London Economics and Ipsos 2018). As any good standard, it provides a solution to the "lemon problem" (Akerlof 1970), that is, the information asymmetries between buyers and sellers, which go to the disadvantage of the quality and size of markets. The energy label reduces customer uncertainty and transaction cost, and it has become a shorthand for communicating potential energy savings. The label has therefore proven to be a win-win for EU-based home appliance industry and EU regulators alike.

Compliance Through Litigation? the Example of "Hoovergate"

The reliability and trustworthiness of an environmental label hinge upon the extent to which the advertised performance lives up to reality when a product is used by the end consumer. The requirements set by the EU Energy Label for the product group of vacuum cleaners, as well as the compliance of manufacturers with these requirements, have been targeted by visible litigation activity. The British inventor Sir James Dyson sued competitors for alleged non-compliance with energy efficiency standards, and Dyson urged the Commission to alter its regulatory approach with respect to testing requirements. As discussed in Chapter 2, litigation can serve as a powerful "business tool" (Forcier 1994: 140) to challenge and potentially revoke existing regulation. The story of litigation started in 2012 when the UK-based electronics producer Dyson discovered a mole from Bosch inside the firm, who allegedly sent back information to Bosch. The companies settled the dispute out of court (Burn-Callander 2015). The legal dispute continued, however, and triggered litigant action on both sides. In 2014, Bosch accused Dyson of advertising incorrect values on the energy labels for its appliances, leading to German courts ruling that Dyson had to change the information (Elektrojournal 2014). In 2015, Dyson brought cases to national courts in Germany, Belgium, France and the Netherlands against BSH Hausgeräte with its brands Bosch and Siemens. Dyson argued that the competitors' advertising and communication of vacuum cleaners were misleading. The energy efficiency rating would be based on testing vacuum cleaners under laboratory conditions with empty bags rather than under real-life conditions with dust-loaded bags. Due to these testing practices, he argued, his bagless vacuum cleaner would be discriminated against by EU regulation. He made a case that only a dust-loaded test method, such as the one devised by the IEC, would provide accurate information. This led him to argue that Bosch and Siemens vacuum cleaners would not meet the standards as advertised by BSH. Dyson even drew an analogy with "Dieselgate", claiming that Bosch and Siemens had misled consumers in "behaviour akin to the Volkswagen scandal" (Farrell 2015). Bosch, in a public response, emphasised that "all Bosch and Siemens vacuum cleaners are measured in compliance with European energy regulations. Appliance performance at home is consistent with laboratory performance – and any suggestion to the contrary is grossly misleading" (BSH 2015). The Commercial Court of Antwerp in Belgium asked for a preliminary ruling by the European Court of Justice (ECJ). With respect to the directive on unfair commercial practices (2005/29/EC), it asked whether BSH was misleading consumers by failing to mention that the tests were carried out with an empty dust bag. In July 2018 (Case C-632/16), the ECJ ruled that providing information on the testing conditions resulting in energy classification was not required by law. Therefore, not providing such information did not amount to a "misleading omission", as argued by the plaintiff. However, the court also ruled that BSH's practice to add supplementary labels was unlawful (ECJ 2018).

At the European level, Dyson challenged the testing requirements under the Ecodesign and Energy Labelling Schemes. In May 2013, Dyson applied for annulment of a Commission delegated regulation concerning the energy labelling of vacuum cleaners (regulation (EU) no. 665/2013). Dyson's request to annul the Commission's regulation was initially rejected by the General Court in November 2015 (Case T-544/13 Dyson v Commission) ruling he had "failed to demonstrate that there were more reliable, accurate and reproducible tests than the one endorsed by the Commission" (EGC 2015). In May 2017, Dyson won his appeal at the ECJ, and the claim was sent back to the EGC for judgement (Case C-44/16 P *Dyson Ltd v Commission*). The ECJ argued that the efficiency ratings should be based on how the devices are used in practice, ruling that the previous court decision had failed to appreciate the full range of evidence provided. The EGC delivered its final judgement in November 2018 (Case T-544/13 *RENV Dyson Ltd v Commission*), by which it overturned its initial decision adopted in 2015. The General Court upheld Dyson's argument and annulled the regulation on the energy labelling of vacuum cleaners. The EGC held that the calculation method to measure the energy performance adopted by the Commission did not comply with essential elements of the Ecodesign directive, namely to provide information for consumers on the energy efficiency of products during use (EGC 2018). The Commission did not appeal the decision within the deadline set. As a consequence, there is currently no regulation for this product group in place, which leaves industry with the uncertainty as to how they can secure compliance (Interview home appliance industry 2019b). Clearly, industry would have preferred to avoid such a "limbo" (Interview home appliance industry 2019a).

These court battles between the German and British producers show the extent to which compliance with energy efficiency and related testing requirements has become a visible matter of a firm's reputation. Moreover, it illustrates how litigation can feed into the regulatory process. The European Commission asked the standardisation body CENELEC to revise harmonised standards for vacuum cleaners already in 2015, with an explicit mandate to review the measurement of energy consumption as well as dust pickup and dust re-emission with a partly loaded rather than an empty receptacle (mandate 540, 20.07.2017). Further, while the court decisions were pending, NGOs have raised concerns whether the energy label would continue to be trusted by consumers where testing requirements under laboratory conditions would diverge significantly from real-life conditions of actual use (CLASP et al. 2017: 9). And, finally, the EGC ruling in 2018 *revoked* applicable regulation, requiring policymakers and stakeholders to come up with new rules and testing procedures in order to comply with Ecodesign requirements. Beyond the regulatory uncertainty created, the litigation and ensuing decision have caused reputational damage to the way in which thresholds and adequate testing procedures are agreed upon (Interview home appliance industry 2019b).

The Regulatory Power of the Home Appliance Industry

The home appliance industry holds significant regulatory power under the Ecodesign (implementing acts) and Energy Labelling (delegated acts) procedures in setting product-specific requirements and testing procedures. While industry operates in a legislative context, there is strong third-party involvement (Tanasescu 2009: 11). Differently from VAs, the European Parliament and the Council as well as member state representatives are involved in post-legislative rule-setting, yet industry is an influential player. Industry representatives provide extensive expert input and are frequently mandated with standardisation. Representing the home appliance industry, the European association APPLiA (formerly CECED) is a recognised stakeholder in the Ecodesign Design Consultation Forum, which includes representatives from EU countries, industries and civil society (on the process leading to setting up the Forum rf. Tanasescu 2009: 162–172). Notably, the Consultation Forum has the task of assessing the effectiveness of VAs as implementing measures. Further, APPLiA participates in the European Circular Economy Stakeholder Platform Coordination Group (European Commission 2018g) and also in the European Innovation Partnership on Raw Materials High-Level Steering Group (European Commission 2018i).

A good example for industry-led rule-setting is the 2010 Energy Label recast, which added additional efficiency classes to the top-performing A category rather than engaging in rescaling. Studies have shown that consumers are less inclined to pay a higher price for increased energy efficiency within the A category, when compared to a simple A-G scheme (Heinzle and Wüstenhagen 2009). The over-crowded A-categories thus generated a reputational gain for industry, which is why it fervently opposed the rescaling scheme (ZVEI 2018; Crisp 2015a). Despite industry opposition rescaling was finally decided in 2017. The new scheme will regroup products into lower efficiency classes, and products from the A(+++) categories will likely be relegated to a C rating or possibly even less. This should leave room for efficiency gains without the need for yet another round of re-regulation over the next decade or longer. Such change has been applauded by NGOs (ANEC and BEUC 2015, Interview ENGO 2019). Industry, in contrast, has argued that the overpopulation of the highest category proves how efficient the product regulation on Ecodesign is, arguing that there is no need to downgrade highly efficient products. Further, they argued that the new scheme will confuse regular consumers rather than providing clarity about energy efficiency. Overall, industry has made a case for regulatory certainty and stability in order to facilitate innovation and keep markets competitive (CECED 2015). This status quo bias of the industry points to "excess inertia" where there is a need for regulatory intervention to switch to a different, more efficient standard (David 1985; Pierson 2000).

That said, the way in which the rescaling will actually be implemented product-by-product in the post-legislative phase is once again driven by (industry) expert input. Immediately after an agreement on the new Energy Labelling Framework Regulation was reached, CECED emphasised that implementation should be "practical and enforceable" (CECED 2017). Rescaling will start with those product groups that were last regulated in 2010 (see Table 5.2), namely refrigerators and freezers, dishwashers and washing machines. Washing machines, for example, have seen a particularly overcrowded top-performing A+++ class with 55% of the market share in 2015 already having the rating (ECOS 2017: 2). Similarly, in 2014, around 94% of dishwashers placed on the European market were classified into the A category (around 53% above the A++ category). In order to prepare new Ecodesign measures for dishwashers, the Commission conducted a review study through its Joint Research Centre between 2014 and 2016 (JRC 2016). The preparatory study for the revision of the dishwasher regulation took note of significant improvements in specific energy and water consumption, of around 34 and 46%, respectively, between 1998 and 2014 (Boyano et al. 2017: 13–14). The preparatory study saw further potential to improve the energy efficiency performance at an incremental level (drastic increases could only be reached by a massive switch to heat pump-equipped dishwashers sold at a high purchase price, ibid.: 28) and a need to introduce resource efficiency requirements. More specifically, it was recommended that the energy label classes should be rescaled, and that devices should be designed so as to implement further technical innovation that generates additional energy savings (ibid.: 22–25). However, the study also highlighted that a potential switch to handwashing or a lower dishwasher market penetration rate was not included in the model (ibid.: 28). This is the focal point of the CECED/APPLiA campaign "What if all Europeans had a dishwasher?" (APPLiA 2018e). The home appliance association posits that, at the aggregate level, setting overly ambitious Ecodesign requirements would ban more affordable products from the market and prevent consumers switching from handwashing to a dishwasher in the first place (Interview home appliance industry 2019a). APPLiA thus pledged for an increase in the penetration of dishwashers across Europe, which in 2018 was at about 50% of all households. Along these lines, an alliance of home appliance manufacturers has urged the Commission to adopt Ecodesign regulations that "account for income inequality […] allowing citizens to access efficient services and products, including when they have a low level of income or they come from countries with lower average incomes" (APPLiA et al. 2018).

The home appliance industry will also be heavily involved in setting up the new database introduced with the 2017 Energy Labelling recast. National and European industry associations lobbied heavily against the introduction of this scheme, bringing forth arguments on intellectual property and data security. Further, they questioned the usefulness of a database that would not deliver to consumers the kind of information they are generally after, namely price and the availability of products. Finally, industry anticipated a work overload for enforcement authorities who would now focus on compliance with new information provision requirements, as opposed to real, physical testing and actual product compliance (Interview home appliance industry 2018a; CECED 2017). The arguments brought forward by industry do to some extent echo the discussion surrounding the introduction of new information requirements under REACH. Drawing on the example of chemical regulation, however, we may as well anticipate that industry will eventually align itself with the new requirements. Being in the driving seat of providing the data, we can expect that by investing in the scheme and further developing implementing methods the European home appliance industry will begin to "own" the process and potentially develop a preference for stricter implementation of information requirements, especially to detect non-compliance and crowd out competitors.

Similarly, the move towards resource efficiency targets under the circular economy framework requires that industry buys into the project and cooperates. For the Ecodesign working plan 2016–2019, the European Commission announced plans to consider resource efficiency aspects for both product groups already covered through Ecodesign measures and new product groups. More specifically, the Commission announced plans to address product-specific or horizontal requirements in areas such as durability, reparability, as well as reuse and recycling (European Commission 2016c: 5, 9). To that end, the European Commission has requested European standardisation bodies (CEN, CENELEC and ETSI) to develop adequate criteria to assess the durability, reparability and recyclability of products, as well as assessing the proportion of re-used components and recycled material content in a product. The mandate (no. 543), issued by the Commission in November 2015 was rejected on first submission. It took the standardisation bodies two years to eventually accept the Commission's request (ECOS 2016) to start working on resource efficiency standardisation. ENGOs take a critical stance on what they consider a process driven by industry, and characterised by "delays and threats" (Interview ENGO 2019). The Joint Technical Committee 10 on Energy-related products and Material Efficiency Aspects for Ecodesign (CEN/CLC/JTC 10) was set up by CEN and CENELEC for this purpose. The industry representative chairing this new committee took a very cautious and pragmatic approach as to the feasibility of this standardisation request and the introduction of new mandatory standards (Interview home appliance industry 2017; CEN-CENELEC 2018). Industry representatives typically refer to enforcement issues to make a case that Ecodesign regulation should not be too onerous or impose too many requirements, and especially those that are not easily measureable, as this all hampers effective enforcement (Interview home appliance industry 2018a, b; APPLiA et al. 2018). They also argue that, to function as an effective pull-factor for consumers, the labelling scheme has to be sufficiently simple and should not overburden the consumer with complex and detailed information. Compared to the co-evolution of industry and regulatory interests in the initial phase of introducing mandatory Ecodesign and Energy Labelling measures, a clear conflict materialises: moving beyond energy efficiency goals to pursue resource efficiency measures is the next natural step for policymakers (Interview COM 2017b; Interview ministry 2017), whereas industry seeks to prevent additional requirements. Industry therefore also prefers to be in the driving seat as the standard setter rather than having to comply with externally imposed requirements. The industry's credo reads: "First standardise, then regulate" (Interview home appliance industry 2018b). By contrast, NGOs promote the opposite: "First regulate, then standardise" (Interview ENGO 2019). From an environmentalist perspective, industry has not only slowed down but captured the process in a setting where policymakers abstain from setting regulatory requirements, or at least threaten to do so (Interview ENGO 2019).

Where we continue to see some co-evolution of regulatory preferences, by contrast, is on enforcement issues around WEEE. For instance, the home appliance industry would welcome stricter regulatory requirements imposing take-back schemes in order to ensure the collection at the end-of-life of products and contribute to solve the problem of WEEE escaping official waste treatment streams (Interview home appliance industry 2018a). Further, industry would welcome reporting duties for all commercial actors handling WEEE, not just producers. What the home appliance industry opposes, however, are new information requirements on hazardous chemicals to be passed on to recyclers (APPLiA 2018d). Policymakers, while discussing the WEEE recast adopted in May 2018, had envisioned the introduction of a database of information on chemical substances of concern, to be accessible to waste treatment operators. To address policymakers' ambition to boost the recycling of WEEE—and to prevent the introduction of binding regulatory requirements—in February 2018, APPLiA and Digital Europe introduced the platform "Information for Recyclers – I4R" (I4R 2018). The platform is hosted by the WEEE Forum, an international association of producer responsibility organisations created in 2002 (WEEE Forum 2018). I4R aims at giving the recycling industry access to information about the presence and location of materials and components in need of separate treatment. In June 2018, several home appliance manufacturers signed two Codes of Conduct for Marking of Appliances for End-of-life Treatment. The signatories voluntarily committed to placing newly designed markings on the back of heat pump tumble dryers, washing machines, washer dryers and dishwashers containing f-gases, as well as refrigerators built with vacuum insulation technology (APPLiA 2018c). The new WEEE directive (2018/849/EU) entered into force in July 2018 and needs to be transposed into national law by July 2020. Member of European Parliaments (MEPs) had voted in favour of making extended producer responsibility schemes mandatory for WEEE, but this was opposed by the Council (Bourguignon 2018: 11).

ICT Industry: The Market Knows Best!

> The choice should be left to the consumer, who buys a device due to its performances and features. The legislator should refrain from "overadvertising" consumers in this respect. (DigitalEurope 2015)

For ICT products, the Ecodesign directive is being currently implemented through three VAs and four implementing regulations, mostly in the absence of Energy Labelling or an uptake of the Ecolabel (Table 5.2). The only ICT product group with an Energy Label and an uptake of the Ecolabel is televisions. As highlighted by the DigitalEurope position, the ICT industry is overall critical of how the Ecodesign framework is being implemented, making a strong case that many of the design issues should be left to market forces and not be subject to cumbersome regulatory requirements.

How can one explain the striking difference between the two industry branches covered in this chapter? Let us first consider the "outlier" in consumer electronics, i.e. televisions. Here we see a move from voluntary to binding measures, very much along the lines of the pattern observed for home appliances. Already in 1997, the association of consumer electronics manufacturers, EACEM (which subsequently became EICTA until it joined DigitalEurope), voluntarily committed to reducing the standby power use of TVs and VCRs (video cassette recorders). This VA complemented the SAVE programme aiming at reducing the power consumption of consumer electronics, as established by the European Council decision 91/556/EEC. The agreement, signed by 15 EACEM member companies, was recognised by the European Commission in 1998 (ten Brink and Morère 2002). The VA represented more than 60% of the respective markets (mure and Fraunhofer 2008). From an industry perspective, labelling was not considered to be an effective tool, notably because the aggregate financial savings for the end consumer were not deemed significant enough (Bruens 2012). The energy saving impact of this VA was assessed as being at a low level (mure and Fraunhofer 2008). In 2003, a new VA was concluded for TVs and DVDs, sub-divided into several commitments, targeting two distinct types of television receivers and DVD players. These commitments were supported by around seven to twelve companies, holding a market share of around 40–50% in 2004, which, for some product groups, had significantly decreased in a short period of time (mure and Fraunhofer 2014e). While EICTA approached a number of companies, the association was not successful in recruiting new signees (EICTA 2005). Moreover, there were rapid shifts caused by technological innovations, such as the transition from analogue to digital TV, the introduction of flat screen display or the significant market increase of DVD receivers (mure and Fraunhofer 2014e; EICTA 2005). Altogether, such change has increasingly blurred established product segmentation, paving the way to personalised and interactive multimedia services. In 2009, the VA was replaced by mandatory requirements under a regulation on Ecodesign (642/2009) and a regulation on Energy Labelling (278/2009). In addition, Ecolabel requirements for TVs were laid down by a Commission decision (2009/300/EC). A major reason for manufacturers to shift to binding regulation was to avoid free-riding—compared to the VAs concluded by the home appliance industry, the consumer electronics manufacturers never secured a similar degree of market coverage. In fact, the VA's coverage did not include the "large majority of the relevant economic sector" stipulated in the 2009 Ecodesign directive (Annex VIII, directive 2009/125/EC) and was significantly below the required threshold of 80% of units placed on the EU market, as laid out in the 2016 Commission guidelines (European Commission 2016b). Accordingly, the Commission, in its impact assessment published in 2009, identified insufficient market penetration of energy-efficient devices driven by market forces alone. The Commission thus recommended an Ecodesign implementing regulation complemented by an energy label in its impact assessment of possible options (European Commission 2009: 4–6). For manufacturers, the energy label and the Ecolabel are instruments to differentiate their product in a crowded market segment and to signal the environmental performance to end consumers or public purchasers. Contrary to the other ICT product groups (rf. Table 5.2), there has been the uptake of the Ecolabel for televisions, with more than 100 devices being listed (European Commission 2018d). The extent to which power consumption levels of televisions actually matter for consumer decisions is rather controversial, with some arguing that energy efficiency is not of prior concern to consumer decisions (Interview ICT industry 2017). Yet there is evidence that consumers are willing to pay more for a higher energy class also in this product segment (London Economics and Ipsos 2018: 17, 37). Consumer demand for high-end and larger displays has, however, clearly been on the rise (DigitalEurope 2017b: 3). This is a factor which explains the significant increase in specific energy consumption of televisions in the period since 1999, depicted in Fig. 5.4, which has slightly decreased since 2011. There have indeed been improvements in the energy efficiency of products placed on the market in the last decade, especially when put in relation to screen size. Digital Europe reports that, between 2011 and 2017, power consumption per square inch dropped by more than 40% (DigitalEurope 2017b: 6). There is therefore a significant rebound effect for this product group with the use of more energy efficient but bigger and more performant devices.

Other ICT product segments covered by implementing regulations, rather than VAs, include single set-top boxes, power supplies, computers and computer servers (Table 5.2). These markets also typically involve a high and diverse number of products. The targets set by such binding regulation proved to be relatively unambitious. Regulation 617/2013 covering computers and computer servers, for instance, opted for the lowest energy efficiency standards considered in the impact assessment (European Commission 2013a). In contrast, the requirements set to be awarded an Ecolabel for portable and personal computers (decision Commission decisions 2016/337/EU) were rather demanding, relating to aspects of energy efficiency, power management and resource efficiency. In contrast to televisions, there was no uptake on the Ecolabel for either personal computers (European Commission 2018e) or portable computers (European Commission 2018f).

Differently from the TV segment, manufacturers of complex set-top boxes (CSTB), imaging equipment and game consoles have opted for VAs rather than Ecodesign implementing regulations. What we observe for all three product groups is a significantly higher degree of market concentration when compared with televisions. Manufacturers of CSTBs have agreed to a VA in 2009, following up on a Code of Conduct for Digital TV Service Systems, which was concluded between hardware manufacturers, software producers and the services industry in 2001. Compared to the rapid decline in sales of single set-top boxes, covered by regulation 107/2009, CSTBs are a growing market (VHK et al. 2014: v). The alleged goal of industry was to avoid Ecodesign implementing regulations, which was considered inappropriate in a rapidly changing market, as well as to replace the rather strict targets of the previous Code of Conduct with more lenient targets under the VA (Klinckenberg and Harmelink 2017: 16, 18; VHK et al. 2014: 148). Further, industry representatives highlighted that Ecodesign regulation would typically target the manufacturer only, while the VA would bring together hardware and software producers and service providers so as to maximise total energy savings (Interview ICT industry 2017). The VA, which entered into force in July 2010, was subject to an impact assessment and stakeholder consultation in the framework of the Ecodesign Consultation process (European Commission 2012), and a regulation was adopted in 2012 (COM (2012) 684). The signatories to this VA are individual companies and not industry associations. While the number of manufacturers involved in the agreement has remained fairly constant during the first five years of the VA, membership of other signatories has varied. The market coverage of the VA, however, cannot be verified (Klinckenberg and Harmelink 2017: 18–19). The VA seeks to improve the energy efficiency of CSTBs without hampering their functionality, setting maximum energy consumption targets and seeking to phase out the least efficient devices (CSBT 2018). The effectiveness of the VA in improving CSTBs' energy efficiency cannot be assessed in the absence of accurate data for power consumption levels prior to the entry into force of the voluntary measures (Klinckenberg and Harmelink 2017: 21).

In 2011, major printing manufacturers have signed a VA on imaging equipment, which, in 2013, was endorsed by a Commission decision

(COM (2013) 23). In 2013, the European Commission also issued a decision (2013/806/EU) on Ecolabel requirements for this product group. Industry preferred voluntary action over binding regulation, and the Commission considered that self-regulation was more appropriate for this "dynamic product sector", providing "flexibility" and "quicker updating of target levels" (European Commission 2013b: 7). The VA is managed by the dedicated association EuroVAprint (EuroVAprint 2018). Following a withdrawal in 2017 by Ricoh, Panasonic and Samsung for reasons of discontinued production or market consolidation, the VA, in 2018, comprised of 13 manufacturers (Brother, Canon, Dell, Epson, HP, Konica, Kyocera, Lexmark, Murata, OKI, Sharp, Toshiba, Xerox) which together achieved market coverage of over 90%. The VA covers printers, copiers, faxes and multifunctional devices. There was no uptake on the Ecolabel by manufacturers, and the label was discontinued in 2017 (European Commission 2017). In terms of the VA's effectiveness, policy experts and NGOs argued that the VA does not add any value in terms of energy savings because imaging equipment was already covered under the Energy Star (discontinued after 2018). In any case, there are no data available on energy consumption levels prior to the VA (Klinckenberg and Harmelink 2017: 32). Compared to the standards set by the VA, the Ecolabel requirements were significantly more ambitious, which, in addition to a lack of an expected pull effect for consumers, might explain why there was no uptake of the label.

The third VA concluded by the ICT industry covers game consoles (Efficient Gaming 2018). The manufacturing of game consoles is a highly concentrated market, which basically consists of three players, namely Sony, Microsoft and Nintendo, with market coverage of around 90%. These three companies negotiated a VA in 2014. Following impact assessment and stakeholder consultation, the Commission, in April 2014, recommended acceptance of the VA, which in 2015 was adopted as an implementing measure under Ecodesign (European Commission 2015d). While the industry commitment does not cover the gaming mode, it suggests power caps for playback and navigation mode, introducing thresholds for both modes to be achieved in 2017 and in 2019, respectively. The reason given is that at this stage no "representative and reproducible measurement tests for energy consumption in gaming mode" have been developed (European Commission 2015a). NGOs have been critical about the VA with respect to both its process of adoption and its targets. The "coolproducts" alliance criticised manufacturers who were buying time by taking six years to negotiate a VA in a first place, and then negotiated a VA which in substance was giving companies leeway to comply with very generous, "business as usual" requirements (coolproducts 2015).

While in these three product groups industry adopted a proactive stance in order to pre-empt binding regulation, no initiatives were taken in other areas targeted under the Ecodesign working programmes. The Commission DG GROW, working on Ecodesign measures in the area of enterprise servers, data storage and ancillary equipment, has asked DigitalEurope to come up with self-regulatory proposals, but no action was taken (Interview COM 2017b). Industry representatives put forward that companies were already voluntarily committing to ambitious goals as members of the international "Green Touch" initiative (GreenTouch 2018), and said that there was no need to duplicate such efforts (Interview ICT industry 2017). Given such non-action under the Ecodesign framework, the Commission, in July 2018, published a draft regulation in order to receive stakeholder feedback. The draft proposed the introduction of energy efficiency and material efficiency requirements for servers and data storage. In its joint reaction, DigitalEurope and the European Data Centre Association (EUDCA) pointed to past industry efforts and successes in reducing the energy footprint of servers, and highlighted the weaknesses and trade-offs in the proposed regulation (DigitalEurope and EUDCA 2018). Overall, the ICT industry argues that market drivers are sufficient to cut the energy cost of servers and data storage, and that inappropriate measurement of idle power would have perverse effects for highly efficient, big installations (Interview ICT industry 2017). Policymakers, in contrast, highlight that there is significant potential for improvement, especially for smaller servers which typically are inactive over longer periods of time (Interview COM 2017b). The Commission proposal has the potential to materialise as a regulatory threat, incentivising industry to become active and engage in self-regulation.

In conclusion, the implementation of the Ecodesign framework for the ICT products has proven difficult in view of the innovative features of the sector. The European Commission, in its fourth working plan and assessment of Ecodesign implementing measures, has taken a critical stance and is acknowledging difficulties:

For ICT products it has proven very difficult to make a reliable estimate of their energy savings potential, given the uncertainty about future market developments. Moreover, for the fast moving ICT product sectors, questions have arisen as to the suitability of the ecodesign/energy labelling process (which takes on average around 4 years) for establishing minimum energy and resource efficiency criteria. At the same time, the voluntary agreements that have been recognised for some electronic product groups (i.e. imaging equipment, game consoles and complex set-top boxes) as alternatives to regulatory measures, have not always proven to be faster in achieving the objectives of Ecodesign. (European Commission 2016c: 8)

Innovation Through Regulation? the Example of Cadmium-Free Technology

The above passage, which discussed evidence on Ecodesign and Energy Labelling, points to significant trade-offs between the lengthy adoption of regulation (and even VA) and fast-moving technological innovation. However, there are also examples where binding requirements boosted innovation. The development of cadmium-free technology for televisions is one such example (Interview EP 2017). Under the RoHS directive as initially adopted in 2002, the use of cadmium had not been banned from the manufacturing process in EEE because no reliable technical alternatives were available back then. Once such alternatives became available for a range of products, however, cadmium was subsequently restricted in 2006. This was not the case for the manufacturing of televisions, given that a significant degree of energy savings was attributed to the use of the substance. Several exemptions were thus granted to TV manufacturers. In 2015, when companies producing quantum dots as part of nanotechnology containing cadmium asked for another exemption, an inter-institutional conflict emerged. The Commission initially wanted to grant another exemption until July 2017 on the grounds that no alternative was available to quantum dots technology. The European Parliament disagreed and vetoed the Commission's plans in a plenary session in May 2015 (European Parliament 2015). MEPs asked for a re-assessment of the use of cadmium in TV sets, arguing that safer alternatives to the toxic and carcinogenic substance were available, and issued a motion (EurActiv 2015). The producers of cadmium-based technology, by contrast, put forward that the ban would involve losses in energy efficiency: "a quantum dot based television will reduce energy consumption by more than

20%—potentially saving more than 3 billion Euros in energy costs and preventing the emission of 7 million tonnes of CO_2 annually", and thus supported the Commission's position (Willis 2015). In August 2017, the Commission did eventually follow the EP's position and announced it would ban the use of cadmium in TVs and displays by October 2019 under the RoHS directive. Producers of cadmium-free technology such as Nanoco welcomed this decision (Compound Semiconductor 2017). According to Nanoco CEO Michael Edelman, "Cadmium-based technology has been a non-starter from the beginning. This is a failed technology that has been abandoned by leading international display manufacturers and rejected by consumers" (Compound Semiconductor 2017). It is therefore apparent that binding regulation can support and speed up the transition towards new technologies, underpinned by co-evolving interests of regulators and front-running companies.

The Regulatory Power of the ICT Industry

Information provided by interviewees suggests that it is unlikely that in the absence of the VA the energy use of CSTBs would have been regulated. As the global market for CSTBs is a rapidly changing one (number and type of functionalities is changing constantly and every 18 months completely new models are placed on the market) the regulatory process is lengthy and the regulator may not have access to the information needed to effectively regulate this market. (Klinckenberg and Harmelink 2017: 21)

The above quote from a comparative international study on voluntary energy efficiency measures summarises why the regulatory output on ICT products looks strikingly different compared to the home appliance sector. Even though the VA in question—on CSTBs—proved unambitious and ineffective, policymakers are not in a position to cast a credible regulatory threat on industry actors engaging in voluntary cooperation. This, naturally, undermines the very design of the Ecodesign directive following the "new approach", which was supposed to use binding regulation as a last resort where voluntary action fails to materialise or produce the desired results (Interview COM 2006a). It explains why there was a rather low degree of regulatory activity on ICT products, considering the type of products listed under the Ecodesign working programmes (see Table 5.1). And it explains why ICT products manufacturers have not been more proactive in many instances, often to the astonishment of Commission officials (Interview COM 2017b). The identification and "flagging" of product groups should have had a much stronger signalling effect indeed.

On top of seriously limited regulatory capacity on the side of policymakers, industry also saw no benefit in lending support to regulation or engaging in VAs. From an industry perspective, the way in which the framework has been implemented, targeting "how" things were to be done rather than "what" was going to be achieved began from the wrong end (Interview ICT industry 2017). The level of rule-specification involved in the post-legislative phase of Ecodesign and Energy Labelling is thus considered to be disproportionate and inappropriate in the fast-moving ICT sector. In addition, there is no perception that advertising energy or resource efficiency product features would generate economic gains, as illustrated by the lack of uptake of the voluntary Ecolabel. It is commonly argued that consumers base their purchasing decisions not on energy savings but on price, technical features and design. In any case, the price of buying a product is more salient for the average consumer than the future cost of using the product. In addition, the energy saving potential might not even materialise for the consumer, given the comparatively short lifespan of electronics products. Finally, engaging in voluntary action was overall considered to be too costly and not beneficial enough. As one interviewee put it, "agreements under Ecodesign are not voluntary, they are forced voluntary" (Interview ICT industry 2017). The VA is adopted in response to regulatory demands and is subject to strict procedural requirements imposed on industry when preparing, adopting and implementing such an agreement (European Commission 2016b). According to the substantive requirements set by the Ecodesign directive, a product group has to be regulated if sales volumes, environmental impact and improvement potential are all significant. More precisely, for a VA to become eligible for endorsement under the Ecodesign framework, it has to be open to participation, provide added value, secure sufficient market coverage, have quantified and staged objectives, involve civil society, implement monitoring and reporting procedures, be cost-effective and sustainable (Annex VII Ecodesign directive, European Commission 2016b). In a way, industry would do the job of the Commission by generating evidence doing the preparatory studies, by envisaging regulatory measures and discussing them with stakeholders, and by overseeing implementation and enforcement (Interview ICT industry 2017). At the same time, as argued by a policy expert at DG Energy, the reputational risk for industry may be even higher in a voluntary setting, given that its performance will be measured against the goals it sets itself (Interview COM 2017c). Companies will thus carefully weigh the costs and benefits of proposing and engaging in voluntary action. In the three examples discussed above, we see a high degree of market concentration and added economic benefits of cooperation.

In view of such evidence, one could envisage a scenario where the ICT industry will no longer be targeted by measures under Ecodesign. As discussed above, the European Commission has acknowledged the difficulties to regulate ICT under the Ecodesign framework and has envisaged a separate track approach (European Commission 2016c: 8; see Table 5.1). Such considerations have alerted ENGOs who campaign intensively to promote the adequacy and advantages to regulate ICT under Ecodesign and Energy Labelling (Fayole and Arditi 2018). In their view, these regulatory instruments can boost industry's and consumers' role in the transition to a sustainable digital society (Haucke et al. 2019; EMF 2018). Leading NGO campaigners urge policymakers and business to take on a leading role in disruptive innovation in order to pave the way towards resource efficiency, framed as a societal and economic win-win situation in a medium and longer term perspective (Crisp 2015b). For example, the "cool products" alliance seeks to exert pressure on the European Commission to regulate mobile phones under Ecodesign. In March 2018, the coalition wrote a public letter to Commission President Jean-Claude Juncker to that end (coolproducts 2018b). Industry experts, in contrast, warn that the European Commission would risk reputational damage by targeting the mobile phone as it is "the iconic product of our times" (Interview ICT industry 2017). In response to repeated demands for binding regulation of consumer electronics, the ICT industry seeks to generate cost-benefit analysis (Valdani Vicari & Associati 2018) to underpin sustainability features of innovative products in the absence of binding regulation. This also seems to be the line of argumentation inside DG Energy, where interview partners have highlighted the inadequacy of the lengthy Ecodesign procedure for adopting regulatory requirements in the fast-moving market segment (Interview COM 2017c).

The regulatory challenge becomes even more pronounced when moving beyond the question of regulating (relatively straightforward) issues around energy usage in order to tackle the entire life cycle of ICT products. With the increasing salience of resource efficiency aspects for consumer electronics and their design (EMF 2018: 4), industry fears that Ecodesign requirements could yet become even more burdensome. To feed into the ongoing debate, in August 2016, Digital Europe presented evidence about best practices in the ICT industry using recycled plastics (DigitalEurope 2016). In April 2017, DigitalEurope followed up with a report on how the digital industry is contributing to "repair, remanufacturing and refurbishment in a Circular Economy" (DigitalEurope 2017a). In a nutshell, the association recommends that related issues should not be addressed under waste legislation, that the potential of the industry contribution should be recognised rather than hampered, and that legislation should not prescribe design measures which impede product innovation (ibid.: 14).

This chapter has discussed two diverse industries, emphasising variation concerning the type of technological and market innovation (incremental versus radical), as well as market structure (fragmented versus concentrated). Accordingly, the industries have pursued quite distinct regulatory strategies under the EU's Ecodesign framework. The home appliance industry has sought and received regulatory endorsement of pre-existing voluntary measures on energy efficiency, securing market coverage and avoiding free-riding. While the sector has experienced substantial innovation during a first phase of reducing energy consumption throughout the 1990s and thereafter, there is now an argument that additional steps can only be incremental, and that industry should not be overburdened with further regulatory requirements. The ICT industry overall opposed binding regulatory requirements on energy efficiency for most products, arguing that the fast-moving technology cannot be matched by a lengthy process of product regulation. It is at this stage uncertain which policy instruments will be used in future to target this sector, and whether regulatory threats such as the proposal to regulate enterprise servers and data centres will materialise either in voluntary or in binding measures. Both the home appliance and ICT industries will, however, come under increasing societal and regulatory pressure with the proliferation of demands for more circularity, at EU-level with the Circular Economy package, but also at national and international level.

REFERENCES

Akerlof GA. (1970) The Market for "Lemons": Quality Uncertainty and the Market Mechanism. *The Quarterly Journal of Economics* 84(3): 488–500.

ANEC and BEUC. (2013) *ANEC/BEUC Comments on the Draft Voluntary Agreement Guidelines.* Brussels: The European Association for the Co-ordination of Consumer Representation in Standardisation, The European Consumer Organisation.

ANEC and BEUC. (2015) *Simplifying the EU Energy Label. Restoring the Successful and Well-Understood Closed A to G Scheme.* Brussels: The European Association for the Co-ordination of Consumer Representation in Standardisation, The European Consumer Organisation.

ANEC and BEUC. (2016) *How Consumers Benefit from Ecodesign Year After Year. Time to Appreciate Ecodesign and to Release the Ecodesign Working Plan 2015–2017.* Brussels: The European Association for the Co-ordination of Consumer Representation in Standardisation, The European Consumer Organisation.

APPLiA. (2018a) *By the Numbers: The Home Appliance Industry in Europe, 2017–2016.* Brussels: Home Appliance Europe. Available at: https://www.applia-europe.eu/statistical-report-2017-2016/documents/APPLiA_SR18.pdf (accessed 24.3.2019).

APPLiA. (2018b) *Bye, Bye CECED. Hello APPLiA.* Press Release 8.3.2018. Brussels: Home Appliance Europe.

APPLiA. (2018c) *Industry Commits on New Marking Symbols That Will Ease Recycling.* Press Release 25.6.2018. Brussels: Home Appliance Europe.

APPLiA. (2018d) *Is EU's Waste Package Making a Step Towards a Circular Society?* Press Release 18.4.2018. Brussels: Home Appliance Europe.

APPLiA. (2018e) *What If All Europeans Had a Dishwasher?* Brussels: Home Appliance Europe. Available at: https://www.applia-europe.eu/campaigns/what-if-all-europeans-had-a-dishwasher (accessed 24.3.2019).

APPLiA, ehi, ehpa, et al. (2018) *Joint Industry Letter on Ecodesign.* 9.7.2018. Brussels: Home Appliance Europe, European Heating Industry, European Heat Pump Association, European Partnership for Energy and the Environment, EUnited Cleaning, LightingEurope.

Bach D and Newman AL. (2007) The European Regulatory State and Global Public Policy: Micro-Institutions, Macro-Influence. *Journal of European Public Policy* 14(6): 827–846.

Barbière C. (2016) Commission Delays Ecodesign Strategy for Fear of Offending UK Businesses. *Euractiv.* 29.4.2016.

Bauer MW and Knill C. (2012) Understanding Policy Dismantling: An Analytical Framework. In: Bauer MW, Jordan A, Green-Pederson C, et al. (eds) *Dismantling Public Policy: Preferences, Strategies, and Effects.* Oxford: Oxford University Press, 30–51.

Bertoldi P and Rezessy S. (2007) Voluntary Agreements for Energy Efficiency: Review and Results of European Experiences. *Energy & Environment* 18(1): 37–73.

BEUC. (2017) *EU Report Confirms Ecolabel Must Keep Benefitting Consumers and the Environment.* Brussels: The European Consumer Organisation.

BEUC. (2018) *Ecodesign & Energy Label*. Brussels: The European Consumer Organisation.

Bourguignon D. (2018) *Briefing. Circular Economy Package. Four Legislative Proposals on Waste*. PE 625.108. Brussels: EPRS European Parliamentary Research Service.

Boyano A, Moons H, Villanueva A, et al. (2017) Follow-Up of the Preparatory Study for Ecodesign and Energy Label for Household Dishwashers. *JRC Technical Reports*. EUR 28808 EN. Sevilla: European Commission, Joint Research Centre.

Bruens W. (2012) The EACEM Commitment for TVs and VCRs. In: Bertoldi P, Ricci A and Wajer BH (eds) *Energy Efficiency in Household Appliances: Proceedings of the First International Conference on Energy Efficiency in Household Appliances*, 10–12 November 1997, Florence, Italy. Berlin, Heidelberg: Springer, 92–99.

BSH. (2015) *BSH Initiates Legal Steps Against Dyson*. Press Release 28.10.2015. München: BSH Hausgeräte GmBH.

Burn-Callander R. (2015) Dyson Counter-Sued by Bosch Over 'Cheating' Allegations. *The Telegraph*: 28.10.2015.

Büthe T and Mattli W. (2011) *The New Global Rulers: The Privatization of Regulation in the World Economy*. Princeton: Princeton University Press.

Cama T. (2018) Trump's Plan for Energy Star Sparks Industry Uproar. *The Hill*: 22.2.2018.

CECED. (2002) *Second Voluntary Commitment on Reducing Energy Consumption of Domestic Washing Machines (2002–2008)*. Brussels: European Committee of Domestic Equipment Manufacturers.

CECED. (2015) *EU Summer Package: Rain & Shine. New Energy Label Regulation Will Cause Unnecessary Delays to Consumer Benefits*. Press Release 15.7.2015. Brussels: European Committee of Domestic Equipment Manufacturers.

CECED. (2017) *Agreement Reached: Focus Needed Now on Practical & Enforceable Implementation*. Press Release 24.3.2017. Brussels: European Committee of Domestic Equipment Manufacturers.

CEN-CENELEC. (2018) *Standardization Complements the European Union's Ecodesign Regulation Towards a European Circular Economy: A View from Richard Hughes, Chairman of CEN/CLC/JTC 10*. Brussels: CEN-CENELEC. Available at: https://www.cencenelec.eu/news/brief_news/Pages/TN-2018-034.aspx (accessed 13.08.2018).

Chandler AD. (2005) *Inventing the Electronic Century: The Epic Story of the Consumer Electronics and Computer Industries, with a New Preface*. Harvard: Harvard University Press.

CLASP, ECOS, EEB, et al. (2017) *Closing the 'Reality Gap': Ensuring a Fair Energy Label for Consumers*. Report 21.6.2017. Brussels: Clean Energy Access

Program, European Environmental Citizens Organisation for Standardisation, European Environmental Bureau. https://www.topten.eu.

Compound Semiconductor. (2017) *Quantum Dot Firm Nanoco Welcomes EC Cadmium Ban.* 10.8.2017. Brussels: coolproducts. Available at: https://www.compoundsemiconductor.net/article/102260/Quantum_Dot_Firm_Nanoco_Welcomes_EC_Cadmium_Ban (accessed 23.6.2018).

coolproducts. (2015) *EC End-of-Level Boss is too Easy to Beat.* Press Release 27.4.2015. Brussels: coolproducts. Available at: https://www.medium.com/@Coolproducts/ec-end-of-level-boss-is-too-easy-to-beat-f87e63b19505 (accessed 28.8.2018).

coolproducts. (2018a) *Cool Products for a Cool Planet: Products Are Changing.* 20.7.2018. Brussels: coolproducts. Available at: https://www.coolproducts.eu (accessed 17.8.2018).

coolproducts. (2018b) *Letter to President Juncker.* 26.3.2018. Brussels: coolproducts.

Crisp J. (2015a) A+ Energy Efficiency Labels Will be Ditched. *Euractiv:* 1.7.2015.

Crisp J. (2015b) EEB: Disruptive Businesses Vital for Ambitious Circular Economy. *Euractiv:* 2.11.2015.

CSBT. (2018) *Voluntary Agreement.* Available at: http://www.cstb.eu/ (accessed 04.08.2018).

David PA. (1985) Clio and the Economics of QWERTY. *The American Economic Review* 75(2): 332–337.

DigitalEurope. (2015) *Ecodesign and Energy Label Review: Maintain Energy Efficiency as the Basis for Measures.* Brussels: Digital Europe.

DigitalEurope. (2016) *Best Practices in Recycled Plastics.* Brussels: DigitalEurope.

DigitalEurope. (2017a) *The Contribution of the Digital Industry to Repair, Remanufacturing and Refurbishment in a Circular Economy.* Report 12.4.2017. Brussels: DigitalEurope.

DigitalEurope. (2017b) *Folow-Up Position on the Proposed Energy Efficiency Requirements in the Display Regulations.* 15.11.2017. Brussels: DigitalEurope.

DigitalEurope. (2018) *DigitalEurope: About Us.* Available at: http://www.digitaleurope.org/About-Us.

DigitalEurope and EUDCA. (2018) *DigitalEurope and EUDCA Concerned About Impact of Proposed Ecodesign Requirements for Servers.* Press Release 30.8.2018. Brussels: DigitalEurope, European Data Centre Association.

ECOS. (2016) *Standardisers Cave In: Material Efficiency Standards for Energy-Related Products Finally to Be Developed.* Press Release 1.7.2016. Brussels: European Environmental Citizens Organisation for Standardisation.

ECOS. (2017) *The Revised Energy Labelling Regulation.* Brussels: European Environmental Citizens Organisation for Standardisation.

ECOS. (2018) *Ecodesign & Energy Labelling*. 23.7.2018. Brussels: European Environmental Citizens Organisation for Standardisation. Available at: http://www.ecostandard.org/category/activities-on-ecodesign (accessed 27.8.2018).

ECOS, EEB, IFIXIT, et al. (2017) *Circular Economy Opportunities for Digital Products*. Brussels: European Environmental Bureau.

EEA. (2016) *Energy Consumption for Electrical Appliances in Households*. Copenhagen: European Environment Agency. Available at: https://www.eea. europa.eu/data-and-maps/daviz/energy-consumption-for-electric-appliances-1#tab-chart_1 (accessed 31.8.2018).

EEB. (2018a) *Briefing on Ecodesign and Energy Labelling for a Circular Economy*. Brussels: European Environmental Bureau.

EEB. (2018b) *Product Policy*. Brussels: European Environmental Bureau. Available at: http://www.eeb.org/work-areas/resource-efficiency/product-policy/ (accessed 27.8.2018).

EEB. (2018c) *Resource Efficiency*. Brussels: European Environmental Bureau. Available at: http://www.eeb.org/work-areas/ (accessed 27.08.2018).

EEB. (2018d) *Towards an EU Product Policy Framework Contributing to the Circular Economy*. Brussels: European Environmental Bureau.

EEB, BEUC, ANEC, et al. (2016) *Let's Reinforce Not Reduce Ecodesign and Ecolabel*. Joint Letter 28.10.2016. Brussels: European Environmental Bureau.

Efficient Gaming. (2018) *Games Consoles Voluntary Agreement*. Available at: http://www.efficientgaming.eu/ (accessed 04.08.2018).

EGC. (2015) *Dyson's Action for Annulment of the Regulation on Energy Labelling of Vacuum Cleaners is Unsuccessful*. Press Release No. 133/15. Luxembourg: General Court of the European Union.

EGC. (2018) *The General Court Annuls the Regulation on the Energy Labelling of Vacuum Cleaners*. Press Release No. 168/18. Luxembourg: General Court of the European Union.

EICTA. (2005) *Industry Self-Commitment to Improve the Energy Performance of Household Consumer Electronic Products Sold in the European Union*. Brussels: European Industry Association for Information Systems, Communication Technologies and Consumer Electronics.

Elektrojournal. (2014) Falsche Labelung? Bosch erwirkt gegen Dyson zwei einstweilige Verfügungen. *Elektrojournal*: 13.10.2014.

EMF. (2018) *Circular Consumer Electronics: An Initial Exploration*. Cowes: Ellen Macarthur Foundation (EMF).

EurActiv. (2015) Toxic Cadmium One Step Closer to EU-Wide Ban. *Euractiv*: 26.5.2015.

Europe Economics. (2015) *The Economic Impact of the Domestic Appliances Industry in Europe*. Report for the European Committee of Domestic Equipment Manufacturers (CECED). London: Europe Economics.

European Commission. (2009) Commission Staff Working Document Accompanying the Document to the Commission Regulation Implementing Directive 2005/32/EC with Regard to *Ecodesign Requirements for Televisions.* SEC (2009) 1012 final, 22.7.2009. Brussels: European Commission.

European Commission. (2010) *Europe 2020. A European Strategy for Smart, Sustainable and Inclusive Growth.* COM (2010) 2020. Luxembourg: Office for Official Publications of the European Communities.

European Commission. (2012) *Report from the Commission to the European Parliament and the Council on the Voluntary Ecodesign Scheme for Complex Set-Top Boxes.* COM (2012) 684 final. Brussels: European Commission.

European Commission. (2013a) Commission Staff Working Document Accompanying the Regulation 617/2013 of the European Parliament and of the Council with Regard to *Ecodesign Requirements for Computers and Computer Servers.* SWD (2013) 219 final. Brussels: European Commission.

European Commission. (2013b) Commission Staff Working Document. Executive Summary of the Impact Assessment Accompanying the Document Report from the Commission to the European Parliament and the Council on the *Voluntary Ecodesign Scheme for Imaging Equipment.* SWD (2013) 14 final, 29.1.2013. Brussels: European Commission.

European Commission. (2015a) *Commission Recognises Voluntary Energy Efficiency Agreement for Game Consoles.* Brussels: European Commission. Available at: https://ec.europa.eu/growth/content/commission-recognises-voluntary-energy-efficiency-agreement-game-consoles-0_hr (accessed 10.8.2018).

European Commission. (2015b) *Digital Single Market.* Brussels: European Commission. Available at: https://ec.europa.eu/digital-single-market/en (accessed 7.9.2018).

European Commission. (2015c) *Europe 2020 Strategy.* Brussels: European Commission. Available at: https://ec.europa.eu/info/business-economy-euro/economic-and-fiscal-policy-coordination/eu-economic-governance-monitoring-prevention-correction/european-semester/framework/europe-2020-strategy_en (accessed 5.4.2018).

European Commission. (2015d) Report from the Commission to the European Parliament and the Council on the *Voluntary Ecodesign Scheme for Games Consoles.* COM (2015) 178 final. Brussels: European Commission.

European Commission. (2016a) *Buying Green! A Handbook on Green Public Procurement.* 3rd ed. Brussels: European Commission, DG Environment.

European Commission. (2016b) Commission Recommendation (EU) 2016/2125 of 30 November 2016 on *Guidelines for Self-Regulation Measures Concluded by Industry* under Directive 2009/125/EC of the European Parliament and of the Council. Brussels: European Commission.

European Commission. (2016c) Communication from the Commission. *Ecodesign Working Plan 2016–2019.* COM (2016) 773 final. Brussels: European Commission.

European Commission. (2016d) *Communication from the Commission. Clean Energy for all Europeans.* COM (2016) 860 Final. Brussels: European Commission.

European Commission. (2017) *Circular Economy: New Chapter for European Green Products and Organisations.* Press Release 3.6.2017. Brussels.

European Commission. (2018b) *Circular Economy: New Rules Will Make EU the Global Front-Runner in Waste Management and Recycling.* Press Release IP-18-3846 22.5.2018. Brussels: European Commission.

European Commission. (2018c) *Energy Star.* Brussels: European Commission. Available at: https://www.ec.europa.eu/energy/en/energy-star.

European Commission. (2018d) *EU Ecolabel.* Brussels: European Commission. Available at: http://www.ec.europa.eu/ecat/category/en/18/televisions.

European Commission. (2018e) *EU Ecolabel Electronic Equipment/ Personal Computers.* Brussels: European Commission. Available at: http://www.ec.europa.eu/ecat/category/en/20/personal-computers.

European Commission. (2018f) *EU Ecolabel Electronic Equipment/ Portable Computers.* Brussels: European Commission. Available at: http://www.ec.europa.eu/ecat/category/en/21/portable-computers.

European Commission. (2018g) *European Circular Economy Stakeholder Platform: A Joint Initiative by the European Commission and the European Economic and Social Committee.* Brussels: European Commission. Available at: http://www.ec.europa.eu/environment/circular-economy/index_en.htm (accessed 20.08.2018).

European Commission. (2018h) *Green Public Procurement.* Brussels: European Commission. Available at: http://www.ec.europa.eu/environment/gpp/eu_gpp_criteria_en.htm.

European Commission. (2018i) *High Level Steering Group of the European Innovation Partnership on Raw Materials (E03391).* Brussels: European Commission. Available at: http://www.ec.europa.eu/transparency/regexpert/index.cfm?do=groupDetail.groupDetail&groupID=3391 (accessed 23.8.2018).

European Parliament. (2015) *MEPs Veto Cadmium Exemption Plans for Displays, Lightings and TVs.* Press Release 20.5.2015. Brussels: European Parliament.

Eurostat. (2018) *Energy Consumption in Households.* Available at: https://www.ec.europa.eu/eurostat/statistics-explained/index.php/Energy_consumption_in_households (accessed 14.8.2018).

EuroVAprint. (2018) *Voluntary Agreement.* Available at: http://www.eurovaprint.eu/pages/voluntary-agreement/ (accessed 4.8.2018).

Farrell S. (2015) German Vacuum Cleaner Firm Set to Sue Dyson Over Energy-Test Claims. *The Guardian*: 28.10.2015.

Fayole C and Arditi S. (2018) We Need More Durable and Reparable Products to Build a Circular Economy. *Euractiv*: 8.2.2018.

Forcier JR. (1994) *Judicial Excess: The Political Economy of the American Legal System*. Lanham, New York, London: University Press of America.

Greenpeace. (2018) *Together We Can: Rethink IT*. Available at: https://www. greenpeace.org/archive-international/en/campaigns/detox/electronics/ Guide-to-Greener-Electronics/ (accessed 12.8.2018).

GreenTouch. (2018) *Mission to Deliver the Architecture, Specifications and Roadmap to Increase Network Energy Efficiency by a Factor of 1000 Compared to 2010 Levels*. Available at: https://s3-us-west-2.amazonaws.com/bell-labs-microsite-greentouch/index.html.

Haucke F, Lenschow A and Pollex J. (2019) Consumption for Sustainability? Exploring Societal and Political Gynamics in Digital Society. In: Boucher JL and Heinonen J (eds) *Sustainable Consumption: Promise or Myth? Case Studies from the Field*. Cambridge: Cambridge Scholars Publishing.

Heinzle S and Wüstenhagen R. (2009) *Consumer Survey on the New Format of the European Energy Label for televisions: Comparison of a 'A-G Closed' Versus a 'Beyond A' Scale Format*. St. Gallen: University of St. Gallen.

Henningsen J. (2011) Energy Savings and Efficiency. In: Birchfield VL and Duffield JS (eds) *Toward a Common European Union Energy Policy: Problems, Progress, and Prospects*. Gordonsville: Palgrave Macmillan, 144–154.

Herring H and Sorrell S. (2009) *Energy Efficiency and Sustainable Consumption. The Rebound Effect*. Houndmills, Basingstoke: Palgrave Macmillan.

I4R. (2018) *WEEE Recycling Information: I4R-Platform*. Available at: http:// www.i4r-platform.eu (accessed 16.8.2018).

IFIXIT. (2018) *Repair Is Noble*. Available at: https://www.ifixit.org/ (accessed 23.8.2018).

Industry Europe. (2011) White Goods Leader in Europe. *Industry Europe*: 10.11.2011.

Interview COM. (2006a) Desk Officer IPP, DG ENTR, Brussels, 3.5.2006.

Interview COM. (2006b) Polic Officer Energy Efficiency, DG TREN, Brussels, 3.5.2006.

Interview COM. (2006c) Policy Officer Sustainable Production and Consumption, DG ENVI, Brussels, 23.3.2006.

Interview COM. (2017a, 2019) Head of Unit, DG ENVI, Brussels, 10.4.2017 and 9.1.2019.

Interview COM. (2017b) Polic Officer Ecodesign Directive, DG GROW, Brussels, 11.4.2017.

Interview COM. (2017c) Policy Officer Energy Efficiency, DG ENERGY, Brussels, 11.4.2017.

Interview ENGO. (2006) Senior Policy Officer, Brussels, 5.5.2006.

Interview ENGO. (2019). Senior Programme Manager, ECOS, Brussels, 10.1.2019.

Interview EP. (2017) Polic Officer Greens/EFA, Brussels, 12.4.2017.

Interview home appliance industry. (2017) Technical Executive, AMDEA, Phone 10.10.2017.

Interview home appliance industry. (2018a) Managing Director Small and Large Domestic Electrical Appliances Divisions, ZVEI, Frankfurt/Main, 23.3.2018.

Interview home appliance industry. (2018b) Head of Unit and Team Member Environment, Resources and Work Security BSH, Munich, 27.3.2018.

Interview home appliance industry. (2019a) Energy Policy Director and Environment Policy Director, APPLIA, Brussels, 10.1.2019.

Interview home appliance industry. (2019b) Senior Expert of EU Technical Government Affairs, BSH, Brussels, 10.1.2019.

Interview ICT industry. (2017) Director, Team Members, Sustainability Policy, Digital Europe, Brussels, 11.4.2017.

Interview ministry. (2017) Senior Project Manager Home and Local Energy, BEIS, London, 23.10.2017.

JRC. (2016) *EU Ecodesign for Dishwashers*. Ispra: Joint Research Centre. Available at: http://www.susproc.jrc.ec.europa.eu/Dishwashers/index.html.

JRC. (2018) *The 2018 Predict Key Facts Report. An Analysis of ICT R&D in the EU and Beyond*. Sevilla: European Commission, Joint Research Centre.

Klinckenberg F and Harmelink M. (2017) *Effectiveness of Energy Efficiency Voluntary Agreements*. Report Prepared for the Executive Committee of the 4E Technology Collaboration programme. London, Utrecht: The Policy Partners, SQ Consult.

Knill C. (2001) Private Governance across Multiple Arenas: European Interest Associations as Interface Actors. *Journal of European Public Policy* 8(2): 227–246.

London Economics and Ipsos. (2018) *Study on the Impact of the Energy Label: and Potential Changes to It – On Consumer Understanding and on Purchase Decisions*. ENER/ C3/2013-428. Final Report. London: London Economics.

Make resources count. (2018) *End of the World [Not]: Good News Stories from the War against Waste*. Available at: http://www.makeresourcescount.eu/ (accessed 27.08.2018).

Meli L. (1999) The CECED Commitment for Clothes Washers. In: Bertoldi P, Ricci A and Wajer BH (eds) *Energy Efficiency in Household Appliances: Proceedings of the First International Conference on Energy Efficiency in Household Appliances*, 10–12 November 1997, Florence, Italy. Berlin, Heidelberg: Springer, 89–91.

mure and Fraunhofer. (2008) *EU 38 Negotiated Agreement EACEM for VCRs (Stand-By Mode and On-Mode)*. Available at: http://www.measures-odyssee-mure.eu/table3_mr.asp?Cod=EU2/EU23/EU7/EU19/EU21/EU9/EU8/EU35/EU38/EU29/EU34/EU33/EU45/EU46/EU3.

mure and Fraunhofer. (2014a) *EU 2 CECED Voluntary Commitment Washing Machines II*. Available at: http://www.measures-odyssee-mure.eu/table3_mr.asp?Cod=EU2/EU23/EU7/EU19/EU21/EU9/EU8/EU35/EU38/EU29/EU34/EU33/EU45/EU46/EU3.

mure and Fraunhofer. (2014b) *EU 3 CECED Voluntary Commitment on Household Refrigerators, Freezers and Combinations.* Available at: http://www.measures-odyssee-mure.eu/table3_mr.asp?Cod=EU2/EU23/EU7/EU19/EU21/EU9/EU8/EU35/EU38/EU29/EU34/EU33/EU45/EU46/EU3.

mure and Fraunhofer. (2014c) *EU 8 CECED Voluntary Commitment Diswashers.* Available at: http://www.measures-odyssee-mure.eu/table3_mr.asp?Cod=EU2/EU23/EU7/EU19/EU21/EU9/EU8/EU35/EU38/EU29/EU34/EU33/EU45/EU46/EU3.

mure and Fraunhofer. (2014d) *EU 9 CECED Voluntary Commitment Washing Machines.* Available at: http://www.measures-odyssee-mure.eu/table3_mr.asp?Cod=EU2/EU23/EU7/EU19/EU21/EU9/EU8/EU35/EU38/EU29/EU34/EU33/EU45/EU46/EU3.

mure and Fraunhofer. (2014e) *EU 45 EICTA Self-Commitment to Improve the Energy Performance of CRT and Flat LCD Televisions and Stand by Mode for DVD Players.* Available at: http://www.measures-odyssee-mure.eu/table3_mr.asp?Cod=EU2/EU23/EU7/EU19/EU21/EU9/EU8/EU35/EU38/EU29/EU34/EU33/EU45/EU46/EU3.

Pierson P. (2000) Increasing Returns, Path Dependence, and the Study of Politics. *American Political Science Review* 94(2): 251–267.

rreuse. (2018) *Social Enterprises Active in Reuse, Repair and Recycling.* Available at: https://www.rreuse.org/team (accessed 23.8.2018).

Schnabl G. (2005) The Evolution of Environmental Agreements at the Level of the European Union. In: Croci E (ed) *The Handbook of Environmental Voluntary Agreements: Design, Implementation and Evaluation Issues.* Berlin, Heidelberg and New York: Springer, 93–106.

Senet S. (2018) Thailand: The Rich World's New Dumpsite for e-waste. *Euractiv:* 3.7.2018.

Sorrell S. (2009) The Rebound Effect: Definition and Estimation. In: Evans J (ed) *International Handbook on the Economics of Energy.* Cheltenham: Edward Elgar, 199–233.

Tanasescu I. (2009) *The European Commission and Interest Groups: Towards a Deliberative Interpretation of Stakeholder Involvement in EU Policy-Making.* Brussels: Brussels University Press.

ten Brink P and Morère M. (2002) Monitoring Mechanisms for Efficient Environmental Agreements. In: ten Brink P (ed) *Voluntary Environmental Agreements: Process, Practice and Future Use.* London, New York: Routledge, 437–460.

Valdani Vicari & Associati. (2018) *Study for the Introduction of an e-labelling Scheme in Europe. Cost Benefit Analysis.* Brussels: Digital Europe, Mobile & Wireless Forum.

VHK and ARMINES. (2015) *Ecodesign & Labelling Review Household Refrigeration.* Preparatory/Review Study Commission Regulation (EC)

No. 634/2009 and Commission (Delegated) Regulation (EU) 1060/2010. VHK, VITO, VM, Wuppertal Institute, ARMINES.

VHK, VITO, VM, et al. (2014) *"Omnibus" Review Study on Cold Appliances, Washing Machines, Dishwaschers, Washer-Driers, Lighting, Set-top Boxes and Pumps*. Brussels, Delft: VHK, VITO, VM, Wuppertal Institute for Climate.

Vogel D. (2012) *The Politics of Precaution: Regulating Health, Safety and Environmental Risks in Europe and the United States*. Princeton: Princeton University Press.

WEEE Forum. (2018) *What Is the WEEE Forum*. Available at: http://www.weee-forum.org/what-is-the-weee-forum (accessed 16.8.2018).

Willis J. (2015) Cadmium Ban in TVs: Balancing Innovation and Regulation. *Euractiv*: 18.5.2015.

Woersdorfer JS. (2017) *The Evolution of Household Technology and Consumer Behavior, 1800–2000*. London, New York: Routledge.

zerowasteeurope. (2018) Available at: https://www.zerowasteeurope.eu/about/ (accessed 23.8.2018).

ZVEI. (2018) *Neues Energielabel: Umdenken wird gefordert*. Press Release 6.12.2018. Frankfurt: ZVEI.

CHAPTER 6

The Operator:
Providing an Essential Service

Transmission system operators (TSOs) play a crucial role in the operation of an interconnected electricity grid, both within and beyond
national remits. For grid operators and politicians alike, the worst case
is a blackout, and it is the paramount goal of energy regulation to avoid
this scenario. With the increasing interconnectedness of the electricity
infrastructure in the European context, providing a public good—secure,
reliable operation of the grid and continuous supply of electricity, that
is—becomes a European endeavour. Moreover, TSOs have assumed a
central role in building a European integrated electricity market. They
are at the heart of realising a key objective of European energy policy, as
stated in the Lisbon treaty (Article 194 TFEU): ensuring the functioning of the energy market and promoting the interconnection of energy
networks.

As *operators* of infrastructure, these actors dispose of structurally
important assets. They have to ensure short term that existing capacity is
ready to respond when it is needed in operation to meet the actual load.
Medium and long term they have to make sure that there is enough
capability installed and expected available capacity to meet demand.
TSOs are thus the guarantors of both short term security and mid to
long term adequacy. To manage the infrastructure effectively, TSOs as
the operation *experts* draw on a high level of technical information and
knowledge; in the context of digitalisation, they increasingly play a role
as *innovators* in developing new technological solutions.

© The Author(s) 2019   185
S. Eckert, *Corporate Power and Regulation*,
International Series on Public Policy,
https://doi.org/10.1007/978-3-030-05463-2_6

This chapter follows the following structure: a first part presents European TSOs as key actors in the electricity markets of Continental Europe and the policy-making process of the EU. The second part examines in more detail whether and to what extent system operators assume a regulatory rather than a purely operational role in the EU context, drawing on evidence from various issues in infrastructure regulation.

EUROPEAN TRANSMISSION SYSTEM OPERATORS

There is a long-standing legacy of cross-border technical cooperation between electricity infrastructure operators in Continental Europe, which predates the creation and integration of markets in the European Community and Union for decades. Since European policymakers lack the possibility to adopt measures regarding the ownership of infrastructure, they have taken two alternative routes of market creation: they have prioritised non-discriminatory access to the infrastructure, plus they have opted for legal and organisational unbundling (Buchan 2009: Chapter 6, 2010: 404). Infrastructure-related aspects are thus a cornerstone of European energy policy, both because of the legacy of voluntary cross-border cooperation and the specificities of European policy-making.

European Transmission System Operators

Transmission system operators (TSOs) run the high-voltage grids that transport electricity. TSOs operate, maintain and develop transmission facilities. Their second task is the management of physical flow and transmission network access. They ensure a real-time physical balance between supply and demand, and convey the cost of imbalances to the responsible parties. Infrastructure operators thus dispose of structurally important assets, technical capacity and information, which are all needed in providing a common good to society, namely security of supply. In view of this particular role, it is adequate to consider TSOs as high reliability organisations. This type of organisation "must not make serious errors because their work is too important and the effects of their failures too disastrous" (La Porte and Consolini 1991: 19). The paramount goal therefore is to ensure "failure-free organizational performance" (ibid.: 20), which for electricity means security of supply by all means and at all times. As guarantors of secure electricity supply, TSOs hold an immense source of power, which may enable them to play a role in the policy process well beyond their immediate operational task.

In economic terms, this costly infrastructure is considered a natural monopoly, given it is inefficient to duplicate the grids. This is why the operation of the distribution and transportation lines is highly regulated. In a competitive environment, the monopoly position of network owners furthermore raises questions about how to regulate the ownership of the infrastructure in two aspects: first, whether ownership should be in public or private hands; second, whether vertical integration, where one company owns the infrastructure but at the same time engages in production and trade activities, bears the risk of abuse of a dominant position. European policymakers cannot impose the privatisation of public utilities on member states, yet they can define rules with respect to liberalisation and the organisation of markets. TSOs only came into existence as separate entities when in the context of liberalisation vertically integrated companies had to unbundle. That is, they had to separate tasks related to the operation of the grid and other business areas. Partly as a result of different paths of market liberalisation across countries, the TSOs in Europe diverge considerably in regard to their capacity, status and resources (Rious et al. 2008). Figure 6.1 shows the variation between national TSOs across Europe in terms of ownership and unbundling. Under European law, three types of TSOs are compliant with separation requirements, namely full ownership unbundling (OU), the Independent System Operator (ISO) model and the Independent Transmission Operator (ITO) model. Under the ISO model, the ownership and operation of the transmission grid must be separated; that is, the system operator does not dispose of the grid assets, which do still belong to an integrated company. Under the ITO model, TSOs may remain part of a vertically integrated undertaking but have to comply with a minimum degree of organisational separation, operating the network through a subsidiary. All of these three models do exist across Europe, while full unbundling and ITO are the two models most frequently used (Fig. 6.1). It further shows that only the UK has fully privatised its network, whereas most countries still have partial or full state ownership.

Depending on the history and degree of unbundling, TSOs can have a different outlook, either being more technical, operational in orientation or more economically oriented with a strategic vision. Some, especially TSOs within vertically integrated firms, are often merely the

Country	Unbundling model	Ownership Structure
Albania	OU	Fully State Owned
Austria	ITO	Mostly State Owned
Belgium	OU	Mostly Private
Bulgaria	ITO	Fully State Owned
Croatia	ITO	Fully State Owned
Czechia	OU	Fully State Owned
Denmark	OU	Fully State Owned
Estonia	OU	Fully State Owned
Finland	OU	Mostly Private
France	ITO	Mostly State Owned
Germany	OU, ITO	Mostly Private
Greece	ITO	Mostly State Owned
Hungary	ITO	Fully State Owned
Ireland	ISO	Fully State Owned
Italy	OU	Mostly State Owned
Latvia	ISO	Fully State Owned
Lithuania	OU	Fully State Owned
Luxemburg	ITO	Mostly State Owned
Netherlands	OU	Fully State Owned
Norway	OU	Fully State Owned
Poland	OU	Fully State Owned
Portugal	OU	Fully State Owned
Romania	OU	Mostly State Owned
Slovakia	OU	Fully State Owned
Slovenia	OU	Fully State Owned
Spain	OU	Mostly State Owned
Sweden	OU	Fully State Owned
Switzerland	ITO	Mostly State Owned
United Kingdom	OU, ISO	Fully Private

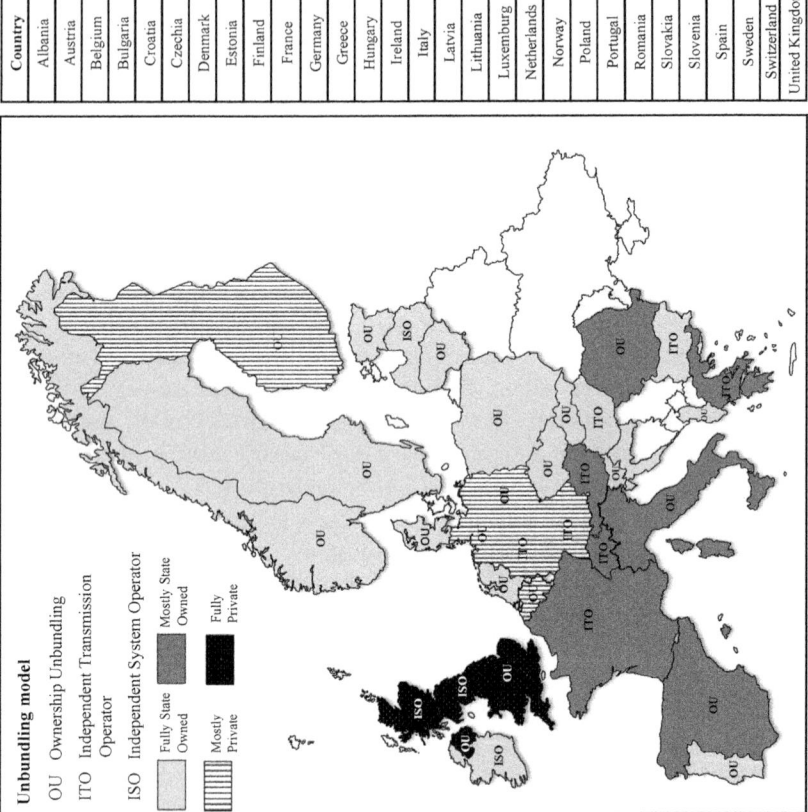

Unbundling model

OU   Ownership Unbundling
ITO   Independent Transmission Operator
ISO   Independent System Operator

Fully State Owned
Mostly State Owned
Mostly Private
Fully Private

Fig. 6.1   TSOs' unbundling and ownership structure in Europe (*Source* Own figure based on Meletiou et al. [2018])

technical expert units, lacking resources and status within their firm. In contrast, independent TSOs will have more of a strategic and managerial business orientation. The Nordic countries have been amongst the first to introduce independent regulation and to unbundle their network operators. Central-Western European countries, by contrast, underwent transformative change around a decade later (triggered by the EU), followed by the Central-Eastern and South-Eastern European countries.

The operation of high-voltage grids involves a cross-border aspect where electricity moves freely across the interconnected grid. This is another source of operational power for TSOs. Whatever the patterns of political, intergovernmental and international cooperation, TSOs have to come to terms with the technical necessity to cooperate across borders. They typically dispose of authority for historic reasons (Cutler et al. 1999: 4) where they have acquired long-standing experience in dealing with cross-border issues. In order to address the technical and financial issues resulting from such cross-border flows, grid operators have created organisational structures to engage in cooperation in accordance with existing infrastructure patterns post-war. Back then, firms were mostly integrated, which is why the European association brought together producer as well as transmission system interests inside the Union for the Coordination of Production and Transmission of Electricity (UCPTE) for Central-Western Europe. Infrastructure operators from France, Germany and Switzerland created UCPTE in 1951. In 1999, resulting from the spin-off of producer interests, UCPTE was transformed into the Union for the Coordination of Transmission of Electricity (UCTE). Over time, the regional scope of the UCTE expanded to include up to 29 TSOs from 24 Central European countries. Other regional bodies followed the example of UCTE, such as NORDEL gathering the Nordic countries in 1963, or the United Kingdom Transmission System Operators Association (UKTSOA) as well as the Association of the Transmission System Operators of Ireland (ATSOI), which were both established in 1999.

These four regional associations were the founding members of the European Transmission System Operators (ETSO) association, starting to cooperate informally inside Union of the electricity industry in Europe (EURELECTRIC) from 1999 onwards. ETSO was created as a response to an emerging European policy agenda, but its centralised structure was also seen as more appropriate to address cross-border technical issues. The persisting divergence of national and regional practice materialised to be a potential threat to secure operation in an increasingly interconnected grid (Interview TSO 2007a). In 2001, ETSO became an international association with direct membership of 32 Transmission System Operator (TSO) companies from the 15 countries of the European Union plus Norway and Switzerland. ETSO subsequently enlarged its membership towards the TSOs of East and South-East European countries.

All of the previously mentioned regional sub-organisations and ETSO itself were eventually combined with the creation of the European Network of Transmission System Operators for Electricity (ENTSO-E) in 2009. The creation of ENTSO-E has externally empowered TSOs to overcome organisational fragmentation with the creation of a single EU-wide association. ENTSO-E was established in December 2008 and became fully operational in July 2009. At the time of writing, the organisation comprises 43 electricity TSOs from 36 countries across Europe. TSOs have operated a number of voluntary schemes inside ETSO, for instance on inter-TSO compensation (ITC) or on grid security. Cooperation on grid security originates in an immediate reaction to the November 2006 blackout discussed in the Introduction.

It is therefore apparent that TSOs as the owners of the high-voltage grids to transport electricity have a key role to play in operating the infrastructure safely and reliably, and contributing to the integration of European markets. Private authority in this field relies on a long-standing legacy, and legitimacy has been acquired both through the "special expertise" and the "historical role of private sector participants" (Cutler et al. 1999: 4). Dedicated TSO interests have only entered the picture in the context of liberalisation and unbundling. Beyond the secure operation of the (existing) interconnected grid, the single market agenda of EU policymakers further magnifies the centrality of these actors. With the objective to integrate national markets, issues such as the allocation of costs for the cross-border use of infrastructure and investment in required infrastructure become crucial—and these are issues where infrastructure operators sit in the driving seat. What is more, some of the TSOs' fundamental economic interests correspond with the European market integration agenda. As owners and operators of infrastructure, they have a natural interest in expanding their asset base, for instance by investing in interconnectors (Eyre 2016: 136; Interview COM 2017, 2019b).

Market Participants, NGOs and Consumers

The European landscape of organised interests and stakeholders has changed dramatically over the last decades as a consequence of liberalising and reorganising the sector. In this section, the role of various market participants will first be discussed, next it will go on to shed light on the relevance of environmental and consumer-related interests.

As mentioned previously, TSOs as separate entities have only come into existence in the course of EU-induced market opening, with a varying degree of organisational, legal and economic independence. With the unbundling agenda, vertically organised firms have been restructured, splitting up generation, transmission, distribution, supply, exchange and trading activities. Some of them, such as the vertically integrated German company Eon, have started to sell their power grid as a reaction to the Commission's sector inquiry conducted in 2005 and 2006. While initially the sector was unified and organised in the single business association EURELECTRIC since 1989, new associational structures have emerged over time. This also meant that interest constellations underwent change. At the time when the Internal Energy Market (IEM) discussion unleashed, there was only EURELECTRIC representing the sector, alongside the member states and the European institutions. Electricity firms organised inside EURELECTRIC massively lobbied against market liberalisation in the mid-1990s, but failed to forestall the reform (Eising 2002, 2009: 138; Eising and Jabko 2001). Back then there were no independent regulators, nor was there a distinction within the electricity sector between various business activities. Initially, most of the European energy companies were fervently opposed to the liberalisation agenda, with the exception of the Anglo-Saxon and Nordic companies who took a more accommodating stance. European TSO cooperation, encouraged by the Commission, was initiated inside EURELECTRIC when TSOs started to cooperate informally as of 1999. They then set up a proper association with direct membership and a programme in 2001 (Interview ETSO 2007a). Other market actors also created their associative structures independent from EURELECTRIC, e.g. the European Federation of Energy Traders (EFET) created in 1999 or the Association of European Energy Exchanges (EuroPEX) created in 2001.

Inside the industry, there is a fundamental divide between users of infrastructure and providers of infrastructure as to the question of maximising capacity versus maximising security of supply. Business actors such as traders or generators are in favour of maximising the available capacity and suspect that existing capacity is not being used efficiently by TSOs for economic reasons (Interview energy industry 2007a, b). TSOs, by contrast, take a more cautious approach to the use of capacity for security reasons, i.e. their preference is on the side of maximum security (Interview TSO 2007a, b).

Compared to the other industry branches studied in this book, TSOs are not heavily exposed to public or NGO pressure (except in the case of a blackout), nor are consumer interests particularly well organised or represented at the EU-level. Most visible resistance against TSO activities takes the form of public opposition to the construction of new power lines at the local level. This opposition frequently involves environmental concerns and ENGO mobilisation. By contrast, the impact of the cost of infrastructure on individual consumers is rather abstract, and the share of network cost in consumer end prices is comparatively small, as Fig. 6.2 illustrates, which further highlights considerable variation across countries. Nevertheless, there have been attempts at the European level to address the concerns of both these aspects by European policymakers and stakeholders. As the cost for the transmission infrastructure is ultimately born by consumers and taxpayers, efficient use of existing infrastructure and new investment must be a policy priority.

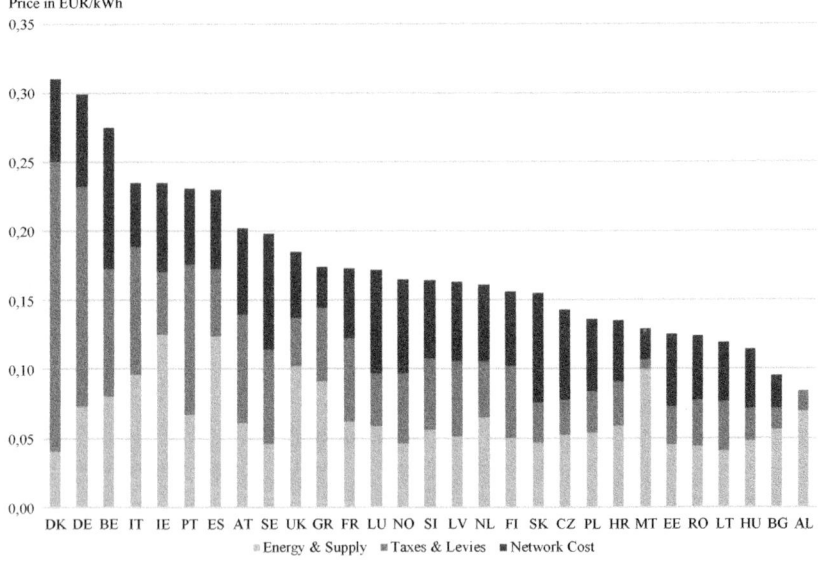

Fig. 6.2 Electricity prices components for household consumers (*Source* 2016 data, Eurostat [online data codes: nrg_pc_204_c])

Generating public acceptance for the construction of new infrastructure has become more acute in meeting the double challenge of market integration and the transition to renewable energy (Solorio and Jörgens 2017). In order to facilitate exchange and cooperation beyond the national context, the Renewable Grid Initiative (RGI) was created in 2009 (Interview ENGO 2017). The RGI seeks to build an advocacy coalition, joining the interests of transmission system operators and ENGOs in the transition to renewable energies. In 2018, RGI was composed of 18 members, 10 TSOs and 8 NGOs. The concept behind the RGI is the idea that TSOs should drive the transition towards renewables, and the RGI seeks to push them in this direction. As experts regarding the technical feasibility and operational security in the process of allocating energy from renewables, TSOs are the actors who can effectively reassure policymakers that no risk is involved in the energy transition. On the other hand, the RGI seeks to convince ENGOs that grid expansion is needed to allocate production from renewable energy and that they thus need to team up with TSOs in the pursuit of a common cause. The organisation is financed by membership contributions and through third-party funding, and financially supports the work of ENGOs on grid aspects. The declared goal is to create new knowledge and expertise inside the ENGO community. Another goal of the RGI is to identify suitable ways of dealing with environmental impacts and engaging with the public when constructing new infrastructure. In 2011, the RGI assembled a coalition of 24 organisations including: World Wide Fund for Nature (WWF), Greenpeace, Birdlife International, and Friends of the Earth (FoE) Europe as signatories of the "European Grid Declaration on Electricity Network Development and Nature Conservation" (EGD). The goals of the EGD are a sustainable grid development taking into account biodiversity considerations. Overall, therefore, the RGI is reliant on voluntary cooperation and seeks to establish visible examples of best practice. It exemplifies how business and ENGO interests may actually co-evolve.

Consumer interests have been at the heart of the liberalisation agenda from the outset, given that the European Commission expected benefits from the market opening for all types of consumers, whether they are large or small (European Commission 1991: 3–4). As end prices have been on the rise for a variety of reasons over the last decades, energy costs have become an increasingly salient issue (Bouzarovski and Petrova 2015). Consumer organisations such as BEUC work on energy-related issues and have, for instance, provided input on the consumer-related aspects in the Clean Energy Package (BEUC 2017). The informal gathering of national regulatory authorities (NRAs) inside the Council of European Energy Regulators (CEER) has further sought to build up EU-level capacity on consumer issues (Interview regulator 2017; Interview CEER 2007). As energy and especially network costs are regulated, the price issue is of particular importance to NRAs gathered inside CEER. Further, the European Parliament has been vocal on consumer-related interests and has been successful in including energy poverty as an objective of European energy policy with the Third Energy Package, against the initial reluctance of the European Commission (Haber 2018: 321). Since then, the European Commission has taken on board the issue. A study as well as a communication on energy prices and costs in Europe (European Commission 2014) was part of the European Commission's proposals for the energy and climate goals for 2030. The study attributed price increases to the combined effect of higher network tariffs and energy taxes as well as renewable subsidies, while also emphasising price differences across member states. Based on these findings, the Commission proposed "a new" or "fair deal for consumers" in the 2015 Energy Union Strategy and Clean Energy Package (European Commission 2015: 11; 2016a: 9–11). The Commission suggests to include consumer-related goals into the new governance framework, requiring that member states report on energy poverty and related measures, and to set up an Energy Poverty Observatory (European Commission 2016a: 11). While the European Parliament has focused on vulnerable customers and energy poverty as a non-desirable side effect of liberalisation (Haber 2018), the European Commission continues to build on the market-approach, promoting the "phasing-out of all regulated prices" (European Commission 2015: 12). In the proposed recast of the electricity directive (European Commission 2016b), the Commission inserted consumer participation and the free choice of electricity suppliers for all customers as well as protecting energy poor or vulnerable customers as goals of energy policy. According to the Commission, vulnerable consumers should be protected through the general welfare system at member state and local level rather than through sector-specific social regulation.

The TSOs' Role in European Energy Governance

The realisation of an IEM pre-supposed building up governance capacity at the European level in order to tackle cross-border issues (a detailed discussion is provided in Mathieu 2016: 85–125). As I have discussed elsewhere, both regulatory governance networks and self-regulation by industry have been constitutive elements in the evolution of European energy governance (Eckert 2016). The timeline in Fig. 6.3 shows how European regulation and TSO cooperation have evolved over time.

In order to build up policy expertise and competence, the European Commission initiated dedicated energy fora by the late 1990s, following the first energy directives—one for gas located in Madrid and one for electricity located in Florence. The Florence Electricity Forum (FEF) first met in 1998 and brought together market participants and regulators. The effectiveness of the FEF has been intensely discussed in the literature (Eberlein 2003, 2008; Vasconcelos 2001; Héritier 2003). The FEF more or less failed as a decision-making device, yet it triggered the creation of institutional structures such as ETSO in 1999 and the Council of European Regulators (CEER) in 2000. The introduction of independent regulators became a mandatory requirement with the new

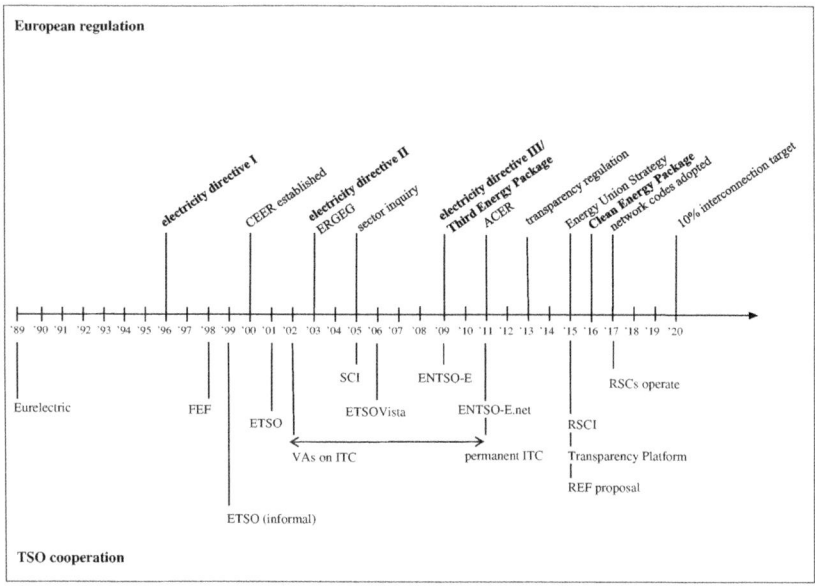

Fig. 6.3 Timeline of European energy regulation and industry cooperation (*Source* Author's illustration)

legislation adopted in 2003, which also formalised their cooperation within a European Regulators Group for Electricity and Gas (ERGEG, created by Commission decision 2003/796 EC). ERGEG has a formal mandate to provide policy advice to the Commission, while the CEER continues to exist as an informal cooperation structure (also discussed by Eberlein 2008: 86). With the Third Energy Package adopted in 2009, ERGEG was transformed into the Agency for the Cooperation of Energy Regulators (ACER). ACER started to operate in 2011. The willingness of these national regulators to cooperate transnationally is pronounced in comparison with other sectors, given the degree of interdependence and the need for cross-border coordination in electricity (Maggetti and Gilardi 2014). ACER does integrate stakeholder input through its Electricity Stakeholder Advisory Group (AESAG) established in 2011. It includes the major sector associations such as ENTSO, EURELECTRIC and EFET but also the associations of major energy users such as the chemical industry. The role of TSOs in the policy realm has been consolidated with the Third Energy Package. The third electricity directive did also impose more detailed rules in terms of unbundling, whereas the second electricity directive laid down that member states designate TSOs, specify their tasks and comply with some minimum requirements (Articles 8–10 directive 2003/54/EC). While the unbundling options laid down in the directive allowed some leeway for member states—as a result of massive national resistance from Germany and France—the sector enquiry, conducted by DG Competition in 2005 and 2007 (European Commission 2007a), proved de facto more effective in incentivising integrated companies such as Eon to sell their grid in order to pre-empt competition cases (Buchan 2009: Chapter 7).

Hence, both networks bringing together TSOs and NRAs have seen their role formalised in the subsequent rounds of legislation. The forum process triggered institution-building and thus prepared the ground for later steps in the process, namely to set up ACER and ENTSO-E. An important difference between the NRAs' and TSOs' European organisations is that on the regulators' side formal cooperation (inside ERGEG, later ACER) is institutionally separated from informal cooperation (inside the CEER), while on the TSOs' side it is not. As a result, ENTSO-E as an organisation is double-hatted, allowing for both cooperation to fulfil a mandate formalised in EU law *and* informal cooperation. Here, the comparison with organisational structures in the gas sector is insightful: Eurogas, the lobbying arm of the industry, is an organisation separate from ENTSO-G, which fulfils a formal mandate. Differently from ENGSO-G, where membership is limited to EU countries, ENTSO-E does include non-EU countries (discussed in further detail in Chapter 7). This gives ENTSO-E additional flexibility in terms of territorial coverage and inclusiveness, which can turn out to be a wild card vis-à-vis regulators in the context of a physically interconnected market.

Once established as a distinct player in European energy policy, TSOs effectively voiced their interests through their new association. According to policy insiders, early on in the process TSOs were trusted more by the Commission than by the regulators (Interview TSO 2007a). Indeed, some national regulators proved reluctant to support the European agenda. Further, TSOs proved more effective in their cooperation. For example, TSOs managed to agree on a common stance on cross-border traffic, whereas the regulators failed to achieve the required consensus in their group (Interview TSO 2007a, c). The formal role attributed to TSOs in the Third Package can be seen as proof of this trust. In fact, the revised legislative framework established ENTSO-E as a "fundamental regulatory agent" (Mathieu 2016: 113), a move which gave rise to quite some political controversy and opposition from NRAs. In the run-up to the Third Package, ETSO lobbied intensely to see its role enhanced, fearing a loss of influence where the regulators' body could become more powerful with the introduction of some ERGEG+model. The Commission then put forward a proposal which was envisaging a strikingly weak role for the regulatory network. In fact, regulators would have merely formed a consulting body with hardly any direct competencies (European Commission 2007b: 11–12, 25–27). By contrast, the Commission suggested giving a rather encompassing mandate to a formalised TSO network. The development of EU-wide market and technical codes formed part of this mandate (European Commission 2007b: 13–15), as DG Energy and Transport was of the opinion that only TSOs held the required expertise to develop these codes. This allocation of power seemed unbalanced, and national regulators were highly critical of the proposal. In their view, it risked "codifying a model of principally self-regulation by network operators at EU level" (CEER 2008b). Interestingly, the CEER managed to build an advocacy coalition amongst Member of European Parliaments (MEPs) rather than with member states. Rapporteur Alejo Vidal-Quadras (Spain, EPP-ED) argued that several tasks attributed to TSOs "should be in the hands of the regulatory authorities instead" (European Parliament 2008: 33).

More specifically, he argued that the agency, rather than the TSOs, should be in charge of developing technical codes in areas such as trading and market transparency and consulting stakeholders (European Parliament 2008: 33–34). Inside the Parliament, support was voiced for a much stronger agency. However, along the lines of the famous "Maroni doctrine" the Commission pointed to the constraints of delegating tasks to a single agency (Chamon 2016: 208–209). The outcome was a more powerful agency than previously envisioned, yet still a body that functioned more as a formal network of national regulators with a centralised office rather than as a supranational agency per se (Thatcher and Coen 2008). The role of the ACER "is not the execution of delegated regulatory Commission competencies, but the coordination of the regulatory decisions of independent national regulators" (European Commission 2016d: 22). ACER can adopt positions and recommendations addressed at TSOs, NRAs and EU institutions, as well as decisions on specific cross-border aspects. ACER was formally established in March 2011, two years later than the TSO network which started to operate in 2009. There was thus an alliance of TSOs and the Commission on the one hand as well as regulators and the European Parliament on the other. Indeed, the Council did not support an enhanced role for some kind of supranational regulatory body given the member states' preference to safeguard regulatory power within the national remits (Jevnaker 2015: 930, 936). At the same time, there is reason to believe that member states were not entirely opposed to give the TSOs some leeway. This is not surprising given the fact that TSOs continue to operate under national regulation in their territories and that, for the time being, their ownership structure is predominantly national (see Fig. 6.1).

Beyond the immediate influence of TSOs in the policy formulation stages and their institutionalised role, network operators have significantly shaped policy outcomes in the process of implementing European law, and through voluntary cross-border and regional cooperation. TSOs drafted the networks codes as part of the implementation of the Third Energy Package; they concluded voluntary agreements on ITC until a binding scheme was introduced; and further, they started to cooperate on security issues. In a first step, they set up the Security Coordination Initiative (SCI) in 2005, which was transformed into the Regional Security Coordination Initiatives (RSCIs) in 2015 (ENTSO 2015) and were institutionalised as Regional Security Coordinators

(RSCs) in 2017. Through their cross-border cooperation, TSOs frequently prepared the way for subsequent policy measures adopted at European level. This also holds for the most recent policy proposal put forward by the European Commission in 2016 as the so-called Clean Energy Package.

Network Aspects in the Clean Energy Package

Another round of revisions of electricity market regulation is underway since 2015. These revisions are part of the "Energy Union" agenda, a key project of the Juncker Commission. The Commission's Vice President for the Energy Union, Maros Sefcovic, proposed an overarching strategy in February 2015 (European Commission 2015). The Council endorsed the proposal in its March 2015 meeting (European Council 2015). In November 2016, the Commission adopted a package of proposals entitled "Clean Energy for all Europeans", usually referred to as the Clean Energy Package (European Commission 2016a). Out of altogether eight proposals seven constitute revisions, while a new piece of legislation tackles overarching governance issues. The new measures on energy efficiency standards for buildings and for renewable energy use were adopted in May and in June 2018, respectively (European Commission 2018). Further, in December 2018, policymakers closed negotiations on the energy efficiency directive as well as the new regulation on the governance of the Energy Union (regulation (EU) 2018/1999). In the same month European negotiators forged a deal on the internal electricity market and ACER regulations, both awaiting member state approval at the time of writing (Simon 2018; Council of the European Union 2018).

The overarching goal of the Clean Energy Package is to complete market integration, while ensuring security of supply and increasing the share of renewables. The 2015 Commission strategy identified five broad priority areas: security of supply, solidarity and trust; a fully integrated energy market; energy efficiency; de-carbonisation; and research, innovation and competitiveness. The Commission highlights the need for investment in infrastructure in order to secure a well-interconnected European network (European Commission 2016a: 8). Member states called for building infrastructure and interconnections especially to peripheral regions, for fully implementing and enforcing the energy acquis, and for putting priority on security of supply issues (European Council 2015: 2).

Institution-wise, the package mostly suggested an incremental evolution of the institutional framework (Interview COM 2017, 2019a). The only leap in building up regulatory capacity was the Commission's proposal to create "Regional Operational Centres" (ROCs). In regard to the cooperation between regulators and TSOs, the strategy emphasised that the existing bodies "still reflect national views" and that cross-border cooperation needed to be strengthened and improved. The Commission envisioned "significant reinforcement of the powers and independence of ACER" currently holding "very limited decision-making rights". That said, the proposal discards the option to transform ACER "to something closer to a pan-European regulator" (European Commission 2016d: 16). Giving ACER more power would require significant change in the agency's budget and staff. Furthermore, the Commission argued that a more centralised structure would unduly weaken the NRAs' role (European Commission 2016d: 16, 22). The Commission has thus been cautious to delegate further power to the European agency, which since its creation has managed to have a say in most ongoing policy discussions (Interview COM 2017, 2019b). At the same time, simply safeguarding the status quo would fail to address the "regulatory gap as regard NRAs' regulatory functions at regional level" (European Commission 2016d: 17). Instead, the Commission proposed "a system of coordinated regional decisions and oversight of certain topics by NRAs of the region" (European Commission 2016d: 17). The creation of ROCs would thus come along with enhanced regulatory oversight at the regional level. This would, of course, also affect the voluntary regional cooperation of TSOs. With respect to infrastructure operators, it was argued that "Transmission system operation will need to become much more integrated" (European Commission 2016d: 58) and that there was a need "to better define the role of ENTSO-E in order to strengthen its coordination role and render its decision-making process more transparent" (European Commission 2016c: 8). By contrast, industry actors (other than TSOs) wanted to see regulatory oversight through ACER strengthened, especially where appeal routes and checks and balances are concerned (Eyre 2016: 144–145).

The creation of regional operational centres (ROCs) was by far the most controversial issue in the negotiations (Baker et al. 2017: 4–5; Interview COM 2017, 2019a). ENTSO-E, bluntly speaking, had an interest in maintaining the status quo and in *preventing* enhanced regional oversight. To that end, TSOs argued that the Regional Security Coordinators (RSCs), introduced in 2017 as part of the network code process, were sufficient in addressing security of supply issues. Rather than introducing a new layer of regulatory capacity, ENTSO-E suggested to opt for a forum process. Regional Energy Forums (REFs) were proposed as new structures in order to address political areas of cooperation (ENTSO 2017). It is not surprising that TSOs were backed by member states, opposed to shifting power towards the European level, in their positioning. The Council, in its negotiation position agreed in December 2017, opposed the introduction of the ROCs and instead suggested to maintain the RSCs (Council of the European Union 2017). What is more surprising, however, is that MEPs this time around did not support the call for more regulatory capacity on cross-border issues—in sharp contrast with negotiations on the Third Package where the European Parliament was the major ally of regulators in fighting for a more powerful agency (Jevnaker 2015). The reporting duty on the electricity directive was with the committee for Industry, Transport and Energy (ITRE), the committee for Environment (ENVI) gave an opinion. The ITRE report suggested the creation of "coordination" rather than "operational" centres. While the report identified a need to enhance regulatory oversight through ACER at regional level, it argued that the resources of these regional coordination centres should be limited as much as possible (European Parliament 2018a). The committee's rapporteur Krišjānis Kariņš (EPP, Latvia) stated that the "ultimate responsibility for the security of the system has to remain with the transmission system operators" rather than the regional centres (European Parliament 2018a: 107). Similarly, the ENVI rapporteur Ivo Belet (EPP, Belgium) argued that regional cooperation should not be imposed top-down but should be developed bottom-up by TSOs (European Parliament 2018b: 109). MEPs may well be aware of the reluctance to support further shifts of competencies towards the European level in their constituencies. However, this lack of support to strengthen European administrative and regulatory capacity may go to the advantage of TSOs. The compromise struck in December 2018 was to introduce coordination centres, managed by the TSOs, while also enhancing regional regulatory oversight. This solution secures a balance between national and supranational interests, and between TSOs and the regulators (Interview COM 2017, 2019a).

Subsequent rounds of EU regulation show that TSOs have been particularly apt in organising and making their voice heard at EU-level.

Already the timing of the creation of ETSO and the CEER indicates that the first move was on the side of system operators and not NRAs. TSOs created their European association before it was due, and also managed to swiftly provide the resources needed (Interview COM 2017, 2019a). To be clear, I do not deny the type of collective action problems ENTSO-E faces in accommodating different preferences of TSOs, diverging in their ownership and unbundling structure, and operating in quite distinct national and regional environments. In the run-up to the Third Energy Package, for instance, ETSO could not formulate a common position on unbundling given its very diverse membership including vertically integrated firms (Interview TSO 2007c). Nevertheless, TSOs share an interest in safeguarding their architectonical role in integrating markets and in expanding the interconnected grid. Hence, they usually manage to find workable compromises and generally act as a united bloc (Interview regulator 2017). The evolution of EU energy governance underpins the argument that TSOs have effectively built up trust amongst policymakers and thus acquired and consolidated their authority. In the negotiations of the Clean Energy Package industry was concerned that the regulatory straightjacket might become too tight with a stronger, more centralised agency, which is why industry representatives kept emphasising that there was no need for yet another round of regulation (Interview TSO 2017). While TSOs will have to comply with a number of new requirements once the Package is fully adopted, they certainly can live with the outcome.

Operator or Regulator?

The evolution of energy governance illustrates how TSOs have proactively shaped the emerging architecture and secured themselves an important role in the European energy market. Here, I will discuss in further detail three examples where TSOs have undertaken a central role, namely in allocating the cost for the use of infrastructure across borders, in managing congestion, in contributing to network development, and in drafting network codes.

Allocating the Cost for the Use of Infrastructure

Remuneration schemes were historically designed within the remits of nation states, yet electricity flows do not stop at the borders. Trading electricity therefore involved practices of "pancaking" national tariffs, i.e. of accumulating taxes at national borders for the usage of neighbouring electricity grids. This practice is incompatible with the idea to integrate national markets into one bigger regional market. An appropriate mechanism to cover the cost of transmission losses and the infrastructure cost to host transit flows thus had to be found. This was one of the priorities for the European Commission when launching the IEM. Lacking the required technical expertise, information and regulatory capacity, the Commission sought to systematically involve stakeholders in the problem-solving process in the framework of the FEF created in 1998. The Forum was supposed to develop an adequate solution, bringing on board regulators and market actors. However, the issue turned out to be highly controversial in the subsequent discussions (Eberlein 2003). Decision-making was stalled on several instances, as the non-binding coordination failed to resolve the conflicts and to compensate for the Commission's lack of hierarchical powers vis-à-vis diverging national and stakeholder interests (Eberlein 2008). Despite lengthy discussions, no policy agreement was reached at the FEF.

When proposing the second legislative package, the Commission did, however, build on the expert input generated in FEF discussions. Regulation (EC) No 1228/2003 on cross-border exchanges in electricity defined the general principles guiding the mechanism, imposed transparency rules on the TSOs and attributed the approval of compensation schemes to NRAs. In its Article 3 on the inter-transmission system operator compensation mechanism, it addressed voluntary cooperation between TSOs. Such voluntary cooperation, it was stipulated, should follow guidelines adopted and amended by the Commission, based on advice from national regulators. The process to agree to such guidelines proved difficult, however, and discussions came to a halt at several instances. NRAs inside ERGEG disagreed significantly on the appropriate design of ITC schemes.

While policymakers and regulators failed to agree on a common framework, infrastructure operators unilaterally began to take measures. To use Jessica Green's conceptualisation, TSOs thereby acquired "entrepreneurial authority" in confronting governance failure (Green 2014: 17). Between 2002 and 2010, European TSOs negotiated several agreements within their European association ETSO. These agreements lasted for varying periods and involved a process of continuous re-negotiation (ITC schemes for 2002, 2003, 2004, 2005–2007, 2007,

2008–2009, 2010). As a result of these agreements, individual fees both for transits (pancaking) and explicit fees for market actors (export fees) were abolished. TSOs developed a highly complex method in order to model infrastructure costs. Each method is a simplification of the reality in cross-border flows and therefore contains flaws. ETSO has worked continuously to improve the methodology. In 2007, difficulties arose in regard to which methodology was appropriate, resulting in delays in the voluntary process, and thus an interim ITC mechanism was implemented. The challenge of agreeing on an ITC mechanism is that it involves visible redistribution between national system operators, the costs of which are ultimately being passed on to national consumers. Agreements between TSOs were repeatedly stalled in a constellation whereby individual TSOs sought to avoid an increase of tariffs in their national constituency. The redistributive conflict line therefore ran between transit countries on the one hand and trading (exporting or importing) countries on the other. Figure 6.4 shows the distribution of physical energy flows across Europe in 2017, displaying clear patterns between importing and exporting countries. Switzerland, for example, is a classical transit country. Italy, Finland and the UK, by contrast, are net importers and thus have to pay more than they receive through ITC.

European policymakers and national regulators faced information asymmetries when seeking to monitor the process. In theory, they could impose a fine on operators for withholding information or giving false information (Article 12 of regulation (EC) No 1228/2003), but in practice this did not occur. Further, the national remit of existing schemes caused collective action problems not only between TSOs but also between national regulators who cooperated rather loosely within ERGEG. They held substantially diverging interests and thus could not agree on a common stance. Using its only power of effective sanctioning, individual national regulatory authorities might disapprove of an agreement reached by TSOs. Yet in practice this instrument proved to strengthen the negotiation position of individual TSOs rather than enhancing regulatory oversight. In line with a two-level game logic (Putnam 1988), individual TSOs sitting at the negotiation table could claim that their hands were tied due to the opposition of their national regulator to certain negotiation outcomes.

The rules governing ITC have been revised as a result of the Third Energy Package, by regulations EC 714/2009 (Article 13) and EC 838/2010. The adoption of the 2010 regulation made the 2009

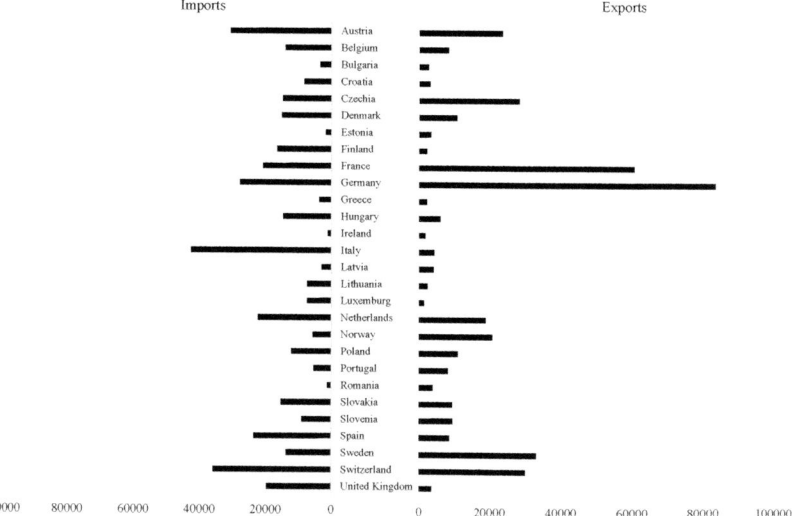

Fig. 6.4 Physical energy flows in Europe (Full year 2017 data, displayed in GWh, incl. physical energy flows between AT, BE, BG, CH, CZ, DE, DK, EE, ES, FI, FR, GR, HR, HU, IR, IT, LT, LU, LV, NL, NO, PL, PT, RO, SI, SK, SE, UK, excludes physical enery flows of these countries with AD, AL, AM, AZ, BA, BY, GE, IQ, IR, MA, ME, MK, MT, RS, RU, SY, TR, UA. Own figure using ENTSO-E power statistics, physical energy and power flows. *Source* https:// www.entsoe.eu/data/power-stats/physical-flows/ [last access 11 May 2018])

voluntary agreement on ITC the last one of its kind (ENTSO-E 2009, see Fig. 6.3). With the new regulatory framework being introduced, we thus move from "entrepreneurial" to "delegated authority" (Green 2014: 33–36). The 2010 regulation includes an annex defining binding guidelines on ITC. These guidelines provide further detail on issues such as the relevant costs, compensation and payment amounts, and attribute oversight and monitoring tasks to ACER. In particular, the agency submits a proposal on how to compensate the provision of infrastructure for cross-border flows. In March 2011, ENTSO-E put in place an enduring (ITC) mechanism. The multiyear agreement lays down compensation mechanisms that, firstly, cover the cost of transmission losses and, secondly, the infrastructure costs to host transit flows. The mechanism to compensate for transmission losses relies on the same model (with and without transit) that had already been used by TSOs previously

(ENTSO-E 2011). In order to compensate TSOs for the additional infrastructure which can be required to host transit flows, a framework fund has been established which is adopted based on a proposal submitted by ACER.

The formalised regulatory framework introduced with the Third Energy Package hence endorsed pre-existing voluntary industry practice. The existing ITC system does not, however, resolve the underlying redistributive conflict. These inefficiencies and flaws in the current system have been addressed in an own-initiative report published by ACER in March 2013 (ACER 2013b). The agency's main criticism was that the method used to assess the cost of making cross-border capacity available would not provide enough incentives to develop the network efficiently. According to an NRA representative and former ENTSO staff, people have "given up" and have accepted the current situation (Interview regulator 2017). A Commission official stated that "lately nobody has complained" and that there was therefore no reason to re-open the issue (Interview COM 2017, 2019a). The rules of inter-transmission system operator compensation therefore remain largely unchanged under the Clean Energy Package.

Managing Congestion

Another challenge related to increased cross-border flows is to effectively manage bottlenecks at interconnectors between national grid systems (congestion management). In the run-up to the Third Energy Package, findings in a sector inquiry showed that most cross-border interconnectors experience sustained congestion (European Commission: SEC 2007a 1724: 172). In the Clean Energy Package, the European Commission highlighted several shortcomings, such as the "persisting problem of significant national limitations to cross-border electricity flows" and a need to "ensure that electricity imports and exports are not restricted by national actors for economic reasons" (European Commission 2016b: 20). Economically speaking, TSOs do indeed have some incentives to reduce congestion inside their zone by pushing it towards the borders, where it is more profitable to them (Interviews energy economics expert 2005, 2008; Glachant and Pignon 2005). Related questions have even led to a court case brought by the Austrian energy regulator and TSO to the attention of the ACER Board of Appeals and the European General Court (EGC) in 2015. ACER had recommended splitting up the German-Austrian electricity price zone, arguing there was structural congestion on the German-Austrian border. E-Control and the Austrian Power Grid AG argued that this congestion was created artificially, to solve grid problems located inside Germany and at the German-Polish border (E-Control 2015). The ACER Board of Appeal rejected the appeal, and the EGC in October 2016 ruled the action inadmissible (Case T-671/15).

Technically, congestion management is complex as it is impossible to predict accurately where the huge amounts of electrons in the network will flow. There are only methods of approximation, but the calculations are not exact. The purpose of the congestion management methodology is to ensure that physical power flows associated with allocated capacity comply with network security standards. There are various methods to manage congestions (e.g. as discussed by Knops et al. 2001), which can be categorised in two groups: market-based methods, such as explicit or implicit auctioning, and non-market-based methods, such as first come, first served. Furthermore, there are transaction-based and non-transaction-based methods, and some methods are more economically oriented, while others are purely technical. Amongst experts, there is little to no consensus about which method to use. None of the methods constitutes a perfect solution, that being 100% energy security (Interviews energy economics expert 2005, 2008). In regard to managing congestion, however, TSOs need to strike a balance between securing the safe functioning of the network and increasing available capacity. There is therefore an apparent conflict between TSOs and other market participants: network operators, who have a preference for maximum energy security, and users of the grid, who have a preference for maximum capacity. In the short run, TSOs have an interest to accumulate congestion rents, and in the long run to invest in new capacity. TSOs will also have differing incentives according to whether or not lines are commercial or regulated. Thus, under certain conditions, TSOs may be tempted to withhold capacity. Withholding available capacity very often equals withholding *information* on available capacity. Overall it is in the TSO's interest not to be completely transparent about its network capacity. When allocating the cost for congestion management amongst TSOs, the redistributive consequences are not clear from the outset, that is, there is initially a veil of ignorance about the ultimate costs for the participants. This is different from the visible redistributive structure of ITC which functions through direct financial transfers. Another difference is that, ultimately, congestion management is a profitable business for all TSOs, since the cost is going to be born by users.

Historically, the number and size of price zones in Europe diverged considerably, as did congestion management methods used by each TSO in their respective zones (ETSO 2006). Cross-border governance of congestion management was based on TSO autonomy in their zones, so that they were able to manage congestion independently and would only coordinate with neighbouring TSOs from "their" side of the border. This situation has only slowly begun to change due to market restructuring as well as European and national regulation. European regulation has sought to tackle such methodological diversity and market fragmentation. A 2003 regulation on access to the network for cross-border exchanges in electricity recommended non-discriminatory, market-based solutions and non-transaction-based methods, specified by guidelines adopted in 2006 as explicit or implicit auctions. The 2009 recast of the 2003 regulation stipulated ENTSO-E's tasks and responsibilities in enhancing cooperation between TSOs, while detailed rules on congestion management were laid out through the adoption of network codes. The network code on capacity allocation and congestion management (CACM) was the second network code developed by ENTSO-E which entered into force in April 2015. The methodology, to be adopted across Europe, is based on flow-based market coupling, with most capacity allocated day-ahead and remaining capacity intra-day. Central-Western Europe, the first region in which CACM became operational, has faced serious problems: the directions of flows have changed, and flows have become more volatile. Further, the current model tends to favour bigger countries over smaller ones (Interview COM 2017, 2019a).

While there is increasing convergence in regard to the methodology used, geographical fragmentation continues to be an obstacle to a truly integrated market. The design of appropriate bidding zones is important to facilitate market-based electricity trading. Within a zone, market participants can exchange energy without capacity allocation, that is, there is no need to acquire transmission capacity to conclude electricity trade. ACER has found evidence that TSOs use capacity allocation to address congestion problems (ACER 2016: 5). The bidding zones' boundaries mostly correspond to national borders, while some member states such as Italy, Denmark, Norway and Sweden are split into several bidding zones. Some countries have also created joint bidding zones, such as Austria and Germany since 2001. Policymakers and regulators have sought to generate evidence about the consequences of the status quo for integrating electricity markets, pushing for transnational and European solutions. In 2013, ACER, in close cooperation with TSOs, launched a consultation on bidding zones in the course of implementing the network code on congestion (ACER 2013a). In the Clean Energy Package the Commission argued that "bidding zones should reflect structural congestion" and that "cross-zonal capacity should not be reduced in order to resolve internal congestion" (European Commission 2016d: 27). To address these issues, the Commission proposed a new, economically driven design of the bidding zones in Europe. These shall be "designed in a way as to maximise economic efficiency and cross-border trading opportunities while maintaining security of supply" (European Commission 2016d: 47), which will essentially not contain any structural congestion. Further, the Commission suggested that TSOs are liable to compensate market participants for the loss of capacity rights. The Commission also proposed to create "price zones" that make sense economically, in disregard of national boundaries. This would, for example, imply that Germany would be split up into two price zones (Interview COM 2017, 2019a). The design of bidding zones is one of the aspects covered in the Clean Energy Package. ENTSO-E conducted a stakeholder consultation and published the results in March 2018 (ENTSO-E 2018). TSOs argued that there was a lack of evidence for reconfiguring the bidding zones and recommended maintaining the existing zones. Other market participants, in particular EFET, voiced disappointment that ENTSO-E followed a political rationale where it wanted to safeguard national borders, prevailing in the current design rather than delivering a "technical analysis" which would "maximise welfare at European level" (EFET 2018). It is highly unlikely that such a radical overhaul of the market structure in Europe would win the necessary support of member state representatives in the Council. In this area, therefore, the market design to be implemented will surely be a far cry from the Commission's initial ambitions.

Contributing to Network Development

Network development is a cornerstone of European energy policy in order to realise the multiple objectives to integrate markets, ensure security of supply, and drive a transition towards clean energy (Buchan 2015; Eckert 2016). Building new capacity is already a daunting task at the national level, yet realising infrastructure projects of a European scale faces many more obstacles. In particular, physical interconnection challenges incumbents and dominant market players, as "competition comes down the pipes and the wires" (Helm 2014: 30). The discussion of network development issues will address the various steps in the process, such as identifying the need for new capacity, which presupposes an appropriate assessment of existing capacity, planning and promoting infrastructure projects, and financing and implementing them.

The discussion of ITC and congestion management has already given us some hints as to the complexity of managing and operating the electricity grid across borders. Many flaws and deficiencies of existing schemes will also feed into the assessment of medium and long term adequacy of supply. Again, TSOs are in a privileged position to generate and analyse the type of information needed to properly assess capacity. TSOs tend to overstate the need for investing in new capacity because they have an interest in underexploiting existing capacity for the purpose of security of supply. Further, they will want to expand their asset base. Overall therefore, TSOs will be favourable to invest in new interconnectors (Eyre 2016: 137), not at least because they can pass on the cost to the consumer (Interview COM 2017, 2019b). Also, they will be particularly eager to invest in those lines that are profitable, i.e. where they link to price zones that are at a comparably or higher level than their own zone. Regulators, by contrast, will urge that investments are based on solid cost-benefit analysis, which is why they may oppose the very idea of setting interconnection targets (Interview COM 2017, 2019b).

In order to allow for some external control by other stakeholders, it is therefore crucial that TSOs offer access to relevant information on a non-discriminatory and transparent basis. Other market participants such as traders, organised inside EFET, typically pledge for more transparency. The need to disclose information was discussed early on in the Florence Energy Forum. In 2006, ERGEG formulated guidelines of good practice in regard to transparency (ERGEG 2006). Responding to augmenting pressure from stakeholders and the Commission, TSOs started to run a transparency platform called ETSOVista in 2006 (Interview TSOs 2007c). ETSOVista, for the first time, provided pan-European data on the operation and capacity allocation of interconnector infrastructure. The threatening potential of the Third Energy Package and the competition law sector inquiry incentivised German TSOs, in particular, to support such a scheme, while up until then this kind of information was provided only by Nordic TSOs for their regional market. ETSO implemented ETSOVista between 2006 and 2010. In the course of implementing the Third Energy Package, the transparency platform was renamed ENTSO-E.net, becoming operational in 2011. As a final step, upgraded and more comprehensive information was provided as of January 2015 on the "Transparency Platform". This newest version of the platform became mandatory as a result of the 2013 transparency regulation (EU No 543/2013) which required fundamental information related to electricity generation, load, transmission and balancing. While these efforts have been acknowledged by experts as a significant improvement, problems in terms of data quality and accessibility remain—according to analysts, these are caused by the TSOs' current incentive structure and governance issues (Hirth et al. 2018).

The European Commission, in its Clean Energy proposals, suggested to not only take the provision but also the assessment of data a step further. To that end ENTSO-E was supposed to conduct a "medium to long-term Union level resource adequacy assessment" (European Commission 2016d: 29) which should provide the basis for capacity mechanisms. Hence, these would no longer be solely national in scope but allow for cross-border participation (European Commission 2016d: 31). It has been argued that significant economic benefit could be generated at an aggregate, European level by taking one of the following measures: permitting cross-border participation of generators in local capacity mechanisms; creating an EU-level common model for capacity mechanisms; or even introducing an EU-wide single capacity mechanism (Hawker et al. 2017). The Commission moreover proposed that TSOs conduct a European resource adequacy assessment for a ten-year period (European Commission 2016d: 54–58), which is supposed to be EU-wide in scope and to include all member states. TSO input would again be substantial, as they would submit to ACER a draft of their methodology, based on the principles outlined in the regulation. ACER could then either approve or request amendments to the methodology. Another goal pursued by the Commission was to eliminate pancaking practices of national capacity mechanisms in order to establish schemes at a regional level. Following that logic, national capacity mechanisms would no longer be permitted where no adequacy concern was identified. In this context the ROCs would have had the task to provide for an annual calculation on entry capacity for cross-border participation for each bidding zone border, while NRAs would have had to ensure non-discriminatory cross-border participation. A political agreement along the lines of the Commission's ambitions is unlikely on several aspects, given that some of the institutional innovations, such as the introduction of the ROCs, are already off the table.

European policymakers have sought to lend visible support to network development through the identification of priority projects and medium to long term planning. Until 2020, the EU strives to achieve a 10% interconnection target, which is to increase to 15% by 2030. The Commission first identified projects in its 2006 priority interconnection plan (COM 2016a, 846). Since 2013, a list of so-called Projects of Common Interest (PCIs) has been compiled on a biannual basis, following impact assessment and comprehensive consultation. The realisation of PCIs is supported through faster-permitting procedures and the right to apply for EU funding—such as the one provided under the Connecting Europe Facility between 2014 and 2020.

Every two years, ENTSO-E proposes a Ten-Year Network Development Plan (TYNDP). TSOs submit a draft plan to the agency for its opinion. In particular, ACER checks for the plan's consistency with national planning. ACER can recommend amendments on both types of plans. However, these TYNDPs are not binding, and decisions are ultimately taken at national level. Usually, ENTSO-E is too accommodating and tends to accept too many proposals (Interview COM 2017, 2019b). The TSO "wish-list" will therefore not go unchecked, because in any case the permit procedures are in the hands of national regulators. Further, ACER has begun to challenge the TSOs expertise, arguing that operators exaggerate the need for new capacity instead of making more efficient use of existing capacity, for instance through the use of up-to-date software tools (Interview COM 2017, 2019b). While in the Clean Energy Package rules on the TYNDP have remained largely unchanged, the Commission does, however, urge TSOs to "conduct an extensive consultation process, and at an early stage and in an open and transparent manner, involving all relevant stakeholders" (European Commission 2016d: 62). As part of the Energy Union Strategy adopted in 2015, the Commission has further created an Energy Infrastructure Forum that meets annually in Copenhagen. The Forum brings together a wide range of stakeholders and covers network development-related issues such as cross-border cost allocation, innovation or public acceptance (European Commission 2017).

The realisation of costly infrastructure projects faces a diverse set of challenges. First of all, there is the question of providing adequate funding for cross-border projects. Back in 2006, the European Commission deplored the low levels of investment in cross-border infrastructure, amounting to around 5% of total annual investment in electricity grids in the EU (European Commission 2006: 5). In 2017, the Commission estimated that up to 2030, about 180 billion Euros would be needed to upgrade and expand European energy networks (European Commission 2017: 2). One of the obstacles to investment is that available funding, such as the congestion income, is used to lower (national) tariffs and not to construct new infrastructure. Seeking to expand their asset base, TSOs privilege investment over lowering tariffs. NRAs, on the other hand, have a general preference to lower the tariffs for national consumers. The Commission sector inquiry launched in 2005 has, however, provided evidence that vertically integrated companies reinvest relatively lower shares of their income than unbundled companies in order to lower transmission tariffs (discussed by Buchan 2009: 58). While some funding may be provided from EU sources, the arsenal of available policy instruments cannot induce the level of investment necessary to establish a well-functioning internal electricity market (Bjørnbye 2006). In the Clean Energy Package, the Commission therefore prioritises the use of income to increase interconnection capacities through new investments (European Commission 2016d: 28, 52–53). Again, it is rather unlikely that member states and their regulators will accept this proposal, as they have an interest to safeguard control on the use of income (Interview COM 2017, 2019a).

Acquiring Regulatory Power?

The Third Energy Package introduced a procedure for the development of EU-wide network codes. In this process, ENTSO-E has arguably become "a fundamental regulatory agent" (Mathieu 2016: 113). TSOs indeed dispose of substantial regulatory power, since the codes are of paramount importance as an implementing tool. It is worth noting that the Commission had initially suggested that the implementation of the network codes would be voluntary, yet the rapporteur in the EP urged that they ought to be binding (European Parliament 2008: 34). He echoed the concerns of regulators who stressed that the process for making the codes binding was vital to providing regulatory certainty for investors and to develop the infrastructure (CEER 2008a). TSOs were, for their part, eager to suppress any notion that the TSO network would become a self-regulatory body (ETSO 2008).

The adoption of the network codes follows a multi-step procedure: the Commission publishes an annual priority list; ACER formulates, on request by the Commission and following consultation of stakeholders, a framework guideline; TSOs conduct stakeholder consultation and draft network codes; ENTSO-E sends a draft network code to ACER; ACER then writes an opinion and sends the code to the Commission; the Commission sends the code to the Electricity Cross-Border Committee of specialists from national energy ministries where they are adopted, with approval of the Council and the EP; and the code finally becomes binding regulation. The Commission suggested in the Clean Energy Package to add a provision which would clarify that ACER can revise draft electricity network codes before submitting them to the Commission (European Commission 2016d: 32). Furthermore, the Commission proposed to mandate distribution system operators (DSOs) with the task to draft network codes. Other market actors voiced their criticism about the operators' role and urged for a more fundamental revision of code development in order to enhance regulatory oversight and transparency. For instance, they have suggested that voting patterns of individual TSOs in network code adoption should be published (Eyre 2016: 141–142, 144). Again, it is unlikely that the procedures established with the Third Energy Package will be subject to major change.

The effectiveness of the current scheme is difficult to assess because the required expertise mainly resides with the TSOs. According to insights gathered through interviews conducted with Commission experts, it seems to be too costly, and even impossible, to obtain a neutral assessment of the status quo. One interviewee argued that in regard to the question whether TSOs unduly benefit from fulfilling their mandate to draft and prepare regulation, a "suspicion remains that they have worked for their own benefit" (Interview COM, 2017, 2019a).

The role of TSOs in the EU regulatory process shows that operators provide public goods, requiring technical expertise and cooperation, which cannot be delivered purely by public governance. Infrastructure operators have been proactive in addressing key policy challenges such as cross-border tariffs, managing congestion in the interconnected

European market, and building up cross-border capacity. Their voluntary cooperation on ITC was anticipated and thus has not only prevented more detailed regulation but also shaped the broader regulatory framework. Regarding congestion management, EU policymakers have sought to tighten the regulatory straightjacket, yet information asymmetries and complexity of the technical process are difficult to overcome, and formalised, binding regulation in many ways have endorsed pre-existing operational practice. Similarly, network development hinges on TSO assessment of existing infrastructure and their contribution to building new cross-border capacity. They are natural allies of the European agenda in that they seek to expand their infrastructure and maximise their income. In short, TSOs are in many respects in the driving seat towards a truly integrated European market. As one interviewee put it:

> Assessing the expertise of the different actors, it can be said that the really smart propositions come from the TSOs, not from the regulators, nor from the Commission. (Interview energy economics expert 2005, 2008)

The case study on the regulatory power of operators conducted in this chapter leads to the following conclusions. First, TSOs were in the driving seat of building up cross-border governance capacity thanks to their legacy of technical cooperation prior to the EU's market creation and integration agenda. They thus derived their authority from this historical role, as argued in the literature (Cutler et al. 1999: 4). Drawing on such technical, operational, but also coordination capacity, TSOs were further in a position to fill a persistent regulatory gap, or compensate for governance failure (Green 2014: 17; Eberlein and Grande 2005). Even in areas, which initially were governed by voluntary cooperation and subsequently covered by binding rules, TSOs continue to hold significant power in rule specification and implementation. The scheme for ITC is a good example. Analytically speaking, we see a move from "entrepreneurial" to "delegated", and thus regulated, authority (Green 2014: 33–36). In practice, however, this has not fundamentally reduced the rule-setting autonomy of TSOs. Simply put, there is just no alternative to the technical and operational capacity held by TSOs that is needed to formulate and specify rules. The persisting lack of European governance and regulatory capacity for cross-border issues enhances this privileged position of the operator. As political willingness to engage in further shifts of competencies towards the European level is clearly in decline, we might even see more power gains of private actors relative to public actors in the near future. Finally, TSOs as high reliability organisations (Bierly and Spender 1995; La Porte and Consolini 1991; La Porte 1996) dispose of a wild card they may play to their advantage in the public discourse: security of supply arguments. No policymaker wants to gamble with the political ramifications of a blackout. As guarantors of uninterrupted energy supply TSOs dispose of a heavy responsibility, which bears powerful threatening potential in regulation.

References

ACER. (2013a) *The Influence of Existing Bidding Zones on Electricity Markets.* Consultation Document PC_2013_E_04. 31.7.2013. Ljubljana: Agency for the Cooperation of Energy Regulators.

ACER. (2013b) *A New Regulatory Framework for the Inter-Transmission System Operator Compensation.* Recommendation of the Agency for the Cooperation of Energy Regulators 05/2013. 23.3.2013. Ljubljana: Agency for the Cooperation of Energy Regulators.

ACER. (2016) *On the Common Capacity Calculation and Redispatching and Countertrading Cost Sharing Methodologies.* Recommendation of the Agency for the Cooperation of Energy Regulators 02/2016. 14.11.2016. Ljubljana: Agency for the Cooperation of Energy Regulators.

Baker P, Finkler J and Kolokathis C. (2017) *Regional Operational Centres: A Review of the Commission's Proposal and Recommendations for Improvement.* Brussels: Regulatory Assistance Project, ClientEarth.

BEUC. (2017) *Energy Markets of the Future: How the EU's Energy Transition Should Work for Consumers.* BEUC Policy Paper. Brussels: The European Consumer Organisation.

Bierly PE and Spender J-C. (1995) Culture and High Reliability Organizations: The Case of the Nuclear Submarine. *Journal of Management* 21(4): 639–656.

Bjørnbye H. (2006) Interconnecting the Internal Electricity Market: A Goal Without a Plan? *Competition and Regulation in Network Industries* 1(3): 333–353.

Bouzarovski S and Petrova S. (2015) The EU Energy Poverty and Vulnerability Agenda: An Emergent Domain of Transnational Action. In: Tosun J, Biesenbender S and Schulze K (eds) *Energy Policy Making in the EU: Building the Agenda.* London: Springer, 129–144.

Buchan D. (2009) *Energy and Climate Change: Europe at the Crossroads.* Oxford, New York: Oxford University Press.

Buchan D. (2010) From Liberalisation to Intervention: Europe, the UK, and the Changing Agenda. In: Rutledge I and Wright P (eds) *UK Energy Policy and the End of Market Fundamentalism*. Oxford: Oxford University Press, Oxford Institute for Energy Studies, 401–420.

Buchan D. (2015) Energy Policy: Sharp Challenges and Rising Ambitions. In: Wallace H, Pollack MA and Young AR (eds) *Policy-Making in the European Union*. 7th ed. Oxford: Oxford University Press, 344–366.

CEER. (2008a) *European Energy Regulators Welcome the European Parliament's Vision*. Press Release 08–04. 25.6.2008. Brussels: Council of European Energy Regulators.

CEER. (2008b) *Making the 3rd Energy Package Proposal More Effective*. Press Release 08–01 16.1.2008. Brussels: Council of European Energy Regulators.

Chamon M. (2016) *EU Agencies: Legal and Political Limits to the Transformation of the EU Administration*. Oxford: Oxford University Press.

Council of the European Union. (2017) Outcome of Proceedings. Subject: Proposal for a Regulation of the European Parliament and of the Council on the Internal Market for Electricity (Recast) 15879/17. 20.12.2017. Brussels: General Secretariat of the Council.

Council of the European Union. (2018) Transport, Telecommunications and Energy Council (Energy). 19.12.2018. Brussels: Council of the European Union.

Cutler CA, Haufler V and Porter TP. (1999) *Private Authority and International Affairs*. Albany, NY: Suny Press.

E-Control. (2015) *E-Control Takes Legal Action Against German–Austrian Price Zone Split*. Appeal Brought Before ACER Board of Appeal; Action Brought Before EU General Court. Press Release 25.11.2015. Vienna: E-Control.

Eberlein B. (2003) Regulationg Cross-Border Trade by Soft Law? The "Florence Process" in the Supranational Governance of the Electricity Markets. *Journal of Network Industries* 4(2): 137–156.

Eberlein B. (2008) The Making of the European Energy Market: The Interplay of Governance and Government. *Journal of Public Policy* 28(1): 73–92.

Eberlein B and Grande E. (2005) Beyond Delegation: Transnational Regulatory Regimes and the EU Regulatory State. *Journal of European Public Policy* 12(1): 89–112.

Eckert S. (2016) The Governance of Markets, Sustainability and Supply. Toward a European Energy Policy. *Journal of Contemporary European Research* 12(1): 502–517.

EFET. (2018) *ENTSO-E Consultation on Its Draft Bidding Zones Review Report*. EFET Response. 9.3.2018. Brussels: European Federation of Energy Traders.

Eising R. (2002) Policy Learning in Embedded Negotiations: Explaining EU Electricity Liberalization. *International Organization* 56(1): 85–120.

Eising R. (2009) *The Political Economy of State-Business Relations in Europe: Interest Mediation, Capitalism and EU Policy Making*. London: Routledge.

Eising R and Jabko N. (2001) Moving Targets: National Interests and EU Electricity Liberalization. *Comparative Political Studies* 34(7): 742–767.

ENTSO. (2015) *Multilateral Agreement on Participation in Regional Security Coordination Initiatives.* Brussels: European Network of Transmission System Operators for Electricity.

ENTSO. (2017) *Power Regions for the Energy Union: Regional Energy Forums as the Way Ahead.* Policy Paper October 2017. Brussels: European Network of Transmission System Operators for Electricity.

ENTSO-E. (2009) *European Electricity Transmission System Operators Reach Agreement on an Interim Solution for Inter-TSO Compensation.* Press Release December 2009. Brussels: European Network of Transmission System Operators for Electricity.

ENTSO-E. (2011) *ENTSO-E puts in place an enduring inter-TSO compensation mechanism.* Press Release March 2011. Brussels: European Network of Transmission System Operators for Electricity.

ENTSO-E. (2018) *First Edition of the Bidding Zone Review.* Draft Version for Public Consultation until 9 March 2018. Brussels: European Network of Transmission System Operators for Electricity.

ERGEG. (2006) *Good Practice on Information Management and Transparency in Electricity Markets.* ERGEG Guidelines E05-EMK-06-10. 2.8.2006. Brussels: European Regulators Group for Electricity and Gas.

ETSO. (2006) *An Overview of Current Cross-Border Congestion Management Methods in Europe.* May 2006. Brussels: European Transmission System Operators.

ETSO. (2008) *Transmission Network Governance: What Does the 3rd Energy Package Envisage?* Presentation at the Florence School of Regulation Workshop on Network Governance, 21.2.2008. Florence: Florence School of Regulation.

European Commission. (1991) *Proposal for a Council Directive Concerning Common Rules for the Internal Market in Electricity and Natural Gas.* COM (91) 548 final. Luxembourg: Office for Official Publications of the European Communities.

European Commission. (2006) Communication. *Priority Interconnection Plan.* COM (2006) 846 final. Luxembourg: Office for Official Publications of the European Communities.

European Commission. (2007a) *DG Competition Report on Energy Sector Inquiry.* Brussels: European Commission.

European Commission. (2007b) Proposal for a Regulation of the European Parliament and of the Council establishing a *European Union Agency for the Cooperation of Energy Regulators.* COM (2007) 530 final. Brussels: European Commission.

European Commission. (2014) Communication. *Energy Prices and Costs in Europe.* COM (2014) 21. Luxembourg: Office for Official Publications of the European Communities.

European Commission. (2015) *Energy Union Package*: Communication from the Commission to the European Parliament, the Council, the European Economic and Social Committee, the Committee of the Regions and the European Investment Bank. A Framework Strategy for a Resilient Energy Union with a Forward-Looking Climate Change Policy. COM (2015) 80 final. Brussels: European Commission.

European Commission. (2016a) *Communication from the Commission. Clean Energy for all Europeans*. COM (2016) 860 final. Brussels: European Commission.

European Commission. (2016b) Proposal for a Directive of the European Parliament and of the Council on *Common Rules for the Internal Market in Electricity*. COM (2016) 864 final. Brussels: European Commission.

European Commission. (2016c) Proposal for a Regulation of the European Parliament and of the Council on the *Governance of the Energy Union*. COM (2016) 759 final. Brussels: European Commission.

European Commission. (2016d) Proposal for a Regulation of the European Parliament and of the Council on the *Internal Market for Electricity*. COM (2016) 861 final. Brussels: European Commission.

European Commission. (2017) Communication on *Strengthening Europe's Energy Networks*. COM (2017) 718 final. Brussels: European Commission.

European Commission. (2018) *Europe Leads the Global Clean Energy Transition: Commission Welcomes Ambitious Agreement on Further Renewable Energy Development in the EU*. Statement/18/4155 14.6.2018. Strasbourg: European Commission.

European Council. (2015) *European Council Conclusions* 19–20 March 2015. EUCO 11/15. Brussels: General Secretariat of the Council.

European Parliament. (2008) *Report on the Proposal for a Regulation of the European Parliament and of the Council Amending Regulation (EC) No 1228/2003 on Conditions for Access to the Network for Cross-Border Exchanges in Electricity* (COM (2007) 0531-C6-0320/2007-2007/0198 (COD)) A6-0228/2008. Brussels: Committee on Industry, Research and Energy. Rapporteur Alejo Vidal-Quadras.

European Parliament. (2018a) Report on the Proposal for a Directive of the European Parliament and of the Council on the *Common Rules for the Internal Market in Electricity* (Recast) (COM (2016) 0864-C8-0495/2016-2016/0380(COD)). Brussels: Committee on Industry, Research and Energy. Rapporteur Krišjānis Kariņš.

European Parliament. (2018b) Report on the Proposal for a Regulation of the European Parliament and of the Council on the *Internal Market for Electricity*

(Recast) (COM (2016) 0861-C8-0492/2016-2016/0397(COD)). Brussels: Committee on Industry, Research and Energy. Rapporteur Krišjānis Kariņš.

Eyre S. (2016) An Industry Perspective: The Primacy of Market-Building. In: Andersen SS, Goldthau A and Sitter N (eds) *Energy Union: Europe's New Liberal Mercantilism?* London: Palgrave Macmillan, 133–146.

Glachant J-M and Pignon V. (2005) Nordic Congestion's Arrangement as a Model for Europe? Physical Constraints vs. Economic Incentives. *Utilities Policy* 13(2): 153–162.

Green JF. (2014) *Rethinking Private Authority: Agents and Entrepreneurs in Global Environmental Governance.* Princeton: Princeton University Press.

Haber H. (2018) Liberalizing Markets, Liberalizing Welfare? Economic Reform and Social Regulation in the EU's Electricity Regime. *Journal of European Public Policy* 25(3): 307–326.

Hawker G, Bell K and Gill S. (2017) Electricity Security in the European Union: The Conflict Between National Capacity Mechanisms and the Single Market. *Energy Research & Social Science* 24: 51–58.

Helm D. (2014) The European Framework for Energy and Climate Policies. *Energy Policy* 64: 29–35.

Héritier A. (2003) New Modes of Governance in Europe: Increasing Political Capacity and Policy Effectiveness? In: Börzel TA and Cichowski RA (eds) *The State of the European Union: Law, Politics, and Society.* Oxford: Oxford University Press, 105–126.

Hirth L, Mühlenpfordt J and Bulkeley M. (2018) The ENTSO-E Transparency Platform: A Review of Europe's Most Ambitious Electricity Data Platform. *Applied Energy* 225: 1054–1067.

Interview COM. (2017, 2019a) *Grid Expert, DG Energy, Brussels,* 12.4.2017 and 10.1.2019.

Interview COM. (2017, 2019b) *National Expert, DG Energy, Brussels,* 11.4.2017 and 10.1.2019.

Interview energy economics expert. (2005, 2008) *Florence,* 4.7.2005 and Paris, 22.4.2008.

Interview energy industry. (2007a) *Grid Expert, EURELECTRIC, EFET, Brussels,* 20.12.2007.

Interview energy industry. (2007b) *Policy Coordination and Communication Unit, EURELECTRIC, Brussels,* 21.12.2007.

Interview ENGO. (2017) *Chief Executive Officer, Renewables Grid Initiative, Berlin,* 30.5.2017.

Interview regulator. (2007) *Deputy Secretary General, ERGEG/CEER, Brussels,* 20.12.2007.

Interview regulator. (2017) *Grid Expert, OFGEM, Former Staff ENTSO, London,* 13.7.2017.

Interview TSO. (2017) *Economic and Legal Experts, ENTSO-E, Brussels,* 11.4.2017.

Interview TSO. (2007a) Former Secretary General, ETSO, Brussels, 17.12.2007.

Interview TSO. (2007b) Member of Steering Committee, ETSO, Brussels, 20.12.2007.

Interview TSO. (2007c) *Secretary General, ETSO, Brussels,* 19.12.2007.

Interview TSO. (2008) *Manager National Grid, Florence,* 21.2.2008.

Jevnaker T. (2015) Pushing Administrative EU Integration: The Path Towards European Network Codes for Electricity. *Journal of European Public Policy* 22(7): 927–947.

Knops HPA, de Vries L and Hakvoort RA. (2001) Congestion Management in the European Electricity System: An Evaluation of the Alternatives. *Journal of Network Industries* 2: 311–351.

La Porte TR. (1996) High Reliability Organizations: Unlikely, Demanding and at Risk. *Journal of Contingencies and Crisis Management* 4(2): 60–71.

La Porte TR and Consolini P. (1991) Working in Practice but Not in Theory: Theoretical Challenges of High Reliability Organizations. *Journal of Public Administration Research and Theory* 1(1): 19–48.

Maggetti M and Gilardi F. (2014) Network Governance and the Domestic Adoption of Soft Rules. *Journal of European Public Policy* 21(9): 1293–1310.

Mathieu E. (2016) *Regulatory Delegation in the European Union: Networks, Committees and Agencies.* London: Palgrave Macmillan.

Meletiou A, Cambini C and Masera M. (2018) Regulatory and Ownership Determinants of Unbundling Regime Choice for European Electricity Transmission Utilities. *Utilities Policy* 50: 13–25.

Putnam RD. (1988) Diplomacy and Domestic Politics: The Logic of Two-Level Games. *International Organization* 42(3): 427–460.

Rious V, Glachant J-M, Perez Y, et al. (2008) The Diversity of Design of TSOs. *Energy Policy* 36(9): 3323–3332.

Simon F. (2018) EU Forges Deal on Coal Phase-Out, with Special Polish Clause. *Euractiv:* 19.12.2018.

Solorio I and Jörgens H. (2017) *A Guide to EU Renewable Energy Policy.* Cheltenham: Edward Elgar.

Thatcher M and Coen D. (2008) Reshaping European Regulatory Space: An Evolutionary Analysis. *West European Politics* 31(4): 806–836.

Vasconcelos J. (2001) Cooperation Between Energy Regulators in the European Union. In: Henry C, Matheu M and Jeunemaître A (eds) *Regulation of Network Utilities: The European Experience.* Oxford: Oxford University Press, 284–289.

CHAPTER 7

Brexit: Corporate Power Undone?

Is the British departure from the European Union (Brexit) unravelling corporate power in regulation? This is the question addressed in this chapter which examines how the unseen event of leaving the EU is going to affect UK-based companies. Both the exact timing and the type of Brexit—with or without a deal—are still unclear at the time of writing. Policymakers and business in the EU-27 and in the UK are in fact preparing for a no-deal scenario. There is a real risk of a hard Brexit a few days ahead of the original date set for Brexit, the 29 March 2019: industry and trade unions alike called for an emergency plan to avoid a no-deal (Partington 2019); MPs in the House of Commons took over control in order to find alternatives to the departure deal struck between the EU and Prime Minister Theresa May which continuously failed to receive parliamentary backing (Kuenssberg 2019); May offered to step down once the House would finally vote in favour of her Brexit deal (Daily Mail 2019). Moreover, even if we assume that the UK will enter the second phase of negotiating the future relations with the EU, we can at this stage only hypothesise about the regulatory alignment and divergence after Brexit (Armstrong 2018). What we do know for certain is that in the vote to leave politics trumped economic rationales (Jensen and Snaith 2016). In a nutshell, "Brexit is a business killing issue" (Interview MP 2017). Further, we know that UK-based business is generally unhappy with the outcome of the referendum, threatening with their own "exit" from the island (Elgot and Savage 2018; Hutton 2018;

© The Author(s) 2019
S. Eckert, *Corporate Power and Regulation*,
International Series on Public Policy,
https://doi.org/10.1007/978-3-030-05463-2_7

Monaghan and Elgot 2018). In response, high-profile Brexiteers disqualified such announcements using strong language, outspokenly so foreign secretary Boris Johnson shortly before he resigned (Crisp et al. 2018). This fierce opposition between Brexiteers and business comes as a paradox if we bear in mind that it was an alliance of UK politicians and companies who have a long-standing track record of criticising Brussels red tape. Accordingly, UK actors have been central protagonists in the EU's deregulation and better regulation agenda. One explanation to dissolve this conundrum is that populist and Eurosceptic attitudes frequently involve a critical stance on corporate power (Fuchs et al. 2017). Against the backdrop of such a specific political context, what type of outcome can we expect for the areas of regulation and sectors studied in this book? First, I will look at chemical and environmental regulation in the four industry sectors covered in earlier Chapters 4 and 5 (paper, plastics, Information and Communication Technology (ITC), home appliance). Second, I will discuss the UK's and their TSOs' role in the (Chapter 6).

CHEMICAL AND ENVIRONMENTAL REGULATION POST-BREXIT

Chemical and environmental policies are two areas where the Europeanisation of national legislation has been particularly prevalent over the past few decades (Töller 2010; Brouard et al. 2011; Heyvaert and Čavoški 2018). Disintegration therefore constitutes a window of opportunity for massive deregulation. The UK would finally have the chance to cut Brussels red tape, as promised by Brexiteers. While at first glance we could expect business to be unequivocal supporters of deregulation, we do however find that in many instances industry prioritises regulatory certainty. In an internationalised business environment industry moreover benefits from a regulatory framework that provides a level playing field beyond the national market. In the following sections I will present the economic importance of the domestic industries in the paper, plastics, home appliance and ICT sector, as well as reflect on the relevant NGO landscape in the UK. Then, I move on to discuss the potential effects of disintegration for the areas of regulation that affect industry's day-to-day business, namely chemicals, waste and resource efficiency regulation.

UK-Based Industries and Brexit

The sectors discussed in this book will be significantly affected by Brexit. This is due to their trade and supply chain patterns as much as to the impact of EU regulation on their day-to-day business. The UK-based chemical, plastics and ICT industries are internationally important sectors, while the paper and home appliance industries heavily rely on imports from EU and non-EU countries. The direct lobbying influence, or "instrumental power" (Fuchs 2007: 7), can thus be expected to be considerable especially for the plastics and ICT industries. Moreover, especially bigger, multinational players dispose of important "structural power" (Fuchs 2007: 7, 58) where they can credibly threaten to dislocate.

The UK chemical sector does not belong to the global top ten countries in chemical sales (CEFIC 2017: 6). It is, however, amongst the largest in Europe. According to 2016 data, the UK generates 7% of chemicals sales in the EU, ranking sixth after Germany, France, Italy, the Netherlands and Spain (CEFIC 2017). Domestically, the chemical industry is the second largest exporter to the EU after the UK automobile industry (EAC 2017a: 3). Its two major associations are the UK Chemical Industries Association (CIA), representing bigger manufacturers, and the Chemical Business Association (CBA), assembling companies further along the value chain. The UK chemical industry employs around 500,000 people, directly and indirectly (CIA 2017). The UK-based plastics industry is of similar economic importance (see Fig. 7.1): in 2016, demand for plastics conversion in the UK amounted to 7.5%, ranking fifth amongst EU countries, again with Germany being the top plastics converter with 24.5% of the European share (PlasticsEurope 2018: 21). The UK branch is represented by the British Plastics Federation (BPF). In 2017, BPF brought together 483 firms, many of which were small and medium-sized enterprises (BPF 2018a), covering approximately 80% of the industry (Interview plastics industry 2017). BPF reported 170,000 employees, 6200 companies, and an annual sales turnover of 23.5 billion GBP for the UK plastics industry in 2015. The same year, exports accounted for 35% of annual sales turnover with 7.5 billion GBP (BPF 2016: 7). The plastics industry presents itself as an employment

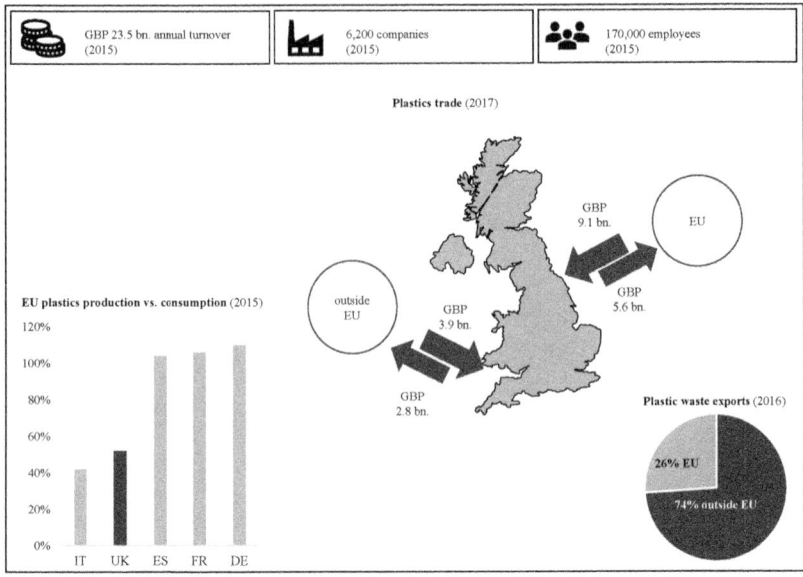

Fig. 7.1   Economic importance and trade patterns UK plastics industry (*Source* BPF 2016, 2017, own illustrations)

generator, coming second in the domestic manufacturing sectors. By way of comparison, manufacturing in chemicals counted 100,000 employees in 2015 (BPF 2016: 19). Plastics trade patterns in 2017 illustrate that the EU is an important trading partner, with a value of 9.1 billion GBP of imports from, and exports at a value of 5.6 billion GBP to EU countries. This compares to exports to non-EU countries of 2.8 billion GBP and imports of 3.9 billion GBP (BPF 2017: 1).

The UK chemical sector, and the plastics sector in particular, will be hit hard by Brexit (Global Economic Dynamics 2015: 9), especially in the case of no deal: in this case, the gross value added in the chemical industry would fall by 16% by current levels, according to a government study (House of Commons 2018). This is due to the fact that the pharmaceutical and chemical industries in the UK are the first and third most dependent on trade with the EU (Extance 2018). According to BPF estimates (BPF 2017), the no deal scenario would lead to a cost increase of around 340 million GBP for exports in the plastics sector and an increase of 540 million GBP for imports, totalling 880 million GBP. In a report based on a BPF members' survey, published in December 2018, the association reiterated concerns about the detrimental economic effects of a no-deal Brexit (BPF 2018d). The UK is a net importer of both plastic raw materials and products, with a high share of European imports (BPF 2016: 56). The UK producers increasingly depend on the import of plastic raw materials. In 2015, the UK industry produced only around 50% of the polymers it consumed, while Germany, France and Spain were net exporters at around 110% (BPF 2016: 31). Further, the UK is the fourth largest consumer of plastics in Europe. In domestic plastics consumption, packaging (44.3%) and building and construction plastics (23.6%) make up the largest share (BPF 2016: 14). The plastics industry in particular has drawn attention to the potentially negative effect of Brexit in respect to the sector's trade deficit (which is particularly high with Germany), calculating that the cost of trade with the EU under WTO tariffs could rise by 880 million GBP (BPF 2017). In 2016, 69% of the industry's trade was with Europe, compared to 16% with Asia or 8% with North America. Finally, the UK has a trade surplus in exporting plastics scrap, mainly to China but also to some European countries (BPF 2017: 3; Tamma 2018a). In 2016, 74% of total plastic waste exports went to Asia (mainly China) and 26% to Europe (see Fig. 7.1). Including material exported for recycling, the UK is in the middle range of EU member states with up to 30% of plastics going to landfill (in the absence of a landfill ban) and about the same amount going to energy recovery and recycling (PlasticsEurope 2018: 32, 33). The UK performs slightly better in recycling packaging waste, where it achieves a rate above the EU-average which is 40% (PlasticsEurope 2018: 37).

The UK paper industry is small compared to the plastics industry and other UK-based manufacturing branches (BPF 2016: 19). The Council of the Paper Industry (CPI) represents the UK-based industry. In 2017, the sector generated an annual turnover of 11.5 billion GBP, and reported 56,000 direct, and some further 86,000 indirect employees along the value chain. CPI members range from big multinational companies to SMEs (Fig. 7.2).

Voicing its concerns in the Brexit negotiations is the "number one policy priority" for the UK-based paper industry. The industry is indeed affected as far as trade patterns in European integrated supply chains post-Brexit and unified product standards are concerned (CPI 2017c: 4).

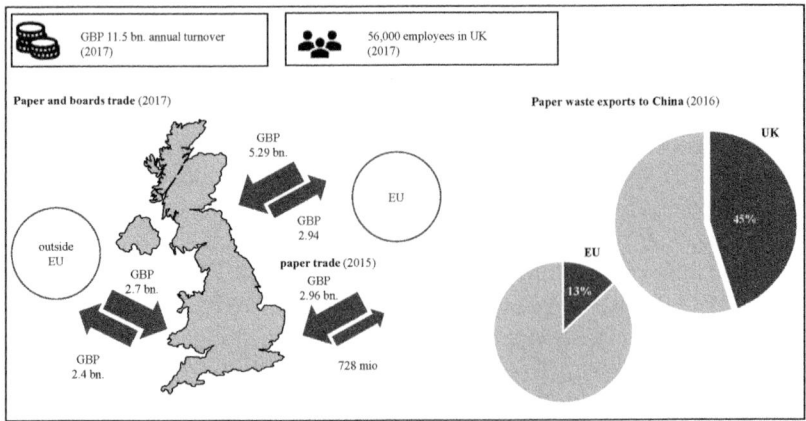

Fig. 7.2 Economic importance and trade patterns UK paper industry (*Source* CPI 2017a, c, 2018a; EPRC 2018, own illustrations)

The UK corrugated paper and paperboard industry is amongst the UK's manufacturing sectors identified as being the most dependent on trade with the EU, at a level of 87.1% trade with the EU for exports (Gasiorek et al. 2018). Conversely, the EU-based exporting companies would bear significant losses (Global Economic Dynamics 2015: 9). The UK is the largest net importer of paper globally and maintains close links especially with EU countries: in 2015, 4.69 million tonnes of paper were imported at a value of 2.96 billion GBP, compared to an export volume of only 798,000 tonnes at a value of 728 million GBP (CPI 2017a). In 2017, the UK paper industry exported paper and boards at a value of 2.94 billion GBP to EU countries, while exports to non-EU countries equalled 2.4 billion GBP. At the same time, the UK imported at a value of 5.29 billion GBP, compared to imports from non-EU countries at 2.7 billion GBP (CPI 2018a: 26). Further, the UK heavily depends on exports of paper waste: close to 8 million tonnes of paper have been collected for recycling in 2016. Out of this total amount 4.9 million tonnes were exported, of which 3.5 million tonnes went to China (CPI 2017c: 20). The UK did thus sent almost half (45%) of the total material collected to China. By way of comparison, the aggregate level of exports in the EU was significantly lower, namely 13% in 2016 (EPRC 2018: 3; CPI 2017c: 20). Including exported material, the UK achieved a 69% recycling rate in

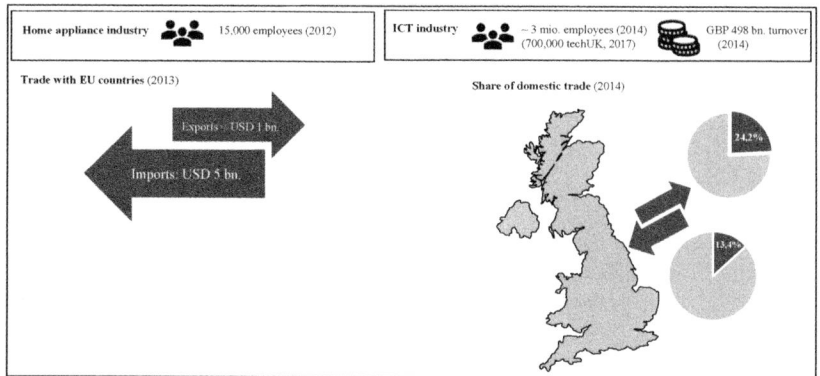

Fig. 7.3 Economic importance and trade patterns UK home appliance and ICT industry (*Source* Europe Economics 2015; frontier economics and techUK 2018; techUK 2018b)

2015, close to the EU-average of 71.9% and at about the same level with North America at 68% (EPRC 2018: 3; CPI 2017c: 20).

Both the UK home appliance and ICT manufacturers are net importers (see Fig. 7.3), yet the trade imbalance is far more significant for the home appliance industry which relies heavily on electronic device imports. In 2016, the Association of Manufacturers of Domestic Appliances (AMDEA) comprised of 35 firms (AMDEA 2017: 16). These members included small as well as bigger companies, such as Dyson or the UK-based branches of BSH Home Appliances, Miele, Samsung or Whirlpool. While AMDEA is the UK national trade association member of the European association APPLiA (formerly CECED), the big companies also hold direct membership in the EU association. For 2016–2017, APPLiA reported that between 5 and 10 manufacturing sites of direct members were based in the UK (APPLiA 2018: 24). In 2012, around 15,000 employees worked in the UK domestic appliances sector (Europe Economics 2015).

Brexit will affect the home appliance industry because it is an internationalised, importing branch (Interview home appliance industry 2017a). The major activity of UK members in APPLiA is the sale of appliances that are produced outside the UK, while a small share of parts and materials is being produced in the UK, to be processed in other countries (CECED 2017: 3). In 2014, the UK imported products at a trade value of above 5 billion US dollars from other EU countries, which compared to exports at a trade value of below 1 billion US dollars (Europe Economics 2015: 34). The UK is the single largest net importer in the EU-28 (Europe Economics 2015: 38). By way of comparison, Germany's exports equalled 9 billion US dollars and imports 8 billion US dollars the same year. In regard to Brexit, the EU home appliance association called for an ambitious trade agreement as well as cooperation between customs authorities for trade with non-EU countries. Further, the industry raised concerns regarding potential future non-tariff barriers, such as diverging regulatory or technical requirements as well as additional administrative and regulatory cost (CECED 2017: 3).

The UK-based ICT sector is a major player in the domestic and European economy. Indeed, the UK is seen as the "European tech champion" (Scott et al. 2018), which gives industry instrumental and structural power. The trade association for the UK technology industry (techUK) in 2017 represented more than 950 companies, employing around 700,000 people, covering about half of all tech sector jobs in the UK (techUK 2018b). Membership covers the digital sector broadly speaking, i.e. companies that either produce or intensively use digital technology. Members include big international leaders alongside innovative start-ups, while the majority are small and medium-sized businesses (Interview ICT industry 2017). In 2014, the digital sector generated a turnover of 498 billion GBP and gross value added (GVA) of 258 billion GBP (frontier economics and techUK 2018: 19). The sector therefore contributed significantly to the UK economy, namely with 15.7% GVA (5.3% digital producing); 15.8% turnover (4.8% digital producing); and 10.1% employment (3.5% digital-using), equalling three million jobs (frontier economics and techUK 2018: 4, 6–7) (Fig. 7.3).

Given the transnational outlook of the sector, techUK has been described as being the "most European" (Interview ICT industry) UK trade association. In 2014 (frontier economics and techUK 2018: 7), the digital sector accounted for 24.2% of domestic exports (7.5% digital producing) and 13.4% of imports (9.7% digital producing). The share of exports was particularly high in services, which amounted to 81% of the digital sector exports, and represented 46% of the total of UK services trade. For digital-producing industries, international supply chains are preeminent: 49% of inputs of goods and services in the producing sector were imported, significantly above the share of 28% economy-wide. Finally, about half of digital sector goods exports and one-third of services exports were with EU countries (frontier economics and techUK 2018: 8). The industry vigorously voices its interests in the Brexit debate. While tariffs on digital goods are determined by WTO rules, the key concerns are about trade in services and non-tariff, regulatory barriers to trade (frontier economics and techUK 2018: 6, 8).

Consumer and Environmental Organisations

Considering the role of UK consumer and environmental organisations is important as these are influential not only at the national but also at the supranational level. As discussed in Chapter 3, many ENGOs receive EU-funding, and the policy fields relevant to them are typically highly Europeanised. UK-based NGOs have been supporting the emergence of an EU-level NGO landscape in various ways (Berny 2008, 2016) and have exerted direct influence on European policies (Haigh 2015). For example, CHEM Trust as a UK registered charity has become one of the most important generators of "counter policy expertise" (Fischer 1990: 28) in European chemical regulation. It was created at the initiative of World Wide Fund for Nature (WWF) chemical experts in 2017 when the organisation ceased to cover the policy field. A new ENGO with a policy-specific outlook was deemed to give higher visibility to the health and environmental aspects of chemical regulation. In the context of the legal uncertainties involved with Brexit, the organisation is considering options to relocate its base in an EU member state (Interview ENGO 2017b). Another example of an important UK-based addition to the ENGO world is Client Earth, which in 2006 was founded in London, and opened its Brussels office in 2008 (Thornton and Goodman 2017). It fills an expanding niche in the ENGO landscape with its focus on litigation as a policy tool in advocacy work. As discussed in Chapters 2 and 3, litigation has become a powerful tool not only for businesses but also for NGOs. By generating non-corporate legal expertise in this field, Client Earth seeks to counterbalance corporate dominance (Smedley 2016). Moreover, other UK-based voluntary organisations have set the environmental agenda globally. The substantive contribution of the Ellen MacArthur Foundation (EMF) to the international diffusion of the circular economy concept (Murray et al. 2017: 374) is a case in point (EMF 2012, 2014). The advocacy work of the EMF has had a significant impact on EU and UK policymakers, setting the policy agenda on plastics (EMF 2016; Interview plastics industry 2017) or consumer electronics (EMF 2018).

In response to the Brexit decision, ENGOs in the UK formed the Greener UK campaign, bringing together 13 major environmental organisations including Greenpeace, WWF and FoE, as well as a number of supporting organisations and cooperation partners (Greener UK 2017). Similarly, academic environmental experts have aligned to maintain a blog about the potential effects of Brexit and the ongoing negotiations (Burns et al. 2016). These activities are motivated by a concern that disintegration of the EU will lead to policy dismantling. UK environmental policy, with the exception of some particularly strong domestic statutory instruments in the area of energy and climate policy, is sourced from the EU. The UK's EU Withdrawal Act, passed in June 2018 (parliament.uk 2018; GOV.UK 2018), seeks to safeguard the EU environmental policy acquis during a transition period. In a 25 Year Environment Plan published in January 2018, the UK environmental secretary Michael Gove further announced to deliver a "Green Brexit" and "to set up a world-leading environmental watchdog, an independent, statutory body to hold Government to account for upholding environmental standards" (DEFRA 2018a: 7; HM Government 2018c). ENGOs and think tanks have, however, expressed their concern about environmental protection and access to justice being weakened post-Brexit. In reaction to the government's plans they have called for stronger powers for the new body and certain guarantees to avoid what they identify as an enforcement gap (Greener UK 2018b; ClientEarth 2018; IEEP 2018). As one of the declared goals of Brexit was to cut Brussels red tape and engage in deregulation, it is seemingly unrealistic that the UK will simply keep the EU acquis in environmental policy in the medium to long term. Some recent policy developments can be taken as initial signals that Britain will engage in a less ambitious environmental policy post-Brexit: for example, coming into office, Prime Minister Theresa May closed the Department for Climate Change (Johnston 2017a); important policy dossiers, such as the Clean Growth Strategy, came with significant delay (Johnston 2017b, c; Ambrose 2018); the budget of the environmental ministry, the Department for Environment, Food & Rural Affairs (DEFRA), is subject to cuts from now until 2020, though it is going to be heavily affected by Brexit. As a matter of fact, DEFRA will have to come up with numerous statutory instruments replacing EU law. At the same time, it lacks legislative experience, given that most of its legislative framework was, until now, European (Owen et al. 2018: 21–22, 26, 36; Howard 2015). Another complication is that the field of environmental policy and the responsibilities of DEFRA are devolved. Because of the unifying force of EU legislation, most of the UK's environmental policy has largely remained aligned across the territory in the past (Heyvaert and Čavoški 2018: 123–124). Waste policies, however, are already diverging between the devolved nations (DEFRA 2018b), given that the EU framework leaves substantial leeway in this area to member states. Such divergence is likely to increase post-Brexit, unless Westminster succeeds in reclaiming shares of policy-making authority.

Overall, we can therefore expect that environmental policy post-Brexit will be more diverse in the nations, and less stable where policies in the antagonistic Westminster system prove responsive to public pressure, corporate lobbying and NGO campaigning. In areas where public or NGO pressure is high, the UK might potentially outperform the EU as an environmental leader. The UK debate on plastics is a good example in this respect (Baker 2018): the EMF published widely discussed strategic reports on the "New Plastics Economy" in 2016 and 2017 (EMF 2016, 2017a, b), and in April 2018, together with the Waste and Resources Action Programme (WRAP) launched a UK "Plastics Pact". The Plastics Pact brought together a network of national and regional initiatives implementing a variety of targets set until 2025, and received support from DEFRA; Sky News launched its Ocean Rescue project in January 2017; UK-based ENGOs also heavily campaigned on plastics issues (e.g. WWF 2018; Plastic Oceans 2018). Greenpeace, for instance, called on the government to introduce a UK-wide deposit-return scheme for drink containers and plastic bottles (Greenpeace 2018a). Typically, such campaigning triggers voluntary action on the business side. This frequently applies to retailers, who are often subject to targeted campaigns and then voluntarily commit to phase out certain products. In 2018, various retailers and fast food restaurants in the UK announced a ban on the use of plastic straws, notably in response to targeted campaigns launched by the NGO SumOfUs (BBC 2018c; SumOfUs 2017). Other companies voluntarily implemented a "latte-tax" on disposable coffee cups, a measure which MPs in the Environmental Audit Committee had proposed to the government (EAC 2018c).

Compared to massive public attention going to plastics products and waste, the issue of paper waste and recycling has not made it on top of the agenda. In fact the UK lacks the waste processing capacity to deal with both, plastic waste and the large amounts of low-quality cardboard waste and mixed paper rubbish that are going to be affected by the Chinese bans and restrictions on imported waste (Laville 2017; Tamma 2018a; Musaddique and Gabbatiss 2017). Similarly, environmental issues around consumer electronics have not hit the headlines, although resource efficiency and the export of electronic waste pose a rapidly growing problem in this thriving market. For instance, the Chinese ban and restrictions on importing waste amplify pressure on domestic waste management capacity. The UK has diverted its e-waste to Thailand, yet following China's example, Thailand has recently decided to restrict the import of electronic waste (Ellis-Petersen 2018). UK-based ENGOs have so far not been particularly active on consumer electronics. Most activities have targeted the international level, such as those of the Basel Action Network (BAN) on e-waste trafficking (ban 2018) and the Greenpeace initiative on "Greener Electronics" (Greenpeace 2018b). These issues might, however, become more topical in the context of the resources and waste strategy, published in December 2018 (HM Government 2018f). Previous to that, the EMF, supported by Google, addressed circular economy aspects for consumer electronics in a dedicated report (EMF 2018).

Chemicals Regulation and Disintegration: Access to Data and Markets

[…] if we don't have the EU REACH or a similar system in place, what else is there? Where do we go from here? REACH is seen as one of the most ambitious pieces of regulation. It is not that it does not come with its flaws, but is there anything that is capable of doing the similar things that REACH does? (Nishma Patel, CIA, EAC 2017b)

We surveyed members across the REACH cross-sector group immediately after the referendum asking what they thought we should do about REACH. We were surprised that so many companies – the vast majority – wanted to stick with REACH. Asked why, it was because they wanted access to the single market. The European market was still the number one destination for their goods. Compliance with REACH they thought would give them not only a better chance of securing a good FTA but would also minimise registry barriers to trade. (Susanne Baker, techUK, EAC 2017b)

The effect of Brexit on UK chemical regulation is one of the key concerns for business and NGOs alike. The main issue regarding Registration,

Evaluation, Authorisation of Chemicals (REACH) is access to information: for industry, because it has invested massively in generating the type of data and expertise required to comply with registration and authorisation obligations (CIA 2018); for NGOs, because they fear that UK consumers will no longer be accurately informed about the risks due to potential exposure to hazardous chemicals (Greener UK 2018c); and for the UK government, because absent access to the REACH database, it would lack the information needed to justify regulatory decisions, which is why it could lose cases in court (Interview ENGO 2017b; Greener UK 2018c).

UK-based business and NGOs form a strange alliance as far as regulatory certainty on chemicals is concerned. Both sides expressed their preference to stay as closely aligned to the REACH system as possible (EAC 2017a: 5). The UK-based chemical industry, having fought REACH from its proposal through adoption and implementation, now praises the benefits of EU regulation, and lobbies hard to stay inside (Interview ENGO 2017b). The main reason is the regulatory cost of leaving the system. The chemicals value chain, including smaller suppliers manufacturing specialised products, has invested massively in the authorisation procedure in order to comply with the REACH registration deadlines, especially so in the run-up to the third and last deadline for registering substances in quantities of 1 to 100 tonnes per year which closed on 31 May 2018. With this last deadline, REACH "is starting to bite" (Interview ENGO 2017a), and the registration duty imposes a regulatory cost which has the potential to crowd out smaller suppliers along the value chain, as observed for the past two deadlines. The unknown consequences of Brexit exacerbate this situation and are likely to cause further market exit (Interview MP 2017; EAC 2017b: Q 38). Business wants to minimise uncertainty and does not want to lose the investment that has gone into the existing scheme:

> We have been involved in complying with the regulations, putting the data together, since its infancy. In our divorce from the EU, to lose that work is going to be a big back step. (Nishma Patel, CIA, EAC 2017b)
> I remember one SME in our membership was quoted £50,000 to register two materials, and just did not have that capital inside their business at that time. They had to stop buying the material, stop supplying it and pass the business on to somebody else. [...] We are waiting until 2018 for the over 1 tonne registration to come in. That is when we don't know exactly how it is going to be because people are going to have to make a stark

choice, either register or pull out of the market. (Douglas Leech, CBA, EAC 2017b)

Another issue for business is continued access to knowledge- and cost-sharing mechanisms provided under REACH. Companies have the possibility to submit joint registrations where they produce or import the same chemical as other companies in the EU, profiting from economies of scale (EAC 2017a: 4). The REACH database is only shared between EU member state firms and those from countries in the European Economic Area (EEA), with EEA countries participating in discussions yet without holding voting rights. Switzerland, for example, being outside the EEA, was not granted access to the REACH database, as it would not accept European Court of Justice (ECJ) rulings. Industry associations repeatedly expressed concern that their industry would suffer badly from Brexit and that there was a need to protect a decade-long investment in EU chemicals regulation, including the cost caused by the 2018 registration deadline (CIA 2017, 2018: 5–7; Extance 2018; ECHA 2018a). It is apparent that there are important sunk costs involved for industry. Post-Brexit, chemicals manufacturers could be obliged to transfer more than 9000 registrations to the EU and new chemicals could end up having to be registered twice, in the UK and EU, with big additional costs (Extance 2018; BBC 2018a; House of Commons 2018). Such additional costs would be particularly harsh for SMEs, whereas big transnational companies can outsource registration to their counterparts based in the EU. REACH does constitute a trade barrier for producers outside the system, which is why there is a real risk that UK-based chemicals manufacturers dislocate (Extance 2018).

Besides the chemical industry and its value chain, it is also downstream users, such as electronics producers organised inside techUK or AMDEA, who are affected by REACH in a number of ways: manufacturers may need to register substances and apply for authorisation; both importers and manufacturers need to comply with restrictions; and in accordance with Article 33, there is a need to disclose SVHCs above a certain threshold in products, including their components, as required by the 2015 ECJ ruling (Case C-106/14). This complex information has to be made accessible to users, waste management industry and recyclers alike, raising issues of practicability (EAC 2017b: Q 89, 90). The electronics and tech products segment, however, has already been subject to similar requirements, prior to REACH, under the Restriction of Hazardous Substances (RoHS) directive first introduced in 2002. Despite the regulatory burden imposed by REACH and other EU regulation, most downstream users expressed their preference to keep REACH in place (techUK 2016).

Finally, from an industry perspective, maintaining close ties with the EU on chemicals is a means to safeguard the UK's influence in EU policy-making and, ultimately, influence for the UK-based chemical industry. The UK's stance in EU chemical policy has been characterised as "balanced, pragmatic and proportionate" (CIA 2018: 6), "risk-based" (Interview plastics industry 2017; Interview MP 2017; EAC 2017b: Q 68; Interview ministry 2017b), "influencing" and "well-respected" (EAC 2017b: Q 49). Staying inside REACH would therefore safeguard influence on European chemical regulation, which is recognised to set standards globally:

> REACH is seen by many as the gold standard for environmental protection and it's taken as reference by other countries that have implemented or are in the process of implementing similar regulations. (CIA 2018: 6)
>
> If you talk about chemicals regulation and the impact it has had on consumers and use, looking at it from a global perspective first, most of our members are dealing with a set of chemicals regulation, whether it is REACH in the EU, whether it is a similar REACH regime in China or Korea, or the TSCA in the US. Increasingly, around 65% of that - 65% of the chemicals produced in the world - respond to REACH-like legislation. REACH is becoming or has become the type of legislation that companies increasingly have to respond to, with some differences, but the overarching principles remain the same. (Nishma Patel, CIA, EAC 2017b)
>
> REACH [...] is the most advanced system in the world for ensuring chemicals are safe for human health and the environment. (Greener UK 2018c: 3)

Being part of REACH therefore means to hold substantive regulatory power, because decisions taken under REACH bear consequences not only for all EU member states in the single market but also beyond, in the global chemical market. From the NGO side, the fact that many other countries such as Turkey or Korea are starting to implement something similar to REACH has been interpreted as a sign that the USA, with its weak and ineffective chemical regulation, has lost global regulatory competition in this sector (Interview ENGO 2017b). While business and NGOs clearly advocate the EU-type scheme for chemicals, an alternative outcome cannot be entirely discarded. If the UK stays outside the single market, remaining a part of REACH will indeed pose a problem, as pointed out by a government representative during the inquiry conducted by the House of Commons Environmental Audit Committee in April 2017 (EAC 2017a):

> You will be aware of the principles the Prime Minister set out. We are not going to be part of the single market and REACH is a single market mechanism. (EAC 2017a)

In the course of 2017, DEFRA repeatedly stated that the UK would leave REACH and replace it with a new UK chemical regime. Both MPs and stakeholders were highly critical of the government's "poor response" (Interview MP 2017) and urged politicians to provide more clarity (Focus 2015). By March 2018, Prime Minister Theresa publicly announced that she would examine "the terms on which the UK could remain part of EU agencies such as those that are critical for the chemicals, medicines and aerospace industries" and that the UK would accept "abiding by the rules of those agencies and making an appropriate financial contribution" in order to avoid a scenario of duplicating regulatory cost (BBC 2018b). This intention was confirmed in the government's "White Paper" published in July 2018, which outlined its Brexit strategy (HM Government 2018b: 8, 20–22). The bitter pill the UK would have to swallow if it was to be aligned with EU chemical regulation is to accept ECJ rulings, a precondition the EU set for Switzerland and which is unlikely to be lifted for the UK (Greener UK 2018a: 5). As a consequence, Swiss authorities are basically copying EU decisions without having access to data. The UK would need to adapt continuously to an evolving and progressing policy framework in all areas related to REACH, including a wide range of post-legislative rules, without having a say in decision-making. According to the assessment of CHEM Trust, the EU can be expected to impose alignment with a number of chemical-related EU laws, going beyond the intentions expressed in the UK government's July 2018 strategy (Young 2018). The UK would thus disengage politically with the EU policy-making on chemicals, yet without de-Europeanising its own domestic policies (Copeland 2016; Burns et al. 2019).

The EU will not allow the UK to cherry-pick in this policy field. In fact, the guidance given by its chemical agency European Chemicals Agency (ECHA) clearly refers to the UK's future status as a third country (ECHA 2018b). Further, EU member states clarified in their guidelines published in March 2018 that the UK will be excluded from

EU decision-making bodies and agencies (European Council 2018: 3). Being outside REACH could mean that industry would need to explore altered trade relations, for instance by strengthening its links with the USA (Interview ENGO 2017a). The US scheme is far less ambitious, especially in its requirements to provide safety information (Vogel 2012; Interview ENGO 2017b). The kind of regulatory relief to which industry could aspire in this context had already become obvious during the negotiations of the Transatlantic Trade and Investment Partnership (TTIP). Back then, US and European chemical industries formed what ENGOs across the Atlantic deplored as a "toxic partnership" (CIEL et al. 2014) to lobby for a business-friendly version of transatlantic regulatory cooperation in the area of chemicals. Concerns have therefore been raised that in future the UK might become a "dumping ground" (Lourie 2017; Greener UK 2018c: 3) for products containing harmful chemicals that are banned in the EU. That said, the cost of adapting to a new scheme is considerable, which is why industry prefers the status quo:

> 94% of our members see Europe because it is closer. The costs of shipping goods across to America are fairly high for the chemical sector, and they have the chemical sector over there. They are doing their own, and in some cases they have cheaper raw materials than we do and less environmental restrictions than we may have, so we cannot compete in costs against them on numerous occasions anyway. No, I think aligning with TSCA [Toxic Substance Control Act] would just cause us more grief and more problems. We have been in Europe for 40 years. We have been in REACH since 2007, and starting to comply and put dossiers together since 2010. We are fairly entwined with that sort of regime, so trying to cut that out may cause a lot more problems. (Douglas Leech, CBA, EAC 2017b)

In the medium to long term UK chemical policy will hence depend on the outcome of negotiations on the future relations with the EU and the type of economic cooperation the partners will adhere to. In its 25 Year Environment Plan published in January 2018, the British government announced the publication of an overarching chemicals strategy "to set our approach as we leave the EU" (HM Government 2018c: 100).

Plastics in the Spotlight and a Looming Waste Crisis

When the United Kingdom leaves the European Union, control of important areas of environmental policy will return to these shores. We will use this opportunity to [...] put the environment first. (Theresa May, HM Government 2018c)

These actions will, we hope, ensure that this country is recognised as the leading global champion of a greener, healthier, more sustainable future for the next generation. (Michael Gove, HM Government 2018c)

Now we must take bold action to become a world leader in tackling the scourge of single-use plastic littering our streets, countryside and coastline. (Philip Hammond, HM Treasury 2018)

As chemical and waste policies are closely intertwined, this raises the question as to the degree to which the UK will align with both the EU's chemical and waste policies, including the recent changes introduced with the new Circular Economy Package. While domestic commitments to chemical policy are on hold with negotiations ongoing, waste-related issues have made headlines and triggered policy reactions: first, the global marine littering campaign proved particularly successful in the UK; second, the waste crisis looming with the Chinese decision to restrict waste imports urges for action. I will first present these two challenges and policy initiatives and then address how these affect the plastics and paper industries.

In the course of 2017 and 2018, the UK government has initiated the first changes to its legislative framework on waste, with a primary focus on plastics. In doing so, government documents repeatedly refer to media coverage, such as the BBC's Blue Planet (HM Treasury 2018: 2), or the strategies proposed by the EMF (HM Government 2018c: 89). It also seems that the UK government seeks to outperform EU plans on plastics, as illustrated by Philip Hammond's statement quoted above. On the issue of the UK's charge on plastic bags, for instance, there was controversy as to whether British policymakers claim ownership of change driven by EU regulation (Stone 2018; Gabbatiss 2017). In its 25-year outlook, DEFRA places strong emphasis on plastic waste (HM Government 2018c: 4, 6, 10, 29, 83–84, 86–87, 89). The plan sets targets to achieve zero avoidable waste by 2050, already announced in the 2017 Clean Growth Strategy and zero avoidable plastic waste by the end of 2042 (HM Government 2017a). It refers to various possible measures to reduce plastic waste: introduce taxes and charges to reduce the amount of single-use plastic waste; reform producer responsibility systems; cooperate with WRAP to explore plastic-free supermarket aisles; consider advice from the Voluntary & Economic Incentives

Working Group set up under the Litter Strategy; cooperate with waste management industry and re-processors to improve collection and recycling; and work with WRAP to develop a joint commitment with business and NGOs to tackle plastic waste, with an initial focus on plastic packaging as suggested by the EMF. In January 2018, the government also announced its "world-leading microbeads ban" (HM Government 2018e), followed by an announcement to introduce a deposit-return scheme for drink containers in England in March 2018 (HM Government 2018a). From March until May 2018, the Treasury conducted a consultation about how taxing and charges could be used to address the problems posed by single-use plastic product waste (HM Treasury 2018). A Resource and Waste Strategy for England (HM Government 2018f), published in December 2018, again put heavy emphasis on issues related to plastics, including instruments such as taxes and charges. While at EU-level, the Commission's desire to use fiscal instruments was met with opposition from member states and was, in the end, not included in the Plastics Strategy (Solletty 2018; Tamma 2018b), the UK could thus take the lead in introducing this type of instrument to reduce plastic waste. On other issues, however, it appears that the UK strategy very much relies on business-driven solutions and voluntary measures.

The Chinese bans and restrictions on imported waste, announced in January and coming into effect in March 2018, further increased the urgency of the plastics dossier. In 2016, 63% of the packaging waste collected in the UK was exported. 74% of total plastic waste exports went to Asia (mainly China), and 26% to Europe. According to Her Majesty's Revenue and Customs (HMRC) data, total plastics exports have fallen from 243 million kg in the first quarter of 2017 to 215 million kg in the respective 2018 period. Exports going to China have fallen by 97% in the first four months following the decision. Instead, exports have gone to Malaysia, becoming the single largest export destination of domestic plastic waste, as well as to Thailand and Taiwan. Export of recovered paper has fallen from above 400 thousand tonnes in January 2018 to around 340 thousand tonnes in February 2018, and recovered paper prices have fallen drastically (HMRC 2018; WRAP 2018b). The UK has diverted its exported paper and cardboard waste to Turkey, Taiwan and Vietnam. In addition to the Chinese ban, UK exports to destinations in EU countries may also experience decline. The UK currently exports around 10% of its waste to EU member states, given it lacks the required energy-from-waste and spare landfill capacity at home (Solletty 2017; Suez 2017). These external factors have triggered a domestic debate about the UK's waste management and recycling capacities, and may have contributed to the U-turn of government departments to give up on behind the scene opposition to the recycling targets in the EU's Circular Economy Package. By March 2018, Resources Minister Thérèse Coffey stated the government would back the package (Carrington 2018a, b). Whitehall further published a new resources and waste strategy (HM Government 2018f), drawing on scientific evidence generated by a Government Office for Science report (2017). ENGOs and opposition take a critical stance on government initiatives and argue that especially in the area of waste policy EU external pressure and the threat to impose fines are important drivers of domestic change, which will be absent post-Brexit (Interview MP 2017; Interview ENGO 2017a). As the responsibilities of DEFRA are devolved, we might also see further divergence across the UK nations, which are already quite pronounced in the area of waste management (DEFRA 2018b).

With "plastics in the spotlight" (Baker 2018), the UK plastics industry faces enormous public and political pressure. Accordingly, reputation has become a key issue for industry, and negative perceptions affect both their customer base and their attractiveness as an employer (BPF 2016: 24; Interview plastics industry 2017). Given the emphasis placed by the UK government on voluntary measures in addressing the plastics issue (HM Government 2018c: 88, 91), there is however also potential for industry to be in the driving seat. BPF sought to be more proactive on sustainability issues, notably through setting up a sustainability working group in 2015. Since its existence, end-of-life-plastics have become a priority of the group, and the BPF expert has dedicated particular attention to the Ellen MacArthur plastics report (Interview plastics industry 2017). The association runs various schemes on reducing and raising awareness about littering and is a signatory to the UK Plastics Pact (WRAP 2018d). This voluntary commitment, advertised as the "world-leading pact to tackle plastic pollution" (WRAP 2018c), brings together actors across the plastic packaging value chain, including manufacturers and suppliers of packaging materials as well as major brands and retailers. It sets various goals for plastic packaging, to be achieved by 2025: eliminating single-use plastic packaging; achieving a recycling rate of 70%; and securing that, on average, packaging products contain 30% recycled content. BPF came up with its own vision for a circular economy in May 2018 (BPF 2018c), committing to zero packaging waste going to landfill by 2025, and minimising plastic items leaking into the environment. Industry also seeks to influence relevant regulation, notably the UK's Packaging Recovery Note (PRN), which is the UK's producer responsibility system. Reforming the PRN is seen by some industry representatives as "the most timely and efficient way to generate more revenue and increase recycling rates", whereas initiatives like plastic-free aisles might have "unintended consequences", as this "could dramatically increase food waste", and introducing a deposit-return scheme would involve "a difficult cost/benefit equation" (Baker 2018). In its vision document, BPF highlights current shortcomings of the PRN as not rewarding difficult-to-recycle activities over easy recycling, and incentivising exporting material over recycling at home. A lowering in the quality of recovered material has been seen as a by-product of the existing scheme. Industry takes the Chinese ban as an opportunity to ask for more financial and regulatory support for domestic collection and recycling activities (BPF 2018c: 5, 22). This could also mean that the UK—assumed it would stay outside REACH post-Brexit—adopts a more pragmatic stance on legacy materials in recycled products. From an industry perspective, REACH often poses an obstacle to recycling.

> For example, let's say the PVC window with a certain additive in, we would say: if it is collected sensibly, and processed properly, there is no risk to the public […] and therefore we would advocate recycling […] the UK has always been a risk versus hazard-based society, we have always looked at the risk, and that's why we would advocate these things, it's promoting the circular economy, and these legacy additives, we are still ensuring that they are not leaching, ensuring that this waste is not going to landfill, you are not incinerating it, you get a resource out of your recycling, which you can use again, and we think that is a good thing. (Interview plastics industry 2017)

BPF also adopts a similar line of reasoning in the discussions on setting limits for persistent organic pollutants (POPs) under the United Nations Stockholm Convention and Basel Convention, warning that very low limits may prevent recycling (BPF 2018b).

In comparison with the attention going to plastic waste, the issue of paper waste has not been addressed to the same extent. Especially in the context of discussions on the Chinese ban on the import of mixed, unsorted paper and cardboard this is surprising, as volume-wise the export of these materials is much more important than the amount of plastics exported (Minister Thérèse Coffey during a hearing at the EAC 2018a). In 2016, 74% of the waste paper the UK exported went to China and, likewise, 13.6% of recovered paper China imported came from the UK at a volume of 3884 thousand tonnes. The UK is the second single largest exporter to China after the USA with 12,790 thousand tonnes (WRAP 2018a). The UK system of separate collection is underdeveloped. From an EU-wide perspective, experts situate it at the low end of the performance continuum (Interview paper industry 2017). Postwar, the UK failed to continue on the path of its wartime legacy in lending governmental support to paper salvage, which back then was used as a source of income to generate resources for military purposes (Irving 2016; Thorsheim 2015). As a consequence, the UK experienced a postwar collapse of paper recycling, and England especially failed to ensure separate collection of good quality material (Gandy 1994: 51–54). The UK paper industry thus lobbies for the adoption of a "consistent, standardised, quality focused collection regime for household collections", stressing that the "increasing adoption of comingled collection" has contributed to a significant decline in the quality of recovered paper over the past decade (CPI 2018b). The paper industry is furthermore concerned that the UK's waste prevention policy could negatively affect the packaging market and urges the government to "abandon policies that seek to reduce it at all costs" (CPI 2017b). On the UK's packaging waste legislation, the CPI opposes radical change but calls for action to improve recovery and facilitate household recycling, which has stagnated over the last decade. To that end, it calls to oblige processors and exporters of secondary material under the system, to bolster collection infrastructure, to promote collection consistency and to improve the quality of materials recovered. Further, industry calls on policymakers to implement a single collection and recovery system for the entire territory of the UK, with no variation across the devolved administrations (CPI 2018b). In regard to recycling, the paper industry points to a need "to promote quality over quantity to drive downstream growth" (CPI 2017b).

Product Regulation and Standards in a Global Britain

We continue to support these policy measures [on EU products policy], which cut energy bills, increase energy security, reduce emissions and help customers make informed choices, and we will keep step with equivalent standards wherever possible and appropriate, or even exceed them where it is in the UK's interest to do so. (HM Government 2017a: 44)

In the longer term, we are concerned that the UK will become a "rule taker" outside the EU, complying with, but unable to influence, rules and standards. If our formal standards diverge too far from those applying in European countries, there is a risk that the UK could become a dumping ground for energy inefficient products. We recommend that the Government retains or mirrors European energy product standards for the immediate future at least and should also, as far as possible, maintain routes to influence their development, for example through active UK participation in European standards bodies. (House of Commons 2017)

Through the EU, British concepts of regulation became world standards – from medicine to mobile phone frequencies – allowing companies such as Vodafone to grow to global dominance. (Hutton 2018)

Compared to waste management issues, product-related regulation and standards seem to be "no-brainers" for policymakers. These are single market issues which are not affected by devolution (Interview ministry 2017a). Indeed, safeguarding such regulation and standards post-Brexit should not be an issue where access to the European market for goods is contingent on compliance. In the area of energy and climate policy, as illustrated by the above quote, the UK government seems to be committed to pursuing their energy efficiency goals, which in their Clean Growth Strategy have been prioritised, putting "efficiency first" (Rosenow and Cowart 2017; HM Government 2017a). That said, there is one important implication for both industry and politics: being outside the EU means to comply with European norms and standards, yet without being a part of the rule-making process. In fact, the waning regulatory power of domestic business has already been seen as an important drawback post-Brexit, for instance in the thriving UK-based ICT sector (Scott et al. 2018). Brexit, therefore, affects the UK's competitiveness in highly Europeanised sectors, which to some extent derives from being one of the most important players in EU policy-making.

By now, product-related environmental regulation has become an important compliance issue for industry manufacturing in, or importing to the EU. Producers and importers need to be aware of SVHCs in their products. REACH, in Article 7.2, requires that companies notify these substances in their products, as well as for components in complex products. Further, the RoHS directive restricts the use of certain hazardous substances in electrical and electronic equipment (EEE). Moreover, energy efficiency requirements apply, and products need to be labelled accordingly. At the end-of-life phase, electronic products are subject to the Waste from Electrical and Electronic Equipment (WEEE) directive. UK-based industry and retailers have repeatedly voiced concern about "onerous" EU regulation such as REACH, "voted the most burdensome piece of EU legislation by SMEs" (techUK 2016). Also, the duplication of requirements such as those under REACH and RoHS is felt as cumbersome and superfluous (Interview home appliance industry 2017a). It was argued that the type of uniform EU regulatory and testing requirements fails to leave room for innovative products, or unduly trumps energy efficiency over other considerations important to end consumers. In the run-up to the Brexit vote, for example, new Ecodesign measures were being postponed. More specifically, standards on toasters and kettles were put on hold, so as to not upset the average British voter against Brussels red tape (Holehouse 2016; Neslen 2017). Visible litigation further contributed to such politicisation of European product policy. British inventor and Brexiteer Sir James Dyson had sought to trigger a "Hoovergate" scandal (Crisp 2016) echoing the "Dieselgate" scandal in the automobile sector. He sued European competitors and successfully filed a case against the European Commission, challenging established energy efficiency testing methods (for a detailed discussion rf. to Chapter 5).

Despite such criticism and examples of legal action, UK-based industry predominantly advocates future alignment with EU regulation. The motives are to maintain market access and, where possible, keep influencing European regulatory developments. TechUK has lobbied the UK government to harmonise future domestic regulation on resource efficiency with the material efficiency product design rules under the Ecodesign directive and to respect the RoHS "repaired as produced" principle for spare parts (techUK 2018a: 4–5, 8). So far, the UK government has announced plans to implement and continue to adapt to EU products standards such as those on energy efficiency, and also to engage in pace-setting in areas such as smart appliances (HM Government 2017a: 44). A challenge for post-Brexit compliance and adaptation in product policy is the constant evolution of EU regulation which, as discussed in Chapter 5, results from decision-making through standard-setting bodies and Comitology. To refer to recent examples: the rescaled Energy Labelling Scheme entered into force in August 2017, and a number of implementing measures (Ecodesign regulations) need to be adopted for all product categories regulated under Ecodesign. Further, as discussed in Chapter 5, new policy proposals push the focus of Ecodesign towards resource efficiency criteria. As part of its Circular Economy Action Plan, the European Commission has requested European standardisation bodies (CEN, CENELEC and ETSI) to develop adequate criteria to assess the durability, reparability and recyclability of products, as well as the proportion of reused components and recycled material content in a product. The objective is to develop a methodology to declare the presence of critical raw materials and to communicate the resource efficiency characteristics of a product. To that end, a new standards committee to consider material efficiency aspects has been set up inside European Committee for Standardisation (CEN) and European Committee for Electrotechnical Standardisation (CENELEC). This newly established Joint Technical Committee 10 on Energy-related products—Material Efficiency Aspects for Ecodesign (CEN/CLC/JTC 10) is currently chaired by an AMDEA expert (Interview home appliance industry 2017b; CEN-CENELEC 2018), and is closely being followed by other UK trade associations such as tech UK (techUK 2018a: 22).

Business representatives are highly concerned that they won't be able to participate in this type of standardisation work post-Brexit and will therefore lose out in influencing not only European but also international rule-setting. Research on standardisation has provided ample evidence that the European system of setting unifying standards through a hierarchical governance structure is by far more effective and more influential in international standard-setting compared to other, more fragmented and decentralised schemes such as the one in the US (Büthe and Mattli 2011: 146–159). CEN and CENELEC have been closely cooperating with their respective international bodies, International Organisation for Standardisation (ISO) and International Electrotechnical Commission (IEC). In fact, the European bodies and the international bodies have frequently coordinated their work and mutually endorsed their decisions, to an extent that the US-side has complained about an undue influence of European standardisation bodies (Büthe and Mattli 2011: 157–158). In order to feed into the European system of standardisation effectively, well-coordinated and hierarchical national systems covering the entire economy are particularly well suited. The British scheme with the uncontested status of the British Standardisation Institute (BSI) fulfils this requirement and is well respected and highly influential (Büthe and Mattli 2011: 153–155). Against this background, it does not come as a surprise that trade associations such as AMDEA have deplored the loss of influence in European standardisation post-Brexit (AMDEA 2018). The home appliance association has pointed out (AMDEA 2018) that full participation in CEN and CENELEC requires current or prospective membership in the European Free Trade Association (EFTA). In the absence of such membership, the BSI would only be eligible for affiliate membership such as the one held by Albania, or could seek a Cooperation Agreement such as the one obtained by Japan and South Korea. The BSI wrote a letter, co-signed by AMDEA, techUK and other stakeholders, expressing their desire to remain involved in European standardisation after Brexit, publishing a position paper urging the government to secure UK experts' continued participation in standardisation bodies (BSI 2018b). The Secretary of State for Business, Enterprise and Industrial Strategy, Greg Clark MP, replied to the paper saying that the government would seek to ensure such continuity. Further, the government's White Paper on the future relations with the EU, published in July 2018, stipulated that "the British Standards Institution (BSI) would retain its ability to apply the 'single standard model' – so that where a voluntary European standard is used to support EU rules, the BSI could not put forward any competing national standards" (HM Government 2018b: 20). In its response to this letter, BSI emphasised that CEN and CENELEC are private associations rather than EU bodies, and that BSI would continue "to work with European partners to make whatever changes are required to the statutes of CEN and CENELEC in order to reflect the UK's status outside the EU" (BSI 2018a). Following a similar line of argument, it has been suggested that regulatory alignment surrounding the use of standards will be secured post-Brexit, irrespective of the negotiation outcomes, given that standard-setting and compliance therewith is a voluntary decision of private actors (Armstrong 2018: 1114).

Whether or not and how such changes will materialise at this stage is still an open question. If the BSI and UK-based industry experts do succeed in securing their influence in European standardisation post-Brexit, this technical venue will gain relative importance. In the absence of direct influence on European secondary law, standardisation may thus be a vehicle to secure British regulatory influence through the backdoor and in areas where it relies on standard-setting. Even then, however, the

UK would still mostly likely be a "rule-taker", as the credentials of EU regulation affecting products—through REACH, RoHs, Ecodesign and Energy Labelling—will still be defined by EU policymakers alongside EU and national experts in regulatory committees.

LEAVING THE INTERNAL ENERGY MARKET

The integration of European energy markets has very much been a history of British regulatory power in Europe. The UK was the first country to engage in liberalisation, privatisation, and unbundling and has in many ways uploaded its domestic model to the European level. This section first revisits the history of British influence on EU regulation and then addresses the future role of the UK in European energy policy.

British Regulatory Power in Europe, Past and Future

We recommend that the Government should seek continued UK influence over the rules of the Internal Energy Market. In particular it should explore continued full membership of the technical institutions for developing the detailed rules of the Internal Energy Market. (House of Commons 2018)

The experience of other countries suggests that the UK is likely to have little influence on EU energy policy post-Brexit. This will be particularly concerning in the event the UK continues to participate in the IEM [Internal Energy Market], given the corresponding requirement to comply with current and future relevant EU legislation. (House of Lords 2018)

The EU wants to have an internal electricity market as one coherent thing, and either you are in it and abide by the rules or you are not in it. [For an exception to be made] you have to have a very strong case that you as a country bring something to the Internal Electricity Market that is indispensable to [its] functioning […] I am not aware of the UK having anything […] which in the countervailing scenario of you not bringing it to the market would put the Internal Energy Market in some sort of jeopardy. (House of Lords 2018: Q 45, Jean-Christophe Füeg, Ambassador, Head of International Energy Affairs at the Swiss Federal Office of Energy)

If full participation in the IEM is not accompanied by an acceptable level of influence, the UK will have to review the situation and if deemed necessary leave the IEM if the pros are outweighed by the cons. (Written evidence from Energy UK [BES0024], House of Lords 2018)

The above quotes from the hearings in the Houses of Parliament indicate that future influence in EU energy policy is of key concern to policymakers and stakeholders alike. The potential loss of power is immense indeed, given the track record of British influence in European energy policy. The very design of the Internal Energy Market was substantially shaped by Anglo-Saxon ideas about liberalisation and regulation. UK actors played a key role in European policy-making and were a driving force in pushing the European energy policy agenda forward (Buchan 2010; Pollitt 2017: 136; Ciambra and Solorio 2014; Interview Ministry 2017c). Further, market creation, the introduction of independent regulation and the use of competition law instruments were all elements of European energy policy where the European Commission drew on both, support by British policymakers and stakeholders, as well as the UK model (Buchan 2010: 402–403; Thatcher 2007; Eurelectric 2017: 1). The domestic reform process kicked off in 1989 when the Electricity Act was adopted. Energy generation and infrastructure were legally unbundled, the liberalisation process launched, and an independent regulatory authority (IRA) for electricity was introduced. Ownership unbundling (OU) led to the creation of independent TSOs across the UK in 1995. As discussed in Chapter 6 (see Fig. 6.1), the Independent System Operator (ISO) and the OU models are being implemented across the UK. In Scotland, the Scottish Power Energy Networks and the Scottish and Southern Electricity Networks follow the ISO model. The Transmission System Operator (TSO) in England and Wales (National Grid [NGET]), as well as the TSO in Northern Ireland (Northern Ireland Electricity), by contrast, are fully unbundled. Across Europe the UK transmission network is the only one that is fully privatised (Meletiou et al. 2018: 14, 15). Based on its domestic reform experience, the UK was pushing forward the EU's policy agenda throughout the process of agreeing on the three electricity directives which were adopted in 1996, 2003 and 2009. The negotiations of the Clean Energy Package (European Commission 2015, 2016), however, coincide with the Brexit negotiations and put UK representatives already on the periphery of the process (Interview Ministry 2017c). Brexit will hence be a landmark change for British influence in energy policy. In the past, British actors took leading positions at EU-level, in particular inside the European Commission: in the Delors Commission, Lord Cockfield influenced the thinking behind an Internal Energy Market (Johnson 2012: 3); his successor, Sir Leon Brittan, advocated breaking-up national monopolies, particularly in the energy sector (Eikeland 2004:

11); finally, Director General for energy, Christopher Jones, was one of the architects of the Third Energy Package. UK actors also took on a leading role in other regulatory and industry bodies. Sir John Mogg, the director of the Office of Gas and Electricity Markets (OFGEM), became president of the CEER and European Regulators' Group for Electricity and Gas (ERGEG) in 2005, and according to policy insiders was a highly influential figure in Brussels (Interview COM 2007a). He managed to align all regulatory authorities in the run-up to the third directive in order to fight for a stronger European agency and to gather support for OU (Interview regulator 2007a; Interview COM 2007b).

In the Brexit debate, MPs in both Houses and stakeholders have predominantly advocated continued UK membership in the Internal Energy Market. Parliamentarians highlighted the economic advantage as well as the need to remain influential in the formulation of new rules (House of Commons 2017: 14–16). Continued membership was further seen as being beneficial for security of supply (House of Lords 2018). These demands, however, cannot be reconciled with the wish to put an end to the primacy of EU law and to no longer respect ECJ case law (HSF et al. 2017: 4). What is more, the decision to leave the Single European Market announced by the UK government in January 2017 would also apply to the energy sector (Virley 2017). A scenario under which the UK would be outside the single market raises the question as to which model of cooperation should then apply. Many policymakers have voiced their preference for a Norwegian model, which grants full participation in the IEM and at least some soft influence over the development of new market rules (Interview TSO 2017; House of Lords 2018: 53). The Norwegian model would, however, be contingent on membership in the EEA and require concessions that the UK is not ready to make, such as accepting ECJ jurisdiction. This leaves the Swiss model, which does not presuppose EEA membership or compliance with ECJ case law (Lowe 2017: 4). Accordingly, in its energy policy inquiry, the House of Lords (HL) invited a Swiss energy expert to discuss possible governance arrangements (House of Lords 2018: 17, 53–55). Switzerland's partial participation in the IEM does come with several conditions, and very limited means to influence EU policy. In the late 1990s, Switzerland was granted observer status in the Florence Energy Forum. Following the establishment of the Council of European Energy Regulators (CEER) in 2000, Switzerland was initially not invited but obtained observer status alongside Macedonia and Montenegro in 2012. By contrast, participation in the formal EU decision-making bodies such as ACER is strictly limited to EU member countries. Regulatory cooperation, once formalised, structurally excludes participation from non-EU member states (Lavenex 2009). The UK could therefore obtain observer status within CEER but its future participation in ACER is questionable. The Swiss example also illustrates that future steps in integrating European energy markets are likely to exclude UK membership. For example, Switzerland cannot participate in the new scheme for market coupling (introduced by Commission regulation (EU) 2015/1222), despite being an important transit country hosting a majority of cross-border flows. The regulation (Article 1.4) stipulates that Switzerland could join the system under condition that it implemented European energy law and that the EU and Switzerland concluded a bilateral agreement on cooperation in the electricity sector. In the absence of these preconditions being met, the EU introduced electricity market coupling without Switzerland participating, which was considered to be a decision detrimental to the interests of the Swiss energy industry (Müller 2018; House of Lords 2018: 54; Höltschi 2015). If the UK was obliged to leave the common system of market coupling, this would, according to a study commissioned by NGET, amount to a loss of 90 million GBP a year (Vivid Economics 2016: 6).

Energy policy has thus far not taken centre stage in the negotiation process and has, for instance, not been attributed a stand-alone negotiation chapter. Concerned about this absence of prioritisation, the leaders of top energy companies present in the UK market urged the negotiation parties to pay closer attention to the effects of Brexit for energy and climate policy in a letter dated April 2018 (Waygood et al. 2018). Henceforth, in its July 2018 strategy the UK government expressed its wish to seek "broad energy cooperation with the EU, including arrangements for trade in electricity and gas, cooperation with EU agencies and bodies, and data sharing to facilitate market operations" (HM Government 2018b: 44). This strategy envisaged both a scenario to leave the IEM and the option to stay inside the IEM. In the first case, the UK wanted to safeguard trade over the interconnectors without participating in the EU's automatic capacity allocation system. In the second case, the UK wanted to comply with shared technical rules for electricity trading and commit to consistent carbon pricing mechanisms but saw no need to align with the EU's "wider environmental and climate change rules" (HM Government 2018b: 41). Further, the UK desired to stay a member in ENTSO-E and its Inter-TSO Compensation (ITC) mechanism, while not referring to continued membership in ACER. The UK thus seeks access to informal bodies both on the side of regulators and TSOs, which are to become far more important for UK actors post-Brexit (Interview Ministry 2017c).

The Rise of Private Governance: Technical Cooperation Trumps Politics?

While the UK may be leaving the EU in political terms, the pipes and wires that connect us remain and we will continue to be joined in physical terms. (Written evidence from Energy Institute [BES0028], House of Lords 2018)

Because we have a very well-functioning, competitive and resilient energy system now … with the technology and so many different sources of electricity and so many ways it can be adjusted in the short, medium and long term, I am not worried about security of supply. (Richard Harrington MP, Minister for Energy and IndustryHouse of Lords 2018)

Post-Brexit, the UK may be more vulnerable to supply shortages in the event of extreme weather or unplanned generation outages. While we note the Minister's confidence in future UK energy security, we urge the Government to set out the means by which it will work with the EU to anticipate and manage cross-continent supply shortages that will affect the UK. (House of Lords 2018)

Given the loss of influence of political and formal decision-making bodies, informal and private cooperation is likely to gain in relative importance. Mechanisms of European private governance have proven to be better suited to include the interests of third-country actors (Lavenex 2015; Prange-Gstöhl 2009). In the field of energy policy, there is evidence that supports the assumption that cooperation amongst market participants becomes more important post-Brexit (Virley 2017). What we may therefore expect is that UK-based infrastructure operators can solidify and increase their regulatory power, notably through their continued membership in ENTSO-E. ENTSO-E does hold a mandate to adopt recommendations relating to the coordination of technical cooperation between EU and third-country TSOs (Article 8 regulation EC no 714/2009, proposed Article 27 recast). In a letter dated 30 March 2017, ENTSO-E urged the Brexit negotiating parties to safeguard close cross-border cooperation and make sure there will be no future obstacles to power exchange between the EU and the UK (ENTSO-E 2017).

Again, the Swiss example is insightful for policymakers in envisioning the future role of UK TSOs in European energy governance. Compared to the limited access to the policy arena of Swiss policymakers and regulators, the Swiss grid operator is a central actor in the cross-border cooperation of European TSOs as a member of ENTSO-E. A Commission official argued that Swiss membership in ENTSO-E is not legally compliant with the requirement that only members from countries that fully implement the acquis can be part of bodies that have a formal mandate in EU policy-making, which is the case of ENTSO-E (Interview COM 2017, 2019). In fact, ENTSO-E has a differentiated governance structure as it restricts access to the working groups and decision-making to TSOs from EU countries when fulfilling its official mandate. That said, the TSO association is known to be very accommodating to the interests of third-country TSOs through informal mechanisms of deliberation (Interview regulator 2017). There is therefore reason to believe that the Swiss TSO exerts influence in ENTSO-E decision-making even when it does not sit at the table and does not hold a voting right. Domestically, the Swiss TSO has become a sort of transmission belt for Swiss influence in Brussels, given that policymakers back home rely on market actors to access relevant insider information and to bring up their domestic preferences in EU discussions. Such channels of influence have become ever more important in the aftermath of the Swiss "Against Mass Immigration" referendum held in February 2014, which caused serious tensions with the EU (Eckert 2018). To some extent, therefore, technical necessity for cooperation trumps politics, and the central position of the Swiss grid operator in the interconnected system has ultimately prevented Switzerland's energy interests from being marginalised (Jegen 2009: 592–595). Drawing on the Swiss example post-Brexit, the UK-based infrastructure operators could therefore take the lead in IEM-related matters thanks to their privileged access to ENTSO-E. Further, regulatory oversight could become weaker in areas where OFGEM depends on information exchange with other national regulators in order to effectively oversee market participants back home (Written evidence from Ofgem [BES0025], House of Lords 2018).

While these insights that draw on the Swiss example are revealing there is also a need to strike a line of caution. Switzerland as a transit country hosting a big share of energy flows in Europe (see Fig. 6.4) is at the heart of the European interconnected electricity grid. Switzerland maintains around 40 interconnectors with neighbouring countries, and in

2015, more than 10% of electricity traded between ENTSO-E countries passed through Swiss lines (Swissgrid 2015). By way of comparison, in 2018 the UK shares four electricity interconnectors with EU countries, connecting England and France (2 GW), England and the Netherlands (1 GW), Northern Ireland and Ireland (0.6 GW), as well as Wales and Ireland (0.5 GW) (BEIS 2017: 111). Compared to Switzerland, the UK is at the peripheries of the IEM. The Swiss have a long-lasting legacy of cooperating with neighbouring TSOs in Continental Europe, whereas the UK have done so gradually, establishing closer ties only with the introduction of a supranational energy policy. The Swiss TSO took over important operational tasks related to data management in the European ITC scheme (Interview TSO 2007). In contrast, the UK TSO initially was not even part of the voluntary agreement on ITC, as the financial implications of cross-border flows were not important enough. And the UK regulator did not approve of the voluntary nature of the scheme, calling for a binding mechanism instead (Interview TSO 2008). In the view of certain policy insiders, the peripheral position of the UK will reduce British influence post-Brexit (Interview Ministry 2017c; Interview regulator 2007b, 2017).

As it stands, the UK relies on imports from the EU, and increasingly so. Figure 7.4 displays the evolution of electricity imports and exports from France, Ireland and the Netherlands since 1998 (HM Government 2018d). It shows that most electricity imports originate from France, while the share imported through the interconnector with the Netherlands is growing since it started to operate in 2011. The net imports from France accounted for 9728 gigawatt hours in 2016, and 7306 gigawatt hours from the Netherlands, compared to 512 gigawatt hours from Ireland. Net electricity imports accounted for 6% of final energy consumption in 2015, and 4.9% in 2016. In view of this comparatively low share of electricity imports, economists predict that the costs of Brexit, caused by price increase, would be close to insignificant. If the electricity imported from Central Europe was becoming more expensive, this would have a minor effect on the total cost of electricity (Pollitt 2017: 136). The share of import dependence is far higher in gas, although the UK, along with the Netherlands, is one of the two major gas-producers in the EU. The huge share in gas imports originates from Norway. In total, UK net imports accounted for 38% of consumed energy in 2015 and for 36% in 2016. Electricity comprised 17.5% of the

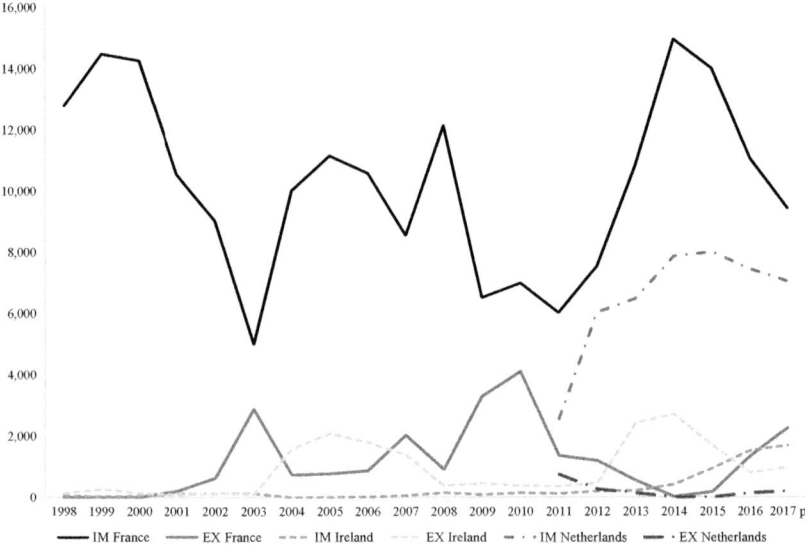

Fig. 7.4 Electricity imports and exports with EU countries (*Source* UK government power statics. Imports, exports and transfers of electricity in GWh [ET 5.6])

UK's final energy consumption in 2016, compared to 17.8% in 2015 and 18.2% in 2014 (BEIS 2016: 11, 115; 2017).

The UK electricity infrastructure is currently under massive reconstruction (Vaughan 2017). Seven additional lines were approved by OFGEM as of February 2018 (see Fig. 7.5, based on Ofgem 2018). These would henceforth connect the UK to Norway, Denmark, Belgium and intensify shared interconnection capacity with France and Ireland. According to a forecast based on eight contracted projects, future UK-EU interconnector capacity will increase from 3.5 gigawatts in 2017 up to about 14.1 gigawatts by 2022. This equals an increase in interconnection capacity from 7% in 2017 to 27% in 2022, of UK peak electricity demand (HSF et al. 2017: 10). In accordance with such grid expansion, interconnection rates evolve rapidly. At the beginning of the New Millennium, the UK was amongst the least interconnected markets in the EU, with only 3% of import capacity out of the installed total capacity (European Commission 2001: 4–5). In 2017, the interconnection level had doubled up to 6%, compared to 9% in Germany and France.

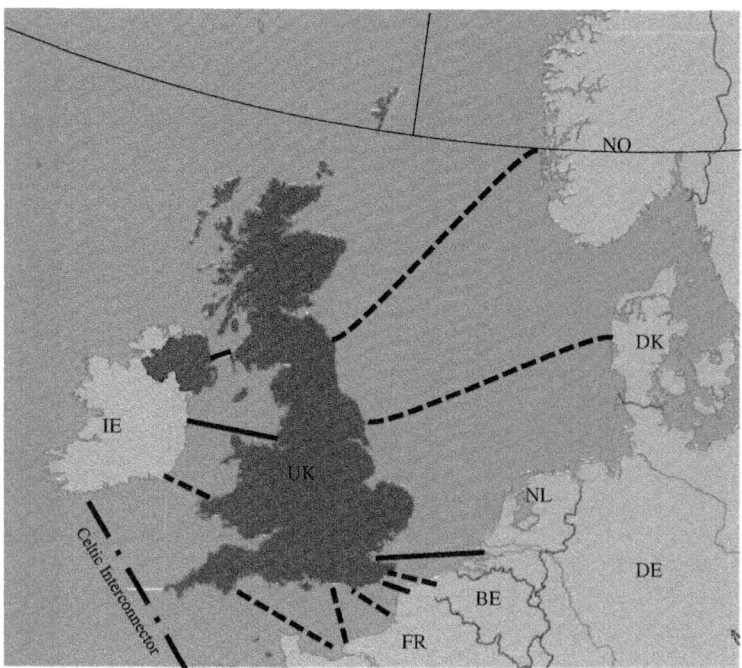

Fig. 7.5 UK cross-border electricity interconnectors. Existing and planned [dotted line] interconnectors as of January 2018 (*Source* House of Lords 2018; Ofgem 2018)

The forecast until 2020 is 8% for the UK, 12% for France and 13% for Germany (European Commission 2017: 10–11).

Some experts do not expect a significant effect on the electricity markets of Brexit. This is assuming that the aforementioned infrastructure projects are completed, no matter what the outcome of the Brexit negotiations is (Pollitt 2017: 136–137; Interview TSO 2017; Morgan 2017a). There are, however, also concerns that the UK being outside the IEM could affect the economic outlook for investment, as well as political support for building new lines connecting to the UK rather than enhancing intra-EU energy flows (Fernandez 2018: 242–243). There is already evidence that a risk premium on investment appeared as a reaction to persistent uncertainty about negotiation outcomes (Vaughan 2017; House of Lords 2018: 36). As illustrated by the quotes, cited at the top of this section, from the hearings in the HL UK policymakers echo this divergence about the potential effect Brexit is going to have on the secure supply of electricity. MPs in both Houses (House of Lords 2018; House of Commons 2017) urged the UK government to address potential supply shortages, as do energy intensive industries (CPI 2017a). The increasing cross-border capacity hints at an increase of net electricity imports to the UK, and the need will become more important in the course of expanding renewable generation in order to realise the goals formulated in the Green Growth strategy (HM Government 2017a).

There is more agreement as to the special situation in Northern Ireland because of the new external border of the EU towards Ireland created by Brexit (HM Government 2017b; Higgins and Costello 2016). The realisation of the Single Electricity Market on the island of Ireland, the I-SEM, is based on European law. This requires that Northern Ireland will fully implement the EU acquis in future (HM Government 2017b: 21–24; HSF et al. 2017: 14). Currently, Northern Ireland relies on imports through the interconnectors to Scotland and Ireland. Between 2004 and 2013, Northern Ireland was a net exporter towards Ireland. Since 2014, however, Northern Ireland became a net importer, though the differential accounted for only a small proportion of total domestic consumption. Between 2002 and 2015, Northern Ireland was a net importer from Scotland, at times with significant shares. In 2016, Northern Ireland for the first time exported some 252 gigawatt hours more than it imported (Department for the Economy 2018: 29). However, Northern Ireland will have to deal with increased intermittent electricity generation in order to achieve its target of producing 40% of its electricity consumption from renewables by 2020, and faces an anticipated supply deficit in 2021. It has therefore been argued that security of supply would be at risk in the medium term if the planned North South Interconnector between Northern Ireland and the Republic of Ireland was not going to be constructed (House of Commons 2017: 18–19). In its strategy for future relations with the EU published in July 2018, the UK government addressed these concerns and announced its intention of "maintaining the Single Electricity Market (SEM) across the island of Ireland in any eventuality" (HM Government 2018b: 41). In the meantime, the UK risks side-lining, literally, by a planned direct interconnection joining France and Ireland known as the Celtic Interconnector (see Fig. 7.5) via a 600-km-long undersea cable, providing capacity for 700 megawatts (Morgan 2017b). The European Commission lends support to the project by allocating 4 million Euros under the Connecting Europe Facility. The French and Irish TSOs, RTE and EirGrid heavily lobby for the project to be realised (EirGrid 2018; RTE 2018). There seems to be both the political momentum and stakeholder support to realise the project (Interview regulator 2017, 2019).

Despite the increased cross-border interconnector capacity between the UK and the EU, the future of energy relations post-Brexit is uncertain, and projects such as the Celtic Interconnector might diminish the political influence of the British. As highlighted by the Swiss energy expert Jean-Christophe Füeg in the hearings at the HL, the UK does not offer anything crucial to the IEM (House of Lords 2018: Q 45). This is different for the Swiss who host a majority of cross-border flows and therefore provide critical infrastructure and dispose of valuable market information. Further, Norway also is different, being an important gas supplier to Europe (Goldthau and Sitter 2014: 70–80). The EU will thus weigh the economic benefits to grant privileged market access to the UK against the cost of accepting British positions in other areas such as free movement of workers (Sumption 2017; Portes and Forte 2017; Pollitt 2017).

It follows from the discussion in this chapter that Brexit to varying extents is going to affect chemicals, waste, product, and energy regulation. Business seeks to achieve close alignment with EU chemicals regulation in order to secure access to markets and knowledge-sharing mechanisms. Further, the energy business seeks to maintain current levels of technical cooperation on infrastructure-related issues with European partners. By contrast, preferences are mixed in regard to the EU's climate and environmental policy ambitions. In the area of product policy industry wishes to maintain its role as a standard-setter and rule-shaper. In the area of waste legislation, industry would, at the contrary, welcome more flexibility, deemed necessary to increase recycling rates. Comparing these areas of regulation, we can thus expect dynamics of differentiated disintegration (Schimmelfennig 2018), resulting in diverse patterns of future regulatory alignment (Armstrong 2018). It is apparent, therefore, that UK-based business—rather than embracing the opportunity to do away with Brussels red tape—predominantly sought to safeguard the status quo. This does not come as a surprise when considering that most of the industry branches will lose out in their power to shape regulation. Brexit, especially under a no-deal scenario, will be a disaster for the regulatory power of UK-based companies.

REFERENCES

Ambrose J. (2018) Government Clean Growth Plan 'Falls Short' on Climate Targets. *The Telegraph:* 17.1.2018.

AMDEA. (2017) *Annual Report 2016–2017.* London: The Association of Manufacturers of Domestic Appliances.

AMDEA. (2018) Newsletter 03.2018. London: The Association of Manufacturers of Domestic Appliances.

APPLiA. (2018) *By the Numbers: The Home Appliance Industry in Europe, 2016–2017.* Brussels: Home Appliance Europe. Available at: https://applia-europe. eu/statistical-report-2017-2016/documents/APPLiA_SR18.pdf   (accessed 24.3.2019).

Armstrong KA. (2018) Regulatory Alignment and Divergence After Brexit. *Journal of European Public Policy* 25(8): 1099–1117.

Baker D. (2018) *Plastics in the Spotlight. An Examination of Current Issues.* Rushden: RPC Group.

ban. (2018) *e-Trash Transparency Project.* Available at: http://www.ban.org/ trash-transparency/ (accessed 12.8.2018).

BBC. (2018a) Brexit Study Warns Over Chemical Industry. *BBC News:* 8.3.2018. London.

BBC. (2018b) In Full: Theresa May's Speech on Future UK–EU Relations. *BBC News:* 2.3.2018. London.

BBC. (2018c) McDonald's to Ditch Plastic Straws. *BBC News:* 15.6.2018.

BEIS. (2016) *Digest of United Kingdom Energy Statistics 2016.* London: Department for Business, Energy and Industrial Strategy.

BEIS. (2017) *Digest of United Kingdom Energy Statistics 2017.* London: Department for Business, Energy and Industrial Strategy.

Berny N. (2008) Le lobbying des ONG internationales d'environnement à Bruxelles. *Revue francaise de science politique* 58(1): 97–121.

Berny N. (2016) Environmental Groups. In: Burns C, Jordan A, Gravey V, et al. (eds) *The EU Referendum and the UK Environment: An Expert Review. How Has EU Membership Affected the UK and What Might Change in the Event of a Vote to Remain or Leave?*

BPF. (2016) *The UK Plastics Industry: A Strategic Vision for Growth.* London: British Plastics Federation.

BPF. (2017) *Understanding Plastics Trade: An Overview of Plastics Import and Export Markets.* London: British Plastics Federation.

BPF. (2018a) *BPF Annual Review 2017.* London: British Plastics Federation.

BPF. (2018b) *Legacy Additives and the Circular Economy*. London: British Plastics Federation.

BPF. (2018c) *Plastics: A Vision for a Circular Economy—Improving the Environment for the Next Generation*. London: British Plastics Federation.

BPF. (2018d) *A BPF Members Survey. Brexit Questionnaire*. December 2018. London: British Plastics Federation.

Brouard S, Costa O and König T. (2011) *The Europeanization of Domestic Legislatures: The Empirical Implications of the Delors' Myth in Nine Countries*. New York: Springer.

BSI. (2018a) *Brexit and Standards Update*. London: British Standards Institution.

BSI. (2018b) *Brexit and Standards: Position Statement*. 1.2.2018. London: British Standards Institution.

Buchan D. (2010) From Liberalisation to Intervention: Europe, the UK, and the Changing Agenda. In: Rutledge I and Wright P (eds) *UK Energy Policy and the End of Market Fundamentalism*. Oxford: Oxford University Press, Oxford Institute for Energy Studies, 401–420.

Burns C, Gravey V, Jordan A, et al. (2019) De-Europeanising or Disengaging? EU Environmental Policy and Brexit. Special Issue: The Future of European Union Environmental Politics and Policy. In: Zito A, Burns S and Lenschow A (eds) *Environmental Politics* 28(2): 271–292.

Burns C, Jordan A, Gravey V, et al. (2016) The EU Referendum and the UK Environment: An Expert Review. How has EU Membership Affected the UK and What Might Change in the Event of a Vote to Remain or Leave? *ESRC UK in a Changing Europe Initiative*, 158.

Büthe T and Mattli W. (2011) *The New Global Rulers: The Privatization of Regulation in the World Economy*. Princeton: Princeton University Press.

Carrington D. (2018a) UK Opposes Strong EU Recycling Targets Despite Plastics Pledge. *The Guardian*: 24.1.2018.

Carrington D. (2018b) UK Reverses Opposition to Tough EU Recycling Targets. *The Guardian*: 29.3.2018.

CECED. (2017) *Impact of Brexit on the EU Industry Producing Household Appliances*. Position Paper. Brussels: European Committee of Domestic Equipment Manufacturers.

CEFIC. (2017) *Facts & Figures 2017 of the European Chemical Industry*. Brussels: The European Chemical Industry Council.

CEN-CENELEC. (2018) *Standardization Complements the European Union's Ecodesign Regulation Towards a European Circular Economy: A View from Richard Hughes, Chairman of CEN/CLC/JTC 10*. Brussels: CEN-CENELEC. Available at: https://www.cencenelec.eu/news/brief_news/Pages/TN-2018-034.aspx (accessed 13.8.2018).

CIA. (2017) *The Chemical Industry: Brexit Priorities for UK Growth*. London: Chemical Industries Association.

CIA. (2018) *Making Brexit Work for the Chemical Industry*. London: Chemical Industries Association.

Ciambra A and Solorio I. (2014) The Liberalisation of the Internal Energy Market: Is the EU Dancing at a British Tempo? In: Tosun J, Schmitt S and Schulze K (eds) *Energy Policy Making in the EU: Building the Agenda*. London: Springer, 142–165.

CIEL, ClientEarth and NRDC. (2014) *Toxic Partnership Revealed*. Washington, New York, London: Center for International Environmental Law, ClientEarth, NRDC.

ClientEarth. (2018) *A New Nature and Environment Commission: Speaking Up for Nature and Holding the Powerful to Account*. London: ClientEarth.

Copeland P. (2016) Europeanization and de-Europeanization in UK Employment Policy: Changing Governments and Shifting Agendas. *Public Administration* 94(4): 1124–1139.

CPI. (2017a) *Brexit. Position Paper*. Swindon, Wiltshire: Confederation of European Paper Industry.

CPI. (2017b) *The Future of UK Paper: A Growth Springboard Sector*. Position Paper. Swindon, Wiltshire: Confederation of European Paper Industry.

CPI. (2017c) *Pride in Paper. CPI Confederation of Paper Industries Review 2016/17*. Swindon, Wiltshire: Confederation of European Paper Industry.

CPI. (2018a) *Paper: The Sustainable, Renewable and Recyclable Choice*. Review 2017/2018. Swindon, Wiltshire: Confederation of European Paper Industry.

CPI. (2018b) *Quality and the Consistency Framework*. Swindon, Wiltshire: Confederation of European Paper Industry.

Crisp J. (2016) Commission Won't Regulate Toasters or Hairdryers After Hoovergate Scandal. *Euractiv*: 8.11.2016.

Crisp J, Foster p and Rayner G. (2018) EU Diplomats Shocked by Boris's 'Four-Letter Reply' to Business Concerns About Brexit. *The Telegraph*: 23.6.2018.

Daily Mail. (2019) Theresa May Offers to Step Down once Brexit Deal is Approved. *MailOnline*: 27.3.2019.

DEFRA. (2018a) *Environmental Principles and Governance After EU Exit*. London: Department for Environment Food & Rural Affairs. Available at: https://consult.defra.gov.uk/eu/environmental-principles-and-governance/ (accessed 6.8.2018).

DEFRA. (2018b) *UK Statistics on Waste*. London: Department for Environment Food & Rural Affairs, Government Statistical Service.

Department for the Economy. (2018) *Energy in Northern Ireland 2018*. Belfast: Analytical Services Division, Department for the Economy.

EAC. (2017a) *The Future of Chemicals Regulation after the EU Referendum*. Eleventh Report of Session 2016–2017. London: House of Commons.

EAC. (2017b) *Oral Evidence: The Future of Chemicals Regulation after the EU Referendum*, HC 912. London: House of Commons.

EAC. (2018a) *Environmental Audit Committee*. Tuesday 30 January 2018. London: House of Commons. Available at: https://parliamentlive.tv/Event/Index/110ad349-e07b-437a-829e-4871223fc050.

EAC. (2018b) *Environmental Audit Committee*. Wednesday 31 January 2018. London: House of Commons. Available at: https://parliamentlive.tv/Event/Index/eeee1757-f244-4b3f-8447-b4c6334d0be5.

EAC. (2018c) MPs Call for "latte levy" on Coffee Cups. 5.1.2018. London: House of Commons.

ECHA. (2018a) *REACH Registration Results*. Helsinki: European Chemicals Agency. Available at: https://echa.europa.eu/de/reach-registrations-since-2008 (accessed 9.8.2018).

ECHA. (2018b) *The UK's Withdrawal from the EU*. Helsinki: European Chemicals Agency. Available at: https://echa.europa.eu/uk-withdrawal-from-the-eu (accessed 9.8.2018).

Eckert S. (2018) The European Commission as a Negotiator: Evidence from the Disintegration Talks with the United Kingdom and Switzerland. In: Jörn E, Bauer MW and Becker S (eds) *The European Commission in Turbulent Times: Assessing Organizational Change and Policy Impact*. Baden-Baden: Nomos, 159–180.

Eikeland PO. (2004) *The Long and Winding Road to the Internal Energy Market: Consistencies and Inconsistencies in EU Policy*. FNI Report. Lysaker: Fridtjof Nansens Institute.

EirGrid. (2018) *Celtic Interconnector*. Dublin: EirGrid. Available at: http://www.eirgridgroup.com/the-grid/projects/celtic-interconnector/the-project/ (accessed 16.08.2018).

Elgot J and Savage M. (2018) Siemens UK Boss Joins Business Leaders' Criticism of Hard Brexit. *The Guardian*: 23.6.2018.

Ellis-Petersen H. (2018) Deluge of Electronic Waste Turning Thailand into 'World's Rubbish Dump'. *The Guardian*: 28.6.2018.

EMF. (2012) *Towards the Circular Economy, Vol. 1: Economic and Business Rationale for a Circular Economy*. Cowes: Ellen Macarthur Foundation (EMF).

EMF. (2014) *Towards the Circular Economy, Vol. 3: Accelerating the Scale-Up Across Global Supply Chains*. Cowes: Ellen Macarthur Foundation (EMF).

EMF. (2016) *The New Plastics Economy: Rethinking the Future of Plastics*. Cowes: Ellen MacArthur Foundation (EMF).

EMF. (2017a) *The New Plastics Economy: Catalysing Action*. Cowes: Ellen MacArthur Foundation (EMF).

EMF. (2017b) *The New Plastics Economy: Rethinking the Future of Plastics & Catalysing Action*. Cowes: Ellen MacArthur Foundation (EMF).

EMF. (2018) *Circular Consumer Electronics: An Initial Exploration*. Cowes: Ellen Macarthur Foundation (EMF).

ENTSO-E. (2017) *Letter from ENTSO-E on Brexit to Michel Barnier and The Rt Hon David Davis MP.* 31.3.2017. Brussels: European Network of Transmission System Operators for Electricity.

EPRC. (2018) *Monitoring Report 2016. European Declaration on Paper Recycling 2016–2020.* Brussels: European Paper Recycling Council.

Eurelectric. (2017) *BREXIT: Maintaining Free and Fair Trade of Electricity and Gas in Europe. A EURELECTRIC Initial Analysis Paper.* Brussels: Union of the Electricity Industry.

Europe Economics. (2015) *The Economic Impact of the Domestic Appliances Industry in Europe.* Report for the European Committee of Domestic Equipment Manufacturers (CECED). London: Europe Economics.

European Commission. (2001) *Mitteilung der Kommission an das Europäische Parlament und den Rat - Europäische Energieinfrastruktur.* KOM (2001) 775 endgültig. Luxemburg: Amt für Veröffentlichungen der Europäischen Kommission.

European Commission. (2015) *Energy Union Package*: Communication from the Commission to the European Parliament, the Council, the European Economic and Social Committee, the Committee of the Regions and the European Investment Bank. A Framework Strategy for a Resilient Energy Union with a Forward-Looking Climate Change Policy. COM (2015) 80 final. Brussels: European Commission.

European Commission. (2016) *Communication. Clean Energy for all Europeans.* COM (2016) 860 final. Brussels: European Commission.

European Commission. (2017) *Communication on Strengthening Europe's Energy Networks.* COM (2017) 718 final. Brussels: European Commission.

European Council. (2018) Guidelines. European Council 23 March 2018. EUCO XT 20001/18. Brussels: Council of the EU.

Extance A. (2018) Brexit Analysis Predicts Chemical Industry Contraction. *Chemistry World:* 15.3.2018.

Fernandez RM. (2018) Conflicting Energy Policy Priorities in EU Energy Governance. *Journal of Environmental Studies and Sciences* 8(3): 239–248.

Fischer F. (1990) *Technocracy and the Politics of Expertise.* Newbury Park: Sage.

Focus. (2015) Neue Öko-Richtlinie: EU drosselt Xbox, Playstation and Wii. *Focus:* 28.4.2015.

frontier economics and techUK. (2018) *The UK Digital Sectors After Brexit.* An Independent Report Commissioined by techUK. Brussels, Cologne, Dublin, London, Madrid: Frontier Economics.

Fuchs D. (2007) *Business Power in Global Governance.* London: Lynne Rienner.

Fuchs D, Gumbert T and Schlipphak B. (2017) Eurosecpticism and Big Business. In: Leruth B, Startin N and Usherwood S (eds) *The Routledge Handbook of Euroscepticism.* New York: Routledge, 317–330.

Gabbatiss J. (2017) How Does the New EU Plastic Strategy Compare to the UK's Plans to Cut Pollution? *The Independent:* 18.1.2017.

Gandy M. (1994) *Recycling and the Politics of Urban Waste.* New York: St. Martin's Press.

Gasiorek M, Serwicka I and Smith A. (2018) *Which Manufacturing Sectors Are Most Vulnerable to Brexit?* Briefing Paper 16. February 2018. Fulmer: UK Trade Policy Observatory (UKTPO), University of Sussex.

Global Economic Dynamics. (2015) *GED Study: Costs and Benefits of a United Kingdom Exit from the European Union.* Gütersloh: Bertelsmann Stiftung.

Goldthau A and Sitter N. (2014) A Liberal Actor in a Realist World? The Commission and the External Dimension of the Single Market for Energy. *Journal of European Public Policy* 21(10): 1452–1472.

GOV.UK. (2018) *Policy Paper: Information About the Withdrawal Bill.* London: Department for Exiting the European Union. Available at: https://www.gov.uk/government/publications/information-about-the-withdrawal-bill (accessed 23.2.2019).

Government Office for Science. (2017) *Report of the Government Chief Scientific Adviser 2016: From Waste to Resource Productivity.* London: The Government Office for Science.

Greener UK. (2017) *Greener UK.* Available at: http://greeneruk.org (accessed 4.8.2018).

Greener UK. (2018a) *Brexit Risk Tracker.* February 2018–April 2018.

Greener UK. (2018b) *Environmental Principles and Governance After the UK Leaves the EU.* Position Paper. 31.7.2018. London: Greener UK.

Greener UK. (2018c) *What Would a No Deal Brexit Mean for the Environment?* 9.7.2018. London: Greener UK.

Greenpeace. (2018a) *The Evidence Is Clear: We Need a UK-Wide Deposit Return Scheme.* London: Greenpeace UK.

Greenpeace. (2018b) *Together We Can: Rethink IT.* Available at: https://www.greenpeace.org/archive-international/en/campaigns/detox/electronics/Guide-to-Greener-Electronics/ (accessed 12.8.2018).

Haigh N. (2015) *EU Environmental Policy: Its Journey to Centre Stage.* London: Routledge.

Heyvaert V and Čavoški A. (2018) UK Environmental Law Post-Brexit. In: Dougan M (ed) *The UK After Brexit: Legal and Policy Challenges.* Cambridge: Intersentia, 115–133.

Higgins P and Costello R. (2016) *IIEA Policy Brief. What Does Brexit Mean for the Energy Sector in Ireland?* Dublin: The Institute of International and European Affairs.

HM Government. (2017a) *The Clean Growth Strategy. Leading the Way to a Low Carbon Future.* London: BEIS.

HM Government. (2017b) *Northern Ireland and Ireland.* Position Paper. 16.8.2017. London: Department for Exiting the European Union.

HM Government. (2018a) *Deposit Return Scheme in Fight Against Plastic.* Press Release 28.3.2018. London: DEFRA.

HM Government. (2018b) *The Future Relationship Between the United Kingdom and the European Union.* Presented to Parliament by the Prime Minister by Command of Her Majesty. Cm 9593. London: UK Government.

HM Government. (2018c) *A Green Future: Our 25 Year Plan to Improve the Environment.* London: DEFRA.

HM Government. (2018d) *UK Government Power Statistics: Imports, Exports and Transfers of Electricity (ET 5.6).* Available at: https://www.gov.uk/government/statistics/electricity-section-5-energy-trends (accessed 10.8.2018).

HM Government. (2018e) *World-Leading Microbeads Ban Takes Effect.* Press Release 9.1.2018. London: DEFRA.

HM Government. (2018f) *Our Waste, Our Resources: A Strategy for England.* London: Her Majesty's Stationery Office, DEFRA.

HM Treasury. (2018) *Tackling the Plastic Problem. Using the Tax System or Charges to Address Single-Use Plastic Waste.* London: HM Treasury.

HMRC. (2018) *Trade Statistics.* Available at: https://www.uktradeinfo.com/Pages/Home.aspx (accessed 10.08.2018).

Holehouse M. (2016) EU to Launch Kettle and Toaster Crackdown After Brexit Vote. *The Telegraph:* 11.5.2016.

Höltschi R. (2015) Strom-Binnenmarkt der EU. Vorerst ohne die Schweiz. *Neue Zürcher Zeitung:* 27.7.2015.

House of Commons. (2017) *Leaving the EU: Negotiation Priorities for Energy and Climate Change Policy.* London: House of Commons.

House of Commons. (2018) *EU Exit Analysis Cross Whitehall Briefing.* January 2018. London: House of Commons.

House of Lords. (2018) Brexit: Energy Security. *Report of Session 2017–19.* London: House of Lords, European Union Committee.

Howard E. (2015) DEFRA Hit by Largest Budget Cuts of Any UK Government Department, Analysis Shows. *The Guardian:* 11.11.2015.

HSF, BCG and GC. (2017) *Strong Currents: Navigating the Post-Brexit Energy Market.* London: The Boston Consulting Group, Global Counsel, Herbert Smith Freehills.

Hutton W. (2018) Enough Already: In the National Interest, We Must Stop a Hard Brexit. *The Guardian:* 24.6.2018.

IEEP. (2018) *Brexit Negotiations: Equivalence, Environmental Standards and Risks.* London: Institute for European Environmental Policy.

Interview COM. (2007a) Advisor to Energy Commissioner, Brussels, 18.12.2007.

Interview COM. (2007b) Grid Expert DG TREN, Brussels, 19.12.2007.

Interview COM. (2017, 2019) Grid Expert DG Energy, Brussels, 12.4.2017 and 10.1.2019.

Interview ENGO. (2017a) Director of Programmes, Client, London, 20.10.2017.

Interview ENGO. (2017b) Executive Director, CHEM Trust, London, 17.7.2017.

Interview home appliance industry. (2017a) Chief Executive, Association Executive, AMDEA, London, 18.7.2017.

Interview home appliance industry. (2017b) Technical Executive, AMDEA, Phone, 10.10.2017.

Interview ICT industry. (2017) Head of Programme, Environment & Compliance, techUK, London, 20.10.2017.

Interview ministry. (2017a) Senior Project Manager Home and Local Energy, BEIS, London, 23.10.2017.

Interview ministry. (2017b) Team Leader REACH, Senior Policy Advisor, DEFRA, London, 17.7.2017.

Interview ministry. (2017c) UK Negotiation Leader in European Energy Policy, BEIS, London, 23.10.2017.

Interview MP. (2017) Environmental Audit Committee, House of Commons, London, 20.10.2017.

Interview paper industry. (2017) Deputy Director General, CEPI, Brussels, 11.4.2017.

Interview plastics industry. (2017) Sustainability Issues Executive, Senior Industrial Issues Executive, BPF, London, 19.7.2017.

Interview regulator. (2007a) Deputy Secretary General, ERGEG/CEER, Brussels, 20.12.2007.

Interview regulator. (2007b) Technical Expert Finnish Energy Regulator, CEER/ERGEG, Brussels, 17.12.2007.

Interview regulator. (2017) Grid Expert, OFGEM, former Staff ENTSO, London, 13.7.2017.

Interview regulator. (2017, 2019) Secretary General, CEER, Brussels, 10.4.2017 and 11.1.2019.

Interview TSO. (2007) Former Secretary General, ETSO, Brussels, 17.12.2007.

Interview TSO. (2008) Manager National Grid, Florence, 21.2.2008.

Interview TSO. (2017) Technical Expert National Grid, London, 19.10.2017.

Irving H. (2016) Paper Salvage in Britain During the Second World War. *Historical Research* 89(244): 373–393.

Jegen M. (2009) Swiss Energy Policy and the Challenge of European Governance. *Swiss Political Science Review* 15(4): 577–602.

Jensen DM and Snaith H. (2016) When Politics Prevails: The Political Economy of a Brexit. *Journal of European Public Policy* 23(4): 1–9.

Johnson J. (2012) *Britain Must Defend the Single Market*. Brussels: Centre for European Reform.

Johnston I. (2017a) Climate Change Department Closed by Theresa May in 'Plain Stupid' and 'Deeply Worrying' Move. *The Independent*: 14.7.2017.

Johnston I. (2017b) Government Given 21 Days to Explain Climate Change Failures or Face Legal Action. *The Independent*: 11.4.2017.

Johnston I. (2017c) UK Government has Breached Air Pollution Laws and Failed to Take Enough Action on Emissions, High Court rules. *The Independent*: 2.11.2017.

Kuenssberg L. (2019) Brexit: MPs Vote to Take Control of Brexit Process for Indicative Votes. *BBC News*: 26.3.2019.

Lavenex S. (2009) Switzerland's Flexible Integration in the European Union: A Conceptual Framework. *Swiss Political Science Review* 15(4): 547–575.

Lavenex S. (2015) The External Face of Differentiated Integration: Third Country Participation in EU Sectoral Bodies. *Journal of European Public Policy* 22(6): 836–853.

Laville S. (2017) China Waste Clampdown Could Create UK Cardboard Recycling Chaos, Say Industry Experts. *The Guardian*: 15.12.2017.

Lourie B. (2017) Without EU Regulations on Chemicals, the UK Will be a Toxic Dumping Ground. *The Guardian*: 1.6.2017.

Lowe P. (2017) *Brexit and Energy: Time to Make Some Hard Choices*. Brussels: Centre for European Reform.

Meletiou A, Cambini C and Masera M. (2018) Regulatory and Ownership Determinants of Unbundling Regime Choice for European Electricity Transmission Utilities. *Utilities Policy* 50: 13–25.

Monaghan A and Elgot J. (2018) More Firms May Follow Airbus in Brexit Threat, Says CBI. *The Guardian*: 22.6.2018.

Morgan S. (2017a) Brexit Impact on Energy Markets Could be 'limited', Study Says. *Euractiv*: 21.11.2017. Brussels.

Morgan S. (2017b) Commission Funds France-Ireland Power Link That Bypasses UK. *Euractiv*: 6.7.2017. Brussels.

Müller GV. (2018) Abseitsstehen vom Strombinnenmarkt kommt die Schweiz teuer zu stehen. *Neue Zürcher Zeitung*: 24.4.2018.

Murray A, Skene K and Haynes K. (2017) The Circular Economy: An Interdisciplinary Exploration of the Concept and Application in a Global Context. *Journal of Business Ethics* 140(3): 369–380.

Musaddique S and Gabbatiss J. (2017) China's Ban on Imported Plastic Leads to 'Impending Crisis' for UK Waste Recycling. *The Independent*: 7.12.2017.

Neslen A. (2017) EU's Ban on Inefficient Toasters Delayed to Avoid Pro-Brexit Press Attack. *The Guardian*: 28.2.2017.

Ofgem. (2018) *Electricity Interconnectors*. London: Office of Gas and Electricity Markets. Available at: https://www.ofgem.gov.uk/electricity/transmission-networks/electricity-interconnectors (accessed 14.8.2018).

Owen J, Lloyd L and Rutter J. (2018) Preparing Brexit, How Ready Is Whitehall? London: Institute for Government.

parliament.uk. (2018) *EU (Withdrawal) Bill Royal Assent.* Available at: https://www.parliament.uk/business/news/2018/january/lords-debates-eu-with-drawal-bill/ (accessed 09.08.2018).

Partington R. (2019) CBI and TUC Bosses Warn UK Faces National Emergency over Brexit. *The Guardian:* 21.3.2019.

Plastic Oceans. (2018) *Changing Attitudes Towards Plastic.* Available at: http://plasticoceans.uk/news (accessed 8.6.2018).

PlasticsEurope. (2018) *Plastics: The Facts 2017. An Analysis of European Plastics Production, Demand and Waste Data.* Brussels, Wemmel: Association for Plastics Manufacturers, European Association of Plastics Recycling.

Pollitt MG. (2017) The Economic Consequences of Brexit: Energy. *Oxford Review of Economic Policy* 33(S1): S134–S143.

Portes J and Forte G. (2017) The Economic Impact of Brexit-Induced Reductions in Migration. *Oxford Review of Economic Policy* 33(S1): S31–S44.

Prange-Gstöhl H. (2009) Enlarging the EU's Internal Energy Market: Why Would Third Countries Accept EU Rule Export? *Energy Policy* 37(12): 5296–5303.

Rosenow J and Cowart R. (2017) UK Needs to Put 'Efficiency First' After Release of Clean Growth Strategy. *Euractiv:* 18.10.2017.

RTE. (2018) *Celtic Interconnector: Electrical Interconnector Between France and Ireland.* Paris: Réseau de Transport d'Electricité. Available at: https://www.rte-france.com/en/project/celtic-interconnector-electrical-interconnec-tor-between-france-and-ireland (accessed 16.8.2018).

Schimmelfennig F. (2018) Brexit: Differentiated Disintegration in the European Union. *Journal of European Public Policy* 25(8): 1154–1173.

Scott M, Dickson A and Contiguglia C. (2018) France Battles to Topple Britain as Europe's Top Tech Nation. *Politico:* 10.6.2018.

Smedley T. (2016) At Work with the FT Interview: James Thornton, ClientEarth. *Financial Times,* 11.5.2016.

Solletty M. (2017) Britain's EU Rubbish: One of the EU's Biggest Waste Exporters May Have to Find New Ways to Burn or Recycle Its Trash at Home. *Politico:* 31.8.2017.

Solletty M. (2018) Plastic Tax Proposal Faces Resistance. *Politico:* 15.1.2018.

Stone J. (2018) Theresa May Ridiculed in European Parliament for Claiming Credit for EU Regulations. *The Independent:* 16.1.2018.

Suez. (2017) *Long Term Waste Treatment Capacity Shortfall Likely to Hit British Business and Taxpayers' Pockets as Millions of Tonnes of Waste Destined for Landfill over Next Decade, according to Latest Research.* Press Release 16.8.2017. Berkshire: Suez Recycling and Recovery UK.

SumOfUs. (2017) *McDonald's Is Polluting Our Oceans.* Available at: https://actions.sumofus.org/a/mcdonalds-is-polluting-our-oceans?source=campaigns (accessed 4.8.2018).

Sumption M. (2017) Labour Immigration After Brexit: Questions and Trade-Offs in Designing a Work Permit System for EU Citizens. *Oxford Review of Economic Policy* 33(S1): S45–S53.

Swissgrid. (2015) Netzdaten 2015. Laufenburg: Swissgrid AG.

Tamma P. (2018a) China's Trash Ban Forces Europe to Confront Its Waste Problem. *Politico*: 21.2.2018.

Tamma P. (2018b) EU's Plastics Strategy Doesn't Include Plastic Tax. *Politico*: 16.1.2018.

techUK. (2016) *Initial techUK Views on Chemical Legislation After EU Exit*. 26.10.2016. London: techUK.

techUK. (2018a) *Reuse | Repair | Remanufacture in the ICT Sector*. London: techUK.

techUK. (2018b) *techUK Representing the Future*. London: techUK. Available at: http://www.techuk.org/about (accessed 11.8.2018).

Thatcher M. (2007) *Internationalisation and Economic Institutions: Comparing European Experiences*. Oxford: Oxford University Press.

Thornton J and Goodman M. (2017) *ClientEarth*. Melbourne: Scribe Publications.

Thorsheim P. (2015) *Waste into Weapons*. New York: Cambridge University Press.

Töller AE. (2010) Measuring and Comparing the Europeanization of National Legislation: A Research Note. *Journal of Common Market Studies* 48(2): 417–444.

Vaughan A. (2017) Brexit and Energy: Does 'Taking Back Control' Mean Losing Power? *The Guardian*: 6.5.2017.

Virley SC. (2017) *Brexit and the Energy Market: Article 50 Has Been Triggert, But What Happens Next? A New Free Trade Agreement Will Be Needed to Maintain the Current Tariff-Free Trading on Gas and Electricity*. London: KPMG.

Vivid Economics. (2016) *The Impact of Brexit on the UK Energy Sector. An Assessment of the Risks and Opportunities for Electricity and Gas in the UK*. London: Vivd Economics.

Vogel D. (2012) *The Politics of Precaution: Regulating Health, Safety and Environmental Risks in Europe and the United States*. Princeton: Princeton University Press.

Waygood S, Simpson P, Gardiner W, et al. (2018) *Letter of Leading European and UK Companies and Investors to Negotiation Leaders Barnier and Davis*. 20.4.2018. United Kingdom. Available at: https://www.euractiv.com/wp-content/uploads/sites/2/2018/04/Brexit-coalition-letter-FINAL.pdf (accessed 27.3.2019).

WRAP. (2018a) *The Facts: China's Tighter Controls on the Quality of Waste Imports*. 16.2.2018. Oxon: The Waste and Resources Action Programme.

WRAP. (2018b) *Recovered Paper Imports & Exports*. Oxon: The Waste and Resources Action Programme. Available at: http://www.wrap.org.uk/content/recovered-paper-imports-exports (accessed 10.8.2018).

WRAP. (2018c) *UK Businesses Make World-Leading Pact to Tackle Plastic Pollution*. Oxon: The Waste and Resources Action Programme.

WRAP. (2018d) *The UK Plastics Pact: Together We Can Create a Sustainable System for Plastics*. Oxon: The Waste and Resources Action Programme. Available at: http://www.wrap.org.uk/content/the-uk-plastics-pact (accessed 26.04.2018).

WWF. (2018) *Plastics: Why We Must Act Now*. Gland: World Wide Fund for Nature. Available at: https://www.wwf.org.uk/updates/plastics-why-we-must-act-now (accessed 10.8.2018).

Young K. (2018) *UK Government White Paper on Brexit Includes a Wish to Stay in EU Chemicals Law, but Are its Commitments Enough?* 12.7.2018. London: CHEMTrust.

CHAPTER 8

Conclusion: The Corporate Challenge to Regulators

This book began by presenting four intriguing cases in which corporate actors came under considerable pressure through media coverage, NGO campaigning and subsequent regulatory activism. Even in these constellations, however, corporate actors proved rather powerful in the ensuing process of regulation. In this concluding chapter I revisit the book's central argument in the light of the empirical findings and provide answers to the research questions that were initially posed. In a nutshell, I posit that, in the areas of regulation studied in the book, policymakers have limited capacity to effectively pose a regulatory threat, while corporate actors do, in turn, pose a real challenge to regulation. In what follows, I will briefly summarise the case study findings on the role of experts, innovators and operators in the regulatory process (see Table 8.1). Further, I will sum up the contributions made to existing literature and identify possible avenues for future research. Finally, I will conclude with some thoughts about the findings' policy implications.

NGO Pressure and Regulatory Threats

My first research question was about *the extent to which corporations are threatened by regulation, as well as the extent to which they themselves pose a challenge to regulation.* This question addresses the dynamics involved in the interaction between corporate actors and regulators. The case studies

© The Author(s) 2019
S. Eckert, *Corporate Power and Regulation,*
International Series on Public Policy,
https://doi.org/10.1007/978-3-030-05463-2_8

Table 8.1 Case study findings

Case studies	Expert	Innovator			Operator
Industry sectors	Paper industry	Plastics industry	Home appliance industry	ITC industry	Transmission system operators
Regulatory threat	Recycled content, food contact materials	Bans and restrictions of materials and products, recycled content	Resource efficiency, reporting duties	Energy and resource efficiency	Ownership unbundling (third package)
Regulatory role of corporations	VA as a pre-emptive strike and planning instrument, seeking stringent regulation	VA as a pre-emptive strike, seeking regulatory flexibility, litigating regulation	Seeking binding energy efficiency standards, litigating non-compliance	Preventing regulation, reluctant on VAs	Anticipating and shaping regulation (VAs, network codes)

Source Author's illustration

discussed in Chapters 4–6 explored the dynamic relationship between European regulation and industry initiatives, illustrated by the timelines presented for each case (see Figs. 4.3, 5.3, and 6.3). I will begin with the first sub-question on regulatory threats.

Both the paper and plastics industry were "threatened" by NGO activism and costly regulation at some stage. This regulatory threat triggered (plastics industry), or at least contributed to (paper industry), the emergence of voluntary initiatives on recycling (as previously discussed in Héritier and Eckert 2008, 2009). Regarding paper and cardboard products, NGOs have sought to raise awareness on resource use, sustainable consumption, as well as health and safety risks. International campaigns addressed issues around deforestation, the reduction of paper use and, more recently, on legacy and toxic substances in recycled packaging and food contact materials. To address resource issues, European policymakers on various occasions envisioned the introduction of binding regulatory requirements for recycled content and further sought to pull consumers to sustainable consumption through instruments such as the Ecolabel. Moreover, chemicals regulation is a powerful tool to eliminate substances of concern. To address health and safety issues, policymakers further strive for regulatory responses for recycled materials, which can prove problematic for packaging and food contact applications. Pressure from the public or NGOs, however, is by far more prevalent on plastics. Identified as a material raising particular environmental and health concerns, PVC was targeted by NGO campaigning at both the national and European levels throughout the 1980s and 1990s. By the start of the New Millennium, policymakers envisaged material-specific regulation and even bans. Further, the industry was affected by restrictions of specific substances, mostly additives such as phthalates. In recent years, massive NGO and media campaigning have put the entire plastics industry under pressure. Campaigning has brought the problem of marine littering to the spotlight, pointing to the negative effects of plastic waste for wildlife but also for human health once microplastics contaminate soil, water and food. Various international NGO coalitions advocated a fundamental transformation of the economy in order to go plastic free. The Chinese ban on waste imports created further momentum to act for European and national policymakers. The EU adopted a Plastics Strategy in the context of its Circular Economy Package, and banned a number of single-use plastics. UK policymakers introduced various measures to address plastics pollution, aiming for global leadership in this respect. The plastics industry, and the PVC branch in particular, therefore, continuously had to face public and regulatory pressure. NGO pressure and regulatory threats addressed at the paper industry, in comparison, were less frequent and powerful.

The home appliance and ICT industries were not to the same extent subject to NGO campaigning. Some NGO and regulatory pressure emerged, especially with respect to the waste phase of electrical and electronic products. International NGO activism addresses the somewhat scandal-prone export of electronic waste outside Europe. Moreover, ENGOs have sought to push industry towards accepting more ambitious energy, and resource efficiency standards both by using campaigning tools and by providing counter-evidence in standardisation procedures. European policymakers have regulated the energy usage of home appliances since the 1990s and have subsequently sought to expand energy efficiency requirements to consumer electronics and ICT under the Ecodesign framework. So far, binding regulation has covered only home appliance products and much less so ICT products. For the home appliance industry a regulatory threat scenario did not materialise for energy efficiency, where industry proactively sought regulatory support to avoid free-riding problems in fragmented market segments. The rescaling of relevant standards mirrored the increasingly incremental innovation in the home appliance segment, often to the disappointment of ENGOs. In the fast-moving ICT sector, characterised by "radical" (Freeman and Soete 1997) or "seismic" (Ford 2017) innovation, regulators mostly failed to cast a credible threat, potentially due to a lack of product and market specific technological know-how. The Commission even acknowledged that the Ecodesign framework may not be fit to regulate ICT products and that a separate track approach may be needed. In the absence of such pressure industry either was not regulated at all or got away with rather unambitious VAs. Regulatory pressure for both industry sectors has, however, taken up speed with the Circular Economy agenda and a move to consider additional regulatory requirements beyond the use phase on resource efficiency. In this area, we see an alliance between ENGOs and certain business segments (i.e. those engaging in repair services, recycling businesses, etc.) lobbying for more sustainable and greener devices, promoting reuse, reparability and recycling. The majority of the home appliance and ICT industry, however, seeks to prevent additional regulatory requirements.

Energy infrastructure operators are far less subject to public and NGO pressure, given that they do run a highly technical, somehow invisible infrastructure—provided that operation runs smoothly. Their business comes to public attention only when new infrastructure needs to be permitted and built, or when things go wrong. Permitting and construction procedures indeed often prove lengthy at national and local level, also due to ENGO campaigning and grass-root contestation. TSOs have thus been involved in national consultation procedures, and an industry-ENGO alliance such as the Renewables Grid Initiative seeks to fuel support for new infrastructure. The most damaging, worst-case scenario for operators, however, is a blackout. Therefore, for policymakers and operators alike, the prior goal is to safeguard reliable operation of the grid and provide a secure supply of electricity. Given this alliance of interests, it is hardly the case that we can discern an explicit regulatory threat. A rare example in European energy governance is the threatening potential of the ownership unbundling measures envisioned in the run-up to the Third Energy Directive adopted in 2009, backed up by sector inquiries and competition policy intervention in the years before. Case study findings on NGO and regulatory pressure thus underline that merely approaching governance and regulation from a demand-side perspective misses out an important part of the picture. In fact, the preconditions for a credible shadow of hierarchy (Héritier and Lehmkuhl 2008; Héritier and Rhodes 2010; Börzel 2010), or regulatory and legislative threats (Halfteck 2008; Glachant 2003) to materialise are quite demanding and are not frequently met. Further, these concepts lose out of sight constellations where interests coevolve between public and private actors, for instance when forming a green alliance. It is thus necessary to turn our attention to the supply side of the equation, considering what private actors have to offer as experts, operators and innovators.

EXPERTS, OPERATORS AND INNOVATORS

In response to the second part of the question regarding the extent to which corporations pose a challenge to regulation, I have suggested examining in more detail the power resources available to them and their regulatory role throughout the policy process. This leads me to my second research question about the ways in which *corporations use various power resources in order to prevent, shape, make or revoke regulation*. The central argument developed in this book is, in line with resource dependence theory (Pfeffer and Salancik 2003), that distinct power resources are mobilised by *experts, operators and innovators*. In what follows, I will briefly revisit the findings of the case studies conducted in Chapters 4, 5 and 6. I will further add some insights from Chapter 7 which addressed the possible effects of Brexit for the regulatory power of corporations.

In Chapter 4, I have discussed the role of industry as *experts* in the transition towards the circular economy thanks to their specialised knowledge and information about the complex materials and substances they produce. Case study analysis has shown how the paper industry challenges proposals for new regulation and seeks to shape regulation, on the grounds of its legacy as a recycling expert. In its discourse, the paper industry cultivates an image as the global leader in paper recycling and as an industry model for circularity. It does so when publicising the achievements of its EU-wide voluntary agreement on paper recycling implemented since 2000, the European Paper Declaration. The Declaration has also proven beneficial to industry as a planning instrument, as it helps to cope with the uncertainties related to the quantities and quality of recovered materials available. Moreover, the paper industry promotes the notion of the bioeconomy, positioning itself as a user of renewable biomass and recyclable feedstocks. Overall, therefore, the paper industry managed to generate significant structural and discursive power (Fuchs 2007) in the regulatory process. With its reliance on finite fossil fuels, the plastics industry, with the exception of producers of bioplastics, has not embraced the idea of a bioeconomy. The circular economy, by contrast, has been an important point of reference in the industry's public discourse. The plastics industry refers to one of the circular economy "Rs" (Kirchherr et al. 2017; Ghisellini et al. 2016) in particular, namely the one for recycling. The plastics industry has invested massively to improve its environmental reputation, in particular to prove the recyclability of the materials and applications produced. In response to targeted ENGO campaigning and regulatory pressure, the PVC industry engaged in a costly voluntary recycling scheme from 2000 onwards (Vinyl 2010 and VinylPlus). The global marine littering campaign and mounting regulatory pressure have fuelled wider industry initiatives at international and European level in the last years. In 2018, the European plastics industry committed to voluntary action in order to address sustainability issues, specifically those raised in the European Commission's Plastics Strategy. Both the paper and plastics industries have an interest in separate collection of high-quality material, wanting to dispose of more and better quality recovered material. A major difference is that the paper industry is asking for more stringent regulation of hazardous substances, as these make the lives of recyclers more difficult. The plastics industry, in contrast, asks to relax regulatory requirements especially for legacy materials in order to facilitate recycling activities and increase recycling rates. The discussion of Brexit has further illustrated that once industry participates in a costly regulatory scheme such as REACH, it has incentives to safeguard the status quo and to avoid change. The European chemical regulatory regime enables industry to pool resources and expertise, and notably the scenario of no longer having access to the REACH database is perceived as a loss by industry experts. This chapter thus shows how in areas such as chemicals regulation the politics of expertise (Boswell 2009; Fischer 1990) and knowledge (Radaelli 1999) prevail, and that industry experts in particular hold epistemic authority (Quack 2016; Sending 2015), at least to the extent that NGOs do not generate sufficient counter policy expertise (Fischer 1990: 28).

Chapter 5 has focused on the manufacturers of home appliances and ICT products in their role as *innovators* in the transition towards resource efficiency. The comparison of these two industry branches was insightful to the extent that two distinct types of innovation were discernible: incremental (Freeman and Soete 1997) or sedimental (Ford 2017) innovation in the case of the home appliance industry, and radical (Freeman and Soete 1997) or seismic (Ford 2017) innovation in the case of the ICT industry. Accordingly, their role in the regulatory process diverged considerably. The home appliance industry sought to make a case that the potential for future energy savings is comparatively low at this stage and that, therefore, binding requirements should not be overambitious. That said, in the past, industry preferred binding over voluntary regulation, which is illustrated by the fact that pre-existing voluntary commitments on energy efficiency were replaced by product-specific regulations under Ecodesign. Visible energy labelling gave these products an additional competitive edge, and mandatory requirements helped to overcome the problem of freeriding in a fragmented product markets. The extent to which market actors attribute reputational gains to the European Energy Label has become evident in the course of litigation concerning alleged non-compliance. The "Hoovergate scandal" triggered by the British inventor Sir James Dyson brought along an ECJ ruling which annulled existing regulation and created a regulatory limbo. This underpins the argument that litigation is by now a powerful business tool (Forcier 1994) also in the European context of mounting adversarial legalism (Kagan 2001; Kelemen 2011). To the contrary, the ICT industry intervened in order to prevent binding regulation, pledging for flexibility and market-driven solutions on the ground that onerous regulation would be detrimental to product and market innovation. In doing so, however, industry committed to voluntary agreements under Ecodesign in only very few cases. Any such voluntary action proved economically beneficial to the participants, mostly in highly concentrated market segments, rather than that it was driven by a background regulatory threat. With the move of policymaking from energy efficiency targets towards wider resource efficiency targets, however, both branches do share a common interest to prevent what they consider onerous regulation. The analysis of industry's role in the standardisation work of the CEN/CENELEC committee for material efficiency has proven this point, as there were clearly efforts to slow down the process and lower the level of ambition. Considering Brexit in this analysis further shows that both industry branches in the UK fear losing out in rule-shaping power to merely become rule-takers. This loss in regulatory power could even negatively affect innovative potential, especially of the ICT industry. The UK-based home appliance industry, though not an important manufacturer, has played a central role in European and international standardisation bodies and fears to lose not only influence but also access to such bodies. The ICT industry is an important branch of the UK economy which also draws its power from being an influential rule-shaper inside the EU. Losing such regulatory power could ultimately be detrimental for its market power. Innovation is thus indeed posing a "regulatory challenge" (Ford 2017: 3), especially where it goes beyond incremental, product-specific innovations and takes on the form of radical market or paradigm innovations (Autio and Lumme 1998), as illustrated by the ICT industry. Moreover, the chapter makes a case that in order to grasp corporate power in regulation, we clearly need to look beyond the legislative arena. Standardisation procedures, in particular, are a formidable venue for private ruling (Büthe and Mattli 2010), and the Brexit debate just underpins how dear it is to industry.

Finally, the case study on the role of TSOs in the European electricity markets presented in Chapter 6 shows to what extent the industry and regulatory sides are intertwined. As *operators* of a critical infrastructure these actors dispose of structurally important assets. They have to ensure that, in the short term, existing capacity is ready to respond when it is needed in operation to meet the actual load. In the medium to long term, they have to make sure that there is enough installed and expected available capacity to meet demand. TSOs are thus the guarantors of both short term security and medium to long term adequacy. In essence, they have to live up to their role as high reliability organisations (La Porte and Consolini 1991). The cross-border cooperation of European TSOs has become a cornerstone of European energy governance. TSOs have assumed a regulatory role (Mathieu 2016) in allocating the costs of the use of cross-border infrastructure, managing congestion, network development and the formulation of network codes. The findings suggest that European TSOs effectively use their power resources in order to prevent, shape and even make regulation on highly technical infrastructure issues. Most of the time infrastructure operators anticipated subsequent regulatory measures, and by that means, they were able to drive the development of the rules instead of having to implement externally imposed requirements. The discussion of possible governance options for involving the UK in energy policy post-Brexit further underpins this argument about the prevalent role of TSOs. Contrary to policymakers and regulators, TSOs will still be able to fully participate in technically driven cross-border cooperation inside the European association (ENTSO-E). Once the UK is outside the Internal Energy Market, private governance on cross-border issues will thus become even more important for the domestic energy sector. In a nutshell, Chapter 6 shows that TSOs as operators have considerable structural and discursive power (Fuchs 2007) resources at their disposal. They master the regulatory game (Coen 2005) to an extent that they have become de facto rule makers. In doing so, they draw on their authority (Cutler 1999) acquired through a legacy of technically driven cooperation which predates European market integration. Further, they engage in a securitisation discourse (Buzan et al. 1998), putting security of supply issues first. And there is hardly any politician who dares to put into doubt this priority in energy policy.

Contribution and Future Research

This book contributes to three strands in the literature: first, to the literature on governance and regulation; second, to research on private actors in International Political Economy; and third, to various fields of policy analysis. With regard to the first two strands of literature, I have suggested moving from demand-side arguments about the shadow of hierarchy (Héritier and Lehmkuhl 2008; Héritier and Rhodes 2010; Börzel 2010), legislative or regulatory threats (Halfteck 2008; Glachant 2003) and authority (Cutler 1999, Green 2014) to considering what private actors have to offer on the supply side. Further research is needed to underpin and develop the arguments presented in this book. In particular, the conceptual framework developed on the basis of exploratory case studies could be used to conduct a more systematic and comprehensive stocktaking of the extent to which corporations prevent, shape, make and revoke regulation. The regulatory power of corporations merits further attention, and it is an endeavour that goes beyond capturing lobbying activities and interest politics. Rather, corporate actors have a substantive impact on the regulatory process, in particular in the non-legislative arena. We therefore need to take a comprehensive, integrated approach which considers the various policy instruments in combination and goes beyond a dichotomy opposing binding legislation versus voluntary self-regulation. More specifically, further research is needed on the role of private actors with respect to agency governance, committee procedures, standardisation and court proceedings. These are all areas which have been covered extensively in the existing literature (Trondal et al. 2012; Scully and van Schendelen 2004; Büthe and Mattli 2011; Bouwen and McCown 2007), yet often in a rather disconnected way, and often with a focus on public rather than private actors. Contributions to the literature on the evolving European administrative space (e.g. Jevnaker 2015), for instance, tend to overstate regulatory centralisation and underrate the role of private governance. Moreover, while the overall trend towards adversarial legalism has been acknowledged for the EU context (Kagan and Axelrod 2000; Kelemen 2011), the role of corporate actors in "regulation by litigation" (Morriss et al. 2009) has been neglected. Public policy analysis needs to dedicate far greater attention to the rising importance of litigation in the regulatory process. First, because of the important temporal dimension involved, as litigation usually allows buying time and putting certain decisions on hold. Second, because it is an important business tool (Forcier 1994), especially when corporations are repeat players (Galanter 1974). And third, because of the substantive effects litigation has on policy outputs and outcomes.

This book further contributes to the vast literature on European public policy. In particular, it makes a contribution to the role of private governance (Knill 2001; Lenschow and Rottmann 2010) in European integration, which is considered central to the case of the internal electricity market. This aspect has so far been neglected in the literature on European energy policy. It has further brought attention to the role of corporations in the area of regulating risks (Vogel 2012; Tosun 2013) and how they strategically use their expertise in the regulatory power game. Concerning the rich literature on environmental policy (e.g. Lenschow 2015; Greenwood 2017), the book draws our attention to the hidden faces of European governance, namely committee governance, agency governance, standardisation bodies and litigation. Addressing the power balance between corporate and diffuse interests (Eising 2016), we risk missing a large part of the picture when solely focusing on the legislative process. Litigation is one of the power resources used by corporate but increasingly also by NGO actors to make a difference in the regulatory game, the consequences of which can be far-reaching. Finally, the book gives us some first clues about the EU's current environmental policy agenda in the age of multiple crises and disintegration, thus contributing to an emerging field of research (e.g. Burns et al. 2019). In fact, a concept such as the circular economy, while bearing promises if taken to its full environmentalist potential, can also be interpreted in a way so as to result in policy dismantling (Bauer and Knill 2012).

THE CORPORATE CHALLENGE TO REGULATION: WHY BOTHER?

Finally, beyond the academic and scholarly interest in policy dynamics and the regulatory process, the findings provided in this book bear important implications for regulatory practice and future policy developments. The case study findings have corroborated the expectation that there is an eminent risk of acquired regulation in terms of rewarding gatekeeping (expert), protecting market position (innovator) and amplifying autonomy (operator).

First, in order to address these challenges to regulation, there is a need to secure sufficient levels of counter-expertise as well as regulatory oversight throughout the policy process. While a regulatory scheme such as REACH depends on the expertise business feeds into the system, the principle of "no data, no market" requires strict enforcement practice. The debate around Brexit and the potential losses for UK-based industry operating outside REACH illustrates the merits of the European scheme, as do the diffusion processes of EU-style chemical regulation around the world. To keep this upward momentum in global regulatory competition, European policymakers should resist current temptations to engage in policy dismantling and deregulation.

Second, protecting the (acquired) market position of innovators bears the risk to miss out on future opportunities—both in terms of new products and markets, as well as in terms of environmental progress. There are striking examples to this end, such as the delays in banning cadmium in TVs despite safe alternatives being available. The current regulatory battle is about the question whether or not Ecodesign is the appropriate instrument to address sustainability features of products throughout their life cycle. Indeed, the instrument is only as effective as its enforcement, and if requirements become too cumbersome, a leaner framework may prove more effective. There is also a need to re-assess the continued energy saving potential through product regulation, as in this area innovation is already generating decreasing returns on investment. Other areas such as housing and mobility have thus moved into the focus of European energy efficiency policy, and rightly so. The future challenges for the EU's ambition to strive towards a circular economy will be around resource efficiency and the waste issue. Market developments, such as increasing prices for raw materials, as well as regulatory decisions, such as China's ban and restrictions on waste imports, both create pressure for change, but purely reactive regulation will not suffice to set the pace in international regulatory competition. The current momentum should be used to engage in bold action in order to live up to a truly sustainable policy.

Third, dealing with operators, there is an inherent challenge not to amplify autonomy. This risk is particularly eminent in the European multi-level setting, where further shifts of competencies towards the European level are contested in the member states. In central areas, as discussed in Chapter 6, this leaves us with a regulatory gap which is filled in by private authority. Yet such lateral shifts of authority should not be left unchecked. In order to live up to the ambition to realise a truly integrated European energy market, there will be a need to overcome some of the dependencies found in the current governance architecture. At the same time, the political world needs to acknowledge the rationale for functional cooperation beyond territorially bound entities such as the EU. De facto arrangements with non-EU countries such as Switzerland

and future arrangements to be struck with the UK point in that direction. It is possible that actual levels of differentiated integration will need to be acknowledged and supported politically.

In short, the analysis of the industry case studies and the potential policy implications of Brexit provided in this book back up the argument that corporations do not simply strive for deregulation but for *power in regulation*.

REFERENCES

Autio E and Lumme A. (1998) Does the Innovator Role Affect the Perceived Potential for Growth? Analysis of Four Types of New, Technology-Based Firms. *Technology Analysis & Strategic Management* 10(1): 41–55.

Bauer MW and Knill C. (2012) Understanding Policy Dismantling: An Analytical Framework. In: Bauer MW et al. (eds) *Dismantling Public Policy: Preferences, Strategies, and Effects*. Oxford: Oxford University Press, 30–51.

Börzel TA. (2010) European Governance: Negotiation and Competition in the Shadow of Hierarchy. *Journal of Common Market Studies* 48(2): 191–219.

Boswell C. (2009) *The Political Uses of Expert Knowledge: Immigration Policy and Social Research*. Cambridge: Cambridge University Press.

Bouwen, P and McCown M. (2007) Lobbying Versus Litigation: Political and Legal Strategies of Interest Representation in the European Union. *Journal of European Public Policy* 14(3): 422–443.

Burns C, Gravey V, Jordan A, et al. (2019) De-Europeanising or Disengaging? EU Environmental Policy and Brexit. Special Issue: The Future of European Union Environmental Politics and Policy. In: Zito A, Burns S and Lenschow A (eds) *Environmental Politics* 28(2): 271–292.

Büthe T and Mattli W. (2010) International Standards and Standard-Standard-Setting Bodies. In: Coen D, Grant W and Wilson GK (eds) *The Oxford Handbook of Business and Government*. Oxford: Oxford University Press, 440–471.

Büthe T and Mattli W. (2011) *The New Global Rulers: The Privatization of Regulation in the World Economy*. Princeton: Princeton University Press.

Buzan B, Wæver O and de Wilde J. (1998) *Security: A New Framework for Analysis*. Boulder, CO: Lynne Rienner.

Coen D. (2005) Business-Regulatory Relations: Learning to Play Regulatory Games in European Utility Markets. *Governance* 18(3): 375–398.

Cutler CA, Haufler V and Porter TP. (1999) *Private Authority and International Affairs*. Albany, NY: Suny Press.

Eising R. (2016) Interest Groups and the European Union. In: Cini M and Pérez-Solórzano Borragán N (eds) *European Union Politics*. Oxford: Oxford University Press.

Fischer F. (1990) *Technocracy and the Politics of Expertise*. Newbury Park: Sage.

Forcier JR. (1994) *Judicial Excess: The Political Economy of the American Legal System*. Lanham, New York, London: University Press of America.

Ford C. (2017) *Innovation and the State: Finance, Regulation, and Justice*. New York: Cambridge University Press.

Freeman C and Soete L. (1997) *The Economics of Industrial Innovation*. Cambridge, MA: MIT Press.

Fuchs D. (2007) *Business Power in Global Governance*. London: Lynne Rienner.

Galanter M. (1974) Why the 'Haves' Come Out Ahead: Speculations on the Limits of Legal Change. *Law & Society Review* 9(1): 95–160.

Ghisellini P, Cialani C and Ulgiati S. (2016) A Review on Circular Economy: The Expected Transition to a Balanced Interplay of Environmental and Economic Systems. *Journal of Cleaner Production* 114: 11–32.

Glachant M. (2003) Voluntary Agreements Under Endogenous Legislative Threats. *FEEM Working Paper* No. 36.2003.

Green JF. (2014) *Rethinking Private Authority: Agents and Entrepreneurs in Global Environmental Governance*. Princeton: Princeton University Press.

Greenwood J. (2017) *Interest Representation in the European Union*. London: Palgrave Macmillan.

Halfteck G. (2008) Legislative Threats. *Stanford Law Review* 61: 629–710.

Héritier A and Eckert S. (2008) New Modes of Governance in the Shadow of Hierarchy: Self-Regulation by Industry in Europe. *Journal of Public Policy* 28(1): 113–138.

Héritier A and Eckert S. (2009) Self-Regulation by Associations: A Collective Action Problem in Environmental Regulation. *Business and Politics* 11(1): 1–22.

Héritier A and Lehmkuhl D. (2008) The Shadow of Hierarchy and New Modes of Governance. *Journal of Public Policy* 28(1): 1–17.

Héritier A and Rhodes M. (2010) *New Modes of Governance in Europe: Governing in the Shadow of Hierarchy*. Basingstoke, New York: Palgrave Macmillan.

Jevnaker T. (2015) Pushing Administrative EU Integration: The Path Towards European Network Codes for Electricity. *Journal of European Public Policy* 22(7): 927–947.

Kagan RA. (2001) *Adversarial Legalism: The American Way of Law*. Cambridge, MA: Harvard University Press.

Kagan RA and Axelrad L. (2000) Regulatory Encounters: Multinational Corporations and American Adversarial Legalism. *California Series in Law, Politics and Society*. Berkeley: University of California Press.

Kelemen RD. (2011) *Eurolegalism: The Transformation of Law and Regulation in the European Union*. Cambridge, MA: Harvard University Press.

Kirchherr J, Reike D and Hekkert M. (2017) Conceptualizing the Circular Economy: An Analysis of 114 Definitions. *Resources, Conservation and Recycling* 127: 221–232.

Knill C. (2001) Private Governance Across Multiple Arenas: European Interest Associations as Interface Actors. *Journal of European Public Policy* 8(2): 227–246.

La Porte TR and Consolini P. (1991) Working in Practice but Not in Theory: Theoretical Challenges of High Reliability Organizations. *Journal of Public Administration Research and Theory* 1(1): 19–48.

Lenschow A. (2015) Environmental Policy. Contending Dynamics of Policy Change. In: Wallace H, Pollack MA and Young AR (eds) *Policy-Making in the European Union.* Oxford: Oxford University Press, 319–243.

Lenschow A and Rottmann K. (2010) The Evolving Role of Industry in European Union Environmental Governance. In: O'Connor A (ed) *Managing Economies, Trade and International Business.* Houndmills, Basingstoke: Palgrave Macmillan, 67–85.

Mathieu E. (2016) *Regulatory Delegation in the European Union: Networks, Committees and Agencies.* London: Palgrave Macmillan.

Morriss AP, Yandle B and Dorchak A. (2009) *Regulation by Litigation.* New Haven, London: Yale University Press.

Pfeffer J and Salancik GR. (2003) *The External Control of Organizations: A Resource Dependence Perspective.* Stanford: Stanford Business Books.

Quack S. (2016) Expertise and Authority in Transnational Governance. In: Cotterrell R and Del Mar M (eds) *Authority in Transnational Legal Theory. Theorising Across Disciplines.* Cheltenham, Northampton: Edward Elgar.

Radaelli CM. (1999) The Public Policy of the European Union: Whither Politics of Expertise? *Journal of European Public Policy* 6(5): 757–774.

Scully R and van Schendelen R. (2004) *The Unseen Hand.* London: Routledge.

Sending OJ. (2015) *The Politics of Expertise: Competing for Authority in Global Governance.* Ann Arbor, MI: University of Michigan Press.

Tosun J. (2013) *Risk Regulation in Europe: Assessing the Application of the Precautionary Principle.* New York: Springer Verlag.

Trondal J, Busuioc M and Groenleer M. (2012) *The Agency Phenomenon in the European Union.* Manchester, New York: Manchester University Press.

Vogel D. (2012) *The Politics of Precaution: Regulating Health, Safety and Environmental Risks in Europe and the United States.* Princeton: Princeton University Press.

REFERENCES

#breakfreefromplastic. (2018) *Break Free from Plastic Global Movement*. Available at: https://www.breakfreefromplastic.org/about/ (accessed 4.8.2018).

Abbott KW, Genschel P, Snidal D, et al. (2014) Two Logics of Indirect Governance: Delegation and Orchestration. *Social Science Research Network* 46: 719–729.

ACER. (2013a) *The Influence of Existing Bidding Zones on Electricity Markets*. Consultation Document PC_2013_E_04. 31.7.2013. Ljubljana: Agency for the Cooperation of Energy Regulators.

ACER. (2013b) *A New Regulatory Framework for the Inter-Transmission System Operator Compensation*. Recommendation of the Agency for the Cooperation of Energy Regulators 05/2013. 23.3.2013. Ljubljana: Agency for the Cooperation of Energy Regulators.

ACER. (2016) *On the Common Capacity Calculation and Redispatching and Countertrading Cost Sharing Methodologies*. Recommendation of the Agency for the Cooperation of Energy Regulators 02/2016. 14.11.2016. Ljubljana: Agency for the Cooperation of Energy Regulators.

Adelle C and Anderson J. (2013) Lobby Groups. In: Jordan A and Adelle C (eds) *Environmental Policy in the EU: Actors, Institutions and Processes*. 3rd ed. London, New York: Routledge, 152–169.

AEA Technology. (2000) *Economic Evaluation of PVC Waste Management*. A Report Produced for European Commission Environmental Directorate. Oxfordshire: AEA Technology.

S. Eckert, *Corporate Power and Regulation*,
International Series on Public Policy,
https://Doi.org/10.1007/978-3-030-05463-2

Aghion P and Tirole J. (1997) Formal and Real Authority in Organizations. *Journal of Political Economy* 105(1): 1–29.

Akerlof GA. (1970) The Market for "Lemons": Quality Uncertainty and the Market Mechanism. *The Quarterly Journal of Economics* 84(3): 488–500.

Alter KJ and Vargas J. (2000) Explaining Variation in the Use of European Litigation Strategies: European Community Law and British Gender Equality Policy. *Comparative Political Studies* 33(4): 452–482.

Ambrose J. (2018) Government Clean Growth Plan 'Falls Short' on Climate Targets. *The Telegraph*: 17.1.2018.

Ambrus M, Arts K, Hey E, et al. (2014) *The Role of 'Experts' in International and European Decision-Making Processes: Advisors, Decision Makers or Irrelevant Actors?* Cambridge: Cambridge University Press.

AMDEA. (2017) *Annual Report 2016–2017*. London: The Association of Manufacturers of Domestic Appliances.

AMDEA. (2018) Newsletter 03.2018. London: The Association of Manufacturers of Domestic Appliances.

Anderson A. (2010) Communicating Chemical Risks: Beyond the Risk Society. In: Eriksson J, Gilek M and Rudén C (eds) *Regulating Chemical Risks: European and Global Challenges*. Dordrecht: Springer, 29–44.

Anderson AG. (2014) *Media, Environment and the Network Society*. Houndmills, Basingstoke: Palgrave Macmillan.

ANEC and BEUC. (2013) *ANEC/BEUC Comments on the Draft Voluntary Agreement Guidelines*. Brussels: The European Association for the Co-ordination of Consumer Representation in Standardisation, The European Consumer Organisation.

ANEC and BEUC. (2015) *Simplifying the EU Energy Label. Restoring the Successful and Well-Understood Closed A to G Scheme*. Brussels: The European Association for the Co-ordination of Consumer Representation in Standardisation, The European Consumer Organisation.

ANEC and BEUC. (2016) *How Consumers Benefit from Ecodesign Year After Year. Time to Appreciate Ecodesign and to Release the Ecodesign Working Plan 2015–2017*. Brussels: The European Association for the Co-ordination of Consumer Representation in Standardisation, The European Consumer Organisation.

Angelova M, Dannwolf T and König T. (2012) How Robust Are Compliance Findings? A Research Synthesis. *Journal of European Public Policy* 19(8): 1269–1291.

APPLiA. (2018a) *APPLiA. About Us*. Available at: https://www.applia-europe.eu/about-us (accessed 24.10.2018).

APPLiA. (2018b) *By the Numbers: The Home Appliance Industry in Europe, 2017–2016*. Brussels: Home Appliance Europe. Available at: https://www.applia-europe.eu/statistical-report-2017-2016/documents/APPLiA_SR18.pdf (accessed 24.3.2019).

APPLiA. (2018c) *Bye, Bye CECED. Hello APPLiA.* Press Release 8.3.2018. Brussels: Home Appliance Europe.

APPLiA. (2018d) *Industry Commits on New Marking Symbols That Will Ease Recycling.* Press Release 25.6.2018. Brussels: Home Appliance Europe.

APPLiA. (2018e) *Is EU's Waste Package Making a Step Towards a Circular Society?* Press Release 18.4.2018. Brussels: Home Appliance Europe.

APPLiA. (2018f) *What If All Europeans Had a Dishwasher?* Brussels: Home Appliance Europe. Available at: https://www.applia-europe.eu/campaigns/what-if-all-europeans-had-a-dishwasher (accessed 24.3.2019).

APPLiA, ehi, ehpa, et al. (2018) *Joint Industry Letter on Ecodesign.* 9.7.2018. Brussels: Home Appliance Europe, European Heating Industry, European Heat Pump Association, European Partnership for Energy and the Environment, EUnited Cleaning, LightingEurope.

ARGUS. (2000) *The Behaviour of PVC in Landfill.* Final Report February 2000. Brussels: European Commission DGXI.E.3.

Armstrong KA. (2018) Regulatory Alignment and Divergence After Brexit. *Journal of European Public Policy* 25(8): 1099–1117.

Arras S and Braun C. (2017) Stakeholders Wanted! Why and How European Union Agencies Involve Non-state Stakeholders. *Journal of European Public Policy* 25(9): 1257–1275.

Autio E and Lumme A. (1998) Does the Innovator Role Affect the Perceived Potential for Growth? Analysis of Four Types of New, Technology-Based Firms. *Technology Analysis & Strategic Management* 10(1): 41–55.

Ayres I and Braithwaite J. (1992) *Responsive Regulation: Transcending the Deregulation Debate.* New York: Oxford University Press.

Bach D and Newman AL. (2007) The European Regulatory State and Global Public Policy: Micro-Institutions, Macro-Influence. *Journal of European Public Policy* 14(6): 827–846.

Bachrach P and Baratz MS. (1962) Two Faces of Power. *The American Political Science Review* 56(4): 947–952.

Bachrach P and Baratz MS. (1970) *Power and Poverty: Theory and Practice.* London, Toronto: Oxford University Press.

Baker D. (2018) *Plastics in the Spotlight. An Examination of Current Issues.* Rushden: RPC Group.

Baker P, Finkler J and Kolokathis C. (2017) *Regional Operational Centres: A Review of the Commission's Proposal and Recommendations for Improvement.* Brussels: Regulatory Assistance Project, ClientEarth.

ban. (2018) *e-Trash Transparency Project.* Available at: http://www.ban.org/trash-transparency/ (accessed 12.08.2018).

Barbière C. (2016) Commission Delays Ecodesign Strategy for Fear of Offending UK Businesses. *Euractiv:* 29.4.2016.

Bartley T. (2018) *Rules Without Rights: Land, Labor, and Private Authority in the Global Economy.* Oxford: Oxford University Press.

Basbanes NA. (2013) *On Paper: The Everything of Its Two-Thousand-Year History.* New York: Knopf Doubleday Publishing Group.

Bauer MW. (2005) Administrative Costs of Reforming Utilities. In: Héritier A and Coen D (eds) *Refining Regulatory Regimes: Utilities in Europe.* Cheltenham, Northampton: Edward Elgar, 53–88.

Bauer MW and Knill C. (2012) Understanding Policy Dismantling: An Analytical Framework. In: Bauer MW et al. (eds) *Dismantling Public Policy: Preferences, Strategies, and Effects.* Oxford: Oxford University Press, 30–51.

BBC. (2018a) Brexit Study Warns Over Chemical Industry. *BBC News.* 8.3.2018. London.

BBC. (2018b) In Full: Theresa May's Speech on Future UK–EU Relations. *BBC News.* 2.3.2018. London.

BBC. (2018c) McDonald's to Ditch Plastic Straws. *BBC News.* 15.6.2018.

BEIS. (2016) *Digest of United Kingdom Energy Statistics 2016.* London: Department for Business, Energy and Industrial Strategy.

BEIS. (2017) *Digest of United Kingdom Energy Statistics 2017.* London: Department for Business, Energy and Industrial Strategy.

Belkhir L and Elmeligi A. (2018) Assessing ICT Global Emissions Footprint: Trends to 2040 and Recommendations. *Journal of Cleaner Production* 177: 448–463.

Bell S. (2008) Rethinking the Role of the State: Explaining Business Collective Action at the Business Council of Australia. *Polity* 40(4): 464–487.

Berny N. (2008) Le lobbying des ONG internationales d'environnement à Bruxelles. *Revue francaise de science politique* 58(1): 97–121.

Berny N. (2016) Environmental Groups. In: Burns C, Jordan A, Gravey V, et al. (eds) *The EU Referendum and the UK Environment: An Expert Review. How Has EU Membership Affected the UK and What Might Change in the Event of a Vote to Remain or Leave?*

Bertoldi P and Rezessy S. (2007) Voluntary Agreements for Energy Efficiency: Review and Results of European Experiences. *Energy & Environment* 18(1): 37–73.

BEUC. (2017a) *Energy Markets of the Future: How the EU's Energy Transition Should Work for Consumers.* BEUC Policy Paper. Brussels: The European Consumer Organisation.

BEUC. (2017b) *EU Report Confirms Ecolabel Must Keep Benefitting Consumers and the Environment.* Brussels: The European Consumer Organisation.

BEUC. (2018) *Ecodesign & Energy Label.* Brussels: The European Consumer Organisation.

Beyers J, Eising R and Maloney W. (2008) Researching Interest Group Politics in Europe and Elsewhere: Much We Study, Little We Know? *West European Politics* 31(6): 1103–1128.

Bickerton C and Accetti CI. (2017) Populism and Technocracy: Opposites or Complements? *Critical Review of International Social and Political Philosophy* 20(2): 186–206.

Bierly PE and Spender J-C. (1995) Culture and High Reliability Organizations: The Case of the Nuclear Submarine. *Journal of Management* 21(4): 639–656.

bio by Deloitte. (2014) *Technical Assistance Related to the Review of REACH with Regard to the Registration Requirements on Polymer*. Final Report Prepared for the European Commission (DG ENV), in collaboration with PIEP. Brussels: European Commission.

Bioplastics E. (2018a) *Members & Membership*. Available at: https://www.europe-an-bioplastics.org/about-us/members-membership/ (accessed 07.01.2019).

Bioplastics E. (2018b) Single-Use Plastics Directive Fails to Acknowledge Potential of Biodegradable Plastics.

Birchfield VL and Duffield JS. (2011) *Toward a Common European Union Energy Policy: Problems, Progress, and Prospects*. Houndmills, Basingstoke: Palgrave Macmillan.

Bjørnbye H. (2006) Interconnecting the Internal Electricity Market: A Goal Without a Plan? *Competition and Regulation in Network Industries* 1(3): 333–353.

Black J. (2002) Critical Reflections on Regulation. *Australian Journal of Legal Philosophy* 27: 1–35.

Blom-Hansen J and Brandsma GJ. (2009) The EU Comitology System: Intergovernmental Bargaining and Deliberative Supranationalism? *Journal of Common Market Studies* 47(4): 719–740.

Blomsma F and Brennan G. (2017) The Emergence of Circular Economy: A New Framing Around Prolonging Resource Productivity. *Journal of Industrial Ecology* 21(3): 603–614.

Bondarouk E and Mastenbroek E. (2018) Reconsidering EU Compliance: Implementation Performance in the Field of Environmental Policy. *Environmental Policy and Governance* 28(1): 15–27.

Borrás S, Koutalakis C and Wendler F. (2007) European Agencies and Input Legitimacy: EFSA, EMeA and EPO in the Post-delegation Phase. *Journal of European Integration* 29(5): 583–600.

Borrello et al. (2016) The Seven Challenges for Transitioning into a Bio-based Circular Economy in the Agri-food Sector. *Recent Patents on Food, Nutrition & Agriculture* 8(1): 39–47.

Börzel TA. (2001) Non-compliance in the European Union: Pathology or Statistical Artefact? *Journal of European Public Policy* 8(5): 803–824.

Börzel TA. (2002) Pace-Setting, Foot-Dragging, and Fence-Sitting: Member-State Responses to Europeanization. *Journal of Common Market Studies* 40(2): 193–214.

Börzel TA. (2008) Der „Schatten der Hierarchie". Ein Governance-Paradox? Special Issue: Governance in einer sich wandelnden Welt. *Politische Vierteljahresschrift* 41: 118–131.

Börzel TA. (2010) European Governance: Negotiation and Competition in the Shadow of Hierarchy. *Journal of Common Market Studies* 48(2): 191–219.

Börzel TA and Risse T. (2006) Europeanization: The Domestic Impact of European Union Politics In: Jørgensen KE, Pollack MA and Rosamond B (eds) *Handbook of European Union Politics*. London: Sage, 483–504.

Boswell C. (2009) *The Political Uses of Expert Knowledge: Immigration Policy and Social Research*. Cambridge: Cambridge University Press.

Bourguignon D. (2015) *Understanding Waste Streams. Treatment of Specific Waste*. Briefing July 2015. PE 564.398. Brussels: EPRS European Parliamentary Research Service. Available at: http://www.europarl.europa.eu/EPRS/EPRS-Briefing-564398-Understanding-waste-streams-FINAL.pdf (accessed 18.3.2019).

Bourguignon D. (2018) *Briefing. Circular Economy Package. Four Legislative Proposals on Waste*. PE 625.108. Brussels: EPRS European Parliamentary Research Service.

Bouwen P. (2002) Corporate Lobbying in the European Union: The Logic of Access. *Journal of European Public Policy* 9(3): 365–390.

Bouwen P. (2004) Exchanging Access Goods for Access: A Comparative Study of Business Lobbying in the European Union Institutions. *European Journal of Political Research* 43(3): 337–369.

Bouwen P. (2009) The European Commission. In: Coen D and Richardson J (eds) *Lobbying the European Union: Institutions, Actors, and Issues*. Oxford: Oxford University Press, 19–38.

Bouwen P and McCown M. (2007) Lobbying Versus Litigation: Political and Legal Strategies of Interest Representation in the European Union. *Journal of European Public Policy* 14(3): 422–443.

Bouzarovski S and Petrova S. (2015) The EU Energy Poverty and Vulnerability Agenda: An Emergent Domain of Transnational Action. In: Tosun J, Biesenbender S and Schulze K (eds) *Energy Policy Making in the EU: Building the Agenda*. London: Springer, 129–144.

Boyano A, Moons H, Villanueva A, et al. (2017) Follow-Up of the Preparatory Study for Ecodesign and Energy Label for Household Dishwashers. *JRC Technical Reports*. EUR 28808 EN. Sevilla: European Commission, Joint Research Centre.

BPF. (2016) *The UK Plastics Industry: A Strategic Vision for Growth*. London: British Plastics Federation.

BPF. (2017) *Understanding Plastics Trade: An Overview of Plastics Import and Export Markets*. London: British Plastics Federation.

BPF. (2018a) *BPF Annual Review 2017*. London: British Plastics Federation.

BPF. (2018b) *Legacy Additives and the Circular Economy*. London: British Plastics Federation.

BPF. (2018c) *Plastics: A Vision for a Circular Economy—Improving the Environment for the Next Generation*. London: British Plastics Federation.

BPF. (2018d) *A BPF Members Survey. Brexit Questionnaire*. December 2018. London: British Plastics Federation.

Bradley KSC. (1997) The European Parliament and Comitology: On the Road to Nowhere? *European Law Journal* 3(3): 230–254.

Bradley KSC. (2008) Halfway House: The 2006 Comitology Reforms and the European Parliament. *West European Politics* 31(4): 837–854.

Brandsma GJ. (2013) *Controlling Comitology: Accountability in a Multi-Level System*. London, New York: Palgrave Macmillan.

Brett W. (2013) What's an Elite to Do? The Threat of Populism from Left, Right and Centre. *The Political Quarterly* 84(3): 410–413.

Brouard S, Costa O and König T. (2011) *The Europeanization of Domestic Legislatures: The Empirical Implications of the Delors' Myth in Nine Countries*. New York: Springer.

Brousseau E and Fares Mh. (2000) Incomplete Contracts and Governance Structures: Are Incomplete Contract Theory and New Institutional Economics Substitutes or Complements? In: Ménard C (ed) *Institutions, Contracts and Organizations: Perspectives from New Institutional Economics*. Cheltenham, Northampton: Edward Elgar, 399–421.

Bruens W. (2012) The EACEM Commitment for TVs and VCRs. In: Bertoldi P, Ricci A and Wajer BH (eds) *Energy Efficiency in Household Appliances: Proceedings of the First International Conference on Energy Efficiency in Household Appliances*, 10–12 November 1997, Florence, Italy. Berlin, Heidelberg: Springer, 92–99.

BSH. (2015) *BSH Initiates Legal Steps Against Dyson*. Press Release 28.10.2015. München: BSH Hausgeräte GmbH.

BSI. (2018a) *Brexit and Standards Update*. London: British Standards Institution.

BSI. (2018b) Brexit and Standards: Position Statement. London: British Standards Institution.

Buchan D. (2009) *Energy and Climate Change: Europe at the Crossroads*. Oxford, New York: Oxford University Press.

Buchan D. (2010) From Liberalisation to Intervention: Europe, the UK, and the Changing Agenda. In: Rutledge I and Wright P (eds) *UK Energy Policy and the End of Market Fundamentalism*. Oxford: Oxford University Press, Oxford Institute for Energy Studies, 401–420.

Buchan D. (2015) Energy Policy: Sharp Challenges and Rising Ambitions. In: Wallace H, Pollack MA and Young AR (eds) *Policy-Making in the European Union*. 7th ed. Oxford: Oxford University Press, 344–366.

Bundgaard AM, Mosgaard MA and Remmen A. (2017) From Energy Efficiency Towards Resource Efficiency Within the Ecodesign Directive. *Journal of Cleaner Production* 144: 358–374.

Bunea A. (2013) Issues, Preferences and Ties: Determinants of Interest Groups' Preference Attainment in the EU Environmental Policy. *Journal of European Public Policy* 20(4): 552–570.

Burgelman RA and Sayles LR. (1986) *Inside Corporate Innovation: Strategy, Structure, and Managerial Skills.* New York: Free Press.

Burn-Callander R. (2015) Dyson Counter-Sued by Bosch Over 'Cheating' Allegations. *The Telegraph.* 28.10.2015.

Burns C. (2013) The European Parliament. In: Jordan A and Adelle C (eds) *Environmental Policy in the EU: Actors, Institutions and Processes.* 3rd ed. London, New York: Routledge, 132–151.

Burns C and Carter N. (2010) Is Co-decision Good for the Environment? An Analysis of the European Parliament's Green Credentials. *Political Studies* 58(1): 123–142.

Burns C and Carter N. (2012) Environmental Policy. In: Jones E, Menon A and Weatherill S (eds) *The Oxford Handbook of the European Union.* Oxford: Oxford University Press, 511–525.

Burns C, Gravey V, Jordan A, et al. (2019) De-Europeanising or Disengaging? EU Environmental Policy and Brexit. Special Issue: The Future of European Union Environmental Politics and Policy. In: Zito A, Burns S and Lenschow A (eds) *Environmental Politics* 28(2): 271–292.

Burns C, Jordan A, Gravey V, et al. (2016) The EU Referendum and the UK Environment: An Expert Review. How has EU Membership Affected the UK and What Might Change in the Event of a Vote to Remain or Leave? *ESRC UK in a Changing Europe Initiative,* 158.

Business Wire. (2017) Corrugated Box Market in Europe to Grow at a CAGR of 6.2% by 2021: Key Players are DS Smith, Georgia-Pacific, International Paper, Mondi, Smurfit Kappa & WestRock—Research and Markets. *Business Wire:* 22.8.2017.

Büthe T. (2003) Governance Through Private Authority? Non-state Actors in World Politics. *Journal of International Affairs* 57(1): 245–253.

Büthe T. (2010) Private Regulation in the Global Economy: A (P)Review. *Business and Politics* 12(3): 1–38.

Büthe T and Mattli W. (2010) International Standards and Standard-Standard-Setting Bodies. In: Coen D, Grant W and Wilson GK (eds) *The Oxford Handbook of Business and Government.* Oxford: Oxford University Press, 440–471.

Büthe T and Mattli W. (2011) *The New Global Rulers: The Privatization of Regulation in the World Economy.* Princeton: Princeton University Press.

Buzan B, Wæver O and de Wilde J. (1998) *Security: A New Framework for Analysis.* Boulder, CO: Lynne Rienner.

Cadot O and Webber D. (2017) Banana Splits: Policy Process, Particularistic Interests, Political Capture, and Money in Transatlantic Trade Politics. *Business and Politics* 4(1): 5–39.

Cafaggi F. (2006) Rethinking Private Regulation in the European Regulatory Space. *SSRN Electronic Journal.*

Cama T. (2018) Trump's Plan for Energy Star Sparks Industry Uproar. *The Hill:* 22.2.2018.

Carus M and Dammer L. (2018) *The "Circular Bioeconomy"—Concepts, Opportunities and Limitations.* Hürth: nova-Institute Institute for Ecology and Innovation.

Carrington D. (2018a) UK Opposes Strong EU Recycling Targets Despite Plastics Pledge. *The Guardian:* 24.1.2018.

Carrington D. (2018b) UK Reverses Opposition to Tough EU Recycling Targets. *The Guardian:* 29.3.2018.

CECED. (2002) *Second Voluntary Commitment on Reducing Energy Consumption of Domestic Washing Machines (2002–2008).* Brussels: European Committee of Domestic Equipment Manufacturers.

CECED. (2015) *EU Summer Package: Rain & Shine. New Energy Label Regulation Will Cause Unnecessary Delays to Consumer Benefits.* Press Release 15.7.2015. Brussels: European Committee of Domestic Equipment Manufacturers.

CECED. (2017a) *Agreement Reached: Focus Needed Now on Practical & Enforceable Implementation.* Press Release 24.3.2017. Brussels: European Committee of Domestic Equipment Manufacturers.

CECED. (2017b) *Impact of Brexit on the EU Industry Producing Household Appliances.* Position Paper. Brussels: European Committee of Domestic Equipment Manufacturers.

CEER. (2008a) *European Energy Regulators Welcome the European Parliament's Vision.* Press Release 08–04. 25.6.2008. Brussels: Council of European Energy Regulators.

CEER. (2008b) *Making the 3rd Energy Package Proposal More Effective.* Press Release 08–01 16.1.2008. Brussels: Council of European Energy Regulators.

CEFIC. (2017) *Facts & Figures 2017 of the European Chemical Industry.* Brussels: The European Chemical Industry Council.

CEN-CENELEC. (2018) *Standardization Complements the European Union's Ecodesign Regulation Towards a European Circular Economy: A View from Richard Hughes, Chairman of CEN/CLC/JTC 10.* Brussels: CEN-CENELEC. Available at: https://www.cencenelec.eu/news/brief_news/Pages/TN-2018-034.aspx (accessed 13.8.2018).

CEPI. (2005) *Sustainable Forest Management.* Position Paper: 1.3.2015. Available at: http://www.cepi.org/position-paper/sustainable-forest-management (accessed 18.3.2019).

CEPI. (2010) *Annual Statistics 2009*. European Pulp and Paper Industry. Brussels: Confederation of European Paper Industry. Available at: http://www.cepi.org/system/files/public/documents/publications/statistics/Annual%20Statistics%202009.pdf (accessed 18.3.2019).

CEPI. (2013) *End-of-Waste = End of Recycling?* Brussels: Confederation of European Paper Industry. Available at: http://www.cepi.org/press-release/end-waste-end-recycling (accessed 18.3.2019).

CEPI. (2017) *Key Statistics 2016. European Pulp and Paper Industry*. Brussels: Confederation of European Paper Industry. Available at: http://www.cepi.org/publication/key-statistics-2016 (accessed 18.3.2019).

CEPI. (2018a) *Key Statistics 2017. European Pulp and Paper Industry*. Brussels: Confederation of European Paper Industry. http://www.cepi.org/keystatistics2017 (accessed 18.3.2019).

CEPI. (2018b) *Latest Market Data Demonstrates Strong Performance for the European Pulp and Paper Industry in 2017*. Press Release: 16.07.2018. Brussels: Confederation of European Paper Industry. Available at: Latest Market Data Demonstrates Strong Performance for the European Pulp and Paper Industry in 2017 (accessed 18.3.2019).

CEPI, ETS, EuroCommerce, et al. (2016) Letter to the European Commission President Juncker and First Vice-President Timmermans: 19.12.2016. *Concerns on the Potential Discontinuation of EU Ecolabel Product Groups*. Brussels: Council of the European Paper Industry, European Tissue Symposium, The European Consumer Organisation, European Environmental Bureau. Available at: http://www.cepi.org/press-release/letter-european-commission-president-juncker-and-first-vice-president-timmermans (18.3.2019).

Chamon M. (2016) *EU Agencies: Legal and Political Limits to the Transformation of the EU Administration*. Oxford: Oxford University Press.

Chandler AD. (2005) *Inventing the Electronic Century: The Epic Story of the Consumer Electronics and Computer Industries, with a New Preface*. Harvard: Harvard University Press.

CHEM Trust. (2016) *Chemicals in Food Contact Materials: A Gap in the Internal Market, a Failure in Public Protection*. Policy Briefing. Brussels. Available at: https://chemtrust.org/food-contact (accessed 18.3.2019).

CHEM Trust. (2018) UK Government White Paper on Brexit Includes a Wish to Stay in EU Chemicals Law, but Are Its Commitments Enough? Brussels.

Chemisches und Veterinäruntersuchungsamt Stuttgart, Landesuntersuchungsanstalt für das Gesundheits- und Veterinärwesen Sachsen, Technische Universität Dresden, et al. (2012) *Abschlussbericht zur wissenschaftlichen Studie. Ausmaß der Migration unerwünschter Stoffe aus Verpackungsmaterialien aus Altpapier in Lebensmitteln*. Bonn: Bundesministerium für Ernährung, Landwirtschaft und Verbraucherschutz.

chemsec. (2018) *The International Chemical Secretariat.* Available at: http://chemsec.org/about-us/ (accessed 4.8.2018).

Chick M. (2010) Network Utilities: Technological Development, Market Structure, and Forms of Ownership. In: Coen D, Grant W and Wilson GK (eds) *The Oxford Handbook of Business and Government.* Oxford: Oxford University Press, 685–702.

Christiansen T and Dobbels M. (2012) Comitology and Delegated Acts After Lisbon: How the European Parliament Lost the Implementation Game. *European Integration online Papers (EIoP)* 16.

CIA. (2017) *The Chemical Industry: Brexit Priorities for UK Growth.* London: Chemical Industries Association.

CIA. (2018) *Making Brexit Work for the Chemical Industry.* London: Chemical Industries Association.

Ciambra A and Solorio I. (2014) The Liberalisation of the Internal Energy Market: Is the EU Dancing at a British Tempo? In: Tosun J, Schmitt S and Schulze K (eds) *Energy Policy Making in the EU: Building the Agenda.* London: Springer, 142–165.

CIEL, ClientEarth and NRDC. (2014) *Toxic Partnership Revealed.* Washington, New York, London: Center for International Environmental Law, ClientEarth, NRDC.

CITPA, CEPI, ACE, et al. (2017) *Letter to European Commission Vice President Timmermans on Plastics Strategy.* 16.11.2017. Brussels: CITPA et al. Available at: http://www.cepi.org/news/letter-european-commission-vice-president-timmermans-plastics-strategy (accessed 18.3.2019).

Clapp J and Fuchs D. (2007) *Corporate Power in Global Agrifood Governance: Challenges and Strategies.* Boston: MIT Press.

Clarke HD, Goodwin M and Whiteley P. (2017) *Brexit: Why Britain Voted to Leave the European Union.* Cambridge: Cambridge University Press.

CLASP, ECOS, EEB, et al. (2017) *Closing the 'Reality Gap': Ensuring a Fair Energy Label for Consumers.* Report 21.6.2017. Brussels: Clean Energy Access Program, European Environmental Citizens Organisation for Standardisation, European Environmental Bureau. https://www.topten.eu.

ClientEarth. (2017) *10 Years In: Time for ECHA to Disseminate Strategic Information to Empower Third Parties.* Brussels: ClientEarth. Available at: https://www.documents.clientearth.org/wp-content/uploads/library/2017-12-18-10-years-in-time-for-echa-to-disseminate-strategic-information-to-empower-third-parties-ce-en.pdf (accessed 18.3.2019).

ClientEarth. (2018a) *A New Nature and Environment Commission: Speaking Up for Nature and Holding the Powerful to Account.* London: ClientEarth.

ClientEarth. (2018b) *Poland's Forests.* Available at: https://www.clientearth.org/polands-forests/ (accessed 4.8.2018).

ClientEarth and chemsec. (2018) *How to Find and Analyse Alternatives in the Authorisation Process*. London, Stockholm: ClientEarth, International Chemical Secretariat. Available at: https://chemsec.org/publication/authorisation-process,reach/how-to-find-and-analyse-alternatives-in-the-authorisation-process (accessed 8.3.2019).

ClientEarth, EEB, chemsec, et al. (2018) *Call for Evidence on Microplastics: Concerns and Recommendations*. London: ClientEarth.

Coe JM and Rogers D. (2012) *Marine Debris: Sources, Impacts, and Solutions*. New York: Springer.

Coen D. (2005) Business-Regulatory Relations: Learning to Play Regulatory Games in European Utility Markets. *Governance* 18(3): 375–398.

Coen D. (2009) Business Lobbying in the European Union. In: Coen D and Richardson J (eds) *Lobbying the European Union: Institutions, Actors, and Issues*. Oxford: Oxford University Press, 145–168.

Coen D. (2010) European Business-Government Relations. In: Coen D, Grant W and Wilson GK (eds) *The Oxford Handbook of Business and Government*. Oxford: Oxford University Press, 285–306.

Coen D and Richardson J. (2009a) Learning to Lobby the European Union: 20 Years of Change. In: Coen D and Richardson J (eds) *Lobbying the European Union: Institutions, Actors, and Issues*. Oxford: Oxford University Press, 3–15.

Coen D and Richardson J. (2009b) Lobbying the European Union: Institutions, Actors, and Issues. *Lobbying the European Union: Institutions, Actors, and Issues*. Oxford: Oxford University Press.

Collins H and Evans R. (2017) *Why Democracies Need Science*. Hoboken: Wiley.

Compound Semiconductor. (2017) *Quantum Dot Firm Nanoco Welcomes EC Cadmium Ban*. 10.8.2017. Brussels: coolproducts. Available at: https://www.compoundsemiconductor.net/article/102260/Quantum_Dot_Firm_Nanoco_Welcomes_EC_Cadmium_Ban (accessed 23.6.2018).

Conant LJ. (2002) *Justice Contained: Law and Politics in the European Union*. Ithaca, NY: Cornell University Press.

Confino J. (2015) Future of Europe's Circular Economy Mired in Controversy. *The Guardian*: 3.2.2015.

Considine M. (1998) Making Up the Government's Mind: Agenda Setting in a Parliamentary System. *Governance* 11(3): 297–317.

coolproducts. (2015) *EC End-of-Level Boss is too Easy to Beat*. Press Release 27.4.2015. Brussels: coolproducts. Available at: https://www.medium.com/@Coolproducts/ec-end-of-level-boss-is-too-easy-to-beat-f87e63b19505 (accessed 28.8.2018).

coolproducts. (2018a) *Cool Products for a Cool Planet: Products Are Changing*. 20.7.2018. Brussels: coolproducts. Available at: https://www.coolproducts.eu (accessed 17.8.2018).

coolproducts. (2018b) *Letter to President Juncker*. 26.3.2018. Brussels: coolproducts.

Cooper T. (2008) Challenging the 'Refuse Revolution': War, Waste and the Rediscovery of Recycling, 1900–50. *Historical Research* 81(214): 710–731.

Copeland P. (2016) Europeanization and de-Europeanization in UK Employment Policy: Changing Governments and Shifting Agendas. *Public Administration* 94(4): 1124–1139.

Corso M and Pellegrini L. (2007) Continuous and Discontinuous Innovation: Overcoming the Innovator Dilemma. *Creativity and Innovation Management* 16(4): 333–347.

Council of the European Union. (2017) Outcome of Proceedings. Subject: Proposal for a Regulation of the European Parliament and of the Council on the Internal Market for Electricity (Recast) 15879/17. 20.12.2017. Brussels: General Secretariat of the Council.

Council of the European Union. (2018) Transport, Telecommunications and Energy Council (Energy). 19.12.2018. Brussels: Council of the European Union.

CPI. (2017a) *Brexit. Position Paper.* Swindon, Wiltshire: Confederation of European Paper Industry.

CPI. (2017b) *The Future of UK Paper: A Growth Springboard Sector.* Position Paper. Swindon, Wiltshire: Confederation of European Paper Industry.

CPI. (2017c) *Pride in Paper. CPI Confederation of Paper Industries Review 2016/17.* Swindon, Wiltshire: Confederation of European Paper Industry.

CPI. (2018a) *Paper: The Sustainable, Renewable and Recyclable Choice.* Review 2017/2018. Swindon, Wiltshire: Confederation of European Paper Industry.

CPI. (2018b) *Quality and the Consistency Framework.* Swindon, Wiltshire: Confederation of European Paper Industry.

Cram L. (1993) Calling the Tune Without Paying the Piper? Social Policy Regulation: The Role of the Commission in European Community Social Policy. *Policy & Politics* 21(2): 135–146.

Crisp J. (2015a) A+ Energy Efficiency Labels Will be Ditched. *Euractiv.* 1.7.2015.

Crisp J. (2015b) EEB: Disruptive Businesses Vital for Ambitious Circular Economy. *Euractiv.* 2.11.2015.

Crisp J. (2016) Commission Won't Regulate Toasters or Hairdryers after Hoovergate Scandal. *Euractiv.* 8.11.2016.

Crisp J. (2017) A+ Energy Efficiency Labels Will be Ditched. *Euractiv.*

Crisp J, Foster p and Rayner G. (2018) EU Diplomats Shocked by Boris's 'Four-Letter Reply' to Business Concerns About Brexit. *The Telegraph.* 23.6.2018.

Croley SP. (2011) Beyond Capture: Towards a New Theory of Regulation. In: Levi-Faur D (ed) *Handbook on the Politics of Regulation.* Cheltenham, Northampton: Edward Elgar, 50–69.

CSBT. (2018) *Voluntary Agreement.* Available at: http://cstb.eu/ (accessed 04.08.2018).

Cuff M. (2017) Climate Change Minister: Clean Growth Plan Coming This Autumn. BusinessGreen.

Cutler CA, Haufler V and Porter TP. (1999) *Private Authority and International Affairs*. Albany, NY: Suny Press.

Daily Mail. (2019) Theresa May Offers to Step Down once Brexit Deal is Approved. *MailOnline*: 27.3.2019.

D'Amato et al. (2017) Green, Circular, Bio Economy: A Comparative Analysis of Sustainability Avenues. *Journal of Cleaner Production* 168: 716–734.

David PA. (1985) Clio and the Economics of QWERTY. *The American Economic Review* 75(2): 332–337.

De Bruycker I. (2017) Politicization and the Public Interest: When Do the Elites in Brussels Address Public Interests in EU Policy Debates? *European Union Politics* 18(4): 603–619.

De Figuiredo J and De Figuieredo RJP. (2002) The Allocation of Resources by Interest Groups: Lobbying, Litigation and Administrative Regulation. *Business and Politics* 4(3): 343.

DEFRA. (2018a) *Environmental Principles and Governance After EU Exit*. London: Department for Environment Food & Rural Affairs. Available at: https://consult.defra.gov.uk/eu/environmental-principles-and-governance/ (accessed 6.8.2018).

DEFRA. (2018b) *UK Statistics on Waste*. London: Department for Environment Food & Rural Affairs, Government Statistical Service.

Delreux T and Happaerts S. (2016) *Environmental Policy and Politics in the European Union*. London, New York: Palgrave Macmillan.

Dennison J and Geddes A. (2018) Brexit and the Perils of 'Europeanised' Migration. *Journal of European Public Policy* 25(8): 1137–1153.

Department for the Economy. (2018) *Energy in Northern Ireland 2018*. Belfast: Analytical Services Division, Department for the Economy.

DigitalEurope. (2015) *Ecodesign and Energy Label Review: Maintain Energy Efficiency as the Basis for Measures*. Brussels: Digital Europe.

DigitalEurope. (2016) *Best Practices in Recycled Plastics*. Brussels: DigitalEurope.

DigitalEurope. (2017a) *The Contribution of the Digital Industry to Repair, Remanufacturing and Refurbishment in a Circular Economy*. Report 12.4.2017. Brussels: DigitalEurope.

DigitalEurope. (2017b) *Folow-Up Position on the Proposed Energy Efficiency Requirements in the Display Regulations*. 15.11.2017. Brussels: DigitalEurope.

DigitalEurope. (2018) *DigitalEurope: About Us*. Available at: http://www.digitaleurope.org/About-Us (accessed 27.7.2018).

DigitalEurope and EUDCA. (2018) *DigitalEurope and EUDCA Concerned About Impact of Proposed Ecodesign Requirements for Servers*. Press Release 30.8.2018. Brussels: DigitalEurope, European Data Centre Association.

Dinan D. (2010) *Ever Closer Union: An Introduction to European Integration.* London: Palgrave Macmillan.

Directorate General Enterprise. (2000) *Recycling Forum.* Final Report. Brussels: European Commission.

Directorate General Environment. (2000) *Study on Minimum Quantity of Recycled Material in Certain Paper and Cardboard Applications.* Darmstadt: Technische Universität Darmstadt, Institut für Papierfabrikation.

Dogwood Alliance. (2017) *The Great American Stand. US Forsts and the Climate Emergency: Why the United States Needs an Aggressive Forest Protection Agenda Focused in Its Own Backyard.* Asheville: Dogwood Alliance.

Doner RF and Schneider BR. (2000) Business Associations and Economic Development: Why Some Associations Contribute More Than Others. *Business and Politics* 2(3): 261–288.

Dougan M. (2018) *The UK After Brexit: Legal and Policy Challenges.* Cambridge: Intersentia.

Dreger J. (2014) *The European Commission's Energy and Climate Policy: A Climate for Expertise.* Houndmills, Basingstoke: Palgrave Macmillan.

Dür A. (2008) Interest Groups in the European Union: How Powerful Are They? *West European Politics* 31(6): 1212–1230.

Dür A, Bernhagen P and Marshall D. (2015) Interest Group Success in the European Union: When (and Why) Does Business Lose? *Comparative Political Studies* 48(8): 951–983.

Dür A and Mateo G. (2014) Public Opinion and Interest Group Influence: How Citizen Groups Derailed the Anti-counterfeiting Trade Agreement. *Journal of European Public Policy* 21(8): 1199–1217.

Dür A and Mateo G. (2016) *Insiders Versus Outsiders: Interest Group Politics in Multilevel Europe.* Oxford: Oxford University Press.

Dür A, Marshall D and Bernhagen P. (2019) *The Political Influence of Business in the European Union.* Ann Arbor: University of Michigan Press.

E-Control. (2015) *E-Control Takes Legal Action Against German–Austrian Price Zone Split.* Appeal Brought Before ACER Board of Appeal; Action Brought Before EU General Court. Press Release 25.11.2015. Vienna: E-Control.

EAC. (2017a) *The Future of Chemicals Regulation after the EU Referendum.* Eleventh Report of Session 2016–2017. London: House of Commons.

EAC. (2017b) *Oral Evidence: The Future of Chemicals Regulation after the EU Referendum,* HC 912. London: House of Commons.

EAC. (2018a) *Environmental Audit Committee.* Tuesday 30 January 2018. London: House of Commons. Available at: https://parliamentlive.tv/Event/Index/110ad349-e07b-437a-829e-4871223fc050.

EAC. (2018b) *Environmental Audit Committee.* Wednesday 31 January 2018. London: House of Commons. Available at: https://parliamentlive.tv/Event/Index/eeee1757-f244-4b3f-8447-b4c6334d0be5.

EAC. (2018c) MPs Call for "latte levy" on Coffee Cups. 5.1.2018. London: House of Commons.

Easton D. (1957) An Approach to the Analysis of Political Systems. *World Politics* 9(3): 383–400.

Eberlein B. (2003a) Regulating Cross-Border Trade by Soft Law? The Florence Process in the Supranational Governance of Electricity Markets. *Journal of Network Industries* 4(2): 137–155.

Eberlein B. (2003b) Regulationg Cross-Border Trade by Soft Law? The "Florence Process" in the Supranational Governance of the Electricity Markets. *Journal of Network Industries* 4(2): 137–156.

Eberlein B. (2005) Regulation by Cooperation: The Third Way in Making Rules for the Internal Energy Market. In: Cameron P (ed) *Legal Aspects of EU Energy Regulation: Implementing the New Directives on Electricity and Gas Across Europe.* Oxford: Oxford University Press, 59–88.

Eberlein B. (2008) The Making of the European Energy Market: The Interplay of Governance and Government. *Journal of Public Policy* 28(1): 73–92.

Eberlein B. (2012) Inching Towards a Common Energy Policy: Entrepreneurship, Incrementalism, and Windows of Opportunity. In: Richardson J (ed) *Constructing a Policy-Making State? Policy Dynamics in the EU.* Oxford: Oxford University Press, 147–169.

Eberlein B and Grande E. (2005) Beyond Delegation: Transnational Regulatory Regimes and the EU Regulatory State. *Journal of European Public Policy* 12(1): 89–112.

ECHA. (2016) REACH 2018: *Registration Deadline for Low-Volume Chemicals.* Press Release REACH 2018: 1.4.2018. Helsinki: European Chemicals Agency. Available at: https://echa.europa.eu/de/press/press-material/pr-for-reach-2018 (accessed 18.3.2019).

ECHA. (2018a) *REACH Registration Results.* Helsinki: European Chemicals Agency. Available at: https://echa.europa.eu/de/reach-registrations-since-2008 (accessed 9.8.2018).

ECHA. (2018b) *Summary: The REACH 2018 Deadline.* ECHA REACH 2018 Registration Results. Helsinki: European Chemicals Agency.

ECHA. (2018b) *The UK's Withdrawal from the EU.* Helsinki: European Chemicals Agency. Available at: https://echa.europa.eu/uk-withdrawal-from-the-eu (accessed 9.8.2018).

ECJ. (2018) Not Providing Consumers with Information on the Testing Conditions That Resulted in the Energy Classification Indicated on the Energy Label of Vacuum Cleaners Does Not Constitute a 'Misleading Omission'. *Press Release No. 117/18.* Luxembourg: Court of Justice of the European Union.

Eckert S. (2015) *The Social Face of the Regulatory State: Reforming Public Services in Europe.* Manchester: Manchester University Press.

Eckert S. (2016) The Governance of Markets, Sustainability and Supply. Toward a European Energy Policy. *Journal of Contemporary European Research* 12(1): 502–517.

Eckert S. (2018) The European Commission as a Negotiator: Evidence from the Disintegration Talks with the United Kingdom and Switzerland. In: Jörn E, Bauer MW and Becker S (eds) *The European Commission in Turbulent Times: Assessing Organizational Change and Policy Impact*. Baden-Baden: Nomos, 159–180.

ECOS. (2016) *Standardisers Cave In: Material Efficiency Standards for Energy-Related Products Finally to Be Developed*. Press Release 1.7.2016. Brussels: European Environmental Citizens Organisation for Standardisation.

ECOS. (2017) *The Revised Energy Labelling Regulation*. Brussels: European Environmental Citizens Organisation for Standardisation.

ECOS. (2018) *Ecodesign & Energy Labelling*. 23.7.2018. Brussels: European Environmental Citizens Organisation for Standardisation. Available at: http://www.ecostandard.org/category/activities-on-ecodesign (accessed 27.8.2018).

ECOS, EEB, IFIXIT, et al. (2017) *Circular Economy Opportunities for Digital Products*. Brussels: European Environmental Bureau.

ECPI. (2003) *US Product Safety Authority Agrees with Use of DINP in Toys*. ECPI Press Release. Brussels: European Council for Plasticisers and Intermediates.

ECPI. (2005) *EU Decision to Restrict Use of Phthalates in Toys Ignores EU Risk Assessment*. Brussels: European Council for Plasticisers and Intermediates.

EDC Free Europe. (2018) *The EDC-Free Europe Coalition of Public Interest Groups*. Available at: http://www.edc-free-europe.org/about-us/ (accessed 4.8.2018).

EEA. (2009) *Diverting Waste from Landfill: Effectiveness of Waste-Management Policies in the European Union*. Copenhagen: European Environment Agency.

EEA. (2016) *Energy Consumption for Electrical Appliances in Households*. Copenhagen: European Environment Agency. Available at: https://www.eea.europa.eu/data-and-maps/daviz/energy-consumption-for-electric-appliances-1#tab-chart_1 (accessed 31.8.2018).

EEB. (2018a) *Briefing on Ecodesign and Energy Labelling for a Circular Economy*. Brussels: European Environmental Bureau.

EEB. (2018b) *The European Commission Steps Forward to Cut Down on Single-Use Plastics: But It's Just the Beginning*. EEB Press Release: 28.5.2018. Brussels: European Environmental Bureau. Available at: https://eeb.org/european-commission-steps-forward-to-cut-on-single-use-plastics-but-its-just-the-beginning (accessed 18.3.2019).

EEB. (2018c) *Product Policy*. Brussels: European Environmental Bureau. Available at: http://www.eeb.org/work-areas/resource-efficiency/product-policy/ (accessed 27.8.2018).

EEB. (2018d) *Resource Efficiency.* Brussels: European Environmental Bureau. Available at: http://www.eeb.org/work-areas/ (accessed 27.08.2018).

EEB. (2018e) *Towards an EU Product Policy Framework Contributing to the Circular Economy.* Brussels: European Environmental Bureau.

EEB, BEUC, ANEC, et al. (2016) *Let's Reinforce Not Reduce Ecodesign and Ecolabel.* Joint Letter 28.10.2016. Brussels: European Environmental Bureau. The European Consumer Organisation. European Association for the Coordination of Consumer Representation in Standardisation. European Environmental Citizens Organisation for Standardisation.

EFET. (2018) *ENTSO-E Consultation on Its Draft Bidding Zones Review Report.* EFET Response. 9.3.2018. Brussels: European Federation of Energy Traders.

EFET I. (2007) *Policy Officer at the EU Liaison Office, Brussels, 19.12.2007.*

Efficient Gaming. (2018) *Games Consoles Voluntary Agreement.* Available at: http://efficientgaming.eu/ (accessed 04.08.2018).

EGC. (2015) *Dyson's Action for Annulment of the Regulation on Energy Labelling of Vacuum Cleaners is Unsuccessful.* Press Release No. 133/15. Luxembourg: General Court of the European Union.

EGC. (2018) *The General Court Annuls the Regulation on the Energy Labelling of Vacuum Cleaners.* Press Release No. 168/18. Luxembourg: General Court of the European Union.

EICTA. (2005) *Industry Self-Commitment to Improve the Energy Performance of Household Consumer Electronic Products Sold in the European Union.* Brussels: European Industry Association for Information Systems, Communication Technologies and Consumer Electronics.

Eikeland PO. (2004) *The Long and Winding Road to the Internal Energy Market: Consistencies and Inconsistencies in EU Policy.* FNI Report. Lysaker: Fridtjof Nansens Institute.

EirGrid. (2018) *Celtic Interconnector.* Available at: http://www.eirgridgroup.com/the-grid/projects/celtic-interconnector/the-project/ (accessed 16.08.2018).

Eising R. (2002) Policy Learning in Embedded Negotiations: Explaining EU Electricity Liberalization. *International Organization* 56(1): 85–120.

Eising R. (2007) The Access of Business Interests to EU Institutions: Towards Élite Pluralism? *Journal of European Public Policy* 14(3): 384–403.

Eising R. (2009) *The Political Economy of State-Business Relations in Europe: Interest Mediation, Capitalism and EU Policy Making.* London: Routledge.

Eising R. (2016) Interest Groups and the European Union. In: Cini M and Pérez-Solórzano Borragán N (eds) *European Union Politics.* Oxford: Oxford University Press.

Eising R and Jabko N. (2001) Moving Targets: National Interests and EU Electricity Liberalization. *Comparative Political Studies* 34(7): 742–767.

Elektrojournal. (2014) Falsche Labelung? Bosch erwirkt gegen Dyson zwei einstweilige Verfügungen. *Elektrojournal*: 13.10.2014.

Elgot J and Savage M. (2018) Siemens UK Boss Joins Business Leaders' Criticism of Hard Brexit. *The Guardian*: 23.6.2018.

Ellis-Petersen H. (2018) Deluge of Electronic Waste Turning Thailand into 'World's Rubbish Dump'. *The Guardian*: 28.6.2018.

EMF. (2012, 2013) *Towards a Circular Economy. Vol. 1. Economic and Business Rationale for an Accelerated Transition*. First published 25.1.2012. Cowes: Ellen MacArthur Foundation. Available at: https://www.ellenmacarthurfoundation.org/assets/downloads/publications/Ellen-MacArthur-Foundation-Towards-the-Circular-Economy-vol.1.pdf (accessed 20.3.2019).

EMF. (2014) *Towards the Circular Economy, Vol. 3: Accelerating the Scale-up across Global Supply Chains*. Cowes: Ellen MacArthur Foundation. Available at: https://www.ellenmacarthurfoundation.org/publications/towards-the-circular-economy-vol-3-accelerating-the-scale-up-across-global-supply-chains (accessed 20.3.2019).

EMF. (2016) *The New Plastics Economy: Rethinking the Future of Plastics*. Cowes: Ellen MacArthur Foundation.

EMF. (2017a) *The New Plastics Economy: Catalysing Action*. Cowes: Ellen MacArthur Foundation (EMF).

EMF. (2017b) *The New Plastics Economy: Rethinking the Future of Plastics & Catalysing Action*. Cowes: Ellen MacArthur Foundation (EMF).

EMF. (2018) *Circular Consumer Electronics: An Initial Exploration*. Cowes: Ellen Macarthur Foundation (EMF).

ENTSO. (2015) *Multilateral Agreement on Participation in Regional Security Coordination Initiatives*. Brussels: European Network of Transmission System Operators for Electricity.

ENTSO. (2017) *Power Regions for the Energy Union: Regional Energy Forums as the Way Ahead*. Policy Paper October 2017. Brussels: European Network of Transmission System Operators for Electricity.

ENTSO-E. (2009) *European Electricity Transmission System Operators Reach Agreement on an Interim Solution for Inter-TSO Compensation*. Press Release December 2009. Brussels: European Network of Transmission System Operators for Electricity.

ENTSO-E. (2011) *ENTSO-E puts in place an enduring inter-TSO compensation mechanism*. Press Release March 2011. Brussels: European Network of Transmission System Operators for Electricity.

ENTSO-E. (2017) *Letter from ENTSO-E on Brexit to Michel Barnier and The Rt Hon David Davis MP*. 31.3.2017. Brussels: European Network of Transmission System Operators for Electricity.

ENTSO-E. (2018a) *ENTSO-E: About. Our Members*. Available at: https://www.entsoe.eu/about (accessed 6.7.2018).

ENTSO-E. (2018b) *First Edition of the Bidding Zone Review*. Draft Version for Public Consultation until 9 March 2018. Brussels: European Network of Transmission System Operators for Electricity.

EPN. (2015) *Letter to the Minister for Climate and the Environment, Government of Sweden*. Lochinver: Environmental Paper Network Europe.

EPN. (2017) *Annual Report 2016. Europe and Beyond*. Lochinver: European Environmental Paper Network.

EPN. (2018) *Environmental Paper Network*. Available at: http://environmental-paper.org/ (accessed 04.08.2018).

EPRC. (2018) *Monitoring Report 2016. European Declaration on Paper Recycling 2016–2020*. Brussels: European Paper Recycling Council.

Erfle S, McMillan H and Grofman B. (1990) Regulation Via Threats: Politics, Media Coverage, and Oil Pricing Decisions. *Public Opinion Quarterly* 54(1): 48–63.

ERGEG. (2006) *Good Practice on Information Management and Transparency in Electricity Markets*. ERGEG Guidelines E05-EMK-06-10. 2.8.2006. Brussels: European Regulators Group for Electricity and Gas.

ERPC. (2007) *European Declaration on Paper Recycling 2006–2010. Monitoring Report 2007*. Brussels: European Recovered Paper Council.

ERPC. (2016a) *European Declaration on Paper Recycling 2011–2015. Monitoring Report 2015*. Brussels: European Recovered Paper Council.

ERPC. (2016b) *European Paper Declaration 2016–2020*. Brussels: European Recovered Paper Council.

ERPC. (2016c) *Paper Recycling Chain Exceeds its Voluntary Commitment*. Press Release: 20.10.2016. Brussels: European Recovered Paper Council. Available at: http://www.cepi.org/press-release/paper-recycling-chain-exceeds-its-voluntary-commitment (accessed 18.3.2019).

ESPA. (2018) *European Plasticisers*. Available at: https://www.europeanplasticisers.eu/about-us (accessed 4.8.2018).

ETSO. (2006) *An Overview of Current Cross-Border Congestion Management Methods in Europe*. May 2006. Brussels: European Transmission System Operators.

ETSO. (2008) *Transmission Network Governance: What Does the 3rd Energy Package Envisage?* Presentation at the Florence School of Regulation Workshop on Network Governance, 21.2.2008. Florence: Florence School of Regulation.

EUBP (2018a) *Members & Membership*. Brussels: European Bioplastics. Available at: https://www.european-bioplastics.org/about-us/members-membership (accessed 7.1.2019).

EUBP (2018b) *Single-Use Plastics Directive Fails to Acknowledge Potential of Biodegradable Plastics*. Position Paper: 23.1.2019. Brussels: European Bioplastics. Available at: https://www.european-bioplastics.org/single-use-plastics-directive-fails-to-acknowledge-potential-of-biodegradable-plastics (accessed 18.3.2019).

EuPC. (2018) *European Plastics Converters.* Available at: https://www.plastics-converters.eu (accessed 4.8.2018).

EurActiv. (2009) Barroso Seizes Control of 'Better Regulation' Agenda. *Euractiv*, 21.9.2009.

EurActiv. (2015) Toxic Cadmium One Step Closer to EU-Wide Ban. *Euractiv*: 26.5.2015.

Eurelectric. (2017) *BREXIT: Maintaining Free and Fair Trade of Electricity and Gas in Europe. A EURELECTRIC Initial Analysis Paper.* Brussels: Union of the Electricity Industry.

Europe Economics. (2015) *The Economic Impact of the Domestic Appliances Industry in Europe.* Report for the European Committee of Domestic Equipment Manufacturers (CECED). London: Europe Economics.

European Bioeconomy Alliance. (2018) *About Us.* Available at: https://bioeconomyalliance.eu/about-euba-bioeconomyalliance (accessed 7.1.2019).

European Commission. (1991) *Proposal for a Council Directive Concerning Common Rules for the Internal Market in Electricity and Natural Gas.* COM (91) 548 final. Luxembourg: Office for Official Publications of the European Communities.

European Commission. (1996) Communication from the Commission. *On Environmental Agreements.* COM (96) 561 final. Luxembourg: Office for Official Publications of the European Communities.

European Commission. (1999) *Ban of Phthalates in Childcare Articles and Toys.* Press Release IP-99-829:10.11.1999. Brussels: European Commission.

European Commission. (2000) *Green Paper. Environmental Issues of PVC.* COM (2000) 469 final. Brussels: Commission of the European Communities.

European Commission. (2001a) *European Governance: A White Paper.* COM (2001) 428. Luxembourg: Office for Official Publications of the European Communities.

European Commission. (2001b) *Mitteilung der Kommission an das Europäische Parlament und den Rat - Europäische Energieinfrastruktur.* KOM (2001) 775 endgültig. Luxemburg: Amt für Veröffentlichungen der Europäischen Kommission.

European Commission. (2002a) Communication from the Commission. *Action plan 'Simplifying and Improving the Regulatory Environment'.* COM (2002) 278 final. Luxembourg: Office for Official Publications of the European Communities.

European Commission. (2002b) Communication from the Commission. *Environmental Agreements at Community Level.* Within the Framework of the Action Plan on the Simplification and Improvement of the Regulatory Environment. COM (2002) 412 final. Luxembourg: Office for Official Publications of the European Communities.

European Commission. (2005a) Communication from the European Commission. *Better Regulation for Growth and Jobs in the European Union.*

COM (2005) 97 final. Luxembourg: Office for Official Publications of the European Communities.

European Commission. (2005b) *Communication from the European Commission to the European Parliament, the Council, the European Economic and Social Committee and the Committee of the Regions. EU Regulatory Fitness.* COM (2012) 746 final. Luxembourg: Office for Official Publications of the European Communities.

European Commission. (2006) Communication. *Priority Interconnection Plan.* COM (2006) 846 final. Luxembourg: Office for Official Publications of the European Communities.

European Commission. (2007a) *DG Competition Report on Energy Sector Inquiry.* Brussels: European Commission.

European Commission. (2007b) Proposal for a Regulation of the European Parliament and of the Council establishing a *European Union Agency for the Cooperation of Energy Regulators.* COM (2007) 530 final. Brussels: European Commission.

European Commission. (2009) Commission Staff Working Document Accompanying the Document to the Commission Regulation Implementing Directive 2005/32/EC with Regard to *Ecodesign Requirements for Televisions.* SEC (2009) 1012 final, 22.7.2009. Brussels: European Commission.

European Commission. (2010) *Europe 2020. A European Strategy for Smart, Sustainable and Inclusive Growth.* COM (2010) 2020. Luxembourg: Office for Official Publications of the European Communities.

European Commission. (2012a) *Innovating for Sustainable Growth: A Bioeconomy for Europe.* Brussels: European Commission. Directorate General for Research and Innovation.

European Commission. (2012b) *Report from the Commission to the European Parliament and the Council on the Voluntary Ecodesign Scheme for Complex Set-Top Boxes.* COM (2012) 684 final. Brussels: European Commission.

European Commission. (2013a) Commission Staff Working Document Accompanying the Regulation 617/2013 of the European Parliament and of the Council with Regard to *Ecodesign Requirements for Computers and Computer Servers.* SWD (2013) 219 final. Brussels: European Commission.

European Commission. (2013b) Commission Staff Working Document. Executive Summary of the Impact Assessment Accompanying the Document Report from the Commission to the European Parliament and the Council on the *Voluntary Ecodesign Scheme for Imaging Equipment.* SWD (2013) 14 final, 29.1.2013. Brussels: European Commission.

European Commission. (2014a) Communication. *Energy Prices and Costs in Europe.* COM (2014) 21. Luxembourg: Office for Official Publications of the European Communities.

European Commission. (2014b) *Communication: Towards a Circular Economy: A Zero Waste Programme for Europe.* COM (2014) 398 final. Brussels: European Commission.

European Commission. (2015a) *Commission Recognises Voluntary Energy Efficiency Agreement for Game Consoles.* Brussels: European Commission. Available at: https://ec.europa.eu/growth/content/commission-recognises-voluntary-energy-efficiency-agreement-game-consoles-0_hr (accessed 10.8.2018).

European Commission. (2015b) *Digital Single Market.* Brussels: European Commission. Available at: https://ec.europa.eu/digital-single-market/en (accessed 7.9.2018).

European Commission. (2015c) *Energy Union Package*: Communication from the Commission to the European Parliament, the Council, the European Economic and Social Committee, the Committee of the Regions and the European Investment Bank. A Framework Strategy for a Resilient Energy Union with a Forward-Looking Climate Change Policy. COM (2015) 80 final. Brussels: European Commission.

European Commission. (2015d) *Europe 2020 Strategy.* Brussels: European Commission. Available at: https://ec.europa.eu/info/business-economy-euro/economic-and-fiscal-policy-coordination/eu-economic-governance-monitoring-prevention-correction/european-semester/framework/europe-2020-strategy_en (accessed 5.4.2018).

European Commission. (2015e) Report from the Commission to the European Parliament and the Council on the *Voluntary Ecodesign Scheme for Games Consoles.* COM (2015) 178 final. Brussels: European Commission.

European Commission. (2015f) *Closing the Loop: An EU Action Plan for the Circular Economy.* COM (2015) 614 final. Brussels: European Commission.

European Commission. (2016a) *Buying Green! A Handbook on Green Public Procurement.* 3rd ed. Brussels: European Commission, DG Environment.

European Commission. (2016b) Commission Recommendation (EU) 2016/2125 of 30 November 2016 on *Guidelines for Self-Regulation Measures Concluded by Industry* under Directive 2009/125/EC of the European Parliament and of the Council. Brussels: European Commission.

European Commission. (2016c) Communication from the Commission. *Ecodesign Working Plan 2016–2019.* COM (2016) 773 final. Brussels: European Commission.

European Commission. (2016d) *Communication. Clean Energy for all Europeans.* COM (2016) 860 final. Brussels: European Commission.

European Commission. (2016e) Proposal for a Directive of the European Parliament and of the Council on *Common Rules for the Internal Market in Electricity.* COM (2016) 864 final. Brussels: European Commission.

European Commission. (2016f) Proposal for a Regulation of the European Parliament and of the Council on the *Governance of the Energy Union.* COM (2016) 759 final. Brussels: European Commission.

European Commission. (2016g) Proposal for a Regulation of the European Parliament and of the Council on the *Internal Market for Electricity.* COM (2016) 861 final. Brussels: European Commission.

European Commission. (2016h) *Report from the Commission on the Implementation of Regulation (EU) 187/2011.* COM (2016) 92. Luxembourg: Office for Official Publications of the European Communities.

European Commission. (2017a) *Circular Economy: New Chapter for European Green Products and Organisations.* Press Release 3.6.2017. Brussels.

European Commission. (2017b) *Communication on Strengthening Europe's Energy Networks.* COM (2017) 718 Final. Brussels: European Commission.

European Commission. (2017c) *Expert Group Report: Review of the EU Bioeconomy Strategy and Its Action Plan.* Brussels: European Commission. Directorate General for Research and Innovation.

European Commission. (2018a) *Circular Economy: Implementation of the Circular Economy Action Plan.* Available at: http://ec.europa.eu/environment/circular-economy/index_en.htm (accessed 7.8.2018).

European Commission. (2018b) *Circular Economy: New Rules Will Make EU the Global Front-Runner in Waste Management and Recycling.* Press Release IP-18-3846 22.5.2018. Brussels: European Commission.

European Commission. (2018c) *Commission General Report on the Operation of REACH and Review of Certain Elements: Conclusions and Actions.* COM (2018) 116 final. Brussels: European Commission.

European Commission. (2018d) *Communication on the Implementation of the Circular Economy Package: Options to Address the Interface Between Chemical, Product and Waste Legislation.* COM (2018) 32 final. Brussels: European Commission.

European Commission. (2018e) *Communication: A European Strategy for Plastics in a Circular Economy.* COM (2018) 28 Final. Brussels: European Commission.

European Commission. (2018f) *Energy Star.* Brussels: European Commission. Available at: https://www.ec.europa.eu/energy/en/energy-star.

European Commission. (2018g) *EU Ecolabel.* Brussels: European Commission. Available at: http://www.ec.europa.eu/ecat/category/en/18/televisions.

European Commission. (2018h) *EU Ecolabel Electronic Equipment/ Personal Computers.* Brussels: European Commission. Available at: http://www.ec.europa.eu/ecat/category/en/20/personal-computers.

European Commission. (2018i) *EU Ecolabel Electronic Equipment/ Portable Computers.* Brussels: European Commission. Available at: http://www.ec.europa.eu/ecat/category/en/21/portable-computers.

European Commission. (2018j) *EU Ecolabel Paper Products.* Available at: http://ec.europa.eu/ecat/category/en/35/printed-paper (accessed 18.3.2019).

European Commission. (2018) *Europe Leads the Global Clean Energy Transition: Commission Welcomes Ambitious Agreement on Further Renewable Energy Development in the EU.* Statement/18/4155 14.6.2018. Strasbourg: European Commission.

European Commission. (2018l) *European Circular Economy Stakeholder Platform: A Joint Initiative by the European Commission and the European Economic and Social Committee.* Brussels: European Commission. Available at: http://www.ec.europa.eu/environment/circular-economy/index_en.htm (accessed 20.08.2018).

European Commission. (2018m) *Green Public Procurement.* Brussels: European Commission. Available at: http://www.ec.europa.eu/environment/gpp/eu_gpp_criteria_en.htm.

European Commission. (2018n) *High Level Steering Group of the European Innovation Partnership on Raw Materials (E03391).* Brussels: European Commission. Available at: http://www.ec.europa.eu/transparency/regexpert/index.cfm?do=groupDetail.groupDetail&groupID=3391   (accessed 23.8.2018).

European Commission. (2018o) *Single-Use Plastics: New EU Rules to Reduce Marine Litter.* Press Release IP-18-3927: 28.5.2018. Brussels: European Commission.

European Commission. (2018p) *A Sustainable Bioeconomy for Europe: Strengthening the Connection Between Economy, Society and the Environment.* Updated Bioeconomy Strategy. Brussels: European Commission. Directorate General for Research and Innovation.

European Council. (2015) European Council Conclusions 19–20 March 2015. EUCO 11/15. Brussels: General Secretariat of the Council.

European Council. (2018a) Guidelines. European Council 23 March 2018. EUCO XT 20001/18. Brussels: Council of the EU.

European Council. (2018b) *Single-Use Plastics: Presidency Reaches Provisional Agreement with Parliament.* Press Release 818/18: 19.12.2018. Brussels: Council of the EU. Available at: https://www.consilium.europa.eu/de/press/press-releases/2018/12/19/single-use-plastics-presidency-reaches-provisional-agreement-with-parliament (accessed 18.3.2019).

European Council. (2018c) *Waste Management and Recycling: Council Adopts New Rules.* Press Release 259/18: 22.5.2018. Brussels: Council of the EU. Available at: https://www.consilium.europa.eu/en/press/press-releases/2018/05/22/waste-management-and-recycling-council-adopts-new-rules (accessed 18.3.2019).

European Parliament. (2008) *Report on the Proposal for a Regulation of the European Parliament and of the Council Amending Regulation (EC) No 1228/2003 on Conditions for Access to the Network for Cross-Border Exchanges in Electricity* (COM (2007) 0531-C6-0320/2007-2007/0198 (COD)) A6-0228/2008. Brussels: Committee on Industry, Research and Energy. Rapporteur Alejo Vidal-Quadras.

European Parliament. (2015a) *Don't Allow Recycling of Plastics that Contain Toxic Phthalate DEHP, Warn MEPs.* Press Release: 25.11.2015. Brussels: European Parliament. Available at: http://www.europarl.europa.eu/news/

en/press-room/20151120IPR03616/don-t-allow-recycling-of-plastics-that-contain-toxic-phthalate-dehp-warn-meps (accessed 18.3.2019).

European Parliament. (2015b) *MEPs Veto Cadmium Exemption Plans for Displays, Lightings and TVs*. Press Release 20.5.2015. Brussels: European Parliament.

European Parliament. (2018a) Report on the Proposal for a Directive of the European Parliament and of the Council on the *Common Rules for the Internal Market in Electricity* (Recast) (COM (2016) 0864-C8-0495/2016-2016/0380(COD)). Brussels: Committee on Industry, Research and Energy. Rapporteur Krišjānis Kariņš.

European Parliament. (2018b) Report on the Proposal for a Regulation of the European Parliament and of the Council on the *Internal Market for Electricity* (Recast) (COM (2016) 0861-C8-0492/2016-2016/0397(COD)). Brussels: Committee on Industry, Research and Energy. Rapporteur Krišjānis Kariņš.

European Parliament. (2019) *Parliament Seals Ban on Throwaway Plastics by 2021*. Press Release 27.3.2019. Strasbourg: European Parliament.

Eurostat. (2018a) *Energy Consumption in Households*. Available at: https://www.ec.europa.eu/eurostat/statistics-explained/index.php/Energy_consumption_in_households (accessed 14.8.2018).

Eurostat. (2018b) *Packaging Waste Statistics. Statistics Explained*. Brussels: Eurostat. Available at: https://ec.europa.eu/eurostat/statistics-explained/index.php/Packaging_waste_statistics (accessed 1.10.2018).

EuroVAprint. (2018) *Voluntary Agreement*. Available at: http://www.eurovaprint.eu/pages/voluntary-agreement/ (accessed 4.8.2018).

Everson M and Joerges C. (2006) Re-conceptualising Europeanisation as a Public Law of Collisions: Comitology, Agencies and an Interactive Public Adjudication. In: Hofmann HCH and Türk AH (eds) *EU Administrative Governance*. Cheltenham, Northampton: Edward Elgar, 512–540.

Extance A. (2018) Brexit Analysis Predicts Chemical Industry Contraction. *Chemistry World*: 15.3.2018.

Eyes on the Forest. (2011) *The Truth Behind APP's Greenwash. Investigative Report Eyes on the Forest*. Eyes on the Forest: Riau, Sumatra.

Eyre S. (2016) An Industry Perspective: The Primacy of Market-Building. In: Andersen SS, Goldthau A and Sitter N (eds) *Energy Union: Europe's New Liberal Mercantilism?* London: Palgrave Macmillan, 133–146.

Falkner G, Hartlapp M, Leiber S, et al. (2004) Non-compliance with EU Directives in the Member States: Opposition Through the Backdoor? *West European Politics* 27(3): 452–473.

Falkner G, Hartlapp M and Treib O. (2007) Worlds of Compliance: Why Leading Approaches to European Union Implementation Are Only 'Sometimes-True Theories'. *European Journal of Political Research* 46(3): 395–416.

Falkner R. (2007) The Political Economy of 'Normative Power' Europe: EU Environmental Leadership in International Biotechnology Regulation. *Journal of European Public Policy* 14(4): 507–526.

Farrell S. (2015) German Vacuum Cleaner Firm Set to Sue Dyson Over Energy-Test Claims. *The Guardian*: 28.10.2015.

Faure M, Fernhoiut F and Philipsen N. (2013) No Cure, No Pay and Contingency Fees. In: Tuil M and Visscher L (eds) *New Trends in Financing Civil Litigation in Europe: A Legal, Empirical, and Economic Analysis.* Cheltenham, Northampton: Edward Elgar, 33–56.

Fayole C and Arditi S. (2018) We Need More Durable and Reparable Products to Build a Circular Economy. *Euractiv*: 8.2.2018.

Fenichell S. (1996) *Plastic: The Making of a Synthetic Century.* Grand Rapids, MI: Harper Business.

Fernandez RM. (2018) Conflicting Energy Policy Priorities in EU Energy Governance. *Journal of Environmental Studies and Sciences* 8(3): 239–248.

Fischer C. (2011) The Development and Achievements of EU Waste Policy. *Journal of Material Cycles and Waste Management* 13(1): 2–9.

Fischer F. (1990) *Technocracy and the Politics of Expertise.* Newbury Park: Sage.

Fischer KH. (1997) *Lobbying und Kommunikation in der Europäischen Union.* Berlin: Berliner Wissenschaftsverlag.

Fleck J, Faulkner W and Williams R. (2016) *Exploring Expertise: Issues and Perspectives.* Houndmills, Basingstoke: Palgrave Macmillan.

Fligstein N and Stone Sweet A. (2002) Constructing Polities and Markets: An Institutionalist Account of European Integration. *American Journal of Sociology* 107(5): 1206–1243.

Focus. (2015) Neue Öko-Richtlinie: EU drosselt Xbox, Playstation and Wii. *Focus*: 28.4.2015.

Forcier JR. (1994) *Judicial Excess: The Political Economy of the American Legal System.* Lanham, New York, London: University Press of America.

Ford C. (2017) *Innovation and the State: Finance, Regulation, and Justice.* New York: Cambridge University Press.

Freeman C and Soete L. (1997) *The Economics of Industrial Innovation.* Cambridge, MA: MIT Press.

frontier economics and techUK. (2018) *The UK Digital Sectors After Brexit.* An Independent Report Commissioined by techUK. Brussels, Cologne, Dublin, London, Madrid: Frontier Economics.

Fuchs D. (2007) *Business Power in Global Governance.* London: Lynne Rienner.

Fuchs D, Gumbert T and Schlipphak B. (2017) Eurosecpticism and Big Business. In: Leruth B, Startin N and Usherwood S (eds) *The Routledge Handbook of Euroscepticism.* New York: Routledge, 317–330.

Gabbatiss J. (2017) How Does the New EU Plastic Strategy Compare to the UK's Plans to Cut Pollution? *The Independent*: 18.1.2017.

Galanter M. (1974) Why the 'Haves' Come Out Ahead: Speculations on the Limits of Legal Change. *Law & Society Review* 9(1): 95–160.

Gandy M. (1994) *Recycling and the Politics of Urban Waste.* New York: St. Martin's Press.

Gasiorek M, Serwicka I and Smith A. (2018) *Which Manufacturing Sectors Are Most Vulnerable to Brexit?* Briefing Paper 16. February 2018. Fulmer: UK Trade Policy Observatory (UKTPO), University of Sussex.

Gehring T and Krapohl S. (2007) Supranational Regulatory Agencies Between Independence and Control: The EMEA and the Authorization of Pharmaceuticals in the European Single Market. *Journal of European Public Policy* 14(2): 208–226.

Geissdoerfer M, Savaget P, Bocken NMP, et al. (2017) The Circular Economy: A New Sustainability Paradigm? *Journal of Cleaner Production* 143: 757–768.

Genschel P and Zangl B. (2014) State Transformations in OECD Countries. *Annual Review of Political Science* 17(1): 337–354.

German Environment Aid. (2018) *Deutsche Umwelthilfe befürwortet EU-Verbot von Plastikgeschirr und fordert verbindliche Einführung von Mehrwegalternativen.* Berlin: Deutsche Umwelthilfe.

Ghisellini P, Cialani C and Ulgiati S. (2016) A Review on Circular Economy: The Expected Transition to a Balanced Interplay of Environmental and Economic Systems. *Journal of Cleaner Production* 114: 11–32.

Glachant M. (2003) Voluntary Agreements Under Endogenous Legislative Threats. *FEEM Working Paper* No. 36.2003.

Glachant J-M and Pignon V. (2005) Nordic Congestion's Arrangement as a Model for Europe? Physical Constraints vs. Economic Incentives. *Utilities Policy* 13(2): 153–162.

Glencross A. (2016) *Why the UK Voted for Brexit: David Cameron's Great Miscalculation.* Houndmills, Basingstoke: Palgrave Macmillan.

Global Economic Dynamics. (2015) *GED Study: Costs and Benefits of a United Kingdom Exit from the European Union.* Gütersloh: Bertelsmann Stiftung.

Goldthau A and Sitter N. (2014) A Liberal Actor in a Realist World? The Commission and the External Dimension of the Single Market for Energy. *Journal of European Public Policy* 21(10): 1452–1472.

GOV.UK. (2018) *Policy Paper: Information About the Withdrawal Bill.* London: Department for Exiting the European Union. Available at: https://www.gov.uk/government/publications/information-about-the-withdrawal-bill (accessed 23.2.2019).

Government Office for Science. (2017) *Report of the Government Chief Scientific Adviser 2016: From Waste to Resource Productivity.* London: The Government Office for Science.

Grant W, Matthews D and Newell PJ. (2000) *The Effectiveness of European Union Environmental Policy.* Houndmills, Basingstoke: Palgrave Macmillan.

Graz J-C and Nölke A. (2008) *Transnational Private Governance and Its Limits*, London: Routledge.

Green JF. (2014) *Rethinking Private Authority: Agents and Entrepreneurs in Global Environmental Governance*. Princeton: Princeton University Press.

Greener UK. (2017) *Greener UK*. Available at: http://greeneruk.org (accessed 04.08.2018).

Greener UK. (2018a) *Brexit Risk Tracker*. February 2018–April 2018.

Greener UK. (2018b) *Environmental Principles and Governance After the UK Leaves the EU*. Position Paper. 31.7.2018. London: Greener UK.

Greener UK. (2018c) *What Would a No Deal Brexit Mean for the Environment?* 9.7.2018. London: Greener UK.

Greenpeace. (2000) *Hazardous Chemicals in PVC Flooring*. A Report Compiled for He Healthy Flooring Network, Greenpeace Research Laboratories Technical Note No. 14/00. Exeter: Greenpeace Research Laboratories, Department of Biological Sciences, University of Exeter.

Greenpeace. (2001) *Toxic Chemicals in a Child's World: An Investigation into PVC Plastic Products*. Exeter: Greenpeace Research Laboratories, Department of Biological Sciences, University of Exeter.

Greenpeace. (2002) *Exposing the Dirty Path of PVC*. Amsterdam: Greenpeace International.

Greenpeace. (2003) *PVC-Free Future: A Review of Restrictions and PVC free Policies Worldwide—A List Compiled by Greenpeace International*. 9th ed. June 2003. Amsterdam: Greenpeace International.

Greenpeace. (2012) PVC ist übel. Die harte Wahrheit über weiches PVC. *Greenpeace Magazin* 2012(6), Hamburg: Greenpeace Deutschland.

Greenpeace. (2018a) *The Evidence Is Clear: We Need a UK-Wide Deposit Return Scheme*. London: Greenpeace UK.

Greenpeace. (2018b) *Together We Can: Rethink IT*. Available at: https://www.greenpeace.org/archive-international/en/campaigns/detox/electronics/Guide-to-Greener-Electronics/ (accessed 12.8.2018).

GreenTouch. (2018) *Mission to Deliver the Architecture, Specifications and Roadmap to Increase Network Energy Efficiency by a Factor of 1000 Compared to 2010 Levels*. Available at: https://s3-us-west-2.amazonaws.com/bell-labs-microsite-greentouch/index.html.

Greenwood J. (2017) *Interest Representation in the European Union*. London: Palgrave Macmillan.

Groenleer M. (2011) Regulatory Governance in the European Union: The Role of Committees, Agencies and Networks. In: Levi-Faur D (ed) *Handbook on the Politics of Regulation*. Cheltenham: Edward Elgar, 548–560.

Groenleer M, Kaeding M and Versluis E. (2010) Regulatory Governance Through Agencies of the European Union? The Role of the European Agencies for Maritime and Aviation Safety in the Implementation of

European Transport Legislation. *Journal of European Public Policy* 17(8): 1212–1230.

Gullberg AT. (2008a) Lobbying Friends and Foes in Climate Policy: The Case of Business and Environmental Interest Groups in the European Union. *Energy Policy* 36(8): 2964–2972.

Gullberg AT. (2008b) Rational Lobbying and EU Climate Policy. *International Environmental Agreements: Politics, Law and Economics* 8(2): 161–178.

Haas PM. (1992) Introduction: Epistemic Communities and International Policy Coordination. *International Organization* 46(1): 1–35.

Haber H. (2018) Liberalizing Markets, Liberalizing Welfare? Economic Reform and Social Regulation in the EU's Electricity Regime. *Journal of European Public Policy* 25(3): 307–326.

Haigh N. (2015) *EU Environmental Policy: Its Journey to Centre Stage.* London: Routledge.

Halfteck G. (2006) *A Theory of Legislative Threats.* Tel Aviv: Tel Aviv University.

Halfteck G. (2008) Legislative Threats. *Stanford Law Review* 61: 629–710.

Hall PA and Soskice D. (2001) *Varieties of Capitalism.* Oxford: Oxford University Press.

Hall RB and Biersteker TJ. (2002) *The Emergence of Private Authority in Global Governance.* Cambridge: Cambridge University Press.

Hansen LG. (1999) Environmental Regulation Through Voluntary Agreements. In: Carraro C and Lévêque F (eds) *Voluntary Approaches in Environmental Policy.* Dordrecht: Springer, 27–54.

Hansen S. (2018) *A Storm Is Raging Over the EU Plastics Packaging Sector.* January 2018. Utrecht: RaboResearch Food & Agribusiness.

Harlow C and Rawlings R. (2013) *Pressure Through Law.* London, New York: Taylor & Francis.

Haucke F, Lenschow A and Pollex J. (2019) Consumption for Sustainability? Exploring Societal and Political Gynamics in Digital Society. In: Boucher JL and Heinonen J (eds) *Sustainable Consumption: Promise or Myth? Case Studies from the Field.* Cambridge: Cambridge Scholars Publishing.

Haufler V. (2001) *A Public Role for the Private Sector: Industry Self-Regulation in a Global Economy.* Washington: Carnegie Endowment for International Peace.

Hawker G, Bell K and Gill S. (2017) Electricity Security in the European Union: The Conflict Between National Capacity Mechanisms and the Single Market. *Energy Research & Social Science* 24: 51–58.

Hayes-Renshaw F. (2009) Least Accessible But Not Inaccessible: Lobbying the Council and the European Council. In: Coen D and Richardson J (eds) *Lobbying the European Union: Institutions, Actors, and Issues.* Oxford: Oxford University Press, 70–88.

HEAL. (2018) *HEAL's Response to the EU Commission's Proposed Roadmap 'Towards a More Comprehensive Framework on Endocrine Disruptors'*. Brussels: Health and Environment Alliance (HEAL).

Heath R. (2017) Commission's Better Regulation Agenda Slammed in New Study. *Politico*, 29.1.2017.

Hébert RF and Link AN. (2006) The Entrepreneur as Innovator. *The Journal of Technology Transfer* 31(5): 589.

Heidbreder EG. (2011) Structuring the European Administrative Space: Policy Instruments of Multi-Level Administration. *Journal of European Public Policy* 18(5): 709–727.

Heinelt H and Meinke-Brandmeier B. (2006) Comparing Civil Society Participation in European Environmental Policy and Consumer Protection. In: Smismans S (ed) *Civil Society and Legitimate European Governance*. Cheltenham: Edward Elgar, 196–218.

Heinzle S and Wüstenhagen R. (2009) *Consumer Survey on the New Format of the European Energy Label for televisions: Comparison of a 'A-G Closed' Versus a 'Beyond A' Scale Format*. St. Gallen: University of St. Gallen.

Helm D. (2014) The European Framework for Energy and Climate Policies. *Energy Policy* 64: 29–35.

Hendry JR. (2003) Environmental NGOs and Business: A Grounded Theory of Assessment, Targeting, and Influencing. *Business & Society* 42(2): 267–276.

Henningsen J. (2011) Energy Savings and Efficiency. In: Birchfield VL and Duffield JS (eds) *Toward a Common European Union Energy Policy: Problems, Progress, and Prospects*. Gordonsville: Palgrave Macmillan, 144–154.

Héritier A. (1987) *Policy Analyse: Eine Einführung*. Frankfurt/New York: Campus Verlag.

Héritier A. (2003) New Modes of Governance in Europe: Increasing Political Capacity and Policy Effectiveness? In: Börzel TA and Cichowski RA (eds) *The State of the European Union: Law, Politics and Society*. Oxford: Oxford University Press, 105–126.

Héritier A and Eckert S. (2008) New Modes of Governance in the Shadow of Hierarchy: Self-Regulation by Industry in Europe. *Journal of Public Policy* 28(1): 113–138.

Héritier A and Eckert S. (2009) Self-Regulation by Associations: A Collective Action Problem in Environmental Regulation. *Business and Politics* 11(1): 1–22.

Héritier A and Lehmkuhl D. (2008a) New Modes of Governance and the Shadow of Hierarchy: Sectoral Governance and Territorially Bound Democratic Government. Special Issue. *Journal of Public Policy* 28(1): 113–138.

Héritier A and Lehmkuhl D. (2008b) The Shadow of Hierarchy and New Modes of Governance. *Journal of Public Policy* 28(1): 1–17.

Héritier A, Moury C, Bischoff CS, et al. (2013) *Changing Rules of Delegation: A Contest for Power in Comitology*. Oxford: Oxford University Press.

Héritier A and Rhodes M. (2010) *New Modes of Governance in Europe: Governing in the Shadow of Hierarchy*. Basingstoke, New York: Palgrave Macmillan.

Herring H and Sorrell S. (2009) *Energy Efficiency and Sustainable Consumption: The Rebound Effect*. Houndmills, Basingstoke: Palgrave Macmillan.

Herweg N. (2017) *European Union Policy-Making: The Regulatory Shift in Natural Gas Market Policy*. Cham: Palgrave Macmillan.

Heyvaert V. (2007) No Data, No Market: The Future of EU Chemicals Control Under the Reach Regulation. *Environmental Law Review* 9(3): 201–206.

Heyvaert V and Čavoški A. (2018) UK Environmental Law Post-Brexit. In: Dougan M (ed) *The UK After Brexit: Legal and Policy Challenges*. Cambridge: Intersentia, 115–133.

Higgins P and Costello R. (2016) *IIEA Policy Brief. What Does Brexit Mean for the Energy Sector in Ireland?* Dublin: The Institute of International and European Affairs.

Hilty LM and Aebischer B. (2014) *ICT for Sustainability: An Emerging Research Field*. London: Springer.

Hirth L, Mühlenpfordt J and Bulkeley M. (2018) The ENTSO-E Transparency Platform: A Review of Europe's Most Ambitious Electricity Data Platform. *Applied Energy* 225: 1054–1067.

HM Government. (2017a) *The Clean Growth Strategy. Leading the Way to a Low Carbon Future*. London: BEIS.

HM Government. (2017b) *Northern Ireland and Ireland*. Position Paper. 16.8.2017. London: Department for Exiting the European Union.

HM Government. (2018a) *Deposit Return Scheme in Fight Against Plastic*. Press Release 28.3.2018. London: DEFRA.

HM Government. (2018b) *The Future Relationship Between the United Kingdom and the European Union*. Presented to Parliament by the Prime Minister by Command of Her Majesty. Cm 9593. London: UK Government.

HM Government. (2018c) *A Green Future: Our 25 Year Plan to Improve the Environment*. London: DEFRA.

HM Government. (2018d) *UK Government Power Statistics: Imports, Exports and Transfers of Electricity (ET 5.6)*. Available at: https://www.gov.uk/government/statistics/electricity-section-5-energy-trends (accessed 10.8.2018).

HM Government. (2018e) *World-Leading Microbeads Ban Takes Effect*. Press Release 9.1.2018. London: DEFRA.

HM Government. (2018f) *Our Waste, Our Resources: A Strategy for England*. London: Her Majesty's Stationery Office, DEFRA.

HM Treasury. (2018) *Tackling the Plastic Problem. Using the Tax System or Charges to Address Single-Use Plastic Waste*. London: HM Treasury.

HMRC. (2018) *Trade Statistics*. Available at: https://www.uktradeinfo.com/ Pages/Home.aspx (accessed 10.08.2018).

Hodges C. (2009) From Class Actions to Collective Redress. *Civil Justice Quarterly* 28(1): 41–66.

Hofman A. (2019) Left to Interest groups? On the Prospects for Enforcing Environmental Law in the European Union. Special Issue: The Future of the European Union in Environmental Politics and Policy. Eds. A. Zito, S. Burns and A. Lenschow. *Environmental Politics* 28(2): 342–364.

Hogwood BW and Peters BG. (1983) *Policy Dynamics*. Brighton, Sussex: Wheatsheaf Books.

Holburn GLF and Vanden Bergh RG. (2000) Policy and Process: A Game-Theoretic Framework for the Design of Non-market Strategy. *Advances in Strategic Management* 19: 33–66.

Holehouse M. (2016) EU to Launch Kettle and Toaster Crackdown After Brexit Vote. *The Telegraph*: 11.5.2016.

Höltschi R. (2015) Strom-Binnenmarkt der EU. Vorerst ohne die Schweiz. *Neue Zürcher Zeitung*: 27.7.2015.

Holzinger K, Knill C and Lenschow A. (2009) Innovative Governance in the European Union. In: Tömmel I and Verdun A (eds) *Innovative Governance in the European Union: The Politics of Multilevel Policymaking*. Boulder, CO: Rienner, 45–61.

Hontelez J. (2012) The Influence of Non-governmental Environmental Organisations on EU Policies. In: Wijen F, Zoeteman K and Pieters J (eds) *A Handbook of Globalisation and Environmental Policy, Second Edition: National Government Interventions in a Global Arena*. Cheltenham, Northampton: Edward Elgar, 663–683.

Hooghe L and Marks G. (2009) A Postfunctionalist Theory of European Integration: From Permissive Consensus to Constraining Dissensus. *British Journal of Political Science* 39(1): 1–23.

House of Commons. (2017) *Leaving the EU: Negotiation Priorities for Energy and Climate Change Policy*. London: House of Commons.

House of Commons. (2018) *EU Exit Analysis Cross Whitehall Briefing*. January 2018. London: House of Commons.

House of Lords. (2018) Brexit: Energy Security. *Report of Session 2017–19*. London: House of Lords, European Union Committee.

Howard E. (2015) DEFRA Hit by Largest Budget Cuts of Any UK Government Department, Analysis Shows. *The Guardian*: 11.11.2015.

Howarth D and Quaglia L. (2017) Brexit and the Single European Financial Market. *Journal of Common Market Studies* 55(S1): 149–164.

Howells G, Twigg-Flesner C and Wilhelmsson T. (2017) *Rethinking EU Consumer Law*. Abingdon: Taylor & Francis.

HSF, BCG and GC. (2017) *Strong Currents: Navigating the Post-Brexit Energy Market*. London: The Boston Consulting Group, Global Counsel, Herbert Smith Freehills.

Hunter D. (1978) *Papermaking: The History and Technique of an Ancient Craft*. New York: Dover Publications.

Hutton W. (2018) Enough Already: In the National Interest, We Must Stop a Hard Brexit. *The Guardian*: 24.6.2018.

I4R. (2018) *WEEE Recycling Information: I4R-Platform*. Available at: http://www.i4r-platform.eu (accessed 16.8.2018).

IEEP. (2018) *Brexit Negotiations: Equivalence, Environmental Standards and Risks*. London: Institute for European Environmental Policy.

IFIXIT. (2018) *Repair Is Noble*. Available at: https://www.ifixit.org/ (accessed 23.8.2018).

Industry Europe. (2011) White Goods Leader in Europe. *Industry Europe*: 10.11.2011.

Inglehart RF and Norris P. (2016) Trump, Brexit, and the Rise of Populism: Economic Have-Nots and Cultural Backlash. *HKS Faculty Research Working Paper Series* August 2016.

Interview CEER. (2007) Secretary General, Brussels, 10.04.2017.

Interview ClientEarth. (2017) Programmes Director, London, 20.10.2017.

Interview COM. (2005a) Legislative Officer and Acting Head of Unit, DG ENVI, Brussels, 23.11.2005.

Interview COM. (2005b) Policy Officer Sustainable Production and Consumption, DG ENVI, Brussels, 23.11.2005.

Interview COM. (2006a) Desk Officer IPP, DG ENTR, Brussels, 3.5.2006.

Interview COM. (2006b) Polic Officer Energy Efficiency, DG TREN, Brussels, 3.5.2006.

Interview COM. (2006c) Policy Officer Sustainable Production and Consumption, DG ENVI, Brussels, 23.3.2006.

Interview COM. (2007a) Advisor to Energy Commissioner, Brussels, 18.12.2007.

Interview COM. (2007b) Grid Expert DG TREN, Brussels, 19.12.2007.

Interview COM. (2017, 2019a) Grid Expert, DG Energy, Brussels, 12.4.2017 and 10.1.2019.

Interview COM. (2017, 2019b) Head of Unit, DG ENVI, Brussels, 10.4.2017 and 9.1.2019.

Interview COM. (2017, 2019c) National Expert, DG Energy, Brussels, 11.4.2017 and 10.1.2019.

Interview COM. (2017d) Polic Officer Ecodesign Directive, DG GROW, Brussels, 11.4.2017.

Interview COM. (2017e) Policy Officer Energy Efficiency, DG ENERGY, Brussels, 11.4.2017.

Interview Consumer Organisation. (2017) Project Officer, BEUC, Brussels, 12.4.2017.

Interview EEB. (2006) Senior Policy Officer, 05.05.2006, Brussels.

Interview energy industry. (2007a) *Grid Expert, EURELECTRIC, EFET, Brussels*, 20.12.2007.

Interview energy industry. (2007b) *Policy Coordination and Communication Unit, EURELECTRIC, Brussels*, 21.12.2007.

Interview ELECTRABEL. (2007) Grid Expert Active in EURELECTRIC AND EFET, Brussels, 20.12.2007.

Interview energy economics expert. (2005, 2008) Florence, 04.07.2005 and Paris, 22.04.2008.

Interview ENGO. (2006) Head of Office, Greenpeace European Unit, 22.2.2006, Brussels.

Interview ENGO. (2017a) Director of Programmes, Client, London, 20.10.2017.

Interview ENGO. (2017b) Executive Director, CHEM Trust, London, 17.7.2017.

Interview ENGO. (2019) Senior Programme Manager, ECOS, Brussels, 10.1.2019.

Interview ENTSO. (2017) Economic and Legal Experts, Brussels, 11.04.2017.

Interview EP. (2005a) MEP, EPP-DE, IMCO, Brussels, 22.2.2006.

Interview EP. (2005b) MEP, PSE-IT, ENVI, Florence, 2.6.2006.

Interview EP. (2005c) Polic Officer Greens/EFA, Brussels, 23.11.2005.

Interview EP. (2017) Polic Officer Greens/EFA, Brussels, 12.4.2017.

Interview ERGEG/CEER. (2007) Deputy Secretary General, Brussels, 20.12.2007.

Interview TSO. (2007a) Former Secretary General, ETSO, Brussels, 17.12.2007.

Interview TSO. (2007b) Member of Steering Committee, ETSO, Brussels, 20.12.2007.

Interview TSO. (2007c) *Secretary General, ETSO, Brussels*, 19.12.2007.

Interview EURELECTRIC. (2007) Policy Coordination and Communication Unit, Brussels, 21.12.2007.

Interview home appliance industry. (2017a) Chief Executive, Association Executive, AMDEA, London, 18.07.2017.

Interview home appliance industry. (2017b) Technical Executive, AMDEA, Phone, 10.10.2017.

Interview home appliance industry. (2018a) Managing Director Small and Large Domestic Electrical Appliances Divisions, ZVEI, Frankfurt/Main, 23.3.2018.

Interview home appliance industry. (2018b) Head of Unit and Team Member Environment, Resources and Work Security BSH, Munich, 27.3.2018.

Interview home appliance industry. (2019a) Energy Policy Director and Environment Policy Director, APPLIA, Brussels, 10.1.2019.

Interview home appliance industry. (2019b) Senior Expert of EU Technical Government Affairs, BSH, Brussels, 10.1.2019.

Interview ICT industry. (2017a) Director, Team Members, Sustainability Policy, Digital Europe, Brussels, 11.4.2017.

Interview ICT industry. (2017b) Head of Programme, Environment & Compliance, techUK, London, 20.10.2017.

Interview ministry. (2017a) Senior Project Manager Home and Local Energy, BEIS, London, 23.10.2017.

Interview ministry. (2017b) Team Leader REACH, Senior Policy Advisor, DEFRA, London, 17.07.2017.

Interview Ministry. (2017c) UK Negotiation Leader in European Energy Policy, BEIS, London 23.10.2017.

Interview MP. (2017) Environmental Audit Committee, House of Commons, London, 20.10.2017.

Interview NRA. (2007) Technical Expert Finnish Energy Regulator, Brüssels, 17.12.2007.

Interview NRA. (2017) Grid Expert, OFGEM, Former Member ENTSO, London, 13.07.2017.

Interview paper industry. (2006a) Managing Director, Recycling and EU Affairs Manager, GesPaRec, VDP, Bonn, 8.5.2006.

Interview paper industry. (2006b) Recycling Director, CEPI, Brussels, 5.5.2006.

Interview paper industry. (2006c) Deputy Secretary General, FEAD, Phone, 24.1.2006.

Interview paper industry. (2006d) EU Affairs Manager, Technical Director, FEFCO, Brussels, 5.5.2006.

Interview paper industry. (2006e) Managing Director, BVSE, ERPA, Bonn, 8.5.2006.

Interview paper industry. (2017) Deputy Director General, CEPI, Brussels, 11.4.2017.

Interview plastics industry. (2006a) Deputy Director, ECPI, Brussels, 23.2.2006.

Interview plastics industry. (2006b) Director Infraserv Höchst, Frankfurt/Main, 24.4.2006.

Interview plastics industry. (2017) Sustainability Issues Executive, Senior Industrial Issues Executive, BPF, London, 19.07.2017.

Interview plastics industry. (2019) Technical and Environmental Affairs Manager, Public Affairs Senior Manager, ECVM, Brussels, 11.1.2019.

Interview ENGO. (2017) *Chief Executive Officer, Renewables Grid Initiative, Berlin*, 30.5.2017.

Interview regulator. (2007a) Deputy Secretary General, ERGEG/CEER, Brussels, 20.12.2007.

Interview regulator. (2017) Grid Expert, OFGEM, Former Staff ENTSO, London, 13.7.2017.

Interview regulator. (2007b) Technical Expert Finnish Energy Regulator, CEER/ERGEG, Brussels, 17.12.2007.

Interview regulator. (2017, 2019) Secretary General, CEER, Brussels, 10.4.2017 and 11.1.2019.

Interview TSO. (2008) Manager National Grid, Florence, 21.02.2008.

Interview TSO. (2017) Technical Expert National Grid, London, 19.10.2017.

Interview ZVEI. (2018) Managing Director Small and Large Domestic Electrical Appliances Divisions, Frankfurt/Main, 23.03.2018.

Interviews energy economics expert. (2005, 2008) Florence, 04.07.2005 and Paris, 22.04.2008.

Irving H. (2016) Paper Salvage in Britain During the Second World War. *Historical Research* 89(244): 373–393.

Jegen M. (2009) Swiss Energy Policy and the Challenge of European Governance. *Swiss Political Science Review* 15(4): 577–602.

Jensen DM and Snaith H. (2016) When Politics Prevails: The Political Economy of a Brexit. *Journal of European Public Policy* 23(4): 1–9.

Jevnaker T. (2015) Pushing Administrative EU Integration: The Path Towards European Network Codes for Electricity. *Journal of European Public Policy* 22(7): 927–947.

Johnson J. (2012) *Britain Must Defend the Single Market*. Brussels: Centre for European Reform.

Johnston I. (2017a) Climate Change Department Closed by Theresa May in 'Plain Stupid' and 'Deeply Worrying' Move. *The Independent*: 14.7.2017.

Johnston I. (2017b) Government Given 21 Days to Explain Climate Change Failures or Face Legal Action. *The Independent*: 11.4.2017.

Johnston I. (2017c) UK Government has Breached Air Pollution Laws and Failed to Take Enough Action on Emissions, High Court rules. *The Independent*: 2.11.2017.

Jones E. (2018) Towards a Theory of Disintegration. *Journal of European Public Policy* 25(3): 440–451.

Jordan A, Huitema D, van Asselt H, et al. (2010) *Climate Change Policy in the European Union: Confronting the Dilemmas of Mitigation and Adaptation?* Cambridge: Cambridge University Press.

JRC. (2016) *EU Ecodesign for Dishwashers*. Ispra: Joint Research Centre. Available at: http://www.susproc.jrc.ec.europa.eu/Dishwashers/index.html.

JRC. (2018) The 2018 Predict Key Facts Report. An Analysis of ICT R&D in the EU and Beyond. Sevilla: European Commission, Joint Research Centre.

Judge D. (1992) 'Predestined to Save the Earth': The Environment Committee of the European parliament. *Environmental Politics* 1(4): 186–212.

Julian K, Denise R and Marko H. (2017) Conceptualizing the Circular Economy: An Analysis of 114 Definitions. *Resources, Conservation and Recycling* 127: 221–232.

Junk WM. (2016) Two Logics of NGO Advocacy: Understanding Inside and Outside Lobbying on EU Environmental Policies. *Journal of European Public Policy* 23(2): 236–254.

Justin G and Christilla RR. (2015) The 'Europeanization' of the Basel Process: Financial Harmonization Between Globalization and Parliamentarization. *Regulation & Governance* 9(4): 325–338.

Kagan RA. (2001) *Adversarial Legalism: The American Way of Law*. Cambridge, MA: Harvard University Press.

Kagan RA and Axelrad L. (2000) Regulatory Encounters: Multinational Corporations and American Adversarial Legalism. *California Series in Law, Politics and Society*. Berkeley: University of California Press.

Katzenstein PJ and Seybert LA. (2018) *Protean Power: Exploring the Uncertain and Unexpected in World Politics*. Cambridge: Cambridge University Press.

Kelemen RD. (2012) European Union Agencies. In: Jones E, Menon A and Weatherill S (eds) *The Oxford Handbook of the European Union*. Oxford: Oxford University Press, 392–403.

Kelemen RD. (2013) Eurolegalism and the European Legal Field. In: Vauchez A and de Witte B (eds) *Lawyering Europe: European Law as a Transnational Social Field*. Oxford and Portland, OR: Hart Publishing, 243–257.

Kelemen RD. (2011) *Eurolegalism: The Transformation of Law and Regulation in the European Union*. Cambridge, MA: Harvard University Press.

Klinckenberg F and Harmelink M. (2017) *Effectiveness of Energy Efficiency Voluntary Agreements*. Report Prepared for the Executive Committee of the 4E Technology Collaboration programme. London, Utrecht: The Policy Partners, SQ Consult.

Klüver H. (2009) Measuring Interest Group Influence Using Quantitative Text Analysis. *European Union Politics* 10(4): 535–549.

Klüver H. (2011) The Contextual Nature of Lobbying: Explaining Lobbying Success in the European Union. *European Union Politics* 12(4): 483–506.

Klüver H. (2012) Biasing Politics? Interest Group Participation in EU Policy-Making. *West European Politics* 35(5): 1114–1133.

Knill C. (2001) Private Governance across Multiple Arenas: European Interest Associations as Interface Actors. *Journal of European Public Policy* 8(2): 227–246.

Knill C and Liefferink D. (2007) *Environmental Politics in the European Union: Policy-Making, Implementation and Patterns of Multi-Level Governance*. Manchester: Manchester University Press.

Knill C, Tosun J and Bauer MW. (2009) Neglected Faces of Europeanization: The Differential Impact of the EU on the Dismantling and Expansion of Domestic Policies. *Public Administration* 87(3): 519–537.

Knops HPA, de Vries L and Hakvoort RA. (2001) Congestion Management in the European Electricity System: An Evaluation of the Alternatives. *Journal of Network Industries* 2: 311–351.

Kohler-Koch B, Quittkat C, Buth V, et al. (2013) *De-Mystification of Participatory Democracy: EU-Governance and Civil Society.* Oxford: Oxford University Press.

Korten DC. (2015) *When Corporations Rule the World.* Oakland: Berrett-Koehler Publishers.

Krämer L. (2000) Thirty Years of EC Environmental Law: Perspectives and Prospectives. In: Somsen H (ed) *Yearbook of European Environmental Law: Volume 1.* Oxford: Oxford University Press, 155–182.

Kuenssberg, L. (2019) Brexit: MPs vote to take control of Brexit process for indicative votes: *BBC News*: 26.3.2019.

La Porte TR and Consolini P. (1991) Working in Practice but Not in Theory: Theoretical Challenges of High Reliability Organizations. *Journal of Public Administration Research and Theory* 1(1): 19–48.

La Porte TR. (1996) High Reliability Organizations: Unlikely, Demanding and at Risk. *Journal of Contingencies and Crisis Management* 4(2): 60–71.

Labelle MC. (2016) Regulating for Consumers? The Agency for Cooperation of Energy Regulators. In: Andersen SS, Goldthau A and Sitter N (eds) *Energy Union: Europe's New Liberal Mercantilism?* London: Palgrave Macmillan, 147–164.

Lacey J. (2017) *Centripetal Democracy: Democratic Legitimacy and Political Identity in Belgium, Switzerland, and the European Union.* Oxford: Oxford University Press.

Lavenex S. (2009) Switzerland's Flexible Integration in the European Union: A Conceptual Framework. *Swiss Political Science Review* 15(4): 547–575.

Lavenex S. (2015) The External Face of Differentiated Integration: Third Country Participation in EU Sectoral Bodies. *Journal of European Public Policy* 22(6): 836–853.

Laville S. (2017) China Waste Clampdown Could Create UK Cardboard Recycling Chaos, Say Industry Experts. *The Guardian*: 15.12.2017.

Lee JJ. (2018) How Did Sea Turtle Get a Straw Up Its Nose? *National Geographic*: 2.6.2018.

Lehmann W. (2009) The European Parliament. In: Coen D and Richardson J (eds) *Lobbying the European Union: Institutions, Actors, and Issues.* Oxford: Oxford University Press, 39–69.

Lehmkuhl D. (2005) How Private Governance Arrangements May Produce Binding Outcomes. *International Journal of Civil Society Law* 4(3): 34–55.

Lenschow A. (2015) Environmental Policy: Contending Dynamics of Policy Change. In: Wallace H, Pollack MA and Young AR (eds) *Policy-Making in the European Union.* 6th ed. Oxford: Oxford University Press, 319–343.

Lenschow A and Rottmann K. (2010) The Evolving Role of Industry in European Union Environmental Governance. In: O'Connor A (ed) *Managing Economies, Trade and International Business.* Houndmills, Basingstoke: Palgrave Macmillan, 67–85.

Levi-Faur D. (2011a) Regulation and Regulatory Governance. In: Levi-Faur D (ed) *Handbook on the Politics of Regulation.* Cheltenham, Northampton: Edward Elgar, 3–21.

Levi-Faur D. (2011b) Regulatory Networks and Regulatory Agencification: Towards a Single European Regulatory Space. *Journal of European Public Policy* 18(6): 810–829.

Levi-Faur D and Jordana J. (2004) *The Politics of Regulation: Institutions and Regulatory Reforms for the Age of Governance.* Cheltenham, Northampton: Edward Elgar.

Lieder M. and Amir R. (2016) Towards Circular Economy Implementation: a Comprehensive Review in Context of Manufacturing Industry. *Journal of Cleaner Production* 115: 36–51.

Liefferink D and Andersen MS. (1998) Strategies of the 'Green' Member States in EU Environmental Policy-Making. *Journal of European Public Policy* 5(2): 254–270.

Littoz-Monnet A. (2017) *The Politics of Expertise in International Organizations: How International Bureaucracies Produce and Mobilize Knowledge.* Abingdon: Taylor & Francis.

Lodge M. (2008) Regulation, the Regulatory State and European Politics. *West European Politics* 31(1): 280–301.

London Economics and Ipsos. (2018) *Study on the Impact of the Energy Label: and Potential Changes to It – On Consumer Understanding and on Purchase Decisions.* ENER/ C3/2013-428. Final Report. London: London Economics.

Long T. (1995) Shaping Public Policy in the European Union: A Case Study of the Structural Funds. *Journal of European Public Policy* 2(4): 672–679.

Long T and Lörinczi L. (2009) Business Lobbying in the European Union. In: Coen D and Richardson J (eds) *Lobbying the European Union: Institutions, Actors, and Issues.* Oxford: Oxford University Press, 169–185.

Lourie B. (2017) Without EU Regulations on Chemicals, the UK Will be a Toxic Dumping Ground. *The Guardian*: 1.6.2017.

Lowe P. (2017) *Brexit and Energy: Time to Make Some Hard Choices.* Brussels: Centre for European Reform.

Lowi T. (1964) American Business, Public Policy, Case-Studies, and Political Theory. *World Politics* 16(4): 677–715.

Lukes S. (2005) *Power: A Radical View.* Houndmills, Basingstoke: Palgrave Macmillan.

Maggetti M and Gilardi F. (2014) Network Governance and the Domestic Adoption of Soft Rules. *Journal of European Public Policy* 21(9): 1293–1310.

Mahoney C. (2004) The Power of Institutions: State and Interest Group Activity in the European Union. *European Union Politics* 5(4): 441–466.

Mahoney C. (2007) Lobbying Success in the United States and the European Union. *Journal of Public Policy* 27(1): 35–56.

Majone G. (1994) The Rise of the Regulatory State in Europe. *West European Politics* 17(2): 77–101.

Majone G. (1997) From the Positive to the Regulatory State: Causes and Consequences of Changes in the Mode of Governance. *Journal of Public Policy* 17(2): 139–167.

Majone G. (1999) The Regulatory State and Its Legitimacy Problems. *West European Politics* 22(1): 1–24.

Make resources count. (2018) *End of the World [Not]: Good News Stories from the War against Waste.* Available at: http://www.makeresourcescount.eu/ (accessed 27.08.2018).

March L. (2017) Left and Right Populism Compared: The British Case. *The British Journal of Politics and International Relations* 19(2): 282–303.

Marine Litter Solutions. (2001) *Delcaration of the Global Plastics Associations for Solutions on Marine Litter.* Marine Litter Solutions. Available at: https://www.marinelittersolutions.com/about-us/joint-declaration (accessed 22.3.2019).

Marine Litter Solutions. (2018) *The Delcaration of the Global Plastics Associations for Solutions on Marine Litter. 4th Progress Report.* March 2018. Marine Litter Solutions.

Markus B, Hansen T and Klitkou A. (2016) What Is the Bioeconomy? A Review of the Literature. *Sustainability* 8(7): 691.

Maroulis N, Kettenis Pd, Bougas K, et al. (2016) *Cumulative Cost Assessment for the EU Chemical Industry.* Final Report. Brussels: Technopolis group, European Commission.

Marshall D. (2010) Who to Lobby and When: Institutional Determinants of Interest Group Strategies in European Parliament Committees. *European Union Politics* 11(4): 553–575.

Martens M. (2012) Executive Power in the Making: The Establishment of the European Chemicals Agency. In: Trondal J, Busuioc M and Groenleer M (eds) *The Agency Phenomenon in the European Union.* Manchester, New York: Manchester University Press, 42–62.

Mastenbroek E. (2005) EU Compliance: Still a 'Black Hole'? *Journal of European Public Policy* 12(6): 1103–1120.

Mathieu E. (2016) *Regulatory Delegation in the European Union: Networks, Committees and Agencies.* London: Palgrave Macmillan.

Matthews D. (2016) Sustainability Challenges in the Paper Industry. *ChEnected—Where Chemical Engineers Mix Up—Online Community.* 12.10.2016. Available at: https://www.aiche.org/chenected/2016/10/sustainability-challenges-paper-industry (accessed 22.3.2019).

May C. (2006) *Global Corporate Power.* Boulder: Lynne Rienner.

May C. (2015) *Global Corporations in Global Governance*. Oxon, New York: Routledge.

Mayntz R. (2005) Governance Theory als Fortentwicklung der Steuerungstheorie? In: Schuppert GF (ed) *Governance-Forschung: Vergewisserung über Stand und Entwicklungslinien*. Baden-Baden: Nomos, 11–20.

Mazey S and Richardson J. (1992) Environmental Groups and the EC: Challenges and Opportunities. *Environmental Politics* 1(4): 109–128.

Mazey S and Richardson J. (1996) The Logic of Organisation: Interest Groups. In: Richardson J (ed) *European Union: Power and Policy-Making*. London, New York: Routledge, 200–215.

Mazey S and Richardson J. (2003) Interest Groups and the Brussels Bureaucracy. In: Hayward J and Menon A (eds) *Governing Europe*. Oxford: Oxford University Press, 208–227.

McCormick K and Kautto N. (2013) The Bioeconomy in Europe: An Overview. *Sustainability* 5(6): 2589.

McCown M. (2009) Interest Groups and the European Court of Justice. In: Coen D and Richardson J (eds) *Lobbying the European Union: Institutions, Actors, and Issues*. Oxford: Oxford University Press, 89–104.

McCubbins MD and Schwartz T. (1984) Congressional Oversight Overlooked: Police Patrols and Fire Alarm. *American Journal of Political Science* 28(1): 165–179.

McGowan L and Wallace H. (1996) Towards a European Regulatory state. *Journal of European Public Policy* 3(4): 560–576.

McGrath M. (2016) *EU Approves Use of Recycled Plastics Containing DEHP*. Reuters: 21.4.2016.

Meletiou A, Cambini C and Masera M. (2018) Regulatory and Ownership Determinants of Unbundling Regime Choice for European Electricity Transmission Utilities. *Utilities Policy* 50: 13–25.

Meli L. (1999) The CECED Commitment for Clothes Washers. In: Bertoldi P, Ricci A and Wajer BH (eds) *Energy Efficiency in Household Appliances: Proceedings of the First International Conference on Energy Efficiency in Household Appliances*, 10–12 November 1997, Florence, Italy. Berlin, Heidelberg: Springer, 89–91.

Micklitz H-W and Weatherill S. (1993) Consumer Policy in the European Community: Before and After Maastricht. *Journal of Consumer Policy* 16(3): 285–321.

Mikler J. (2018) *The Political Power of Global Corporations*. Cambridge: Polity Press.

Monaghan A and Elgot J. (2018) More Firms May Follow Airbus in Brexit Threat, Says CBI. *The Guardian*: 22.6.2018.

Moravcsik A. (1998) *The Choice for Europe: Social Purpose and State Power from Messina to Maastricht*. Ithaca: Cornell University Press.

Morgan S. (2017a) Brexit Impact on Energy Markets Could be 'limited', Study Says. *Euractiv*: 21.11.2017. Brussels.

Morgan S. (2017b) Commission Funds France-Ireland Power Link That Bypasses UK. *Euractiv*: 6.7.2017. Brussels.

Morriss AP, Yandle B and Dorchak A. (2009) *Regulation by Litigation*. New Haven, London: Yale University Press.

Müller GV. (2018) Abseitsstehen vom Strombinnenmarkt kommt die Schweiz teuer zu stehen. *Neue Zürcher Zeitung*.

mure and Fraunhofer. (2008) *EU 38 Negotiated Agreement EACEM for VCRs (Stand-By Mode and On-Mode)*. Available at: http://www.measures-odyssee-mure.eu/table3_mr.asp?Cod=EU2/EU23/EU7/EU19/EU21/EU9/EU8/EU35/EU38/EU29/EU34/EU33/EU45/EU46/EU3.

mure and Fraunhofer. (2014a) *EU 2 CECED Voluntary Commitment Washing Machines II*. Available at: http://www.measures-odyssee-mure.eu/table3_mr.asp?Cod=EU2/EU23/EU7/EU19/EU21/EU9/EU8/EU35/EU38/EU29/EU34/EU33/EU45/EU46/EU3.

mure and Fraunhofer. (2014b) *EU 3 CECED Voluntary Commitment on Household Refrigerators, Freezers and Combinations*. Available at: http://www.measures-odyssee-mure.eu/table3_mr.asp?Cod=EU2/EU23/EU7/EU19/EU21/EU9/EU8/EU35/EU38/EU29/EU34/EU33/EU45/EU46/EU3.

mure and Fraunhofer. (2014c) *EU 8 CECED Voluntary Commitment Diswashers*. Available at: http://www.measures-odyssee-mure.eu/table3_mr.asp?Cod=EU2/EU23/EU7/EU19/EU21/EU9/EU8/EU35/EU38/EU29/EU34/EU33/EU45/EU46/EU3.

mure and Fraunhofer. (2014d) *EU 9 CECED Voluntary Commitment Washing Machines*. Available at: http://www.measures-odyssee-mure.eu/table3_mr.asp?Cod=EU2/EU23/EU7/EU19/EU21/EU9/EU8/EU35/EU38/EU29/EU34/EU33/EU45/EU46/EU3.

mure and Fraunhofer. (2014e) *EU 45 EICTA Self-Commitment to Improve the Energy Performance of CRT and Flat LCD Televisions and Stand by Mode for DVD Players*. Available at: http://www.measures-odyssee-mure.eu/table3_mr.asp?Cod=EU2/EU23/EU7/EU19/EU21/EU9/EU8/EU35/EU38/EU29/EU34/EU33/EU45/EU46/EU3.

Murray A, Skene K and Haynes K. (2017) The Circular Economy: An Interdisciplinary Exploration of the Concept and Application in a Global Context. *Journal of Business Ethics* 140(3): 369–380.

Musaddique S and Gabbatiss J. (2017) China's Ban on Imported Plastic Leads to 'Impending Crisis' for UK Waste Recycling. *The Independent*: 7.12.2017.

Neslen A. (2017) EU's Ban on Inefficient Toasters Delayed to Avoid Pro-Brexit Press Attack. *The Guardian*: 28.2.2017.

Nesti G. (2018) Strengthening the Accountability of Independent Regulatory Agencies: From Performance Back to Democracy. *Comparative European Politics* 16(3): 464–481.

Newell PJ and Grant W. (2000) Environmental NGOs and EU Environmental Law. In: Somsen H (ed) *Yearbook of European Environmental Law. Volume 1.* Oxford: Oxford University Press, 225–252.

Newman AL and Bach D. (2004) Self-Regulatory Trajectories in the Shadow of Public Power: Resolving Digital Dilemmas in Europe and the United States. *Governance* 17(3): 387–413.

Nichols T. (2017) *The Death of Expertise. The Campaign Against Established Knowledge and Why It Matters.* Oxford: Oxford University Press.

Nollert M. (1997) Verbändelobbying in der Europäischen Union. In: Alemann U and Weßels B (eds) *Verbände in vergleichender Perspektive.* Berlin: Sigma, 107–136.

North DC. (1990) *Institutions, Institutional Change and Economic Performance.* Cambridge: Cambridge University Press.

Oberthür S and Dupont C. (2011) The Council, the European Council and International Climate Policy. In: Wurzel RKW and Connelly J (eds) *The European Union as a Leader in International Climate Change Politics.* London: Routledge, 74–91.

OECD. (1999) *Voluntary Approaches for Environmental Policy: An Assessment.* Paris: Organisation for Economic Co-operation and Development.

OECD. (2004) *Biotechnology for Sustainable Growth and Development.* Paris: Organisation for Economic Cooperation and Development (accessed 6.03.2019).

Ofgem. (2018) *Electricity Interconnectors.* London: Office of Gas and Electricity Markets. Available at: https://www.ofgem.gov.uk/electricity/transmission-networks/electricity-interconnectors (accessed 14.8.2018).

Olson M. (1965) *The Logic of Collective Action.* Cambridge, MA: Harvard University Press.

Ossege C. (2015) Driven by Expertise and Insulation? The Autonomy of European Regulatory Agencies. *Politics and Governance* 3(1): 13.

Owen J, Lloyd L and Rutter J. (2018) *Preparing Brexit, How Ready Is Whitehall?* London: Institute for Government.

Oziel C. (2017) *PlasticsEurope Files Second Case Against Echa Over BPA. Latest Action Focuses on Substance's Candidate List Entry as EDC.* ChemicalWatch: 16.11.2017. Available at: https://chemicalwatch.com/61101/plasticseurope-files-second-case-against-echa-over-bpa (accessed 23.6.2018).

paliament.uk. (2018) *EU (Withdrawal) Bill Royal Assent.* Available at: https://www.parliament.uk/business/news/2018/january/lords-debates-eu-withdrawal-bill/ (accessed 09.08.2018).

Partington, R. (2019) CBI and TUC Bosses Warn UK Faces National Emergency over Brexit. *The Guardian*: 21.3.2019.

Patermann C and Aguilar A. (2018) The Origins of the Bioeconomy in the European Union. *New Biotechnology* 40: 20–24.

PE Europe, IKP Universität Stuttgart, IPU, et al. (2004) *Life Cycle Assessment of PVC and of Principal Competing Materials*. Brussels: European Commission.

Pérez Durán I. (2018) Interest Group Representation in the Formal Design of European Union Agencies. *Regulation & Governance* 12(2): 238–262.

Persson T. (2007) Democratizing European Chemicals Policy: Do Consultations Favour Civil Society Participation? *Journal of Civil Society* 3(3): 223–238.

Pesendorfer D. (2006) EU Environmental Policy Under Pressure: Chemicals Policy Change Between Antagonistic Goals? *Environmental Politics* 15(1): 95–114.

Peters BG. (2013) *Strategies for Comparative Research in Political Science*. Houndmills, Basingstoke: Palgrave Macmillan.

Peters GB and Borrás S. (2010) Governance and European Integration. In: Egan M (ed) *Research Agendas in EU Studies: Stalking the Elephant*. Houndmills, Basingstoke: Palgrave Macmillan, 117–133.

Pfeffer J. (1981) *Power in Organizations*. Marshfield, MA: Pitman Publishing.

Pfeffer J and Salancik GR. (2003) *The External Control of Organizations: A Resource Dependence Perspective*. Stanford: Stanford Business Books.

Pierre J and Peters BG. (2000) *Governance, Politics and the State*. Houndmills, Basingstoke: Palgrave Macmillan.

Pierson P. (2000) Increasing Returns, Path Dependence, and the Study of Politics. *American Political Science Review* 94(2): 251–267.

Plastic Oceans. (2018) *Changing Attitudes Towards Plastic*. Available at: http://plasticoceans.uk/news (accessed 08.06.2018).

PlasticsEurope. (2017) *Plastics: The Facts 2016. An Analysis of European Plastics Production, Demand and Waste Data*. Brussels, Wemmel: Association for Plastics Manufacturers, European Association of Plastics Recycling.

PlasticsEurope. (2018a) *Annual Review 2017–2018*. Brussels: PlasticsEurope.

PlasticsEurope. (2018b) *Industry Urges Commission to Avoid Shortcuts and to Focus on Improving Waste Management. PlasticsEurope Reacts on Directive on Single Use Plastics*. Brussels: PlasticsEurope, 29.5.2018.

PlasticsEurope. (2018c) *Membership*. Available at: https://www.plasticseurope.org/en/about-us/membership (accessed 4.08.2018).

PlasticsEurope. (2018d) *Plastics 2030. PlasticsEurope's Voluntary Committment to Increasing Circularity and Resource Efficiency*. Brussels: PlasticsEurope. Available at: https://www.plasticseurope.org/en/newsroom/press-releases/archive-press-releases-2018/plastics-2030-voluntary-commitment (accessed 22.3.2019).

PlasticsEurope. (2018e) *Plastics: The Facts 2017. An Analysis of European Plastics Production, Demand and Waste Data*. Brussels, Wemmel: Association for Plastics Manufacturers, European Association of Plastics Recycling.

Pollack MA. (1997) Representing Diffuse Interests in EC Policy-Making. *Journal of European Public Policy* 4(4): 572–590.

Pollitt MG. (2017) The Economic Consequences of Brexit: Energy. *Oxford Review of Economic Policy* 33(S1): S134–S143.

Portes J and Forte G. (2017) The Economic Impact of Brexit-Induced Reductions in Migration. *Oxford Review of Economic Policy* 33(S1): S31–S44.

Powell WW. (1990) Neither Market Nor Hierarchy: Network Forms of Organization. *Research in Organizational Behavior* 12: 295–336.

Prange-Gstöhl H. (2009) Enlarging the EU's Internal Energy Market: Why Would Third Countries Accept EU Rule Export? *Energy Policy* 37(12): 5296–5303.

Preuss O. (1997) PVC: Die Recycling-Lüge. *Greenpeace Magazin*: 1997(2). Hamburg: Greenpeace Deutschland.

Price R. (2011) Transnational Civil Society and Advocacy in World Politics. *World Politics* 55(4): 579–606.

Princen S. (2007) Agenda-Setting in the European Union: A Theoretical Exploration and Agenda for Research. *Journal of European Public Policy* 14(1): 21–38.

PROGNOS. (2000) *Mechanical Recycling of PVC Wastes*. Brussels: European Commission DG XI.

Putnam RD. (1988) Diplomacy and Domestic Politics: The Logic of Two-Level Games. *International Organization* 42(3): 427–460.

PVC. (2018) *The PVC Industry*. Available at: http://www.pvc.org/en/p/pvc-industry (accessed 4.8.2018).

Quack S. (2016) Expertise and Authority in Transnational Governance. In: Cotterrell R and Del Mar M (eds) *Authority in Transnational Legal Theory. Theorising Across Disciplines*. Cheltenham, Northampton: Edward Elgar.

Radaelli C. (1995) The Role of Knowledge in the Policy Process. *Journal of European Public Policy* 2(2): 159–183.

Radaelli CM. (1999a) The Public Policy of the European Union: Whither Politics of Expertise? *Journal of European Public Policy* 6(5): 757–774.

Radaelli CM. (1999b) *Technocracy in the European Union*. London and New York: Longman.

Rasmussen MK. (2012) Is the European Parliament Still a Policy Champion for Environmental Interests? *Interest Groups & Advocacy* 1(2): 239–259.

Rasmussen MK. (2015) The Battle for Influence: The Politics of Business Lobbying in the European Parliament. *Journal of Common Market Studies* 53(2): 365–382.

Rauh C. (2016) *A Responsive Technocracy? EU Politicisation and the Consumer Policies of the European Commission*. Colchester: ECPR Press.

Rauh C. (2019) EU Politicization and Policy Initiatives of the European Commission: The Case of Consumer Policy. *Journal of European Public Policy.* 6(3): 344–365.

Rethink Plastic. (2018) *Rethink Plastic Alliance of Leading European NGOs.* Available at: http://www.rethinkplasticalliance.eu/ (accessed 4.8.2018).

Rhodes RAW. (1996) The New Governance: Governing Without Government. *Political Studies* 44(4): 652–667.

Richardson J. (1996) Actor-Based Models of National and EU Policy-Making. In: Kassim H and Menon A (eds) *The European Union and National Industrial Policy.* London: Routledge, 26–51.

Rious V, Glachant J-M, Perez Y, et al. (2008) The Diversity of Design of TSOs. *Energy Policy* 36(9): 3323–3332.

Ripoll Servent A. (2015) *Institutional and Policy Change in the European Parliament: Deciding on Freedom, Security and Justice.* London: Palgrave Macmillan.

RISI. (2015) *Global Paper and Board Production Hit Record Levels in 2014.* Boston: RISI, 17.12.2015.

Rittberger B and Wonka A. (2011) Introduction: Agency Governance in the European Union. *Journal of European Public Policy* 18(6): 780–789.

Rivera León L, Bougas K, Zoboli E, et al. (2016) *An Assessment of the Cumulative Cost Impact of Specified EU Legislation and Policies on the EU Forest-Based Industries.* Final Report. Brussels: Technopolis Group, European Commission.

Ronit K and Schneider V. (1997) Organisierte Interessen in nationalen und supranationalen Politökologien: Ein Vergleich der G7-Länder mit der Europäischen Union. In: Alemann U and Weßels B (eds) *Verbände in vergleichender Perspektive.* Berlin: Sigma, 29–62.

Ronit K and Schneider V. (2000) *Private Organizations in Global Politics.* London and New York: Routledge.

Rosenow J and Cowart R. (2017) UK Needs to Put 'Efficiency First' After Release of Clean Growth Strategy. *Euractiv*: 18.10.2017.

Rottmann K and Lenschow A. (2008) 'Privatising' EU Governance: Emergence and Performance of Voluntary Agreements in European Environmental Policy. In: Conzelmann T and Smith R (eds) *Multi-Level Governance in the European Union: Taking Stock and Looking Ahead.* Baden-Baden: Nomos, 232–254.

rreuse. (2018) *Social Enterprises Active in Reuse, Repair and Recycling.* Available at: https://www.rreuse.org/team (accessed 23.8.2018).

RTE. (2018) *Celtic Interconnector: Electrical Interconnector Between France and Ireland.* Paris: Réseau de Transport d'Electricité. Available at: https://www.rte-france.com/en/project/celtic-interconnector-electrical-interconnector-between-france-and-ireland (accessed 16.8.2018).

Sabel CF and Zeitlin J. (2010) *Experimentalist Governance in the European Union: Towards a New Architecture.* Oxford: Oxford University Press.

Sands P. (1990) European Community Environmental Law: Legislation, the European Court of Justice and Common-Interest Groups. *The Modern Law Review* 53(3): 685–698.

Saurugger S. (2008) Interest Groups and Democracy in the European Union. *West European Politics* 31(6): 1274–1291.

Scharpf FW. (1997) Introduction: The Problem-Solving Capacity of Multi-Level Governance. *Journal of European Public Policy* 4(4): 520–538.

Scharpf FW. (2006) The Joint-Decision Trap Revisited. *Journal of Common Market Studies* 44(4): 845–864.

Schattschneider E. (1975) *The Semi-Sovereign People: A Realist's View of Democracy in America*. Wadsworth: Cengage Learning.

Schimmelfennig F. (2018) Brexit: Differentiated Disintegration in the European Union. *Journal of European Public Policy* 25(8): 1154–1173.

Schnabl G. (2005) The Evolution of Environmental Agreements at the Level of the European Union. In: Croci E (ed) *The Handbook of Environmental Voluntary Agreements: Design, Implementation and Evaluation Issues*. Berlin, Heidelberg and New York: Springer, 93–106.

Schön-Quinlivan E. (2013) The European Commission. In: Jordan A and Adelle C (eds) *Environmental Policy in the EU: Actors, Institutions and Processes*. 3rd ed. London, New York: Routledge, 95–112.

Schrefler L. (2013) *Economic Knowledge in Regulation: The Use of Expertise by Independent Agencies*. Colchester: ECPR Press.

Schubert SR, Pollak J and Kreutler M. (2016) *Energy Policy of the European Union*. Houndmills, Basingstoke: Palgrave Macmillan.

Scott C. (2004) Regulation in the Age of Governance: The Rise of the Post-regulatory State. In: Jordana J and Levi-Faur D (eds) *The Politics of Regulation. Institutions and Regulatory Reforms for the Age of Governance*. Cheltenham, Northampton: Edward Elgar, 145–174.

Scott M, Dickson A and Contiguglia C. (2018) France Battles to Topple Britain as Europe's Top Tech Nation. *Politico*: 10.6.2018.

Scully R and van Schendelen R. (2004) *The Unseen Hand*. London: Routledge.

Sending OJ. (2015) *The Politics of Expertise: Competing for Authority in Global Governance*. Ann Arbor, MI: University of Michigan Press.

Senet S. (2018) Thailand: The Rich World's New Dumpsite for e-waste. *Euractiv*: 3.7.2018.

Shapiro M. (1997) The Problems of Independent Agencies in the United States and the European Union. *Journal of European Public Policy* 4(2): 276–277.

Sherrington P. (2000) *Council of Ministers: Political Authority in the European Union*. London: Bloomsbury Academic.

Simon F. (2016) PVC Boss: We Will Not Change Our Reputation in One Day. *Euractiv*: 16.9.2016.

Simon F. (2018) EU Forges Deal on Coal Phase-Out, with Special Polish Clause. *Euractiv*: 19.12.2018.

Simoncini M. (2018) *Administrative Regulation Beyond the Non-delegation Doctrine: A Study on EU Agencies*. Oxford: Bloomsbury Publishing.

Smedley T. (2016) At Work with the FT Interview: James Thornton, ClientEarth. *Financial Times*, 11.5.2016.

Smismans S. (2008) The European Social Dialogue in the Shadow of Hierarchy. *Journal of Public Policy* 28(1): 161–180.

Smith MP. (2008) All Access Points are Not Created Equal: Explaining the Fate of Diffuse Interests in the EU. *The British Journal of Politics & International Relations* 10(1): 64–83.

Solletty M. (2017) Britain's EU Rubbish: One of the EU's Biggest Waste Exporters May Have to Find New Ways to Burn or Recycle Its Trash at Home. *Politico*: 31.8.2017.

Solletty M. (2018) Plastic Tax Proposal Faces Resistance. *Politico*: 15.1.2018.

Solorio I. (2011) Bridging the Gap Between Environmental Policy Integration and the EU's Energy Policy: Mapping out the 'Green Europeanisation' of Energy Governance. *Journal of Contemporary European Research* 7(3): 396–415.

Solorio I and Jörgens H. (2017) *A Guide to EU Renewable Energy Policy*. Cheltenham: Edward Elgar.

Sorrell S. (2009) The Rebound Effect: Definition and Estimation. In: Evans J (ed) *International Handbook on the Economics of Energy*. Cheltenham: Edward Elgar, 199–233.

Stafford ER, Polonsky MJ and Hartman CL. (2000) Environmental NGO–Business Collaboration and Strategic Bridging: A Case Analysis of the Greenpeace—Foron Alliance. *Business Strategy and the Environment* 9(2): 122–135.

Steinebach Y and Knill C. (2017) Still an Entrepreneur? The Changing Role of the European Commission in EU Environmental Policy-Making. *Journal of European Public Policy* 24(3): 429–446.

Steuwer DS. (2013) *Energy Efficiency Governance: The Case of White Certificate Instruments for Energy Efficiency in Europe*. London: Springer.

Stigler GJ. (1971) The Theory of Economic Regulation. *The Bell Journal of Economics and Management Science* 2(1): 3–21.

Stone J. (2018) Theresa May Ridiculed in European Parliament for Claiming Credit for EU Regulations. *The Independent*: 16.1.2018.

Suez. (2017) *Long Term Waste Treatment Capacity Shortfall Likely to Hit British Business and Taxpayers' Pockets as Millions of Tonnes of Waste Destined for Landfill over Next Decade, according to Latest Research*. Press Release 16.8.2017. Berkshire: Suez Recycling and Recovery UK.

SumOfUs. (2017) *McDonald's Is Polluting Our Oceans*. Available at: https://actions.sumofus.org/a/mcdonalds-is-polluting-our-oceans?source=campaigns (accessed 4.8.2018).

Sumption M. (2017) Labour Immigration After Brexit: Questions and Trade-Offs in Designing a Work Permit System for EU Citizens. *Oxford Review of Economic Policy* 33(S1): S45–S53.

Swissgrid. (2015) Netzdaten 2015. Laufenburg: Swissgrid AG.

Taggart P. (1998) A Touchstone of Dissent: Euroscepticism in Contemporary Western European Party Systems. *European Journal of Political Research* 33(3): 363–388.

Tait N and Sherwood B. (2005) Class Actions Across the Atlantic. *Financial Times*, 16.5.2005.

Tamma P. (2018a) China's Trash Ban Forces Europe to Confront Its Waste Problem. *Politico*: 21.2.2018.

Tamma P. (2018b) EU's Plastics Strategy Doesn't Include Plastic Tax. *Politico*: 16.1.2018.

Tanasescu I. (2009) *The European Commission and Interest Groups: Towards a Deliberative Interpretation of Stakeholder Involvement in EU Policy-Making*. Brussels: Brussels University Press.

techUK. (2016) *Initial techUK Views on Chemical Legislation After EU Exit*. 26.10.2016. London: techUK.

techUK. (2018a) *Reuse | Repair | Remanufacture in the ICT Sector*. London: techUK.

techUK. (2018b) *techUK Representing the Future*. London: techUK. Available at: http://www.techuk.org/about (accessed 11.8.2018).

Teffer P. (2018a) How France Escaped EU Legal Action Over Chemical Ban. *EU Observer*: 18.5.2018.

Teffer P. (2018b) Plastics Lobby in Court to Keep Toxic Item Off EU List. *EU Observer*: 12.3.2018.

ten Brink P and Morère M. (2002) Monitoring Mechanisms for Efficient Environmental Agreements. In: ten Brink P (ed) *Voluntary Environmental Agreements: Process, Practice and Future Use*. London, New York: Routledge, 437–460.

Thatcher M. (2007) *Internationalisation and Economic Institutions: Comparing European Experiences*. Oxford: Oxford University Press.

Thatcher M and Coen D. (2008) Reshaping European Regulatory Space: An Evolutionary Analysis. *West European Politics* 31(4): 806–836.

Thatcher M and Stone Sweet A. (2002) Theory and Practice of Delegation to Non-majoritarian Institutions. *West European Politics* 25(1): 1–22.

Thornton J and Goodman M. (2017) *ClientEarth*. Melbourne: Scribe Publications.

Thorsheim P. (2015) *Waste into Weapons*. New York: Cambridge University Press.

TNO Nutrition and Food Research. (2001) *Migration of Phthalate Plasticisers from Soft PVC Toys and Childcare Articles.* Final Report. Brussels: DG Enterprise, European Commission.

Töller AE. (2010) Measuring and Comparing the Europeanization of National Legislation: A Research Note. *Journal of Common Market Studies* 48(2): 417–444.

Tömmel I and Verdun A. (2009) *Innovative Governance in the European Union: The Politics of Multilevel Policymaking.* Boulder: Lynne Rienner.

Tömmel I and Verdun A. (2017) Political Leadership in the European Union: An Introduction. *Journal of European Integration* 39(2): 103–112.

Toshkov D. (2008) Embracing European Law: Compliance with EU Directives in Central and Eastern Europe. *European Union Politics* 9(3): 379–402.

Tosun J. (2013) *Risk Regulation in Europe: Assessing the Application of the Precautionary Principle.* New York: Springer Verlag.

Tosun J, Schmitt S and Schulze K. (2014) *Energy Policy Making in the EU: Building the Agenda.* London: Springer.

Trondal J, Busuioc M and Groenleer M. (2012) *The Agency Phenomenon in the European Union.* Manchester, New York: Manchester University Press.

Trondal J and Peters BG. (2015) A Conceptual Account of the European Administrative Space. In: Bauer MW and Trondal J (eds) *The Palgrave Handbook of the European Administrative System.* London: Palgrave Macmillan, 79–92.

Trumbull G. (2006) *Consumer Capitalism. Politics, Product Markets, and Firm Strategy in France and Germany.* Ithaca, New York: Cornell University Press.

Trumbull G. (2010) Consumer Policy. In: Coen D, Grant W and Wilson GK (eds) *The Oxford Handbook of Business and Government.* Oxford: Oxford University Press, 622–642.

Two Sides. (2017) *Print and Paper Myths and Facts.* Daventry: United Kingdom.

Two Sides. (2018) *Two Sides Forum from the Graphic Communications Supply Chain.* Available at: https://www.twosides.info/about/ (accessed 4.8.2018).

Valdani Vicari & Associati. (2018) *Study for the Introduction of an e-labelling Scheme in Europe. Cost Benefit Analysis.* Brussels: Digital Europe, Mobile & Wireless Forum.

van Schendelen R. (2004) The In-Sourced Experts. In: Scully R and van Schendelen R (eds) *The Unseen Hand.* London: Routledge, 25–35.

Vasconcelos J. (2001) Cooperation Between Energy Regulators in the European Union. In: Henry C, Matheu M and Jeunemaître A (eds) *Regulation of Network Utilities: The European Experience.* Oxford: Oxford University Press, 284–289.

Vaughan A. (2017) Brexit and Energy: Does 'Taking Back Control' Mean Losing Power? *The Guardian*: 6.5.2017.

Veenman S and Liefferink D. (2012) Different Countries, Different Strategies: 'Green' Member States Influencing EU Climate Policy. In: Wijen F, Zoeteman K and Pieters J (eds) *A Handbook of Globalisation and Environmental Policy, Second Edition: National Government Interventions in a Global Arena*. Cheltenham, Northampton: Edward Elgar, 387–414.

VHK and ARMINES. (2015) *Ecodesign & Labelling Review Household Refrigeration*. Preparatory/Review Study Commission Regulation (EC) No. 634/2009 and Commission (Delegated) Regulation (EU) 1060/2010. VHK, VITO, VM, Wuppertal Institute, ARMINES.

VHK, VITO, VM, et al. (2014) *"Omnibus" Review Study on Cold Appliances, Washing Machines, Dishwaschers, Washer-Driers, Lighting, Set-top Boxes and Pumps*. Brussels, Delft: VHK, VITO, VM, Wuppertal Institute for Climate.

Vinyl 2010. (2001) *The Voluntary Commitment of the European PVC Industry*. Brussels: Vinyl 2010.

Vinyl 2010. (2007) *Vinyl 2010. Progress Report 2007*. Report on the Activities of the Previous Year. Brussels: Vinyl 2010.

Vinyl 2010. (2008) *Vinyl 2010. Progress Report 2008*. Report on the Activities of the Year 2007. Brussels: Vinyl 2010.

VinylPlus. (2011) *The Voluntary Commitment of the European PVC Industry*. Brussels: VinylPlus.

Virley SC. (2017) *Brexit and the Energy Market: Article 50 Has Been Triggert, But What Happens Next? A New Free Trade Agreement Will Be Needed to Maintain the Current Tariff-Free Trading on Gas and Electricity*. London: KPMG.

Vivid Economics. (2016) *The Impact of Brexit on the UK Energy Sector. An Assessment of the Risks and Opportunities for Electricity and Gas in the UK*. London: Vivd Economics.

Vogel D. (2012) *The Politics of Precaution: Regulating Health, Safety and Environmental Risks in Europe and the United States*. Princeton: Princeton University Press.

Vogel D, Toffel M and Post D. (2012) Environmental Federalism in the European Union and the United States In: Wijen F, Zoeteman K and Pieters J (eds) *A Handbook of Globalisation and Environmental Policy, Second Edition: National Government Interventions in a Global Arena*. Cheltenham, Northampton: Edward Elgar, 321–361.

Vollaard H. (2014) Explaining European Disintegration. *Journal of Common Market Studies* 52: 1142–1159.

Warleigh A. (2000) The Hustle: Citizenship Practice, NGOs and 'Policy Coalitions' in the European Union—The Cases of Auto Oil, Drinking Water and Unit Pricing. *Journal of European Public Policy* 7(2): 229–243.

Waygood S, Simpson P, Gardiner W, et al. (2018) *Letter of Leading European and UK Companies and Investors to Negotiation Leaders Barnier and Davis*.

20.4.2018. United Kingdom. Available at: https://www.euractiv.com/wp-content/uploads/sites/2/2018/04/Brexit-coalition-letter-FINAL.pdf (accessed 27.3.2019).

Weale A, Pridham G, Cini M, et al. (2000) *Environmental Governance in Europe: An Ever Closer Ecological Union?* Oxford: Oxford University Press.

Weatherill S. (2013) *EU Consumer Law and Policy.* Cheltenham, Northampton: Edward Elgar.

Weber M. (1978) *Economy and Society.* Berkeley: University of California Press.

Webster E. (2004) Firms' Decisions to Innovate and Innovation Routines. *Economics of Innovation and New Technology* 13(8): 733–745.

WEEE Forum. (2018) *What Is the WEEE Forum.* Available at: http://www.weee-forum.org/what-is-the-weee-forum (accessed 16.8.2018).

Wessels W. (1998) Comitology: Fusion in Action—Politico-Administrative Trends in the EU System. *Journal of European Public Policy* 5(2): 209–234.

Wettig J. (2002) New Developments in Standardisation in the Past 15 Years: Product Versus Process Related Standards. *Safety Science* 40(1): 51–56.

Whitley R and Kristensen PH. (1997) *Governance at Work: The Social Regulation of Economic Relations.* Oxford: Oxford University Press.

Williams G. (2005) Monomaniacs or Schizophrenics? Responsible Governance and the EU's Independent Agencies. *Political Studies* 53(1): 82–99.

Williamson OE. (1975) *Markets and Hierarchies, Analysis and Antitrust Implications: A Study in the Economics of Internal Organization.* New York: Free Press.

Williamson OE. (1979) Transaction-Cost Economics: The Governance of Contractual Relations. *Journal of Law and Economics* 22(2): 233–261.

Williamson OE. (1996) *The Mechanisms of Governance.* New York: Oxford University Press.

Willis J. (2015) Cadmium Ban in TVs: Balancing Innovation and Regulation. *Euractiv.* 18.5.2015.

Wilson JQ (ed). (1980) *The Politics of Regulation.* New York: Basic Books, 357–394.

Witt MA and Jackson G. (2016) Varieties of Capitalism and Institutional Comparative Advantage: A Test and Reinterpretation. *Journal of International Business Studies* 47(7): 778–806.

Woersdorfer JS. (2017) *The Evolution of Household Technology and Consumer Behavior, 1800–2000.* London, New York: Routledge.

Woll C. (2009) Trade Policy Lobbying in the European Union: Who Captures Whom? In: Coen D and Richardson J (eds) *Lobbying the European Union: Institutions, Actors, and Issues.* Oxford: Oxford University Press, 277–297.

Wonka A and Rittberger B. (2010) Credibility, Complexity and Uncertainty: Explaining the Institutional Independence of 29 EU Agencies. *West European Politics* 33(4): 730–752.

WRAP. (2018a) *The Facts: China's Tighter Controls on the Quality of Waste Imports.* 16.2.2018. Oxon: The Waste and Resources Action Programme.

WRAP. (2018b) *Recovered Paper Imports & Exports.* Oxon: The Waste and Resources Action Programme. Available at: http://www.wrap.org.uk/content/recovered-paper-imports-exports (accessed 10.8.2018).

WRAP. (2018c) *UK Businesses Make World-Leading Pact to Tackle Plastic Pollution.* Oxon: The Waste and Resources Action Programme

WRAP. (2018d) *The UK Plastics Pact: Together We Can Create a Sustainable System for Plastics.* Oxon: The Waste and Resources Action Programme. Available at: http://www.wrap.org.uk/content/the-uk-plastics-pact (accessed 26.04.2018).

Wurzel RKW. (2008) Environmental Policy: EU Actors, Leader and Laggard States. In: Hayward J (ed) *Leaderless Europe.* Oxford: Oxford University Press, 66–88.

Wurzel RKW. (2013) Member States and the Council. In: Jordan A and Adelle C (eds) *Environmental Policy in the EU: Actors, Institutions and Processes.* 3rd ed. London, New York: Routledge, 75–94.

Wurzel RKW and Connelly J. (2011) Environmental NGOs: Taking a Lead? In: Wurzel RKW and Connelly J (eds) *The European Union as a Leader in International Climate Change Politics.* London: Routledge, 214–231.

WWF. (2007) *DETOX. Campaigning for Safer Chemicals.* Brussels: World Wildlife Fund for Nature.

WWF. (2018) *Plastics: Why We Must Act Now.* Gland: World Wide Fund for Nature. Available at: https://www.wwf.org.uk/updates/plastics-why-we-must-act-now (accessed 10.8.2018).

Wyatt DWC. (1998) Litigating Community Environmental Law: Thoughts on the Direct Effect Doctrine. *Journal of Environmental Law* 10(1): 9–19.

Young K. (2018) *UK Government White Paper on Brexit Includes a Wish to Stay in EU Chemicals Law, but Are its Commitments Enough?* 12.7.2018. London: CHEMTrust.

zerowasteeurope. (2018) Available at: https://www.zerowasteeurope.eu/about/ (accessed 23.8.2018).

ZVEI. (2018) *Neues Energielabel: Umdenken wird gefordert.* Press Release 6.12.2018. Frankfurt: ZVEI.

INDEX

Printed by Printforce, the Netherlands